THE CAMBRIDGE COMPANION TO
# RELIGIOUS EXPERIENCE

For centuries, theologians and philosophers, among others, have examined the nature of religious experience. Students and scholars unfamiliar with the vast literature face a daunting task in grasping the main issues surrounding the topic of religious experience. *The Cambridge Companion to Religious Experience* offers an original introduction to this topic. Going beyond an introduction, it is a state-of-the-art overview of the topic, with critical analyses of and creative insights into its subject. Religious experience is discussed from various interdisciplinary perspectives, from religious perspectives inside and outside traditional monotheistic religions, and from various topical perspectives. Written by leading scholars in clear and accessible prose, this book is an ideal resource for undergraduate and graduate students, teachers, and scholars across many disciplines.

**Paul K. Moser** is Professor of Philosophy at Loyola University Chicago. His most recent publications include *Understanding Religious Experience* (Cambridge University Press, 2020), *The God Relationship* (Cambridge University Press, 2018), and *The Elusive God* (Cambridge University Press, 2008), which won the national book award from the Jesuit Honor Society. Moser, with Chad Meister, serves as the coeditor of the book series Cambridge Studies in Religion, Philosophy, and Society and Cambridge Elements of Religion and Monotheism.

**Chad Meister** is Professor of Philosophy and Theology at Bethel University. His most recent publications include *Evil: A Guide for the Perplexed, Second Edition* (2018), *Christian Thought: A Historical Introduction, Second Edition* (2016), coauthored with James Stump, and *Contemporary Philosophical Theology* (2016), coauthored with Charles Taliaferro. He is also coeditor, with Charles Taliaferro, of the six-volume work *The History of Evil* (2018).

CAMBRIDGE COMPANIONS TO RELIGION

This is a series of companions to major topics and key figures in theology and religious studies. Each volume contains specially commissioned chapters by international scholars, which provide an accessible and stimulating introduction to the subject for new readers and nonspecialists.

*Other Titles in the Series*

*(continued after index)*

THE CAMBRIDGE COMPANION TO
# RELIGIOUS EXPERIENCE

Edited by

Paul K. Moser
*Loyola University Chicago*

Chad Meister
*Bethel University*

# CAMBRIDGE
### UNIVERSITY PRESS

University Printing House, Cambridge CB2 8BS, United Kingdom

One Liberty Plaza, 20th Floor, New York, NY 10006, USA

477 Williamstown Road, Port Melbourne, VIC 3207, Australia

314–321, 3rd Floor, Plot 3, Splendor Forum, Jasola District Centre,
New Delhi – 110025, India

79 Anson Road, #06–04/06, Singapore 079906

Cambridge University Press is part of the University of Cambridge.

It furthers the University's mission by disseminating knowledge in the pursuit of
education, learning, and research at the highest international levels of excellence.

www.cambridge.org
Information on this title: www.cambridge.org/9781108472173
DOI: 10.1017/9781108575119

© Cambridge University Press 2020

First published 2020

*A catalogue record for this publication is available from the British Library.*

*Library of Congress Cataloging-in-Publication Data*
NAMES: Moser, Paul K., 1957– editor. | Meister, Chad V., 1965– editor.
TITLE: The Cambridge companion to religious experience / edited by Paul K. Moser,
Loyola University Chicago, Chad Meister, Bethel College and Seminary, Minnesota.
DESCRIPTION: Cambridge, United Kingdom ; New York, NY, USA : Cambridge University
Press, 2020. | Series: Cambridge companions to religion | Includes bibliographical
references and index.
IDENTIFIERS: LCCN 2020012999 (print) | LCCN 2020013000 (ebook) | ISBN 9781108472173
(hardback) | ISBN 9781108459112 (paperback) | ISBN 9781108575119 (epub)
SUBJECTS: LCSH: Experience (Religion)
CLASSIFICATION: LCC BL53 .C2545 2020 (print) | LCC BL53 (ebook) | DDC 204/.2–dc23
LC record available at https://lccn.loc.gov/2020012999
LC ebook record available at https://lccn.loc.gov/2020013000

ISBN 978-1-108-47217-3 Hardback
ISBN 978-1-108-45911-2 Paperback

# Contents

# Figures

# Contributors

**Fiona Bowie** is a member of Wolfson College, Oxford, and Visiting Senior Research Fellow in the Department of Theology and Religious Studies at King's College London.

**David Burton** is Senior Lecturer in Religion, Philosophy, and Ethics in the School of Humanities at Canterbury Christ Church University.

**William C. Chittick** is Distinguished Professor at Stony Brook University.

**Francis X. Clooney, SJ** is Parkman Professor of Divinity and Director of the Center for the Study of World Religions at Harvard Divinity School.

**Willem B. Drees** is Professor of Philosophy of the Humanities and Dean of the Tilburg School of Humanities at Tilburg University.

**James D. G. Dunn** is Emeritus Lightfoot Professor of Divinity in the Department of Theology and Religion at Durham University.

**Gwen Griffith-Dickson** is Visiting Professor of Theology and Religious Studies at King's College London and Founder and Director of the Lokahi Foundation.

**Steven T. Katz** is Alvin J. and Shirley Slater Chair in Jewish Holocaust Studies at Boston University.

**Chad Meister** is Chairperson and Professor of Philosophy and Theology at Bethel University.

**Paul K. Moser** is Professor of Philosophy at Loyola University Chicago.

**Michael L. Peterson** is Professor of Philosophy of Religion at Asbury Theological Seminary.

**Ann Taves** is Professor of Religious Studies at the University of California at Santa Barbara.

**Mark Owen Webb** is Professor of Philosophy at Texas Tech University.

**Howard Wettstein** is Professor of Philosophy at the University of California, Riverside.

**Phillip H. Wiebe** was Professor of Philosophy at Trinity Western University.

**Xinzhong Yao** is currently Professor of Ethics, School of Philosophy at Renmin University and Professor Emeritus, King's College London.

# Preface

Scholars and teachers from various disciplines have recently renewed the academic interest in religious experience, or at least in experience that some people take to be religious. This book presents that renewed interest in an interdisciplinary manner accessible to college students and helpful to their teachers. The disciplines represented include religious studies, the psychology of religion, the sociology of religion, the philosophy of religion, Biblical studies, theology, and the history of religion. The chapters make original contributions, while avoiding technical discussions available only to scholars. Each chapter takes a point of view that engages its intended readers.

In a university, college, or seminary setting, this book could be used as either required or supplementary reading in such courses as the following: Introduction to Religion; World Religions; Philosophy of Religion; Psychology of Religion; Introduction to Theology; Philosophical Theology; Religious Epistemology; and Foundations of Theistic/ Christian Belief.

The book is divided into four main parts. Part I, "Characterizing Religious Experience: Interdisciplinary Approaches," focuses on influential methodological approaches to religious experience from the psychology of religion, the philosophy of religion, and the theology of religion. Part II, "Religious Experience in Traditional Monotheism," discusses the major monotheistic traditions of classical Judaism, early Christianity, and traditional Islam. Part III, "Religious Experience outside Traditional Monotheism," examines four influential religious traditions outside traditional monotheism: ancient Confucianism and Daoism, classical Buddhism, traditional Hinduism, and traditional African religion. Part IV, "Prominent Themes and Challenges," attends to some controversies regarding religious experience: the role of mysticism, the function of evidence, the role of miracle, the challenge of evil, the bearing of naturalism, and the question of meaning and social value.

We thank the contributors of this volume for writing their chapters and for their collegiality. Their first-rate scholarship and creative insights have made our editorial task gratifying. We also thank the referees for Cambridge University Press for their helpful suggestions, and the editorial staff at Cambridge University Press for their support of our project. In particular, we thank our publisher Beatrice Rehl for guiding this book to publication.

# Introduction: Religious Experience

PAUL K. MOSER AND CHAD MEISTER

Many religious people hold that their religious commitment should be understood in terms of something that has *happened* to them, and they believe that what has happened to them is a distinctive *experience*, a *religious* experience. This experience, in their perspective, does not reduce to a belief, hypothesis, or theory. Instead, it includes something qualitative that has been *presented* or *given* to them in their direct awareness. It is, in their judgment, a qualitative experience, and it is religious. This book examines the nature, scope, context, and significance of religious experience, in search of a good explanation. In doing so, it raises many questions about religious experience that are important to religious studies, philosophy, theology, psychology, sociology, and history. This introduction clarifies some of these questions.

## EXPERIENCE AS RELIGIOUS

Some theorists doubt that there is a well-formed category of *experience*, but we shall not digress to that extreme view. We can make do now with a notion of experience as qualitative awareness, and let it be illustrated by familiar cases of direct attention-attraction by something qualitative (not to be confused with attention-focusing or attention-selection). We may think of it as broadly "perceptual" or "observational," without reducing it to "sensation" in any narrow sense. So, one might experience, or have a sense of, a duty or an honor, without this being sensation in a narrow sense. Given this approach, one can have an experience of something that is not a sensory object.

A key issue concerns when an experience is *religious*. A quick answer would be when it involves *religion*. Perhaps this is true, but it is not adequately illuminating. The notion of religion is as much in need of clarification now as the notion of religious experience. The terms "religion" and "religious" are among the most elusive in circulation regarding their precise meanings (if such meanings are to be had for them). We call everything from being a sports fan to worshiping God "religious." We thus hear: "His commitment to his baseball team is religious." People, of course, may use words as they wish, but we should not lose a hold on clear communication with our words.

Many people think of being religious as somehow involving God, and thus theology, in some way. We prefer a broader understanding, however, in the light of nontheistic religions, such as some versions of Confucianism, Daoism, and Buddhism. One broader understanding takes being religious to involve *overarching meaning* for a person's life. Such an understanding seems to be indicated by Leo Tolstoy's description of his life-forming religious experience:

> All that was around me came to life and received a meaning ... And I was saved from suicide. When and how this transformation within me was accomplished, I could not say. Just as [earlier in my life] the life force within me was gradually and imperceptibly destroyed, and I encountered the impossibility of life, the halting of life, and the need to murder myself, so too did this life force return to me gradually and imperceptibly ... I returned to the conviction that the single most important purpose in my life was to be better, to live according to this ... (1882, pp. 76–77; trans. first two sentences, Aylmer Maude, and remaining sentences, David Patterson)

Tolstoy had struggled with the prospect of suicide, but this struggle, like his Christian theism, is not essential to his life-changing religious experience.

Something *happened*, or *was presented*, to Tolstoy in his experience, or qualitative awareness, and this was not just a belief, hypothesis, or theory. He directly experienced new *meaning* for his life. This meaning arose for him in all surrounding things as well as "within" him, including in the "transformation within" him. It thus was *overarching* meaning for his life. He comments: "All that was around me came to life and received a meaning." This was something Tolstoy experienced directly, and it engaged him in a practical way. It prompted his forming an intention to become conformed to it, that is, to become "better." So, the life-forming experience was important for his practical life. It was not merely speculative or abstract in the way many philosophical reflections are. We could explore religious experiences with overarching meaning in a range of major religions: Confucianism, Daoism, Buddhism, Hinduism, Judaism, Christianity, and Islam, among others. The book's chapters offer some illuminating examples for further exploration.

A significant question for any experience, including any supposed religious experience, is whether it is veridical, or accurate, regarding reality independent of human minds. In other words, does it go beyond merely subjective experience to an experience of something "objective" as independent of human minds? *Realism* about some religious experiences implies that those experiences are objective, relating one to reality independent of human minds. For instance, an apparent experience of God (however one understands "God") is veridical in a realist sense if, and only if, it relates one to a God whose existence is independent of human minds.

We need a clear distinction between the *ontology* and the *epistemology* of religious experience. The ontology concerns what such experience consists in, regardless of how we come to know what a particular religious experience involves. The epistemology concerns conditions for evidence and knowledge regarding religious experience. One familiar epistemological question is: Does one know, or at least justifiably believe, that God exists, on the basis of a specified religious experience, such as a life-changing experience of the kind identified by Tolstoy. Two questions arise here. First, can one know that God exists on the basis of evidence from a religious experience? Second, what kind of religious experience would be suitable as evidence for the existence of God? These are large questions that call for careful examination, and they resist any quick answers. Some of the book's chapters touch on them.

Some theorists, such as Sigmund Freud (1933), Daniel Dennett (2006), and Richard Dawkins (1996), try to account for religious experience *just* in terms of nonreligious factors, such as human psychology, sociology, or biology alone. In doing so, they seek either to reduce or to eliminate claims to religious experience on the basis of factors that are not religious, such as *merely* psychological, sociological, or biological factors. This is a bold effort if it aims to cover the whole range of religious experience. It would call for a case that bears negatively on *all* religious experiences as reducible or eliminable. It is unclear, however, that we have the evidence needed for such a broad case against religious experiences. For instance, we seem not to have the broad kind of evidence needed to support Freud's sweeping position that all religious experience is ultimately a matter of psychological delusion.

We face three main options regarding religious experience, and they correspond to the theological options of theism, atheism, and agnosticism. First, one can be a *realist* about some religious experiences, claiming that some of them relate us to features of reality (such as God) that do not depend for their existence on human minds. Second, one can be a *nonrealist* about all religious experiences, claiming that none of them relates us to features of reality independent of human minds. Third, one can be a skeptic about all religious experiences, proposing that we lack the needed evidence to affirm either the realist or the nonrealist position. Skeptics thus propose that we withhold judgment on the disagreement between realists and nonrealists about religious experience. They find our evidence inadequate to settle the matter in favor of either group.

Some alleged religious experiences seem more plausible, at least to many of us, than others regarding being veridical. For instance, some ecstatic religious experiences, including altered states of awareness, seem to result from delusions of some sort, such as delusions of guilt or of grandeur. Troubling cases arise when people lose their moral bearings in religious ecstasy, taking leave of anything like ethical discernment regarding their attitudes or actions. Religious experience can go bad in this way, and hence religion can too. The history of religion confirms this lesson, abundantly. An important lesson is that neither religious experience nor religion need be morally good. Each can be morally bad and harmful for people, even if some instances are morally good. The history of each of the major religions gives evidence of religion going bad in some cases, and therefore one must try to separate the good from the bad in religious experience and religion, across the range of major religious perspectives.

If religious experience and religion are anchored in overarching meaning for human life, one might recommend aspiring to *morally good* meaning for a life. So, one might recommend against evil religions as a basis for a meaningful life. This might include the religion of, for example, ISIS (or Daesh) in our own time, on the ground that its evils in practice (murder, rape, torture, and so on) disqualify it as a fitting model for human life. In any case, one can subject religious experience and religion to moral evaluation regarding their bearing on a morally good life. In doing so, one can let go of the view, sometimes circulated, that "all religion is good." It is, we suggest, partly an empirical matter whether some aspects of a particular religion are morally good, and the same is true of a religious experience.

## VALUING RELIGIOUS EXPERIENCE

Why care about religious experience at all? We have a straightforward answer if religious experience contributes importantly to overarching meaning for a human life. Insofar as such meaning is valuable to us, we can find value in religious experience as a significant contributor to that meaning. It can contribute as an experiential ground for life's meaning, as it reportedly did in the case of Tolstoy. Even if one lacks a full explanation of a life-changing experience, that experience can be valuable to one's life by contributing to its overarching meaning.

We can distinguish meaning *in life* from the meaning *of life*. A meaning in life for a person is just an aim, purpose, or goal that person has for life. We can create such meaning, then, with our intentions for life, and we can remove such meaning with a change in our intentions. One's meaning in life does not transfer automatically to meaning in life for other people, because those people need not share one's intentions. Such relativity of meaning is a live option among humans, but it does contrast with what some theorists call "the meaning of life."

If there is such a thing as the meaning of life, it has a singularity foreign to meaning in life. It would bear on all human lives, and thus it would not be just a result of individual human intention. It would have a basis in something less variable than the intentions of individual humans. A controversial issue concerns what that basis would be. If such meaning requires an intention, one might look for its source in an intentional agent of a special sort. Some theorists take God to be that intentional source of the meaning of life. Given that view, the reality of the meaning of life will be as debatable as the existence of God. In addition, the value of the meaning of life for humans then will share the value of God for humans.

One value of God for humans, according to some theorists, is God's sustaining *lasting* meaning for human life, beyond any merely temporal meaning. If God is everlasting and has a lasting overarching purpose for human life, then God would be in a position to support lasting meaning for human life. The meaning of human life, then, could be lasting in virtue of its lasting support from God. If God is omitted, and no lasting replacement arises, meaning for human life will be merely temporary, lasting only as long as its temporary basis or source, whatever that may be. Theorists who favor physicalism, reductive or nonreductive, about reality typically think of life's meaning as merely temporary, lasting only as long as its temporary physical basis. They find no basis for lasting meaning for human life, even if some people would prefer such meaning. The main point now, however, is that God could make a difference in this area. We need to look more carefully at a potential role for God in religious experience.

## RELIGIOUS EXPERIENCE AND GOD

People have described religious experiences of God in vastly different ways, with no clear indication of a common core to the experiences. So, the topic can be confusing and frustrating. A problem results from the widely differing conceptions of God in circulation. People may share the term "God," but they often mean very different things by it. Traditional monotheism seeks to add some conceptual unity by portraying God as worthy of worship and hence morally perfect, without any moral defect. In this approach, God must meet a distinctively high moral standard to satisfy the perfectionist title "God." So, power alone will not qualify one for being God. Moral character matters, and it cannot be defective in the case of God.

We should expect evidence for a God inherently worthy of worship to be morally significant in a way that represents God's perfect moral character. If God is inherently an intentional moral agent, seeking to actualize what is morally good, then any decisive evidence of God's reality will indicate a moral agent at work. It follows that any decisive evidence of God in human experience will be evidence of an intentional moral agent seeking to actualize what is morally good. Inquirers about God, then, should give due consideration to whether such morally significant evidence is present in human experience, such as in moral conscience. If some people find such evidence present and others do not, we should ask what accounts for this difference. In this regard, we should consider whether God would self-reveal in human experience in ways sensitive to the receptivity of inquirers. It could be that God would not want divine self-revelation to alienate inquirers who would not welcome such revelation. This consideration may figure in a kind of divine self-hiding for redemptive purposes. In any case, evidence that does not indicate God's moral character will not yield a God worthy of worship (for relevant discussion, see Paul Moser 2020).

A psalmist in the Hebrew Bible identifies a morally significant kind of religious experience that involves God:

O Lord, you have searched me and known me.
You know when I sit down and when I rise up;
you discern my thoughts from far away.
You search out my path and my lying down,
and are acquainted with all my ways.
Even before a word is on my tongue,
O Lord, you know it completely.
You hem me in, behind and before,

and lay your hand upon me.
Such knowledge is too wonderful for me;
it is so high that I cannot attain it.
(Psalm 139:1–6)

This is a religious experience of being *morally searched* by God, in one's moral conscience. The talk of God's "hemming me in" is talk of a moral challenge from God, a challenge to conform to God's perfect moral character. Moral conscience can be like that: It can nudge one, without coercion, away from what is morally bad and toward what is morally good.

One might think of moral conscience as an avenue for divine moral intervention in human experience. It offers an opportunity for God to self-manifest the divine moral character in a way that challenges and guides cooperative humans in relation to God's will. Being thus challenged and guided can be central to a religious experience of God, if the psalmist is right. Even so, moral conscience is fallible for humans; we can be misled by it at times as a result of various defects in our history and experience. Fallibility, however, does not exclude all genuine moral goodness from conscience. Our visual experience, for instance, is fallible, but it would be rash to portray it as always misleading relative to the visual world.

We can correct for distortions in our moral experience in various ways. For instance, we can compare one moral experience with a range of other moral experiences we have, to check for coherence. In addition, we can compare a moral experience we have with the moral experience of other people, again to check for coherence. We do not have an easy recipe here, but we do have some checks and balances, as in the case of visual experience. As a result, we need not throw the baby (good moral experience) out with the dirty bath water (misleading moral experience). Sometimes people opt for wholesale skepticism in an area too quickly, but good judgment advises against such haste. Religious moral experiences merit our careful attention and discernment, because it is a live option that they will signal moral illumination and even theological illumination.

A person's religious experience, such as the psalmist's moral religious experience, can be best explained for that person by a claim that God has actually intervened in that person's experience. This is an empirical matter, and we should not try to settle it simply on a priori grounds. We therefore need to examine actual religious experiences carefully, to see what they include and what best accounts for them.

Some apparent religious experiences will fail to survive such scrutiny, as they are exposed to be just psychological aberrations. Other religious experiences will not succumb so clearly. For instance, our sciences have not excluded as aberrant all religious experiences of the sort described by the psalmist above; nor has anything else. They are thus candidates worthy of our careful attention.

We face a kind of relativism about experiences in general and religious experiences in particular. All people do not share the same experiences. The fact that you experience the common cold does not require that everyone else does too; many people do not experience the common cold at all. Similarly, some people could have a religious experience while others do not. We cannot exclude this option, and it should temper any quick dismissal of religious experience on the ground that some people do not have any such experience. The people who do not experience the common cold would do well not to infer that nobody experiences the common cold. So, one person's (or a group's) not having a religious experience is not an adequate ground to generalize to the skeptical conclusion that nobody has a religious experience. The person-relativity of experience allows for the person-relativity of evidence from variable experience. Inquiry about religious experience will benefit from attention to these lessons.

## RELIGIOUS EXPERIENCE AND SCIENCE

Our best sciences do not pose a universal threat to the reality of religious experience, including such experience regarding God. Stephen Jay Gould has made a general case that supports this point. His main point is that our best sciences, our academic sciences, operate in an empirical domain different from the domain of religion. Science and religion are "non-overlapping magisteria," in his language, because they are different domains of inquiry and subject matter that do not compete. He comments:

> The net, or magisterium, of science covers the empirical realm: what is the universe made of (fact) and why does it work this way (theory). The magisterium of religion extends over questions of ultimate meaning and moral value. These two magisteria do not overlap, nor do they encompass all inquiry (consider, for example, the magisterium of art and the meaning of beauty). To cite the old clichés, science gets the age of rocks, and religion the rock of ages; science studies how the heavens go, religion how to go to heaven. (1999, p. 6)

Gould rightly observes that neither science nor religion encompasses "all inquiry." The academic sciences permit inquiry in religion that is not part of scientific explanation via what is ultimately nature alone. We can confirm this in the standard textbooks of the academic sciences. Similarly, religion allows for inquiry in the sciences that is not part of religion, as various religious scriptures illustrate. Religion, however, will be "respectful" of science in Gould's sense only if it avoids claims to causal and factual significance that contradict empirically justified scientific claims.

As understood by Gould, religion is not in a position to support a realm of *divine* purposes, meanings, and values identifiable in nature but inaccessible to the sciences. If there were such purposes inaccessible to the sciences, religion would identify something causal and factual in a way that challenges science. Gould nonetheless allows for religion's endorsing a kind of deism in theology. He acknowledges without objection that some scientists "still hold a conception of God (as an imperial clock winder at time's beginning) that leaves science entirely free in its own proper magisterium" (1999, p. 22). His central demand is that religion not affirm anything that contradicts an empirically justified scientific finding.

Gould considers people who acknowledge a God personally concerned with the lives of creatures, thus going beyond a clock winder from deism:

> Such people often take a further step by insisting that their God mark his existence (and his care) by particular factual imprints upon nature that may run contrary to the findings of science. Now, science has no quarrel whatever with anyone's need or belief in such a personalized concept of divine power, but [we should] preclude the additional claim that such a God must arrange the facts of nature in a certain set and predetermined way. For example, if you believe that an adequately loving God must show his hand by peppering nature with palpable miracles, or that such a God could only allow evolution to work in a manner contrary to facts of the fossil record (as a story of slow and steady linear progress toward *Homo sapiens*, for example), then a particular, partisan (and minority) view of religion has transgressed into the magisterium of science by dictating conclusions that must remain open to empirical test and potential rejection. (1999, pp. 93–94)

Acknowledging that "science has no quarrel whatever with anyone's . . . belief in such a personalized concept of divine power," Gould demands

that religion not affirm anything that contradicts an empirically justified scientific thesis. He thus rules out any claim of religion that "God
must arrange the facts of nature in a certain set and predetermined
way," that is, a way indifferent to the evidence of the sciences. His
main demand is that religion avoid "dictating conclusions that must
remain open to empirical test and potential rejection." *Empirical*
claims, in short, demand *empirical* evidence, even if they emerge from
religion.

Supporters of religion and religious experience can accept Gould's
demands for religion, given due caution about which claims "must
remain open to empirical test" and about what the relevant "empirical
test" involves. If one were to demand that all empirical evidence be
socially readily shareable just by human means, as is common in the
sciences, many supporters of religion should balk. We should not take it
as an a priori truth, and arguably not take it as a truth at all, that God
would have to make experience and evidence of divine reality socially
shareable in the way the evidence of the sciences is. So, a supporter of
religion can accept Gould's main demand but deny that the relevant
empirical test is always based on socially readily shareable empirical
evidence. Gould neither affirms nor excludes this option.

Gould remarks: "Science simply cannot (by its legitimate methods)
adjudicate the issue of God's possible superintendence of nature. We
neither affirm nor deny it; we simply can't comment on it as scientists"
(1992, p. 119). Perhaps he means "God's actual superintendence of
nature," because the "possible superintendence" is just a matter of
logical consistency and can be settled by consistent imagination. Gould
apparently grants that God could superintend nature without distorting,
undermining, or identifying as theological the evidence in the domain of
the sciences. This seems right, because God could be suitably elusive in
divine superintendence by hiding all identifiable divine fingerprints. God
could superintend nature in various ways without corrupting or identifying as theological the scientific evidence available to humans. We have
no good reason to deny this; so Gould seems to be on the right track here.

The main lesson now is that the sciences do not exclude religion or
religious experiences so long as neither presumes empirical claims
inaccessible to the sciences. An account of religious experience can
welcome scientific contributions in the light of this consideration.
The sciences may not depend on religious experience, but they may be
able to illuminate, among other things, the various psychological and
sociological contexts of religious experience. Religion can benefit from
the sciences at least in this regard.

## RELIGIOUS DISAGREEMENT

Some people are suspicious of religious experience on the ground that it attracts extensive disagreement about its nature and significance. There is no denying that it does attract such disagreement, but it is a mistake to let mere disagreement about religious experience be a source for denying its reality or significance. Mere disagreement is a function of conflicting beliefs, but such beliefs by themselves do not count against the reality or the significance of a subject of disagreement. We do not allow disagreement about scientific matters, for instance, to lead to wholesale dismissal of the relevance of scientific matters, and we should take an analogous approach to disagreement about religious experience.

The test for the reality and the significance of religious experience should come from our overall relevant *evidence*, and not the popularity or the conflict of mere beliefs. Otherwise, we will neglect our best indicator of the reality and the significance of religious experience. Of course, people can, and often do, disagree about what counts as evidence, but this consideration is not unique to the topic of religious experience. So, it does not pose a special problem in connection with religious experience. Sometimes people work with different specific notions of evidence and thus end up talking past each other. For instance, if an extreme empiricist requires that all evidence be sensory, this will raise a problem for theorists who work with a broader notion of evidence. In that case, different specific notions of evidence will be at work, relative to different underlying theoretical purposes. An extreme empiricist could disown interest in a broader notion of evidence that allows for the evidential relevance of religious experience. In that case, we should not expect agreement between the extreme empiricist and various other theorists.

One important lesson is that human agreement is not the foundation of reasonable human commitment aimed at truth, inside or outside religion. Something deeper will serve as the foundation, and that will be a kind of evidence as a (perhaps fallible) truth-indicator. Human experience figures in such evidence, and the big question concerns *what kinds* of human experience may thus figure. In short, what kinds of human experience are (perhaps fallible) truth-indicators? Some religious experiences are candidates, according to some theorists, because they have the marks of indicating (some features of) reality. Tolstoy would offer his aforementioned religious experience as a life-changing example, and the author of the previously cited Psalm 139 would do likewise. Are we in a position to bar those examples as candidates for evidence? If so, on what grounds? Such questions merit our careful attention, without any quick and easy answers. This book's chapters contribute to this kind of attention, regardless of what one ultimately concludes about the reality and significance of religious experience.

CHAPTER SUMMARIES

The book's chapters fall under four general topics: Part I, "Characterizing Religious Experience: Interdisciplinary Approaches"; Part II, "Religious Experience in Traditional Monotheism"; Part III, "Religious Experience outside Traditional Monotheism"; and Part IV, "Prominent Themes and Challenges." Overall, they illuminate a wide range of issues about the nature and significance of religious experience.

In Chapter 1, "Psychology of Religion Approaches to the Study of Religious Experience," Ann Taves notes that in the early twentieth century religious experience was emphasized in the psychological study of religion. It then declined as certain quantitative and behaviorist approaches came to the fore in the 1920s. It reemerged, however, in the second half of the twentieth century as changes in psychology shifted from behavior to cognition and as developments in religion shifted from a primarily Protestant-centered focus to a broader focus on the various religious traditions. Taves uses William James's *Varieties of Religious Experience* (1902), a widely acknowledged classic in the field of psychology of religion, to highlight major features of the field early on and to gain insight into how it has changed over time. With regard to the current situation, she focuses primarily on the psychology of religion as represented by researchers associated with the International Association for the Psychology of Religion and the American Psychological Association's Division 36.

Taves observes that "as a scientific field, psychology of religion is premised on the measurement of religious and/or spiritual (r/s) constructs, which can be treated either as an object of study in its own right, e.g., religiousness or spirituality, or as a variable that effects something else, e.g., flourishing, depression, or benevolence." It is now routinely the case for works in the field to distinguish between religious, mystical, and spiritual experience, she notes, and current research, in contrast to the past, puts less emphasis on sudden subjective experience and more on ordinary religious/spiritual experiences and gradual spiritual transformations that can occur in everyday life. Taves also examines difficulties in the psychology of religion subdiscipline, and she concludes by sketching new directions in which researchers are creating new measures and methods that attempt to provide a more accurate and effective approach to the study of religious experience.

In Chapter 2, "Philosophy of Religion Approaches to the Study of Religious Experience," Phillip H. Wiebe examines several philosophical approaches to religious experience in western history. He notes that the methodological approaches for the discovery of truth in philosophy have not been divorced from those found in what we now consider the sciences. In the ancient world, deduction was used as a form of reasoning in which indubitable axioms were sought, from which other certain truths could then be inferred. This approach was used in considering transcendent realities, such as the existence of God. Once it was established that God exists (from inferences from the existence or design of the cosmos, or from the idea of the greatest conceivable being), one could then interpret certain human experiences as deriving from the divine. The problem was to find indisputable axiomatic truths for this purpose. Classical modern philosophy, of which Descartes was a founding figure, continued to emphasize indubitable truths but focused on the "immediate content of conscious experience." One challenge was to find deductive inferences to God and an external world that follow from the self or substantial mind that Descartes had acknowledged.

Wiebe examines the shift from deductive to inductive inference and then to abductive methodological approaches in philosophy and science, with regards to their relevance to religious experience. He also examines the Theory of Spirits, which postulates theoretical entities, as well as recent work in Reformed Epistemology, as he expands his examination of approaches to religious experience in the philosophy of religion. He concludes by suggesting that a new epistemology for religion and religious experience, one linked to the sciences, is on the horizon.

In Chapter 3, "Theology, Religious Diversity, and Religious Experience," Gwen Griffith-Dickson argues that theology approaches religious experience differently from other disciplines, such as philosophy or psychology, and that, even within the discipline of theology, there are divergent ways of approaching this topic. One major difference between a theological approach and that of other disciplines with regards to religious experience concerns the concept of experience itself. "For the theologian, religious experience does not uniquely designate an exceptional moment with unusual features; rather, it is our lived experience, puzzling, threatening, awe-inspiring, or love-generating, whose ultimate sense and meaning believers seek in relation to their spiritual tradition." In addition, unlike other disciplines, theology is not religiously neutral, but rather it spawns meaning and understanding for adherents within its own faith community.

Griffith-Dickson notes that, with experience as a starting point for theological reflection, an important recent development in Christian theology has been a rethinking about *whose* experience counts for theological reflection and how we engage with it. She references several key movements that have been significant in this regard, including liberation theology, black theology, and feminist theology. Furthermore, she maintains that while theologians may well focus on the experiences of their own faith tradition, religious experience as experienced in our world includes that of "religious others" – those who believe and practice their faith differently from us. Thus, while it can be fruitful to focus on one particular tradition, for a theological enquiry that seeks to comprehend the significance of religious experience as a whole, it must engage with the reality of religious diversity. Griffith-Dickson explores some ways in which this has been attempted, including through a theology of religions, comparative theology, interreligious theology, and interfaith dialog.

In Chapter 4, "Illumined by Meaning," Howard Wettstein focuses on religious experience from an ancient Jewish perspective in the Hebrew Bible's Book of Job. In the relevant passage, God speaks to the suffering Job from a whirlwind. "The Whirlwind vision goes deep," says Wettstein. "Job, diseased, bereft, sitting alone on a pile of ash, is stunned, lifted up by God's words, again filled with awe. Job remains but dust and ashes – but illumined by meaning." Wettstein notes that there is not just one Jewish approach to religious experience; there are such diverse experiences as Maimonidean contemplation, *kabbalistic* mysticism, intense Talmudic engagement, and affective intimacy with the divine.

The Whirlwind passage is unique, even in biblical literature, because God is here speaking as a poet. God's voice speaks here not of justice, sin, or any doctrinal matter, but it speaks instead of the wonders of creation. The resulting poetic insights are not an attempt at theodicy. With them, God offers Job a perspective of the world from God's own vantage point, speaking of the creation in God's own voice, in the first person. With this vision, Job can be liberated from his own suffering, for the world in which he lives is a wonderful place of "joy-inducing beauty," even though it is also a challenging place of "jaw-dropping coldness." According to Wettstein, the Whirlwind vision is the product of human wisdom and poetic imagination. It is also a religious vision, one in which the complexity of the world and the human condition is reflected as God sees it: beautiful, awful, magical.

In Chapter 5, "Religious Experience in Early Christianity," James D. G. Dunn notes that religious experience played an important role in early Christianity. He also points out that while the notion of religious experience today may be identified with what happened in religious revivals of the past, such as those of early Pentecostalism, it should not be limited to uninhibited emotional events. Some religious experiences consist of deep intellectual reflection or a sense of being loved and valued, for example. Dunn begins his overview with Jesus and then moves on to the earliest days of Christianity as expressed in the writings of the New Testament. In Mark's account of Jesus's baptism experience, Dunn argues, the two main features that were motivating and empowering for Jesus's ministry are manifest: a sense of intimate sonship with his divine Father and his empowerment by the Spirit of God. Regarding earliest Christianity, Dunn argues that there were two foundational types of motivating experiences: postmortem appearances of Jesus and the first disciples' Pentecost experiences. Additional signs and wonders, such as visions, healings, and other events taken to be miracles were also distinctive features of early Christian religious experience.

The experiences of the apostle Paul stand out as especially expressive of early Christianity, including the liberating power of the Spirit, being "in Christ," experiencing the Spirit of God as the Spirit of Jesus, and the shared experience of believers as members of the body of Christ. In the Johannine writings, experience of the Spirit continues to flourish as the Spirit of Jesus is understood to be at work in the lives of all believers. With the exception of the book of Revelation (being unique in the Bible as a series of unbroken revelations), the rest of the New Testament, Dunn suggests, shows only modest interest in religious experience. The reasons for that difference are not obvious.

In Chapter 6, "Religious Experience in Traditional Islam," William C. Chittick places emphasis on Sufism or "Islamic mysticism" given its prominence in Islamic history regarding religious experience. He notes that the mystical trend among Muslims can be traced back to the prophet Mohammad and the Qur'an, and that mystical experience has played an extraordinary role in the development of the Islamic faith. While western scholars often identify Sufism with folk religion, Chittick reminds us that it is not only those in the general population who have been attracted to these mystical practices. Indeed, some of the most elite teachers and scholars of Islamic history, such as Ibn Arabi, have been engaged in Islamic mysticism.

According to the Sufi literature of Ibn Arabi and others, the soul must be prepared for perception and understanding of mystical experience in order to reap the good it has to offer. The unprepared individual who undergoes such experience may falsely believe that he or she has been removed from the discipline and obligation of following the teachings of the Qur'an and Hadith. Nearness to God is the ultimate goal of the human quest, and Sufi teaching with regard to this journey includes a recognition of the role of imagination in human experience, the importance of love in finding divine self-disclosure, and the awareness that God alone is ultimately what is real. Chittick characterizes the role of such factors in an important approach to religious experience in traditional Islam.

In Chapter 7, "Religious Experience in Ancient Confucianism and Daoism," Xinzhong Yao argues that while it is challenging to establish clear boundaries between what are dubbed ancient "Confucianism" and "Daoism," nevertheless religious experience in both of these Chinese traditions can be divided into two broad categories: the human-centered and the transcendent-centered. Yao notes that in early classic Confucian and Daoist texts there is abundant evidence that individuals had such experiences as the following: "felt the influence or control of mystical power, had emotional communication with a spiritual being, were enlightened by a new view of life and death, had a dream that was extraordinary but was believed to be true, went through mysterious feelings such as hearing, seeing, smelling something inexplainable, had a visionary experience either alone or together with others, or experienced the union with the universe or cosmic power, in which one came to become one body with the universe."

Yao suggests that Confucian and Daoist experiences converge in a tendency toward a moderate anthropocentrism that includes an ultimate concern about human life and human destiny reflected in personal, familiar, and social matters. He notes that, in both traditions, emphasis is placed on the significance of self-cultivation for a good life, and that the bulk of their religious experiences are associated with practices that nourish a good life.

In Chapter 8, "Religious Experience in Buddhism," David Burton notes that religious experience in Buddhism, rooted as it is in the Buddha's Enlightenment or Awakening experience, is foundational to Buddhism. Nevertheless, he maintains, Buddhist attitudes to religious experience are complex, as are its various traditions. He suggests that western preconceptions of the religion have often led to an overemphasis on the role of personal experience and a subjectivized notion of

Buddhism. This generates a distorted view of it – one that ignores significant aspects of the religion and its practices, such as its ritual and scriptural components.

Religious experiences – including meditative, visual, and altruistic experiences – are an important dimension of the history and lives of Buddhists, even though their import to Buddhist doctrine and practice is widely debated. One example of this debate is whether religious experience plays a role in justifying Buddhist doctrines, such as the doctrine of not-self – the view that there is no enduring, unchanging self, but only a flow of changing events. Some Buddhist scholars have claimed that introspective experience justifies this doctrine, on the ground that although perceptions, acts of will, feelings, and so on are experienced, no unchanging self is found in experience. Not all Buddhist scholars agree, however. Within Buddhist traditions there are disagreements about what introspective experience reveals and supports. Burton takes up this topic and related topics about the role of religious experience in Buddhism.

In Chapter 9, "Ramanuja's Eleventh Century Hindu Theology of Religious Experience," Francis X. Clooney provides a case study for Hindu religious experience in the work of the Vedantin scholar, Ramanuja (1017–1137). As Clooney shows, Ramanuja's writings – which include philosophical and theological works, prayers, rules for worship, and hermeneutical guides of sacred texts – offer a program for religious experience, in particular a deep desire for and experience of union with God/Brahman. Clooney elucidates the work of Ramanuja before moving to the broader Hindu religious context.

A leader of the south Indian Hindu Srivaishnava community (a denomination revering the goddess Lakshmi and the god Vishnu), Ramanuja takes religious experience to be rooted in the contemplation of scripture and tradition, as well as in ritual practice, and to offer a clearer vision of the divine and of union of the self with the divine. Ramanuja's work, as Clooney argues, is an "integrated and whole Vedanta," crafted to provide the "cognitive, affective, and performative steps" requisite for the sincere reader to advance toward an intense spiritual existence in this life. As a Vishishtadvaita (qualified non-dualism) Vedantin, Ramanuja takes the experience of the divine to overcome the gulf between the divine and human by an awareness of a deeper non-duality. His program of religious experience is illustrative of Hindu religious experience, but it is also unique to the Srivaishnava community. Clooney proposes that, as such, further studies are important for developing a more comprehensive understanding of Hindu religious experience.

In Chapter 10, "Exploring the Nature of Mystical Experience," Steven T. Katz focuses on the interconnection between mystical experience, metaphysics, and epistemology, in order to illuminate some key issues in these philosophical domains that arise through mystical experience. He notes that mystical experiences occur in all of the major religious traditions, and they have been studied by theologians and philosophers for many decades. In the past, the emphasis of study has been on mystical experiences as they are described and reported by those who have had them. Based on these reports, important insights have been gleaned about their content from leading thinkers such as William James (1902), Ninian Smart (1984), and Rudolph Otto (1923). Katz joins this discussion, but he takes a different approach, based on his own readings of mystical texts from across the religious traditions.

Katz advances the phenomenological observation that "the content of mystical experience almost always turns out to be what the mystic wants it to be." This is not intended to be a new insight, but he emphasizes that this similarity in the various traditions is not to be accounted for by the nature of the mystical experience itself. Instead, he appeals to the fact that the ineffable and ecstatic experiences of mystics are expressed by them from within the tradition they know and follow. Their testimony uses the metaphysics, ontology, and doctrines from within their own contexts. Thus, mystical experience and mystical consciousness, Katz argues, are mediated, and this mediation better explains the nature of mystical experience than the typical approach of understanding them as being fundamentally the same. He recognizes that his methodological and metaphysical claims are unconventional and provocative and may be proven wrong, and he recommends further exploration of the subject.

In Chapter 11, "Miraculous and Extraordinary Events as Religious Experience," Fiona Bowie examines the notion of experience and what it is about an experience that identifies it as "religious." An experience, she maintains, can be expressed in verbal form whereby one is referring to the effects of the experience on the individual or how the experience makes the individual feel. The term "experience" can also be used as a noun in describing the process for one's acquiring knowledge through the senses or through such things as seeing or feeling. As there is no agreed upon definition of "religion," Bowie notes that the boundary between religious and nonreligious events can appear arbitrary and contextual. She thus focuses on those experiences that are self-described, or described by others, as being "religious," in order to explore what qualifies an experience to be extraordinary and miraculous.

Bowie uses two case studies to illustrate the role experience plays in extraordinary and miraculous events and the relation they have to mystical experience. Her first study involves the out-of-body near-death experience of an American soldier from the 1940s, George Ritchie. He describes in graphic detail the leaving of his body, the visual experiences and sensations that transpired as he left the hospital, the "stupendous certainty" that he was in the presence of the Son of God, the unconditional love emanating from this being, a sense of regret for not being more loving during his life, and then his return to his body. This experience had a profound effect on his life. Bowie maintains that whatever the religious tradition, near-death experiences such as Ritchie's are widely taken to be religious experiences leading to "a reorientation of priorities and values, and removing the fear of death." People who have had such a near death experience commonly state that they *know* that an afterlife exists and what awaits them when they return. Bowie's second case study involves apparitions of Mary in the small town of Medjugorje. The apparitions are unusual in their longevity, as they have continued for almost three decades. Given the longevity and predictable timing of the episodes, scientific studies have been able to focus on the visionaries. The apparitions are consistent with those of other famous Roman Catholic sites, as they offer calls for peace, apocalyptic warnings, and a series of 'secrets' to be revealed later. Bowie concludes that "it can take an extraordinary or miraculous event to enable people to recognise the miraculous in the experience of everyday, ordinary existence."

In Chapter 12, "Evil, Suffering, and Religious Experience," Michael L. Peterson observes that the universal experience of evil and suffering is inescapably related to the phenomenon of religion. He focuses on theoretical and practical aspects of the approaches to evil and suffering in three world religions: Christianity, Islam, and Hinduism. In these traditions, we find case studies that show not only how, in their different formulations, evil and suffering are problematic in these traditions, but also how they provide intellectual and spiritual resources for responding to evil and suffering.

Regarding the theoretical problem raised by evil and suffering, Peterson proposes that: in Judaism the problem fundamentally relates to God's justice; in Christianity it relates to God's love; and in Islam it relates to God's power and control. This difference of emphasis can be accounted for in part, he notes, by the unique ways evil and suffering are experienced as they are processed through the various categories of the religions. As Peterson says:

Thus, in Judaism, the question was about the apparent unjust distribution of the benefits and burdens of life, while in Christianity it was about the apparent lack of God's loving purposes in the outcomes of human affairs. In Islam, then, the question becomes about the apparent lack of divine control in light of the strong theological assertions of Allah's omnipotence.

While the experience of all manner of suffering and evil is a universal human phenomenon, Peterson argues that the different interpretive categories produce different directives with respect to practical engagement. He concludes by pointing out that the various responses to evil and suffering across religious traditions and cultures are significant ways of engaging with a major aspect of human life and experience, and that such a study of this subject may help us to appreciate the powerful influence of global religion and to increase our awareness of our shared humanity.

In Chapter 13, "Naturalism and Religious Experience," Willem B. Drees proposes that a science-inspired naturalism, such as the one he considers, is committed to a fully naturalistic view of reality, but need not exclude religious experience as a category of human experience. He examines the notion of a science-inspired philosophical naturalism, and he proposes that, on the account under consideration, there are both a priori and a posteriori claims about it. Regarding the former, there is an affirmation that there is one reality – the natural world – and no ontological realm beyond it: no God or angels or soul or heaven. Regarding the latter, naturalism can be understood to be a view of reality that incorporates the work of the natural sciences in forming an empirical understanding of all its various dimensions. Drees also considers two clusters of experience: exceptional experiences (those which seem to conflict with natural events) and experiences that coincide with affective responses, such as awe and wonder.

Exceptional experiences, according to the naturalism envisaged by Drees, are explainable, at least in principle, within a naturalistic purview. Anomalies are not accepted as evidence of realities beyond the natural world; instead, they are viewed as incentives for further analysis. For those experiences that are affectively significant, some naturalists may interpret them in terms of awe, beauty, wonder, or even grace, and they may even consider them to be sufficiently similar to religious experiences (given their prior awareness of religious symbols and expressions) such that they refer to themselves as "religious naturalists." Nevertheless, whether identifying as *religious* naturalists or not, naturalists as considered in this chapter claim that all human experiences are congruous with scientific explanations and the workings of the natural world.

In Chapter 14, "Meaning and Social Value in Religious Experience," Mark Owen Webb argues that one overlooked aspect in the study of religious experience is that it occurs in the setting of a religion that is, typically, a social institution. Within such an institution, the subjects of the experiences participate in rituals and ceremonies with others who share at least some of their beliefs and convictions. Thus, religious experiences, like sensory experiences, are socially embedded, and their social context is significant with regard to understanding and evaluating those experiences and to discovering their epistemic value. While the qualia of the experience are private, there is much more involved than only qualitative experience, just as there is in sensory experience.

Webb suggests that a religious context can offer a sharp contrast with a naturalistic or existentialist view of the world implying that a human life does not intrinsically have meaning. Within a religious setting, religious experiences can offer a sense of meaning or significance to one's life by underwriting a narrative about what is important for human life and about something outside, and far greater than, an individual human. In this connection, according to Webb, social factors can figure importantly in the understanding and the significance of religious experiences.

## References

Dawkins, Richard. *River out of Eden*. New York: Basic Books, 1996.

Dennett, Daniel. *Breaking the Spell: Religion as a Natural Phenomenon*. New York: Viking Penguin, 2006.

Freud, Sigmund. "A Philosophy of Life," in *New Introductory Lectures on Psychoanalysis*. New York: Carlton House, 1933.

Gould, Stephen Jay. "Impeaching a Self-Appointed Judge," *Scientific American* 267 (1992): 118–21. www.stephenjaygould.org/reviews/gould_darwin-on-trial.html.

   *Rocks of Ages: Science and Religion in the Fullness of Life*. New York: Ballantine, 1999.

James, William. *Varieties of Religious Experience*. New York: Modern Library, 1902.

Moser, Paul K. *Understanding Religious Experience: From Conviction to Life's Meaning*. Cambridge: Cambridge University Press, 2020.

Otto, Rudolf. *The Idea of the Holy*. Translated by J. W. Harvey. London: Oxford University Press, 1923.

Smart, Ninian. *The Religious Experience of Mankind*, 3rd ed. New York: Charles Scribner's Sons, 1984.

Tolstoy, Lev (Leo). *My Confession*. 1882. (London: Oxford University Press, 1921 [trans. Aylmer Maude]. New York: Norton, 1983 [trans. David Patterson]).

# Part I

*Characterizing Religious Experience:*
*Interdisciplinary Approaches*

# 1 Psychology of Religion Approaches to the Study of Religious Experience

ANN TAVES

## INTRODUCTION

Psychology can stand in various relations with religion: psychology *and* religion, psychology *as* religion, and psychology *of* religion (Jonte-Pace and Parsons 2001). The first is a subfield within religious studies, the second within theology, and the third within psychology. Research in the psychology of religion overlaps to some extent with the new interest in the cognitive science of religion. Researchers differ in their training, however. Most psychologists of religion are trained in psychology, while most researchers associated with the cognitive science of religion are trained in anthropology, philosophy, or religious studies. This chapter focuses on the way psychologists of religion have approached the study of religious experience.

Religious experience, understood primarily in terms of conversion and mystical experience, played a prominent role in the psychological study of religion in the early decades of the twentieth century. Experience (religious or otherwise) waned as a focus of study as behaviorist and quantitative approaches became more prominent. Religious experience reemerged as a topic in the second half of the twentieth century alongside, and largely distinct from, mystical experience and, more recently, spirituality (Wulff 2001; Emmons and Paloutzian 2003). These shifts reflected changes in psychology as it shifted from studying consciousness to behavior in the 1920s and from behavior to cognition in the 1950s, as well as changes in the study of religion as it shifted from a largely Protestant-centered focus on religious experience to a more even-handed study of various religious traditions and, most recently, an understanding of spirituality as potentially separable from religion (Hill et al. 2000).

Although the psychological study of religion has both European and American roots (Wulff 1997), William James's *The Varieties of Religious Experience* (VRE; 1902/1985) played an outsized role in its development and stands as the only widely recognized classic in the psychology of religion. As such, we can use it to highlight key features of the early psychology of religion and better understand how the subfield has changed over time. Two substantive features stand out: its focus on the conversion experience and on mysticism. For most of the nineteenth century, revivals and awakenings in which people experienced conversion were a staple of Protestantism. By the end of the century, however, liberalizing Protestants sought to downplay the need for a sudden experience in favor of a gradual process of transformation, typically through education. Downplaying conversion, while at the same time questioning traditional sources of authority such as the Bible, heightened liberalizers' interest in other forms of experience, such as mysticism, which until that time encompassed a wide range of experiences that Protestants associated with "superstitious" Catholics and "primitive" peoples. Writing in 1890, James (1983, p. 248) indicated that mysticism included "divinations, inspirations, demoniacal possessions, apparitions, trances, ecstasies, miraculous healings and productions of disease, and occult powers."

In this context, James's *Varieties of Religious Experience* made three key interventions: (1) It offered a psychological interpretation of both sudden and gradual conversion that leveled the playing field between evangelical and liberal Protestants by explaining both types of conversion in terms compatible with a modern, scientific religious sensibility. (2) Along with Ralph Inge (1899) and Evelyn Underhill (1911), James adopted a narrowed definition of mysticism that established a hierarchy of experiential phenomena that placed "authentic" mysticism at the apex and relegated other ostensibly "primitive" or "pseudo-mystical" phenomena to the margins. (3) It explained both conversion and mysticism in light of a psychological theory of religion in which the "common nucleus" of all religions was a transformative process premised on an "uneasiness" that required "a solution."

The solution, according to James (1902/1985, p. 400), was "a sense that we are saved from the wrongness by making proper connection with the higher powers." This connection, he said, was mediated by a "higher part" of the self, which potentially transcends the self, as well as "lower parts" associated with insanity. The connection was experienced as the incursion of a power other than the self. Although he downplayed the connections in the VRE, James's understanding of these "incursions from the subconscious" was grounded in a dissociative view of the mind that he had developed in conversation with psychical researchers studying spiritualist mediums and clinicians treating patients with mental disorders (Taves 2009b).

PART I: CONTEMPORARY APPROACHES

With this as a baseline, we can turn to the current situation, keeping in mind that, from the outset, James was criticized for focusing too much on "individual men in their solitude" (VRE, p. 34) at the expense of collective practices and on "religious geniuses," whom he freely admitted, were "subject to abnormal psychical visitations" (VRE, p. 15) at the expense of ordinary, everyday experience. In depicting the current situation, I will focus primarily on the psychology of religion as represented by researchers associated with the International Association for the Psychology of Religion (IAPR) and American Psychological Association's (APA) Division 36. Over the past several decades, psychologists associated with IAPR and APA have offered overviews of the subfield in graduate (Hood, Hill, and Spilka 2018) and undergraduate textbooks (Paloutzian 2017) and, more recently, in two handbooks (Paloutzian and Park 2005, 2013; Pargament, Exline, and Jones 2013).

If we examine these handbooks and textbooks, we find that they now routinely include "spiritual experience" and consistently distinguish between religious, spiritual, and mystical experience. In contrast to the VRE, religious experience is no longer treated as an overarching category that includes mystical (and now spiritual) experience. Although the *Handbook of the Psychology of Religion and Spirituality* (Paloutzian and Park 2005, 2013) treats all three types of experience in a single chapter on "Mystical, Spiritual, and Religious Experience" (and adds a chapter on "The Neuropsychology of Religious Experience"), the others do not. The second and third editions of *The Psychology of Religion* (Spilka et al. 1996, 2003) have separate chapters on "Religious Experience" and "Mysticism." The fourth and fifth editions (Hood, Hill, and Spilka 2009, 2018) retitle the former as "Religious and Spiritual Experience," which they continue to treat apart from "Mysticism." The *APA Handbook of Psychology, Religion, and Spirituality* (Pargament, Exline, and Jones 2013) has separate chapters on "Mystical Experience" and "Spiritual Experience," while leaving out "Religious Experience" entirely. The most recent edition of the *Invitation to the Psychology of Religion* (Paloutzian 2017) breaks with this pattern by focusing on "Religion, Spirituality, and Experience."

If we consider the experiential dimension of religion and spirituality more broadly, we find the psychologists are still devoting attention to conversion (Spilka et al. 1996, 2003), while expanding its purview to include "Spiritual Transformation" (Paloutzian and Park 2005), and most recently, "Deconversion" as well (Streib et al. 2009; Paloutzian

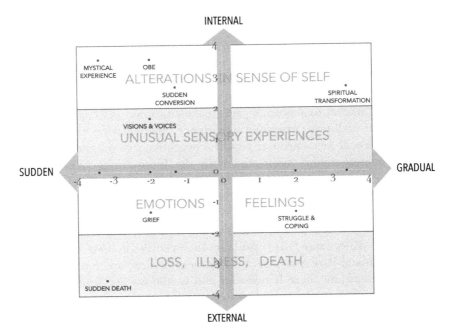

Figure 1.1 Types of experience by dimension (internal/external, sudden/gradual).

and Park 2013; Paloutzian 2017; Hood et al. 2018). There are also chapters we can cluster under the general heading of religious and/or spiritual "struggle and coping" (Paloutzian and Park 2005, 2013; Pargament 2013; Paloutzian 2017; Hood, Hill, and Spilka 2018).

We can make initial sense of these changes as a move away from James's emphasis on sudden, subjective experiences (incursions from the subconscious) to more ordinary (spiritual) experiences and more gradual changes (spiritual transformations) that can take place in the context of practices or everyday life (struggle and coping). Thus, on a continuum from sudden to gradual experience, the focus has shifted from the sudden to the gradual. We also see a shift from an emphasis on experiences that are purely subjective or internal to experiences that are more public and external. If we depict these as two axes (sudden-gradual and internal-external), we can see the work that the terms "mystical" and "spiritual" are now doing (Figure 1.1).

The placement of experiences, though approximate, illustrates the difference between the upper left quadrant, which contains unusual experiences, and the other three quadrants, which contain more ordinary experiences. In the contemporary European and American context, unusual experiences are typically interpreted as mystical, transliminal, or anomalous, or, if translated into psychiatric terms (such that undifferentiated unity = ego dissolution, OBE = dissociation, visions & voices = hallucinations), as pathological. Experiences in the other three quadrants tend to be interpreted as religious, spiritual, or secular.

"Mystical experiences," as psychologists typically define them, appear in the upper left quadrant, along with other sudden internal experiences, while "spirituality" extends to the other three quadrants.[1] The upper right quadrant captures gradual processes of inner spiritual transformation, while the lower right captures more external, public processes that may or may not take place in a formal religious setting. The lower left quadrant contains sudden, observable experiences, such as sudden upwellings of emotion and sudden injury, illness, and death. The latter, which may be accompanied by sudden internal experiences, for example visions and near death experiences, are often treated in nonreligious settings (e.g., hospitals) by personnel increasingly attentive to "spiritual" issues (Sullivan 2019). In this mapping, religious experience has become a "floating signifier" lacking agreed upon associations.

We can deepen our understanding of these experience-related lines of research by turning to the methods psychologists of religion have used to pursue them. Although some like to highlight the subfield's methodological diversity (see, e.g., Hood Jr and Belzen 2013), the majority of studies have relied on questionnaires (also called scales or measures) (Hill and Hood 1999; Hill 2013; Hill and Edwards 2013). As a scientific field, psychology of religion is premised on the measurement of religious and/or spiritual (R/S) constructs, which can be treated either as an object of study in its own right (e.g., religiousness or spirituality), or as a variable that effects something else (e.g., flourishing, depression, or benevolence).

A construct is a hypothetical variable that is not directly observable, such as motivation, intelligence, or, in this case, religiousness or spirituality. As such, it must be operationalized in order to be measured. This can be done by means of a behavior (e.g., how often do you attend church?) or a self-assessment (e.g., how religious are you?) (Oman 2013). Although this gives rise to many different operationalized measures of religion and spirituality, psychologists view this as "the only way [they] can understand religion from a scientific standpoint." (Hood, Hill, and Spilka 2018, p. 17). Of the measures developed by psychologists of

---

[1] In the general population the semantic range of the term "spirituality" is very broad. For an analysis of meanings in the US and Germany, see Streib and Klein (2016).

religion, only a subset focus on experience, whether characterized as religious, mystical, or spiritual (for a list of the more reliable measures, see Hill 2013, pp. 65–67).

To understand how they are approaching religious, spiritual, and mystical experience more clearly, we can return to the topics outlined – religious and mystical experience; spirituality; conversion, deconversion, and spiritual transformation; and struggle and coping – to consider researchers who have shaped the line of inquiry, the questions they are asking, and the tools they use to answer them.

**Religious and Mystical Experience**

Within the psychology of religion, Ralph Hood is widely recognized as the leading expert on religious and mystical experience. Hood created the Religious Experience Episodes Measure (REEM; Hood 1970) using items drawn from the VRE, and the Mysticism Scale (M-Scale; Hood 1975) based on W. T. Stace's criteria for mysticism. Both are well regarded based on the usual measurement criteria (Hill 2013, pp. 65–67) and have been used in numerous studies in the United States. The M-Scale has been used in a number of other cultures as well. In addition to a long history of empirical research, Hood has written most of the overviews of the research in this area. His interdisciplinary *Handbook of Religious Experience* (Hood 1995) was the first, and, until now, only attempt at a comprehensive approach to religious experience. He authored the chapter on "Mystical, Spiritual, and Religious Experiences" in the first and second editions of the *Handbook of the Psychology of Religion and Spirituality* (Paloutzian and Park 2005, 2013) and the chapter on "Mystical Experience" in the *APA Handbook of Psychology, Religion, and Spirituality* (Pargament 2013). He is the first author of the two most recent editions of *The Psychology of Religion* (Hood, Hill, and Spilka 2009, 2018) and bears primary responsibility for its chapters on "Religious and Spiritual Experience" and "Mysticism."

In testing his measures of religious experience (REEM; Hood 1970) and mystical experience (M-Scale; Hood 1975), Hood found that "religious experience" was harder to define and measure across cultures than "mystical experience." In designing the REEM, Hood took what he called "a literary exemplar approach," drawing examples of experiences from James's VRE and asking respondents to rate the extent to which they had experienced something similar. Holm (1982) had difficultly producing a meaningful Swedish equivalent until he replaced the examples drawn from the VRE with examples drawn from Nordic tales.

In light of Holm's efforts, Hood concluded that the REEM was likely best suited to religiously committed North American Protestants.

Hood's experience with the Mysticism Scale, which he based on Stace's (1960) definition of mysticism as an experience of "undifferentiated unity," was quite different. In developing the scale, Hood (2013, pp. 296–97) deliberately rejected James's definition of mysticism, which encompassed "varied forms of intense experiences," as too broad and adopted Stace's definition of mysticism as an experience of "undifferentiated unity." As he explains, "I sought an independent measure of the experience of unity, whether religiously interpreted or not, not a general measure of a variety of transliminal states. I wanted a measure of mysticism as a response to the Real" (p. 297). As Hood elaborated,

> My fascination with James's and Stace's work was fueled by a commitment to what Schuon (1975) has called in an aptly titled book *The Transcendent Unity of Religion*. This controversial view includes the argument that although specific faith traditions must be understood as unique in historical and cultural terms, it is possible that differences in faith tradition mask otherwise identical experiences that are both epistemologically and ontologically identical ... The claim to a transcendent unity to religion (and here "religion" is any articulation of the meaningfulness of mystical experience) rest [sic] upon the ontological claim that in [sic] mystical experience is real. Simply, the report of unitive mystical experience is a report that amounts to an ontological claim about what Hick (1989) simply argued is the Real. (Hood 2013, pp. 301–2)

Hood used Stace's definition to operationalize mysticism because he wanted to test Stace's claim that experiences of "undifferentiated unity" gave access to the Real and thus reflected the underlying unity of religion.

In saying this, he acknowledges (Hood, Hill, and Spilka 2018, p. 356) that "social scientists cannot confirm any ontological claims based on mystical experience; [but] they can construct theories compatible with claims to the existence of such realities" and investigate "hypotheses derived from views about the nature of transcendent reality ..., as long as specific empirical predictions can be made." To test Stace's claim, Hood and collaborators (Hood and Williamson 2000; Hood et al. 2001; Chen et al. 2011) administered the Mysticism Scale to general populations in a number of cultural contexts (the United States, Iran, India, and China) in order to assess the prevalence of such experiences across cultures. Based on these data, Hood (2013) reasserted the case for a "common core" of mystical experience and argued that "mysticism is the best candidate for a distinct, *sui generis* experience that has been recognized across diverse traditions and cultures" (Hood, Hill, and Spilka 2018, pp. 355, 383–88).

Hood relies on this evidence to make a sharp distinction between "mystical experience," which he views as constituting the "common core of religion," and "religious experience," which he views as the product of ordinary attributional processes. Virtually any experience, Hood acknowledges, can be considered religious if it is appraised as such. Mystical experiences, in contrast, are (likely) *sui generis* (a thing in itself) and, thus, inherently mystical regardless of how they are interpreted after the fact, for example as religious, spiritual, or secular.

The separation of the chapters devoted to religious experience and mysticism in the various editions of *The Psychology of Religion* reflect this distinction. Thus, beginning in the 1990s, Spilka et al. (1996) define "religious experience" broadly "as any experience that is identified within faith traditions as religious," adding that "with the possible exception of mystical and numinous experience, it is probably not fruitful to define religious experiences by their inherent characteristics." Perhaps due to Spilka's influence, their textbook takes an emphatically attributional approach to religious experience:

> Whether an experience is religious or not depends upon the experiencer's interpretation of it. Interpretations provide meanings not inherently obvious to those outside the tradition that provides the context for identifying any particular episode as a religious meaningful experience. Almost any experience humans can have can be interpreted as an experience of God. (pp. 183–84)

By way of contrast, "what makes numinous and mystical experiences so important to study is that they are the strongest claims that people can experience foundational realities" (p. 227). This basic distinction between religious and mystical experience is maintained through subsequent editions with minor modifications, such as treating spiritual experience alongside religious experience and downplaying the numinous in later chapters on mysticism.

Hood's approach, as he notes, contrasts with that adopted by Thalbourne, who developed the Mystical Experience Scale (MES; Thalbourne 1991) on "the basis of [his] personal experience [with manic depression] and subsequently refined [it] based on the earlier work by

William James" (Lange and Thalbourne 2007, p. 122).[2] As a result, Thalbourne, like William James and in contrast to Hood and Stace, was far more open to the negative side of such experiences and alert to the potential overlap between experiences characterized as mystical, paranormal, and psychotic. As Thalbourne indicates:

> The possibility that mystical experience involves negative qualities as well was not systematically explored until the 1990s when Thalbourne & Delin (1994) found that magical ideation, mania, and depression correlate with mystical experience ... Whether mystical experience is to be encouraged or cautioned against is a serious issue, as Lukoff's (1985) groundbreaking paper suggests that mystical experience can have psychotic features. (Lange and Thalbourne 2007, p. 122)

As I have argued elsewhere (Taves 2020), Hood is to some extent aware of this issue, though he has not, in my view, adequately dealt with the implications. Thus, his own factor analysis indicates that experiences of unity can be experienced as negative as well as positive. Moreover, based on mental health measures administered along with the M-Scale, he found that, in both the American and Iranian samples, "the introvertive factor was a predictor of psychological dysfunction" (Hood et al. 2001, p. 703). The underlying problem, I think, is that he considers "positive affect," which loads (along with noetic claims, a sense of sacredness, and ineffability) on his interpretive factor "as a secondary quality, *integral to the common core experience of unity*, but on the fringe so to speak" (Hood 2013, 298, emphasis added). He views these secondary qualities as interpretations that are integral to the common core experience, but apparently not as pre-conscious appraisals of a dramatic alteration in the sense of self.

I will discuss the implications of these findings in the next section; for now I will simply note that religious experience, as defined by Hood, Hill, and Spilka, has no general measure and can appear anywhere in Figure 1.1. Thalbourne's MES and his Transliminality Scale (Lange et al. 2000) query a range of unusual experiences that appear in the upper left quadrant, while Hood's mysticism scale focuses on a particular type of experience in which the boundaries of the sense of self blur or disappear based on theories about accessing the Real.

---

[2] His struggle with manic depression was known to many of his collaborators and was discussed more publicly after his death in 2010 (see www.skeptic.org.uk/news/michael-thalbourne-1955-2010/).

**Spirituality**

As already noted, psychologists have embraced the distinction between religion and spirituality, incorporating it into their journals, textbooks, handbooks, and even the name of their APA division. The distinction, though not new, rose to prominence in the latter part of the twentieth century as many Europeans and Americans began characterizing themselves as "spiritual but not religious" (Roof 1993; Zinnbauer, Pargament, and Scott 1999), that is, as embracing non-institutional spirituality but not institutional religion. Faced with the many different ways that both terms had been operationalized, psychologists of religion warned against two dangers: conceptional polarization and losing sight of "the sacred" (Hill et al. 2000). They proposed defining spirituality as "a search for the sacred," where the sacred referred to "a divine being, divine object, Ultimate Reality, or Ultimate Truth as perceived by the individual," and religion as "the means and methods (e.g., rituals or prescribed behaviors) of the search that receive validation and support from within an identifiable group of people" (p. 66).

Building on this understanding of the sacred as the core of both religion and spirituality, Pargament (1999; see also Pargament and Mahoney 2005; Pargament 2013) – consciously following Durkheim's lead – theorized that if spirituality was operationalized in terms of the "sacralization" or "sanctification" of otherwise secular objects, roles, or responsibilities, the consequences of doing so could potentially be measured. Conceived in this way, anything could be spiritualized, including presumably any sort of experience. Thus, as conceived by leading psychologists of religion, virtually any experience can be spiritualized and thus "count" as a spiritual experience. Thus, in contrast to mystical experiences, which, when defined based on Stace, are limited to the upper left quadrant of Figure 1.1, spiritual experiences can appear in any quadrant providing an individual appraises them as such. Religious experiences, too, can appear in any quadrant provided "they receive validation and support from within an identifiable group of people."

Other prominent psychologists of religion have defined spirituality differently. Ralph Piedmont, for example, defines spiritual transcendence as "the capacity of individuals to stand outside of their immediate sense of time and place to view life from a larger, more objective perspective" (Piedmont 1999, p. 988). This definition, which is based on Allport (1950), conceives spiritual transcendence as a personality trait that is found across cultures and plays a distinctive role in human flourishing (Dy-Liacco et al. 2009). His Spiritual Transcendence Scale

(Piedmont 1999) was designed to measure this trait, understood as the "broad domain of motivations that underlie strivings in both secular and religious contexts" (p. 989).

### Conversion, Deconversion, and Spiritual Transformation

Raymond Paloutzian has played a leading role in reconceptualizing conversion as an instance of meaning system change. In placing religious conversion within a meaning systems framework, he situated it as one among many transformational processes. The meaning system framework, which grew out of research on stress (Lazarus and Folkman 1984; Park and Folkman 1997; Park 2005), was concerned from the outset with appraisal processes. Perhaps for that reason, Paloutzian and Park are less concerned with operationalizing religiousness and spirituality than other psychologists of religion. Paloutzian's concern has been with the process of transformation as it is appraised by those who experience it. Relying on the meaning system framework allowed him to consider the fundamental psychological mechanisms on which life changes are based, regardless of whether they are couched in religious or spiritual language (Paloutzian 2005, p. 334). It also allowed him to work with collaborators to integrate new research on "deconversion" in the chapter written for the second edition (Streib et al. 2009; Paloutzian et al. 2013).

### Struggle and Coping

The research on struggle and coping picks up on the valence theme to ask whether religious and spiritual experiences are always positive. This line of research, which Julie Exline has spearheaded in collaboration with Kenneth Pargament, defines religious and spiritual struggles "as experiences of conflict or distress that center on religious or spiritual issues." Their focus has been on events that people attribute to God or a higher power, to the devil or demonic forces, to personal moral failings, or to disagreements that arise in a religious context (Exline and Rose 2013). Items in the Religious and Spiritual Struggles Scale (RSSS; Exline et al. 2014) query these four types of struggles. The items, thus, explicitly target struggles that respondents associate with God, the devil or evil spirits, moral failings, or religion/spirituality, whatever those terms mean for them.

We can contrast this scale with the Global Meaning Violation Scale (GMVS; Park et al. 2016). Whereas the RSSS investigates the extent to which an individual is troubled by religious or spiritual struggles, the GMVS probes the extent to which an individual's sense of global meaning is disrupted by a stressful experience. The RSSS starts with a religious/spiritual construct (R/S struggle), and every item in the scale makes reference to an experience that the researchers consider religious or spiritual in light of their criteria. The GMVS, in contrast, asks the respondent to "think about how [they] felt before and after [their] most stressful experience." Of the thirteen queries, only one refers to God. Others, such as "inner peace," might be construed by participants as religious or spiritual, but the focus is the extent to which the stressful experience violated their meaning system. Although Exline and Park are both interested in stress, struggle, and coping, their scales approach it in different ways.

In this brief overview of psychological approaches to religious, spiritual, and mystical experience, we can see a tension within the field that mirrors the difference in the two scales. On the one hand, we have those, such as Paloutzian and Park, who wish to situate religious and spiritual experiences within a meaning systems framework, which focuses attention on experiences or events that individuals may or may not appraise as religious or spiritual. Others, such as Exline, Piedmont, and Hood, operationalize key terms (religious/spiritual, transcendent, or mystical, respectively) in order to create a scale that allows them to measure a religious, spiritual, transcendent, or mystical construct.

Paloutzian and Park's (2005, 2013) efforts to situate the psychology of religion within a meaning systems perspective, with its concomitant emphasis on appraisal processes, shifts the center of gravity of the field from the psychology of religion and spirituality to the psychology of meaning making. Their efforts have been embraced by some (Murphy 2017; Taves 2018) and met with resistance from others, such as Pargament and Hood. Pargament, building on earlier definitional work (Hill et al. 2000), stresses the need for scholarly definitions of religion and spirituality that allow researchers to distinguish religion and spirituality from other phenomena and from each other. "Without some shared sense of its key parameters," Pargament et al. (2013, p. 10) write, "the boundaries of our subdiscipline become so diffuse that we can lose our professional identity."

Hood's distinction between religious, spiritual, and mystical experience can be viewed as another line of resistance, which, while conceding that appraisal processes are at work in religious and spiritual experiences, argues that they do not play the same determinative role in mystical experiences. Although Hood locates positive valence in the interpretive factor, he nonetheless characterizes the experience of unity as "mystical" rather than more generically as an experience of self-loss or ego dissolution that can be experienced (and thus unconsciously appraised) as either negative or positive.[3] Research on experiences of ego dissolution induced by hallucinogens, such as psilocybin, stress the crucial role of set and setting on the valence of the experience (Carhart-Harris et al. 2018). Although spiritual practices clearly do play an important role in differentiating positive and negative experiences (Kohls and Walach 2007), negative experiences also occur in the context of spiritual practice, as Lindahl et al. (2017) have demonstrated. Current research on disruptions in the sense of self suggests: (1) that such experiences are not simply the product of expectations, as the constructionists might argue, (2) that they can be induced in various ways, including through R/S practices, and (3) that preconscious appraisal processes affect their valence, which in turn affects how they are experienced and characterized (for further discussion, see Taves 2020).

In so far as psychology aspires to approach experience scientifically, concerns regarding disciplinary identity or accessing the Real or Ultimate should not obscure the difficulties researchers face when they attempt to operationalize and measure complex cultural constructs, such as religious, spiritual, and mystical experience. Because appraisal processes (Park 2010) and attribution theory (Spilka, Shaver, and Kirkpatrick 1985) distinguish between events or experiences and the way they are appraised (consciously and unconsciously), these approaches potentially undercut psychology of religion's traditional emphasis on operationalizing religious, spiritual, and mystical experience as an object of study (Taves 2009a). But, as I will argue in the next section, the psychology of religion is not alone in its attempt to operationalize complex constructs. Scales that measure ostensibly different experiential constructs, such as schizotypal, paranormal, exceptional, and psychotic experiences, are also vying for control of the unusual experiences located in the upper left quadrant.

## PART II: PROBLEMS WITH OR LIMITATIONS OF CURRENT PRACTICES

Hill (2013), who has written the major chapters on measurement for the subfield, highlights a range of limitations of measuring R/S constructs,

---

[3] Hood recently acknowledged (Hood, Hill, and Spilka 2018, p. 394) that new studies suggest the role that spiritual practices play in differentiating "positive experiences of ego loss (mysticism) from negative ones (psychoses)" (Kohls and Walach 2007), but this does not lead him to question the distinction he makes between religious and mystical experiences.

some of which are due to the complex nature of the constructs in question and others inherent in measurement more generally. The difficulties are both theoretical, practical, and technical. Theoretically, Hill highlights the lack of conceptual clarity in the subdiscipline, noting that good measurement must be grounded in good theory and a well-defined object of study (i.e., "construct"). Practically speaking, researchers in the psychology of religion, like other psychologists, have relied heavily on American undergraduate psychology students for their data. Such samples are not representative of the United States, much less the rest of the world (on this problem, see Henrich, Heine, and Norenzayan 2010). Moreover, United States samples – historically and to a lesser degree in the present – are skewed toward Protestantism. Although a few measures have been translated and administered in other cultural contexts, the majority have not. This points to the underlying issue of cultural bias, which practical concerns with respect to survey samples have largely obscured. In so far as measures tacitly reflect Euro-American cultural biases and presuppositions about religion and spirituality, we cannot simply translate them into another language, we have to determine if the questions make sense. As a result, cultural differences pose theoretical issues that must be addressed with innovative designs and raise technical issues regarding validity if the questions are not understood as the researchers intend in a given population.

## Theoretical Issues

There are at least three ways to address the problems involved in operationalizing complex constructs, such as religiousness and spirituality: (1) agree on how to operationalize the constructs, as Hill et al. (2000) and Piedmont (2013) advocate, (2) focus on theoretically more robust constructs, such as meaning systems, as Paloutzian and Park advocate, or (3) design measures that treat cross-culturally valid constructs and appraisal queries separately. The RSSS and GMVS illustrate the first two approaches. The RSSS is designed to measure religious and spiritual struggles (a R/S construct), and the GMVS is designed to measure global meaning violations (a construct derived theoretically from a meaning system framework). In the former case, the researchers had to decide what would count as R/S struggles. If they were to test this cross-culturally, they would likely have to modify their construct. God and demons/Satan might not be particularly relevant in an Asian context; moreover, in translating religious and spiritual, the terms would likely take on different meanings in new cultural contexts. In the latter case, since the focus was on a highly stressful event rather than an R/S construct, the researchers' construct (meaning violations) would likely work across cultures, but they might have to modify or add to their queries to reflect the range of violations possible in a given context. Psychologists of religion have not yet considered the third option, which will be discussed in Part III: New Directions.

The theoretical issues involved in measuring complex constructs, such as mystical experience, which fall in the upper left hand quadrant of Figure 1.1, are particularly acute, since very similar experiences are included under different names, e.g., ego dissolution, hallucinations, dissociation, in competing constructs (e.g., paranormal, schizotypal, psychotic experiences) investigated by researchers in other subfields, including psychiatry and anomalistic psychology.

In both, there is growing recognition of the problem. Beginning with the fourth edition, the *Diagnostic and Statistical Manual of Mental Disorders* (DSM-IV, 1994), recognized that (e.g.) hallucinations and dissociation may be a normal part of religious experience in some cultural contexts (Mezzich et al. 1999). Within psychology, there is a recovery of interest in studying anomalous experiences, which has its roots in psychical research and parapsychology, but what counts as anomalous is not well defined. The two editions of the *Varieties of Anomalous Experience* (Cardeña, Lynn, and Krippner 2014), published by the American Psychological Association, include such disparate experiences as synesthesia, lucid dreaming, out-of-body experiences, hallucinations, mental healing, past-lives, near-death experiences, mystical experiences, and alien abductions. The overlap between experiences that are variously categorized as religious, anomalous, and psychiatric looks something like this (see Figure 1.2).

We can think of these complex constructs, such as anomalous, mystical, and psychotic experience, as clusters of items presumed to represent a type of experience. These measures of presumed clusters suffer from two limitations: first, as noted, they often include items that, when considered phenomenologically, seem similar to those in other clusters and, second, with some exceptions, they have not been adequately tested for stability across populations. Similar items may be obscured for different reasons. In some cases, researchers fail to account for similar items because they limit themselves to discipline specific measures. In other cases, the wording of items reflects disciplinary or cultural presuppositions regarding the nature or cause of the experience. The items embed implicit or explicit appraisals of the experience. If constructs are not adequately tested across populations, researchers may assume that they are measuring cross-culturally

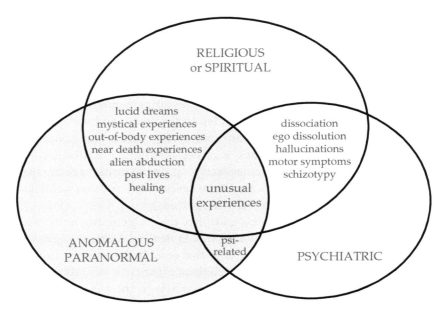

Figure 1.2 Phenomenological overlap between self-reported experiences characterized as religious, anomalous, and pathological.

stable experiences or "natural kinds," when we do not actually know if this is the case. The problem of artificial clusters is not limited to religious, philosophical, or parapsychological constructs, but extends to many psychiatric syndromes as well (Kendell and Jablensky 2003). This is one of the main reasons why the NIMH is encouraging researchers to use the new Research Domain Criteria instead of the DSM categories as the basis for their research (Lilienfeld and Tread-way 2016; Fellowes 2017).

There are three basic strategies for overcoming this problem:

1. As in the psychology of religion, many researchers in psychology, psychiatry, and religious studies stipulate definitions. However, this tends to reinforce disciplinary taxonomies, while overlooking competing constructs.
2. Some are now developing targeted measures of particular experiences, such as of sensed presences (Barnby and Bell 2017) and self-transcendent experiences (Yaden et al. 2017). They are acknowledging the overlap between religious, paranormal, and psychiatric constructs and highlighting our limited knowledge of the mechanisms that differentiate them.

3. Others, studying such disparate topics as religious experience (Taves 2009a), psychosis (Ward et al. 2014; Underwood, Kumari, and Peters 2016), and placebo effects (Ashar, Chang, and Wager 2017) are arguing that appraisal processes – and thus presumably differences in belief and practice – play a crucial role in differentiating experiences.

### Cross-Cultural Issues

Psychologists who focus on anomalous experiences are also calling for more attention to cultural variations, noting that here too researchers tend to assume that anomalous experiences share "widely distributed, universal properties … without sufficient evidence" (Maraldi and Krippner 2019, p. 2). As Maraldi and Krippner point out, we do not know to what extent cultures determine what is nonordinary or anomalous (or supernatural). Obvious differences in this regard lead them to ask whether it is even possible "to develop cross-cultural knowledge about what we currently term anomalous experiences?" They argue that it is possible, but refined methods are needed to do so. They raise several major concerns:

*The problem of framing*: Researchers are not sufficiently attentive to the impact of how questions are framed. When questions include both descriptions of and beliefs about (i.e., appraisal of) an experience, people respond differently than when they are not. In designing the Survey of Anomalous Experiences (SAE), Irwin, Dagnall, and Drinkwater (2013) created items that described paranormal experiences without using terms such as telepathy, precognition, etc., and then asked people if they considered the experiences as paranormal or simply as the result of coincidence or known psychological mechanisms. In doing so, they found that some people reported having had the experiences, but did not consider them as paranormal.

*Culture affects frequency*: Not only does the way experiences are characterized affect the frequency with which experiences are reported, so too does the general cultural or group assessment of their value. Maraldi and Krippner indicate that researchers have demonstrated cross-cultural differences in reported frequency for out-of-body experiences, unusual dreams, and spontaneous childhood past-life experiences.

*The need to get past old debates*: Maraldi and Krippner describe the debate between the cultural and experience sources hypotheses, which parallels, and to some extent overlaps with, the constructionist/common core debates in religious studies, but indicate that the stronger theories acknowledge the interplay of both factors. In their view, the discussion regarding whether culture or universal features has primacy in accounting for AEs seems not particularly fruitful, as both factors are probably present in many if not every AE with different degrees of influence, with some AEs more directly affected by cultural expectations and beliefs (such as mediumship, (Maraldi et al. 2017), whereas other AEs serve as the experiential bases for a wide range of beliefs (such as sleep paralysis, Hufford 1982). (Maraldi and Krippner 2019, p. 8)

Maraldi and Krippner suggest that cross-cultural research with measures that distinguish experiences and beliefs/appraisal could play a significant role in disentangling these factors. This, as they indicate, has important implications for determining whether some AEs are inherently pathological or healthy and/or whether their relation to mental illness is affected by contextual factors.

### Technical Issues

Although some measures of experience, including some used by psychologists of religion, have been validated across cultures, evidence of survey validity is typically based on its internal structure and relation to other variables (Maul 2018). Surveys that are administered across cultures are typically translated into local languages, but researchers typically spend little or no time determining how respondents understand the survey items in the different contexts in which the survey is administered. Cognitive interviews and focus groups can be used to determine how target populations understand items and refine them as needed. In developing the Appraisals of Anomalous Experiences Interview (AANEX) for use in psychosis research, Brett et al. (2007) used focus groups comprised of "high experiencers" drawn from both clinical and general populations to generate neutral descriptions of anomalous experiences.

Because such methods are time consuming and can be impractical, especially when working across cultures, we developed a method for validating survey items online using open-ended meta-surveys to understand how respondents interpret an item and respond to it. This process is iterative; when items are shown to be confusing, cross-culturally unstable, or interpreted differently than we intended, we use participant feedback to make needed revisions, and test these revisions across new samples of respondents (Wolf et al. in press). Item level validation offers a way to refine the wording of questions, eliminate beliefs from descriptive queries, and determine if the neutral descriptions of experiences are recognized and understood in similar ways in different cultural contexts.

These less commonly used types of validation suggest questions that we can use to assess surveys that have been validated with conventional methods:

1.  Is the experience described as generically as possible in terms of bodily sensations (Hinton, Howes, and Kirmayer 2008) or other phenomenological features? Are experiences distinguished from beliefs about and appraisals of the experience (e.g., of its significance, value, or cause) and queried separately?

2.  If the construct is a cluster of several potentially distinguishable experiences, has the universality or stability of the cluster been adequately tested across cultures? Have researchers looked for other constructs that include similar items developed in conjunction with other lines of research? If potentially distinguishable experiences appear in more than one cluster, researchers should consider treating individual experience items as constructs in their own right and investigating how they cluster with other experience items in various cultural and/or clinical contexts.

3.  If a construct is being measured with a questionnaire, have the items been translated into a local language? Have the items been validated to make sure that respondents understand them the way that researchers intend?

## PART III: NEW DIRECTIONS

As scholars of religion are well aware, virtually all religious traditions valorize religious experience, but they do not embrace religious experience in general. Instead, they promote specific experiences that they view as sources of new insight and means of transforming self and world. Traditions not only cultivate some experiences, they actively disparage others. Viewed inclusively, religious experience thus encompasses a wide range of experiences from which traditions select those they choose to valorize in any given context.

Traditional humanities methods are well suited to determine the types of experiences that a given practice tradition officially valorizes as part of its path. Other methods, however, are better suited to determining what people are actually experiencing and how they are interpreting it. Ethnographic interviews and historical sources that give insight into people's experience are of great value in this regard, but inevitably highlight individuals or small groups rather than broader patterns of similarity and difference across cultures and traditions. Well-designed surveys have the potential to collect cross-cultural data that will allow us to determine to what extent the differential valorization of experiences has a measurable effect on their distribution (their frequency and co-occurrence).

Inspired by the two recent measures of anomalous experiences that make a formal distinction between experiences and appraisals – the SAE (Irwin, Dagnall, and Drinkwater 2013) and the AANEX (Brett et al. 2007) – we developed the Inventory of Nonordinary Experiences (INOE) as a tool that will allow us to better understand patterns of similarity and difference across cultures and traditions (Taves and Kinsella 2019).[4] Since neither previous measure included the wide range of items needed to encompass experiences variously appraised as religious, anomalous, and psychiatric, we drew experiences from numerous measures, regardless of what they were designed to assess. Items were stripped of appraisals and combined when similar. In consultation with experts in various traditions, we added experiences that some traditions are known to valorize as religious or spiritual. We developed the appraisal items through an iterative process of consultations and pilot tests. When participants complete the inventory, they indicate if they have had an experience with a yes/no response. If they report having had an experience, they are then asked several context and appraisal questions. At the end, we ask demographic and individual difference questions regarding religious/spiritual identification(s), religiosity, and practice.

In contrast to surveys designed to measure complex experiential constructs, such as spirituality/religiosity, each of the INOE's experience items is a construct in its own right. We are currently in the process of validating each of the experience items in English and Hindi to assess whether the items are understood in similar ways (or even comprehensible) in both contexts. So far, we have been able to revise most items so that they are similarly understood in both India and the United States (for a detailed discussion of our validation process, see Wolf and Ihm 2019; Wolf et al. in press). In asking the experience questions, we do not limit responses to normal waking consciousness, but instead ask respondents to tell us under what conditions the experience occurred (awake, dreaming, while exhausted, under the influence

[4] The INOE was coauthored by myself, Michael Kinsella, and Michael Barlev. The validation team includes myself, Melissa Gordon Wolf, Elliott Ihm, and Maharshi Vyas, plus a technical assistant and coders. The validation and further testing is funded by a grant from the John Templeton Foundation.

of drugs and/or alcohol, or in association with "mind altering" practices). This allows us to sort answers based on context and determine, for example, if experience related dreams are more frequent in some contexts than others.

Of the six appraisal items, three query the valence, significance, and effect of the experience on the person's life (Taves and Kinsella 2019). They allow us to identify the most significant and life-changing experiences regardless of whether they were appraised as religious or spiritual (R/S). The other three appraisals allow us to assess religion-related aspects of the experience. The R/S query asks Americans if they consider the experience religious or spiritual (in English) and Indians if they consider it *adhyatmik ya dharmik* (in Hindi). The Hindi and English terms have culture-specific meanings that we will determine through the validation process and use to interpret responses for the population in question. The other two religion-related appraisals went through many iterations before we arrived at the current "cause" and "reason" questions. The "cause" question asks what respondents believe caused the experience (God, gods, or other deities; other extraordinary or supernatural beings; extraordinary or supernatural forces, powers, or abilities, including your own; mental or physical illness; drugs and/or alcohol; normal mental or physical processes). We deliberately allow more than one response to the cause question because we know that in some contexts, there is no distinction between items (e.g., "Shakti" is both a goddess and an extraordinary force or power). The "reason" question asks why the respondent thinks it happened (to offer a sign or message; to reward them or someone else; to punish them or someone else; for some other reason; for no reason). The responses to the "cause" and "reason" include a range of appraisal options that are sometimes used to distinguish religious, spiritual, and paranormal experiences. In analyzing the data, researchers can collapse the responses in various ways depending on the researcher's interests. In that sense, we tried to avoid privileging a particular definition of religious, spiritual, or paranormal that might or might not work across cultures.

Our goal in designing the INOE was to overcome some of the limitations of extant measures and provide a more effective platform that would allow us to link humanities-style research on the experiential aspects of various religious and cultural traditions with scientific research on unusual experiences. To that end we did the following:

*Artificial Clusters*: Instead of creating a measure of religious, mystical, near death, kundalini, or paranormal experiences premised on the belief that these are cross-culturally stable constructs, we included individual items that are associated with each in order to see if they cluster in different cultural contexts. Because each item is its own construct, researchers do not have to administer the inventory as a whole, but can select items of interest. Although we are interested in mapping what counts as "religious experience" in everyday life across cultures and traditions, the INOE is a very flexible tool that can be used for a variety of purposes.

*Operationalizing Religious, Spiritual, Paranormal, Psychotic, Magical, etc.*: We stripped these connotations from descriptions of experiences and operationalized them in new ways in the appraisals. We retained the terms "religious" and "spiritual" (R/S) in the English version, but we are not operationalizing them. We will determine what respondents mean when they use these terms through the validation process. Moreover, as an appraisal, this item does not have to be translated in the "same" way in every context, for example, it can be translated in terms of "dharma" in India or "dao" in China, and the meaning of the key term for respondents ascertained through the validation process. If a respondent appraises an experience as "spiritual" in the United States and "dharmic" in India, the meaning has to be understood in context. The responses are *not* equivalent. We operationalized explanations typically associated as religious, paranormal, and pathological experiences in the "cause" appraisal, where we allowed respondents to choose more than one cause and researchers to sort responses based on the causes of interest to them. We operationalized what some might view as religion, magic, or superstition in the "reason" appraisal.

Finally, as noted earlier, the inventory cannot (and is not intended to) replace analysis of the experiences that traditions valorize through their teachings and practices, whether in the past or the present. The INOE presupposes this sort of research and seeks to understand how the valorization of certain experiences affects the reported frequency, clustering, and appraisal of experiences in different cultural contexts.

Pilot studies using prevalidated versions of the INOE have demonstrated the potential of this approach (Taves, Barlev, and Kinsella 2017; Barlev 2019). Participants recruited via Amazon Mechanical Turk (MTurk) in the United States (n = 843) and India (n = 721) revealed both commonalities and differences in the frequency, clustering, and appraisal of items. Analysis of our preliminary data indicated that the frequency with which some, but not all, experiences were reported differed. For example, experiences of deja vu, lucid dreaming, dread, loss, and bodily sensations (such as goosebumps) were reported with approximately the same frequency in both contexts, while other experiences, such as revealed messages, past life memories, foreign control of the body, and another self in the body, were reported far more frequently in India than the United States. Furthermore, exploratory factor analysis produced seven culturally recognizable clusters for the United States (e.g., positive and negative emotions, out of body, mysticism, beings), but only two (quite different) clusters for India. Pilot data from the European Summer Research Institute (ESRI, n = 51), which included many meditators (88%), yielded high frequency scores on meditation related items presumably linked to practice. Pilot data collected from college students in each of five countries (the United States [n = 104], China [n = 95], Thailand [n = 106], Vanuatu [n = 99], and Ghana [n = 134]) suggest that experiences of presence, whether of forces, entities, or the dead, are the most commonly appraised as R/S across all five cultures.

CONCLUSION

Within the psychology of religion and spirituality, most researchers have acknowledged that any experience can be appraised as religious or spiritual and, therefore, recognize that what counts as religious or spiritual is a matter of discernment on the part of individuals, groups, cultures, and traditions. Some, such as Hood, hold out the possibility that this does not hold true for mystical experiences, defined as positive experiences of undifferentiated unity. A broader comparative framework, however, indicates that such experiences are more accurately viewed as alterations in the sense of self that are unconsciously appraised as positive or negative. The unconscious appraisal processes can affect how the alterations are experienced and characterized, whether they occur spontaneously, are drug induced, or are cultivated in the context of spiritual practices. Although people typically view these sudden positive transformations as highly significant, they do not offer a basis for declaring mystical experiences sui generis or making scientific claims regarding Ultimate Reality.

Psychologists of religion are currently grappling with the implications of an appraisal-based approach to the study of experience. Like many scholars of religion, some operationalize (i.e., define) their key terms – religiousness and spirituality – both for research purposes and out of a perceived need to preserve their object of study and sense of disciplinary identity. The phenomenological overlap between self-reported experiences characterized as religious, anomalous, and pathological suggests the limitations of a narrowly disciplinary focus. Others, recognizing the importance of appraisal processes, have pushed back against this tendency, arguing that theoretically more robust concepts, such as meaning systems, provide a more solid basis for research.

Due to its traditional reliance on measures administered to North American and European samples, psychologists have only just begun to consider the implications of extending an appraisal-based approach across cultures, traditions, and language groups. As an appraisal-based measure, which we are validating at the item level in two distinct cultures, the INOE is breaking new ground. As a tool, it is designed to identify population level similarities and differences in a linguistically and culturally appropriate way. Although it will allow us to assess the extent to which the differential valorization of experiences has a measurable effect on the frequency with which they are reported and the experiences with which they co-occur in the United States and India, we will – of necessity – rely on historical and ethnographic research in order to interpret our findings. As a measurement-based approach, the INOE is intended to complement historical and ethnographic methods, which are better positioned to identify the types of experiences that practice traditions valorize and to offer nuanced analyses of the way individuals and groups are interpreting their experiences. In developing it, we hope to advance the use of mixed methods in the study of the experiences that are valorized and cultivated by various practice traditions.

### References

Allport, Gordon W. *The Individual and His Religion*. New York: The Macmillan Company, 1950.
Ashar, Yoni K., Luke J. Chang, and Tor D. Wager. "Brain Mechanisms of the Placebo Effect: An Affective Appraisal Account," *Annual Review of Clinical Psychology* 13 (2017): 73–98. https://doi.org/10.1146/annurev-clinpsy-021815-093015.
Barlev, Michael. "Implementation: Preliminary Findings," paper presented in a session on the Inventory of Nonordinary Experiences [INOE] titled "Comparing nonordinary experiences: Surveying, validating, and mapping similarities and differences in the US and India" at the Annual Meeting of the American Academy of Religion, San Diego, CA, November 2019. osf.io/bvaxu.
Barnby, Joseph M., and Vaughan Bell. "The Sensed Presence Questionnaire (SenPQ): Initial Psychometric Validation of a Measure of the 'Sensed Presence' Experience," *PeerJ* 5 (2017): e3149. https://doi.org/10.7717/peerj.3149.
Brett, Caroline, Emmanuelle R. Peters, Louise C. Johns, Paul Tabraham, Lucia Rita Valmaggia, and Philip Mcguire. "Appraisals of Anomalous Experiences Interview (AANEX): A Multidimensional Measure of Psychological

Responses to Anomalies Associated with Psychosis," Br J Psychiatry Suppl 51 (2007): s23–30. https://doi.org/10.1192/bjp.191.51.s23.

Cardeña, Etzel, Steven J. Lynn, and Stanley Krippner (eds.). *Varieties of Anomalous Experience: Examining the Scientific Evidence*, 2nd ed. Washington, DC: American Psychological Association, 2014.

Carhart-Harris, Robin L., Leor Roseman, Eline Haijen, David Erritzoe, Rosalind Watts, Igor Branchi, and Mendel Kaelen. "Psychedelics and the Essential Importance of Context," *Journal of Psychopharmacology* 32 (7) (2018): 725–31. https://doi.org/10.1177/0269881118754710.

Chen, Zhuo, Ralph W. Hood Jr, Lijun Yang, and Paul J. Watson. "Mystical Experience among Tibetan Buddhists: The Common Core Thesis Revisited," *Journal for the Scientific Study of Religion* 50 (2) (2011): 328–38.

Dy-Liacco, Gabriel S., Ralph L. Piedmont, Nichole A. Murray-Swank, Thomas E. Rodgerson, and Martin F. Sherman. "Spirituality and Religiosity as Cross-Cultural Aspects of Human Experience," *Psychology of Religion and Spirituality* 1 (1) (2009): 35–52. https://doi.org/10.1037/a0014937.

Emmons, Robert A., and Raymond F. Paloutzian. "The Psychology of Religion," *Annual Review of Psychology* 54 (1) (2003): 377–402. https://doi.org/10.1146/annurev.psych.54.101601.145024.

Exline, Julie J., Kenneth I. Pargament, Joshua B. Grubbs, and Ann Marie Yali. "The Religious and Spiritual Struggles Scale: Development and Initial Validation," *Psychology of Religion and Spirituality* 6 (3) (2014): 208–22. https://doi.org/10.1037/a0036465.

Exline, Julie J., and Ephraim Rose. "Religious and Spiritual Struggles," in Raymond F. Paloutzian and Crystal L. Park (eds.), *The Handbook of the Psychology of Religion and Spirituality*, 2nd ed. New York: Guilford Press, 2013.

Fellowes, Sam. "Symptom Modelling Can Be Influenced by Psychiatric Categories: Choices for Research Domain Criteria (RDoC)," *Theoretical Medicine and Bioethics* 38 (4) (2017): 279–94. https://doi.org/10.1007/s11017-017-9416-x.

Henrich, Joseph, Steven J. Heine, and Ara Norenzayan. "The Weirdest People in the World?," *The Behavioral and Brain Sciences* 33 (2–3) (2010): 61–83; discussion 83–135. https://doi.org/10.1017/S0140525X0999152X.

Hill, Peter C. "Measurement Assessment and Issues in the Psychology of Religion and Spirituality," in Raymond F. Paloutzian and Crystal L. Park (eds.), *Handbook of the Psychology of Religion and Spirituality*, 2nd ed. New York: Guilford, 2013.

Hill, Peter C., and Evonne Edwards. "Measurement in the Psychology of Religiousness and Spirituality: Existing Measures and New Frontiers," in Kenneth I. Pargament, Julie J. Exline, and James W. Jones (eds.), *APA Handbook of Psychology, Religion, and Spirituality*. Washington, DC: American Psychological Association, 2013.

Hill, Peter C., and Ralph W. Hood (eds.). *Measures of Religiosity*. Birmingham, AL: Religious Education Press, 1999.

Hill, Peter C., Kenneth I. Pargament, Ralph W. Hood, Jr., Michael E. McCullough, James P. Swyers, David B. Larson, and Brian J. Zinnbauer. "Conceptualizing Religion and Spirituality: Points of Commonality, Points of Departure," *Journal for the Theory of Social Behaviour* 30 (1) (2000): 51–77. https://doi.org/10.1111/1468-5914.00119.

Hinton, Devon E., David Howes, and Laurence J. Kirmayer. "Toward a Medical Anthropology of Sensations: Definitions and Research Agenda," *Transcult Psychiatry* 45 (2) (2008): 142–62. https://doi.org/10.1177/1363461508089763.

Holm, Nils G. "Mysticism and Intense Experiences," *Journal for the Scientific Study of Religion* 21 (3) (1982): 268–76. https://doi.org/10.2307/1385891.

Hood, Ralph W. "Religious Orientation and the Report of Religious Experience," *Journal for the Scientific Study of Religion* 9 (4) (1970): 285–91. https://doi.org/10.2307/1384573.

"The Construction and Preliminary Validation of a Measure of Reported Mystical Experience," *Journal for the Scientific Study of Religion* 14 (1) (1975): 29–41. https://doi.org/10.2307/1384454.

(ed.) *Handbook of Religious Experience.* Birmingham, AL: Religious Education Press, 1995.

"Theory and Methods in the Psychological Study of Mysticism," *International Journal for the Psychology of Religion* 23 (4) (2013): 294–306. https://doi.org/10.1080/10508619.2013.795803.

Hood, Ralph W., and Jacob A. Belzen. "Research Methods in the Psychology of Religion and Spirituality," in Raymond F. Paloutzian and Crystal L. Park (eds.), *Handbook of the Psychology of Religion and Spirituality*, pp. 75–93. New York: Guilford Press, 2013.

Hood, Ralph W., Nima Ghorbani, Penny J. Watson, Ahad Framarz Ghramaleki, Mark N. Bing, H. Kristl Davison, Ronald J. Morris, and W. Paul Williamson. "Dimensions of the Mysticism Scale: Confirming the Three-Factor Structure in the United States and Iran," *Journal for the Scientific Study of Religion* 40 (4) (2001): 691–705. https://doi.org/10.1111/0021-8294.00085.

Hood, Ralph W., Peter C. Hill, and Bernard Spilka. *The Psychology of Religion: An Empirical Approach*, 4th ed. New York: Guilford Press, 2009.

*The Psychology of Religion: An Empirical Approach*, 5th ed. New York: Guilford Press, 2018.

Hood, Ralph W., and W. Paul Williamson. "An Empirical Test of the Unity Thesis: The Structure of Mystical Descriptors in Various Faith Samples," *Journal of Psychology and Christianity* 19 (2000): 222–44.

Hufford, David. *The Terror That Comes in the Night: An Experience-Centered Study of Supernatural Assault Traditions.* Publications of the American Folklore Society, v. 7. Philadelphia: University of Pennsylvania Press, 1982.

Inge, William Ralph. *Christian Mysticism; Considered in Eight Lectures Delivered before the University of Oxford.* London: Methuen, 1899.

Irwin, Harvey J., Neil Dagnall, and Kenneth Drinkwater. "Parapsychological Experience as Anomalous Experience plus Paranormal Attribution: A Questionnaire Based on a New Approach to Measurement," *Journal of Parapsychology* 77 (1) (2013): 39–53.

James, William. *Essays in Psychology.* The Works of William James. Cambridge, MA: Harvard University Press, 1983.

*The Varieties of Religious Experience.* Edited by John E. Smith. Cambridge, MA: Harvard University Press, 1985.

Jonte-Pace, Diane E., and William Barclay Parsons (eds.). *Religion and Psychology: Mapping the Terrain; Contemporary Dialogues, Future Prospects*, 1st ed. London: Routledge, 2001.

Kendell, Robert, and Assen Jablensky. "Distinguishing between the Validity and Utility of Psychiatric Diagnoses," *American Journal of Psychiatry* 160 (1) (2003): 4–12. https://doi.org/10.1176/appi.ajp.160.1.4.

Kohls, Niko, and Harald Walach. "Psychological Distress, Experiences of Ego Loss and Spirituality: Exploring the Effects of Spiritual Practice," *Social Behavior and Personality: An International Journal* 35 (10) (2007): 1301–16.

Lange, Rense, Michael A. Thalbourne, James Houran, and Lance Storm. "The Revised Transliminality Scale: Reliability and Validity Data from a Rasch Top-Down Purification Procedure," *Consciousness and Cognition* 9 (4) (2000): 591–617.

Lange, Rense, and Michael A. Thalbourne. "The Rasch Scaling of Mystical Experiences: Construct Validity and Correlates of the Mystical Experience Scale (MES)," *The International Journal for the Psychology of Religion* 17 (2) (2007): 121–40. https://doi.org/10.1080/10508610701244130.

Lazarus, Richard S., and Susan Folkman. *Stress, Appraisal, and Coping*, 1st ed. New York: Springer Publishing Company, 1984.

Lilienfeld, Scott O., and Michael T. Treadway. "Clashing Diagnostic Approaches: DSM-ICD versus RDoC," *Annual Review of Clinical Psychology* 12 (2016): 435–63. https://doi.org/10.1146/annurev-clinpsy-021815-093122.

Lindahl, Jared R., Nathan E. Fisher, David J. Cooper, Rochelle K. Rosen, and Willoughby B. Britton. "The Varieties of Contemplative Experience: A Mixed-Methods Study of Meditation-Related Challenges in Western Buddhists," *PloS One* 12 (5) (2017): e0176239.

Maraldi, Everton de Oliveira, and Stanley Krippner. "Cross-Cultural Research on Anomalous Experiences: Theoretical Issues and Methodological Challenges," *Psychology of Consciousness: Theory, Research, and Practice* 6 (3) (2019): 306–19. https://doi.org/10.1037/cns0000188.

Maraldi, Everton de Oliveira, Stanley Krippner, Maria Cristina Monteiro Barros, and Alexandre Cunha. "Dissociation from a Cross-Cultural Perspective: Implications of Studies in Brazil," *The Journal of Nervous and Mental Disease* 205 (7) (2017): 558–67. https://doi.org/10.1097/NMD.0000000000000694.

Maul, Andrew. "Validity," in Bruce B. Frey (ed.), *The SAGE Encyclopedia of Educational Research, Measurement, and Evaluation*, pp. 1771–75. Thousand Oaks, CA: SAGE Publications, Inc., 2018. https://doi.org/10.4135/9781506326139.

Mezzich, Juan E., Laurence J. Kirmayer, Arthur Kleinman, Horacio Fabrega Jr, Delores L. Parron, Byron J. Good, Keh-Ming Lin, and Spero M. Manson. "The Place of Culture in DSM-IV," *The Journal of Nervous and Mental Disease* 187 (8) (1999): 457–64.

Murphy, James. "Beyond 'Religion' and 'Spirituality': Extending a 'Meaning Systems' Approach to Explore Lived Religion," *Archive for the Psychology of Religion* 39 (2017): 1–26.

Oman, Doug. "Defining Religion and Spirituality," in Raymond F. Paloutzian and Crystal L. Park (eds.), *Handbook of the Psychology of Religion and Spirituality*, pp. 23–47. New York: Guilford Press, 2013.

Paloutzian, Raymond F. "Religious Conversion and Spiritual Transformation: A Meaning-System Analysis," in Raymond F. Paloutzian and Crystal L. Park (eds.), *Handbook of the Psychology of Religion and Spirituality*, 1st ed., pp. 331–347. New York: Guilford Press, 2005.

*Invitation to the Psychology of Religion*, 3rd ed. New York: Guilford Press, 2017. http://ebookcentral.proquest.com/lib/qut/detail.action?docID=4715215.

Paloutzian, Raymond F., and Crystal L. Park (eds.). *Handbook of the Psychology of Religion and Spirituality*. New York: Guilford Press, 2005.

(eds.). *Handbook of the Psychology of Religion and Spirituality*, 2nd ed. New York: Guilford Press, 2013.

Paloutzian, Raymond F., Sebastian Murken, Heinz Streib, and Sussan Rössler-Namini. "Conversion, Deconversion, and Spiritual Transformation: A Multilevel Interdisciplinary View," in Raymond F. Paloutzian and Crystal L. Park (eds.), *Handbook of the Psychology of Religion and Spirituality*, 2nd ed. , pp. 399–421. New York: Guilford, 2013.

Pargament, Kenneth I. "The Psychology of Religion and Spirituality? Yes and No," *International Journal for the Psychology of Religion* 9 (1999): 3–16.

"Searching for the Sacred: Toward a Nonreductionistic Theory of Spirituality," in Kenneth I. Pargament, Julie J. Exline, and James W. Jones (eds.), *APA Handbook of Psychology, Religion, and Spirituality (Vol 1): Context, Theory, and Research*, pp. 257–73. Washington, DC: American Psychological Association, 2013. https://doi.org/10.1037/14045-014.

Pargament, Kenneth I., and Annette Mahoney. "Sacred Matters: Sanctification as a Vital Topic for the Psychology of Religion," *International Journal for the Psychology of Religion* 15 (3) (2005): 179–98.

Pargament, Kenneth I., Julie J. Exline, and James W. Jones (eds.). *APA Handbook of Psychology, Religion, and Spirituality*. APA Handbooks in Psychology. Washington, DC: American Psychological Association, 2013.

Park, Crystal L. "Religion and Meaning," in Raymond F. Paloutzian and Crystal L. Park (eds.), *Handbook of the Psychology of Religion and Spirituality*, 1st ed., pp. 295–314. New York: Guilford Press, 2005.

"Making Sense of the Meaning Literature: An Integrative Review of Meaning Making and Its Effects on Adjustment to Stressful Life Events," *Psychological Bulletin* 136 (2) (2010): 257–301. https://doi.org/10.1037/a0018301.

Park, Crystal L., and Susan Folkman. "Meaning in the Context of Stress and Coping," *Review of General Psychology* 1 (2) (1997): 115–44. https://doi.org/10.1037/1089-2680.1.2.115.

Park, Crystal L., Kristen E. Riley, Login S. George, Ian A. Gutierrez, Amy E. Hale, Dalnim Cho, and Tosca D. Braun. "Assessing Disruptions in Meaning: Development of the Global Meaning Violation Scale," *Cognitive Therapy and Research* 40 (6) (2016): 831–46. https://doi.org/10.1007/s10608-016-9794-9.

Piedmont, Ralph L. "Does Spirituality Represent the Sixth Factor of Personality? Spiritual Transcendence and the Five-Factor Model," *Journal of Personality* 67 (6) (1999): 985–1013. https://doi.org/10.1111/1467-6494.00080.

"A Short History of the Psychology of Religion and Spirituality: Providing Growth and Meaning for Division 36," *Psychology of Religion and Spirituality* 5 (1) (2013): 1–4. https://doi.org/10.1037/a0030878.

Roof, Wade Clark. *A Generation of Seekers: The Spiritual Journeys of the Baby Boom Generation,* 1st ed. San Francisco: HarperSanFrancisco, 1993.

Spilka, Bernard, Ralph W. Hood Jr, Bruce Hunsberger, and Richard Gorsuch. *The Psychology of Religion: An Empirical Approach,* 2nd ed. New York: Guilford Press, 1996.

  *The Psychology of Religion: An Empirical Approach,* 3rd ed. New York: Guilford Press, 2003.

Spilka, Bernard, Phillip Shaver, and Lee A. Kirkpatrick. "A General Attribution Theory for the Psychology of Religion," *Journal for the Scientific Study of Religion* 24 (1) (1985): 1. https://doi.org/10.2307/1386272.

Stace, Walter T. *Mysticism and Philosophy.* London: Macmillan Press, 1960.

Streib, Heinz, and Constantin Klein. "Religion and Spirituality," in Michael Stausberg and Steven Engler (eds.), *The Oxford Handbook of the Study of Religion,* pp. 73–83. Oxford Handbooks in Religion and Theology. New York: Oxford University Press, 2016.

Streib, Heinz, Ralph W. Hood Jr, Barbara Keller, Rosina-Martha Csöff, and Christopher F. Silver. *Deconversion: Qualitative and Quantitative Results from Cross-Cultural Research in Germany and the United States of America.* Research in Contemporary Religion, v. 5. Göttingen: Vandenhoeck & Ruprecht, 2009.

Sullivan, Winnifred Fallers. *Ministry of Presence: Chaplaincy, Spiritual Care, and the Law.* Chicago: University of Chicago Press, 2019.

Taves, Ann. *Religious Experience Reconsidered: A Building-Block Approach to the Study of Religion and Other Special Things.* Princeton, NJ: Princeton University Press, 2009a.

  "William James Revisited: Rereading the Varieties of Religious Experience in Transatlantic Perspective," *Zygon* 44 (2) (2009b): 415–32.

  "What Is Nonreligion? On the Virtues of a Meaning Systems Framework for Studying Nonreligious and Religious Worldviews in the Context of Everyday Life," *Secularism and Nonreligion* 7 (1) (2018): 9. https://doi.org/10.5334/snr.104.

  "Mystical and Other Alterations in Sense of Self: An Expanded Framework for Studying Nonordinary Experiences," *Perspectives on Psychological Science* (2020). Advance online publication. doi:10.1177/1745691619895047.

Taves, Ann, and Michael Kinsella. "Development and Design of the INOE," paper presented in a session on the Inventory of Nonordinary Experiences [INOE] titled "Comparing nonordinary experiences: Surveying, validating, and mapping similarities and differences in the US and India" at the Annual Meeting of the American Academy of Religion, San Diego, CA, November 2019. osf.io/pv5kt.

Taves, Ann, Michael Barlev, and Michael Kinsella. "What Counts as Religious Experience? The Inventory of Nonordinary Experiences as a Tool for Analysis across Cultures and Traditions," paper presented at the Biennial Meeting of the International Association for the Psychology of Religion, Hamar, Norway, August 2017. osf.io/xe8nd.

Thalbourne, Michael A. "The Psychology of Mystical Experience," *Exceptional Human Experience* 9 (1991): 168–86.

Underhill, Evelyn. *Mysticism.* London: Methuen, 1911.

Underwood, Raphael, Veena Kumari, and Emmanuelle Peters. "Cognitive and Neural Models of Threat Appraisal in Psychosis: A Theoretical Integration," *Psychiatry Research* 239 (2016): 131–38. https://doi.org/10.1016/j.psychres.2016.03.016.

Ward, Thomas A., Keith J. Gaynor, Mike D. Hunter, Peter W. R. Woodruff, Philippa A. Garety, and Emmanuelle R. Peters. "Appraisals and Responses to Experimental Symptom Analogues in Clinical and Nonclinical Individuals with Psychotic Experiences," *Schizophrenia Bulletin* 40 (4) (2014): 845–55. https://doi.org/10.1093/schbul/sbt094.

Wolf, Melissa Gordon, and Elliott Ihm. "Validation Methods and Results," paper presented in a session on the Inventory of Nonordinary Experiences [INOE] titled "Comparing nonordinary experiences: Surveying, validating, and mapping similarities and differences in the US and India" at the Annual Meeting of the American Academy of Religion, San Diego, CA, November 2019. osf.io/bnvmc.

Wolf, Melissa Gordon, Elliott Ihm, Andrew Maul, and Ann Taves. "Response Process Evaluation," in Steven Engler and Michael Stausberg (eds.), *The Routledge Handbook of Research Methods in the Study of Religion*, 2nd ed. New York: Routledge, In Press.

Wulff, David M. *Psychology of Religion: Classic and Contemporary*, 2nd ed. New York: John Wiley & Sons, 1997.

"Psychology of Religion: An Overview," in Diane E. Jonte-Pace and William Barclay Parsons (eds.), *Religion and Psychology: Mapping the Terrain; Contemporary Dialogues, Future Prospects*, 1st ed. London: Routledge, 2001.

Yaden, David Bryce, Jonathan Haidt, Ralph W. Hood, David R. Vago, and Andrew B. Newberg. "The Varieties of Self-Transcendent Experience," *Review of General Psychology* 21 (2) (2017): 143–60. https://doi.org/10.1037/gpr0000102.

Zinnbauer, Brian J., Kenneth I. Pargament, and Allie B. Scott. "The Emerging Meanings of Religiousness and Spirituality: Problems and Prospects," *Journal of Personality* 67 (6) (1999): 889–919. https://doi.org/10.1111/1467-6494.00077.

## 2 Philosophy of Religion Approaches to the Study of Religious Experience

PHILLIP H. WIEBE

### INTRODUCTION

The belief that Religious Experience is caused by gods or divinities can be traced back in Western philosophy to at least the Socratic era. In a dialogue between Socrates and Ion, Socrates explains the gift of prophecy: "God takes away the minds of poets" ... [and] "uses diviners and holy prophets in order that we who hear them may know them to be speaking not of themselves ... who utter these priceless words in a state of unconsciousness, but that God himself is the speaker ...; poets are only the interpreters of the God by whom they are severally possessed."[1] Similar remarks can be found in other Platonic dialogues. We do not know exactly how historical these dialogues are, although the view is widely accepted that Plato represents the historical Socrates at least some of the time. Considerable debate has taken place over the meaning given by the early Greek philosophers to the terms 'god' or 'the gods', but I will not try to resolve questions about polytheism or any (implicit) monotheism. My point is that ancient remarks ascribe a causal power to a god generating human experience evidently deemed other-worldly.

Aristotle exhibits comparable respect for the claim that certain experiences – prescient dreams – might find their source in some divinity:

> As to the divination which takes place in sleep, and is said to be based on dreams, we cannot lightly either dismiss it with contempt or give it implicit confidence. The fact that all persons, or many, suppose dreams to possess a special significance, tends to inspire us with belief in it [such divination], as founded on the testimony of experience; and indeed that divination in dreams should, as regards

---

[1] Plato, *Ion*, 534. All Platonic quotes are from Jowett, who uses the pagination of Stephanus.

some subjects, be genuine, is not incredible, for it has a show of
reason.[2]

Plato has been described as the foremost supernaturalist in ancient
times,[3] so his endorsement of divine action upon humans is not surprising, but Aristotle is seldom seen in such a light. Inasmuch as Plato and
Aristotle both had no objection to ascribing a causal role to spiritual
beings, the ground was laid for philosophy's interest in identifying a
possible causal trace from experience to the gods.

## METHODOLOGY

Philosophy has been deeply conscious of modes of argument found
generally in exact studies that we now consider sciences. One ancient
ideal for science was to find indisputable truths – axioms – from which
other truths could be inferred using the most reliable form of reasoning
known to humans, namely deduction. If reasoning begins with truths,
the method of deduction yields only further truths, never falsehoods.
The biggest challenges to this ideal form of structured knowledge –
science – have been to find irrefragable truths and then to apply the
rules of deductive logic correctly. The geometry of Euclid (born ca. 300
BC) was once considered to be an exemplar of such a science; Isaac
Newton's physics is a modern example.

For a long time, deduction was the method of choice when philosophers considered transcendent realities. The existence of God has been
inferred from the very existence of the cosmos;[4] from the idea of God as
the greatest conceivable (or possible) being;[5] and from features of the
universe exhibiting design, pattern, or complexity.[6] With God firmly in
place on these grounds, we could then plausibly *interpret* certain kinds
of human experience as deriving from God. The modern age of Western
Philosophy construes Descartes as one of its founders. He brought in a
focus on 'the immediate content of conscious experience' in ways that
had not been earlier emphasized. The data gleaned from this severely

---

[2] Aristotle, *On Prophesying by Dreams*, pt. 1.
[3] Smith, "Metaphilosophy," p. 213.
[4] Its most famous proponent is St Thomas Aquinas, *Summa Theologiae*, first part,
ques. 2.
[5] St Anselm of Canterbury is its classic source, *Proslogion*, chapters 2–3; Plantinga, ed.,
*The Ontological Argument*, is a modern source.
[6] William Paley, an eighteenth century English philosopher and theologian, is often
credited with giving it full expression in *Natural Theology*.

inward turn might be indubitable, but few significant deductive inferences follow. A 'science of perception' does not rise far above its slim foundations, for from sense data, memory traces, feelings, and similar (supposedly) indubitable experiences even the common-sense world of familiar objects cannot be deduced.

British philosopher Bishop George Berkeley claimed that minds (spirits)[7] are real because he could not conceive of mental contents existing without minds who have or own them. Here was an irrefutable argument, seemingly, from ideas to spirits. However, since Berkeley's position provided no inference to ordinary material objects, as common-sense thinks of these, he was left with a world possessing only minds and the ideas they have. Since our perception of a (supposed) object might occur day after day, but no ordinary material objects exist to give this belief credence, Berkeley construed God as providing the perceptual continuity. Few have followed such phenomenalism that denies the existence of the (so-called) ordinary world and assigns God such a dubious task. Butler exhibits much more interest in the developing sciences than David Hume, his empiricist successor, but he has not had the influence that Hume has.

Hume was influenced by the pattern of thought found in Berkeley, but he could not affirm the existence of minds that are aware of immediate perceptions. He maintained that minds are only constructions of various mental states, famously writing: "I never can catch *myself* at any time without a perception, and never can observe any thing but the perception. When my perceptions are remov'd for any time, as by sound sleep; so long am I insensible of *myself*, and may truly be said not to exist."[8] We might ask: "Who is the self that the I cannot catch?" and "Who is the I at all?" Perhaps Hume's sceptical position might not have lasting interest if it were not for current philosophers who endorse it. Daniel Dennett writes: "The chief fictional character at the center of that autobiography is one's *self*. And if you still want to know what the self *really* is, you're making a category mistake."[9] Hume's sceptical stance toward the common-sense world also means that he could not defend either the past or ordinary objects to be real. Hume tries to rescue common-sense beliefs, but his scepticism, while not as crippling as that of Descartes, leaves us with a world where much is doubtful.

---

[7] Berkeley, "A Treatise concerning the Principles of Human Knowledge," para. 27.
[8] Hume, *A Treatise of Human Nature*, bk. 1, sec. 4, para. 6.
[9] Dennett, "The Self as a Center of Narrative Gravity," p. 114.

Hume is famous for questioning theistic arguments from design, found in his posthumous *Dialogues concerning Natural Religion*, but his view on how inference is involved in assessing Religious Experience is unclear. He puts the following remark in the mouth of the proponent of design, Cleanthes:[10]

> Suppose, therefore, that an articulate voice were heard in the clouds, much louder and more melodious than any which human art could ever reach: Suppose, that this voice were extended in the same instant over all nations, and spoke to each nation in its own language and dialect: Suppose, that the words delivered not only contain a just sense and meaning, but convey some instruction altogether worthy of a benevolent Being, superior to mankind: Could you possibly hesitate a moment concerning the cause of this voice?

Philo, the sceptical person in the *Dialogues* who seems to speak for Hume much of the time, was confounded by the question, not knowing what to reply. According to Nelson Pike, Hume never offers a sceptical rebuttal.[11]

The telling phrase in this quotation from Hume is: "Could you possibly hesitate a moment?" We might legitimately wonder why no hesitation is possible. Are we looking at conventional implication here, not exactly the formal kind found in textbooks of logic?[12] Or did Hume uncover an immediate inference from the imaginary voice speaking simultaneously to all nations in their own languages? Aside from all the evidential issues in ascertaining that it was the same voice heard all over the world, we have the problem of verifying exactly what was said. Perhaps Hume builds into the description the very proposition he is wanting to infer? This is a problem with imaginary cases, which might offer exercises in logic but exhibit little about the cosmos we inhabit.

Hume's imaginary case is very reminiscent of the real allegation in *The Acts of the Apostles*, in the New Testament, of 'the falling of the Holy Spirit' upon the first disciples of the one said to be the Christ. Hume, as an educated Scot, obviously knew this allegation well, since it is featured every year in all liturgical churches. In that experience, people reported hearing a noise very like a strong wind, then saw flames

---

[10]  Hume, *Dialogues concerning Natural Religion*, part 3.
[11]  Cf. Pike, Commentary on Hume's *Dialogues concerning Natural Religion*, pp. 224–34.
[12]  See the distinction discussed by Davis, "Implicature."

of fire resting upon the Christ's disciples, and then heard these disciples speaking languages they had never learned. Coming so closely after the Christ's 'promise of the Holy Spirit', we can understand how people thought that this promise was being kept. Hearing a wind blow and seeing flames alight on heads by themselves would be startling, but would offer no grounds for thinking that some Mind – some Spirit, some Intelligence – was active in the group affected. However, intelligible speech is generated by a mind – an 'object' which Hume understood – and a super Mind is likely to be postulated to exist when intelligible speech simultaneously occurs in numerous languages not known to their speakers. The inference here, however secure it might seem, is not of the deductive kind, but inductive.

## LOGICAL EMPIRICISM (OR POSITIVISM)

Philosophy of religion in general has been profoundly affected in the twentieth century by the rise of Logical Empiricism. Although other 'schools of philosophic thought' are concurrent, such as Marxism, Thomism, Existentialism, and Hegelianism, the Empiricist movement acquired a significant following because of its embrace of the precise developments in Logic, widely credited to Gottlob Frege and Bertrand Russell, and because of its enchantment with the growing sciences. When Empiricism addressed the issue of intelligibility and meaningfulness of religious language, it brought new insights to bear on possible truth and falsehood.

The Vienna Circle[13] is widely credited with having given Empiricism its impetus, its members occupying positions of influence across Western Europe. The three dozen or so mathematicians, physicists, philosophers, and social scientists comprising this group met regularly in Vienna to articulate their views.[14] They scattered when Nazism came into prominence on the European continent. The youthful A. J. Ayer is widely credited with having brought positivism to Britain in a vigorous way, famously asserting that religious and theological claims are not intelligible,[15] so their truth or falsity does not even arise as a question. Logic became especially important in the study of competing views, perhaps giving Frege and Russell's work on logic lasting

---

[13] Cf. Uebel, "Vienna Circle."
[14] See Hempel, "Problems and Changes in the Empiricist Criterion of Meaning," for a helpful overview.
[15] Ayer, *Language, Truth, and Logic*, especially chapter 6.

importance for Philosophy. Six decades after Ayer, John Searle wrote about the scientific and naturalist worldview:

> [it is] not an option. It is not simply up for grabs along with a lot of competing world views. Our problem is not that somehow we have failed to come up with a convincing proof of the existence of God or that the hypothesis of afterlife remains in serious doubt, it is rather that in our deepest reflections we cannot take such opinions seriously.[16]

Another philosopher, Richard Rorty, wrote in 2007 in a vein reminiscent of Ayer: "empirical evidence is irrelevant to talk about God," – a viewpoint that applies equally to theism and atheism.[17] Canadian philosopher Kai Nielsen has quite consistently construed Christian theism as *devoid of factual meaning*: God-talk has not been given intelligible directions for its coherent use, he claims, and nothing could make the propositions about God true.[18] Nielsen asserts that to say that God is that being on which the world depends is to say nothing at all, for no sufficient conditions for dependency have been elaborated, or apparently can be. Also, to speak of God as a self-existent being is to utter another incoherent proposition, he says, for no rules have been discovered for identifying something as self-existent. Similarly, to speak of a being as transcendent is to speak of something obscure, for, if something is experienced, it is *ipso facto* not transcendent. These objections are directed to talk of God, admittedly, but I doubt that he is more forgiving of statements about other spirits. He defends Philosophy's role in critically discussing various forms of life, which, in his judgement, is more rational if lived atheistically.

Karl Popper's emphasis upon the importance of falsifiability[19] of meaningful propositions has also had an impact on views of the peculiar features of religious language. In a famous symposium on the subject in 1955 widely titled as 'Theology and Falsification',[20] British professors Antony Flew, R. M. Hare, Basil Mitchell, and I. M. Crombie debated the nature of religious language. Flew famously asked, using the parable of a

---

[16] Smith, "Metaphilosophy," p. 199; quoted from Searle, *The Rediscovery of the Mind*, pp. 90–91.

[17] Rorty and Vattimo, *The Future of Religion*, p. 33.

[18] Nielsen, *Philosophy and Atheism*, chapter 5, passim.

[19] Popper's *The Logic of Scientific Discovery* was first published in German in 1934, then translated into English in 1959. His Professorship at the University of London gave his work wide consideration.

[20] In Flew and MacIntyre, *New Essays*, pp. 96–130.

garden tended by a gardener who is never seen, or heard, or smelled by bloodhounds, or detected by the electric fence surrounding the garden: "Just how does what you call an invisible, intangible, eternally elusive gardener differ from an imaginary gardener or even from no gardener at all?"[21] The claim about the gardener seems incapable of falsification, or verification, thus rendering it devoid of meaning according to the early criteria of meaningfulness. In this Symposium Hare suggested that having a theological belief is to have a *blik* about theological matters – a feature of beliefs for which no reasons exist, remarking: "It was Hume who taught us that our whole commerce with the world depends upon our *blik* about the world; and that differences between *bliks* about the world cannot be settled by observation of what happens in the world."[22] This discussion occurred in the context of the influence of Wittgenstein upon language and its interpretations, out of which has grown the conviction that religious language might serve some other function than speaking about some actual feature of the cosmos, even though such language appears to be descriptive. A fuller appreciation of religious language requires a closer look at the language of theories that postulate possible unobservable objects, which I will speak of in the following section.

INDUCTION

Probabilistic arguments have taken the place of historic deductive efforts to establish the existence of God. So the existence of God is only probable (or more probable than not) given that a cosmos exists at all; given the fine tuning of vital constants such as gravity;[23] given the development of a mind that knows itself to be a mind;[24] given the presence of a moral order that can be as impressive as the natural order;[25] and given the presence of Religious Experience that 'compels' belief; and so on.[26]

---

[21] Ibid., p. 96.
[22] Hare, in Flew and MacIntyre, ibid., p. 101.
[23] Friederich, "Fine-Tuning."
[24] Augustine was taken with this argument, expressing his views in bk. IX of *On the Trinity*, perhaps his most influential work. This is not the Humean self!
[25] Immanuel Kant advances the view that God is a postulate of practical reason in *Critique of Practical Reason*. For discussion see Evans, "Moral Arguments for the Existence of God."
[26] Richard Swinburne is a foremost articulator of this probabilistic combination of evidences, in *The Existence of God*. For a defense of atheism by a recent atheist,

In an overview of nine prominent theorists of religion, Daniel Pals concludes: "Religion consists of belief and behavior associated in some way with a supernatural realm of divine or spiritual beings."[27] We could pose the question concerning the account mentioned above in which the Holy Spirit is said to have descended on disciples of the Christ: "How *probable* is it that the wind, the flames of fire, and glossolalia were brought about by the Holy Spirit?" Of course, another question first arises over Luke's account: "How likely is it that he described events pretty much as they occurred?" For many critics, religion's capacity to undergird claims about actual events is the most problematic one – we could describe it as the question of *reliability*, in order to avoid confusing the two questions. Many issues arise in an examination of the reliability of an account, including the following:

1.  Is the account first-hand, or is it a hand-me-down from an oral tradition?
2.  How much time has elapsed between an alleged event and its initial description?
3.  Does the source uncritically embrace a highly debatable interpretation of the cosmos, such as ultra-supernaturalistic or magical, or has the source imposed a spiritual interpretation on events?
4.  Did Luke just *use* reporting language, but really intend to write fables having some mythological meaning that inexperienced preachers could use in sermons?[28]

Since nothing in anyone's account of the early activities of the disciples of the Christ suggests that Luke was present when the Holy Spirit was given, the reliability of the account is well below the value of 1, but this value need not be 0. I assume that Luke is the custodian of a report passed down through several hands, which might include first-hand witnesses. The amount of time that elapsed between the alleged event and Luke's record of it is perhaps twenty to thirty years, which is also problematic.

An important additional question about Luke and other narrators relates to contravention of known regularities, namely "Does the report

J. J. C. Smart, and a modern defense of design arguments, by J. J. Haldane, see their jointly-authored *Atheism and Theism*.

[27] Pals, *Nine Theories of Religion*, p. 338.

[28] See Moore, "The Resurrection: A Confusing Paradigm Shift" for comments about this interpretive shift in then-recent criticism. This captures some of the work of Wittgenstein in *Philosophical Investigations*, where he argues that language does not always mean what it appears to mean.

involve events that are contrary to what we know to be laws of nature?" This is a question, in conventional terms, about the alleged event being a miracle. I make a distinction in general between the appearance of a transcendent being and a miracle. For example, the Virgin Mary is famously said to have been visited by the angel Gabriel, and then she is said to have conceived Jesus the Christ without the involvement of any human father. I consider the alleged visitation of Gabriel to have been non-miraculous, for it is not different in principle from a visitation of some kind of being from another planet, but I consider her conception of Jesus without normal sexual intercourse to allege a miracle, for it is contrary to regularities stable enough to be considered laws of nature.

The reliability of Luke's account is apt to be assessed in various ways by different theorists. Perhaps we generally trust Luke, in part because he was a physician in his day and we generally trust physicians in any era. Perhaps we assign a value of 20 per cent to the *reliability* of Luke's account. The remaining question requiring discussion is the *probability* that the Holy Spirit visited the first disciples of the Christ, if Luke described observable events more-or-less accurately. Making a defensible interpretation of the probability value is not easy, but if the wind, the fire, and the intelligible and appropriate speech in various languages not already known did occur, the probability of its source in the Holy Spirit (or a Holy Intelligence) is seemingly high. Among John Stuart Mill's famous grounds[29] for claiming that X causes Y is the discovery that X and Y occur together, or are absent together, or both. These criteria are impossible to apply, however, when one of X or Y is an unobservable entity (being), such as the Holy Spirit. Another methodological approach now comes into view.

## RETRODUCTION OR ABDUCTION

The nineteenth-century American philosopher, Charles Sanders Pierce, is justly famous for insisting that much scientific progress is dependent on a form of thought that postulates the existence of theoretical entities, often unobservable.[30] Here we have a suggestion that is not quite covered by the standard view of induction; in fact, it looks like an instance of the deductive Fallacy of Affirming the Consequent: From 'if p then q' and 'q'

---

[29] Known as Mill's Methods, from his *A System of Logic*, bk. III, chap. 8.

[30] Pierce's views on scientific method are scattered throughout his writings; for a good introduction see Buchler, *Philosophical Writings of Peirce* (1955), especially chapter 11, titled "Abduction and Induction."

infer 'p'. The nineteenth and twentieth centuries exhibit this retroductive thought across the academic spectrum: Atomic theory postulates subatomic particles; Gregor Mendel's theory of invisible 'inheritance factors' (genes) postulates these to account for traits passed from parents to children; Ignaz Semmelweis postulates the existence of invisible 'germs' by which diseases could be transmitted to healthy people.[31]

Charles Darwin's evolutionary theory postulates unobserved mechanisms of natural selection, which is no impediment to its popularity and apparent success; Alfred Wegener's theory of plate tectonics postulates large invisible plates on which Earth's continents rest; Richard Rorty and David Lewis construe the theory of mental states as positing theoretical entities someday identifiable as brain-states; and so on. Of course we must mention that some theories postulating theoretical entities have been refuted, showing that falsifiability can also attach to these theories. Notable is the phlogiston theory advanced by Johann Joachim Becher to account for rusting and combustion, which has been replaced (roughly) by oxidation.[32] Another is the theory of Robert Boyle, Isaac Newton and others, according to which light is transmitted in a luminiferous aether – now widely considered to have been refuted by A. Michelson and E. Morley.[33] A possible interpretation of Hume's discussion of the loud and melodious voice (above) is that he stumbled upon events whose explanation lies in a theory that postulates theoretical entities, but was unsure about what to make of them since retroduction had not come into clear view. He is well known for wanting to stick with observable phenomena, which logical positivism developed into a powerful and dismissive program.

A remarkable statement of the view that 'the gods of Homer' might be construed as the posits of a theory comes from W. V. O. Quine. He writes about the way in which physical objects are postulated to account for immediate perceptions:

> Physical objects are conceptually imported into the situation as convenient intermediaries – not by definition in terms of experience, but simply as irreducible posits comparable, epistemologically, to the gods of Homer. For my part I do, qua lay physicist, believe in physical objects and not in Homer's gods; and I consider it a scientific error to

---

[31] Some controversy exists about his methods and achievements; cf. Tulodziecki, "Shattering the Myth of Semmelweis."
[32] But see Decaen, "Aristotle's Aether and Contemporary Science" for a contrary view.
[33] "Ether: Theoretical Substance," www.britannica.com/science/ether-theoretical-substance (Accessed June 8, 2018).

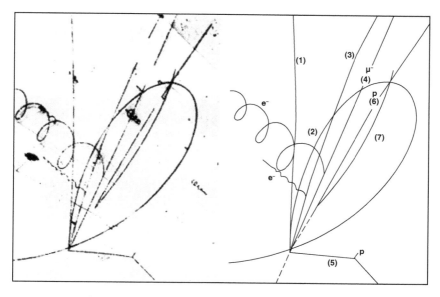

Figure 2.1 Production of a lambda-baryon particle.

believe otherwise. The gods differ only in degree and not in kind. Both
sorts of entities enter our conception only as cultural posits.[34]

Here the groundwork is set for a Theory of Spirits that postulates
theoretical entities, which might also be (or seem) observable under
special circumstances.

The recent history of physics includes remarkable 'interpretations'
of events in cloud-chambers and emulsions through which known particles (particle-waves) pass, such as through a supersaturated vapour, of
propanol, perhaps,[35] which causes droplets to form on the path that a
particle takes. These droplets can be photographed, and so the particle's
path is detected. The following image from the Berkeley Lab[36] describes
circumstances behind the production of a lambda-baryon particle. On
the left-hand side is the photographic image from the particle chamber,
and on the right is a diagrammatic interpretation of it.

A neutrino (devoid of charge) that is not pictured, but corresponding
to the dashed line at the bottom of Figure 2.1 on the right (labelled '*v*'),

[34] Quine, *From a Logical Point of View*, p. 44.
[35] "Cloud Chamber," www2.physics.ox.ac.uk/accelerate/resources/demonstrations/
cloud-chamber (Accessed March 22, 2018).
[36] Close et al., *The Particle Explosion*.

enters the chamber from the bottom and collides with a proton (charged) entering the chamber from the left. This collision produces three positively charged particles (labelled as 2, 3, and 5), two negative ones (1 and 4), and a neutral one (Λ*). This neutral particle, pictured on the right by dashes and identified as Λ*, is the lambda-baryon. This baryon particle has an extremely short life, decaying within one-billionth of a second, and producing a distinctive 'V' when it decays into a proton and a pi-meson (6 and 7, respectively). The existence of this baryon particle is (causally) inferred from the set of observable events shown.

A great deal of physics is presupposed in this 'inference', of course, as well as some assumptions that do not belong exclusively to physics, such as the claim that causality pervades the whole cosmos. Several issues having relevance to Religious Experience come into view:

1.  The reference to the theoretical object is not simply a stand-alone proposition, but is embedded in a cluster of propositions pertaining to subatomic objects. Here *theories*, not *single propositions*, are assessed for plausibility or implausibility. The Flew Symposium did not anticipate this development; neither did early Positivism.

2.  Terms purporting to denote these entities have their meaning deter-mined by the attributes given to the entities, where known, and by the relations, especially causal ones, in which these entities are assigned to other objects, including some whose existence is not in doubt.

3.  Claims about such entities are intelligible, but not in any simple way, since the conceptual links are numerous, and involve many relations to the structure of the known universe. This is why claims about gods might seem ineffable, or devoid of factual meaning, or devoid of sufficient conditions for determining their import.

4.  Other relations besides causality obviously figure in the (full) description of a theoretical object, but causality carries special weight. In first articulating a theory, a term might be introduced with a short definition, but the full import of the term is seen in the whole theory.

5.  Theories evidently attempt to depict a reality whose precise fea-tures might always elude us, but to dismiss a theory prematurely because it gets some small thing wrong is unreasonable.

6.  'Probability' in some important sense is applicable to theories in which theoretical entities are postulated, for we can plausibly say that the existence of the lambda-baryon particle is more probable

given the result shown in Figure 2.1 than on no information at all. Such theories never have a probability of 1, however, for the theoretical entities might need to be reconfigured in just a slightly different way, based on new information.

Terms purporting to denote spirits – purposive beings with volition, beliefs, perception, memory, self-reflection, passions, and perhaps other 'intellectual' features found readily in human beings – of different kinds and ranks have meaning just by virtue of being included in a theory in which the (supposed) denotations are ascribed properties and held to be in relation to things that are not in doubt – including objects accepted as real by commonsense or science. When we speak of spirits of departed persons, for instance, the entities postulated to exist are ascribed properties, and assigned relations to things that are not in doubt, such as the ones who have died. The crucial relation here is between a living person – the bearer of personal identity while a body is alive – and the entity deemed (by the theory) to be the post-mortem bearer of that identity. This (general) theory could be false, of course, although showing this would not be straightforward.

The problem of ongoing identity in post-mortem existence appears to be hardly different than the ongoing identity found in living things generally, which are continually changing. Logic might *teach* the (partial) character of the identity relation by reference to objects having several names or descriptions (such as 'Venus = the Morning Star') or by examples drawn from Arithmetic (such as '7+5 = 12'). However, in actual life we encounter the ongoing identity in a plant, or animal, or human person, where the strict identities favoured by Logic or Arithmetic are just not present. Living organisms all shed some properties when they grow, and acquire new ones, but they retain their identities in spite of such changes.[37] An important proviso for any adequate theory postulating theoretical entities is that extensive links can be found between these entities and the objects that are deemed without qualification, to be real, otherwise the theoretical structure is not adequately anchored in the world of observables.[38]

---

[37] The Humean position on the nature of the self takes advantage of the obscurity in assigning continuing identity by claiming that successive space-time structures are not identities, so that one person, supposedly, is really a set of non-identical states. This position is thinkable, but hardly plausible. The world is more robust than this, arguably.

[38] See Feigl, "The 'Orthodox' View of Theories: Remarks in Defense as well as Critique," which states that the theoretical dimension "floats above" the domain

## THEORY OF SPIRITS IN MODERN EXPERIENCE

In order to show something of how a modern experience exhibits a theoretical object, I will turn to one of the cases that I researched for *Visions of Jesus*.[39] This part of the Theory of Spirits has traditional Hebrew-Christian beliefs as its background – again a vast array of (competitive) claims known best to those brought up in this religion.

### Helen Bezanson

Helen's (first) experience occurred when she was about twenty-one years old, living in Southern Ontario. She went to the Anglican Church as a child, but by the time she married and began a family she was not interested in religion. Her husband's parents took her to a summer camp meeting sponsored by a Pentecostal church. The service ended with an invitation to pray at the front and, when her mother-in-law suggested that she go, Helen did so to please her. Helen returned on the next three nights, going forward each time for prayer because doing so made her feel better about herself. As she prayed on the fourth night she felt a warm presence around her, and thought that someone had touched her. She opened her eyes to see if anyone was nearby, but no one was close enough to be touching her, so she decided to continue praying. She felt a touch again, this time on one of her hands that was raised in prayer. She opened her eyes again to see if anyone was touching her, and again she saw no one, but then she felt that she ought to look up. Her words to me were: "I looked up, my eyes wide open, and I saw Jesus standing just as clear as I can see you sitting there now, and he had both hands out like this [stretched toward her] and he was smiling as though he was accepting me finally." He made a gathering motion with his hands, as though to show her that he was accepting her, and looked so real and alive Helen thought that others must be looking at him too. She looked around to see if others were paying attention to him, but no one else seemed to notice him. She thought to herself, "What's wrong with them? They're not looking at him." She looked back to see if he was still there, and he was.

He stood there some eight to ten feet away, smiling and moving. He looked much as tradition portrays him, although what caught her attention was his eyes and the motion of his hands. Helen also had the sense

---

of experience. Obviously, the "distance" cannot be too great, otherwise the theoretical features link to nothing.

[39] Wiebe, *Visions of Jesus*.

that she was looking at God, which gave the visual impression a characteristic that she was not able to describe. Another unusual feature of the experience was that Jesus seemed to be standing on a pedestal or pillar, for he was not standing on the floor and he did not appear to be floating. Moreover, it seemed as though he stood in an oval doorway on the pedestal, and that a radiance or glow emanated from the oval doorway and surrounded him. As she gazed on him she began talking in another language that she knew nothing about at the time. He gradually faded from view and was gone.

## COMMENTS

The Theory of Spirits is so fully integrated with the Theory of Mind and with other theories belonging to (unreduced) commonsense that separating it might seem artificial. However, atheism in general has no problem with mental states, whatever their eventual scientific destiny, but they do with any kind of spirit. The being that is declared to be a feature of Helen's experience is spiritual, not natural; transcendent, not mundane; and so on. The claims surrounding the Christ form a vast array, since he is embedded in the limitless versions of Hebrew-Christian narrative and explanation. The Christ is construed by Helen as having been the cause of her experience, and in this respect shares a feature found in Plato's account with which I opened this essay.

Helen's experience itself is apt to be variously viewed. Some causal theorists might suggest that spicy food or too much alcohol might have caused Helen's apparition. Such suggestions cannot explain why Helen's experience began with two tactile sensations, followed by visual sensations – surely we cannot point to the way in which different bites of spicy food produce two kinds of sensation. Some views influenced by Freud suggest that sexual deprivation[40] might cause visions and apparitions, but again such efforts cannot show how sexual deprivation produces the two kinds of sensation in close proximity to one another. Julian Jaynes' suggestion[41] that stress might do so is similarly stymied. More promise rests in some variation of The Perceptual Release Theory of Hallucinations, since we know that experience can be hallucinatory. This term is variously interpreted,[42] but a central

---

[40] Michael Carroll offers this explanation for visions of Mary in *The Cult of the Virgin Mary*.

[41] Jaynes, *The Origins of Consciousness*.

[42] See Fulford, *Moral Theory and Medical Practice*, pp. 230–31.

thought is that "sense perceptions and other life experiences leave permanent neural templates or engrams in the brain."[43] These neural engrams are then rearranged in novel ways, and are dropped into conscious experience, much as they generate dreams when we are asleep.

The challenge for the Perceptual Release Theory is to explain the sequence of Helen's perceptual experiences, first the tactile ones and then the visual ones. A particular collection of engrams associated with tactile perception was supposedly dropped into Helen's conscious experience as she had her eyes closed and had the sensation of being touched, and then the (virtually) identical collection was dropped into experience a second time, after she opened her eyes and discovered that no one was standing near enough to her to be touching her. When she opened her eyes to see a figure, she identified it as the Christ (however this was done). Now a different collection of engrams was involved, engrams associated with visual perception. Some of the elements of her perception included features of the building she knew herself to be in, including her knowledge that she was facing the front of the room. The Christic figure was seemingly superimposed on the perceptions that were appropriate for the front of the building, so stored engrams were 'activated' at the same time as her powers of normal visual perception, for she also saw ordinary features of the building.

Helen then attempted 'a reality check', whether consciously or otherwise. She turned to the back of the building and discovered that no one else gave an indication that they were observing that which she had just observed. As she faced the back of the building she saw what would have been normally seen by someone looking at the assembled congregation behind her. The Christic figure did not follow her eye movement, but when she looked again at the front the same figure was visible, and in the same place as before. This would mean that the visual engrams forming the extraordinary figure were dropped into conscious experience, then were removed when she faced the back, and then were dropped into her conscious experience again – the identical engrams – each time occurring in conjunction with the normal visual perceptions of the building she was in. We can see that the Perceptual Release Theory has a great deal to prove, given the variations involved. Meanwhile, Helen thought that a spiritual being – the Christ, however he might be constituted, if he does exist – had appeared to her.

[43] "Perceptual release theory of hallucinations," http://hallucinations.enacademic.com/1415/perceptual_release_theory_of_hallucinations (Accessed July 2, 2018); and Brasic, "Hallucinations."

Given all the promissory notes issued by the Perceptual Release Theory, Helen's claim is not preposterous, in spite of our inability to make sense of the kind of reality the Christ might possess. Helen's experience was unique to her, as I explain using twenty-three variables by which to characterize the modern Christic encounters that I researched.

I cannot go into more detail about the way in which the Theory of Spirits provides accounts of alleged events requiring explanation, and how it postulates beings with properties and relations to other things (animate or inanimate), including relations to things that indubitably exist. An analogy exists between this feature of the Theory and the way in which the theoretical framework in which the postulation of the lambda-baryon particle makes sense. Although we would be unwise to insist too strictly on the form that a theory must take, we can certainly learn from theory structures in various areas.[44] While theories postulating theoretical entities can have falsifiable or corroborative consequences, these are not the only ways such theories have their mettle tested. In *The Web of Belief*, Quine and Ullian discuss some of the properties of 'virtuous' theories, many of which are relevant here, including a theory's simplicity, its not being *ad hoc*, its capacity for receiving confirming and disconfirming evidence, and its capacity to be rendered probable.[45] As many as two dozen of these principles can be found in the literature of the philosophy of science. In their remarks about claims relevant to religion, Quine and Ullian observe that hallucination may rule out some reports deemed vital to religion, that religious claims should not be construed as self-evident, and that people's testimony may be marred by deviousness, self-deception, ignorance, fear, mis-remembering, and misjudging; they observe, however, that evidence for religion might exist.[46]

Another approach to religious experience comes from a movement widely known as Reformed Epistemology, whose best known advocate is Alvin Plantinga. He writes:

> [The] *sensus divinitatis* is a belief-producing faculty (or power, or mechanism) that under the right conditions produces belief that isn't evidentially based on other beliefs. On this model, our cognitive faculties have been designed and created by God; the design plan, therefore, is a design plan in the literal and

---

[44] See Mayr, "The Autonomy of Biology," for comments on the initial negative effects of imposing standards in physics upon biology.

[45] These are found throughout.

[46] Quine and Ullian, *Web of Belief*, pp. 22, 40, 45, and chapter 4.

paradigmatic sense. It is a blueprint or plan for our ways of functioning, and it has been developed and instituted by a conscious, intelligent agent. The purpose of the *sensus divinitatis* is to enable us to have true beliefs about God; when it functions properly, it ordinarily does produce true beliefs about God. These beliefs therefore meet the conditions for warrant; if the beliefs produced are strong enough, then they constitute knowledge.[47]

Plantinga has consistently voiced his objections to having Christian claims and beliefs subjected to the evidence (expressed in probabilities) that inevitably accompany scientific claims. We might wonder whether Helen made the identification of the Christ-figure that appeared to her using her *sensus divinitatis*? No obvious criterion exists by which to determine whether this power is present. In general, no criterion exists by which to determine that the cognitive faculties of those who experience apparitions are functioning properly. We know that hallucinations occur, and also that reliable perception exists, but religious experiences that fall between these two extremes are notoriously difficult to characterize. Reformed Epistemology does not significantly advance philosophical views on Religious Experience.

## ONTOLOGY AND RELIGIOUS EXPERIENCE

In a comprehensive review of religion, Ninian Smart identifies the Experiential and Emotional dimension as one among seven prominent features of religion.[48] The six others consist of (1) the Practical and Ritual dimension; (2) the Narrative and Mythic dimension; (3) Social and Institutional structures; (4) Ethical and Legal teachings; (5) Doctrinal and Philosophic features; and (6) the Material Dimension, consisting of objects or places deemed sacred. Religious experience is clearly in a class of its own when we consider the ontological implications of the various fields in Smart's list. All seven dimensions are of interest, of course, but Experience has the greatest ontological value among the seven.

A new epistemology for religion, certainly for Religious Experience, is coming into view. It requires extricating ourselves from the traditional certainties with which religion has clothed itself, as well as from

---

[47] Plantinga, *Warranted Christian Belief*, p. 149.
[48] Smart, *The World's Religions*, pp. 11–21.

the paralyzing questioning of Descartes or the scepticism of Hume. Our age is wiser and more robust than that of early modern philosophers, who still sought certainty beyond the limits of logic and mathematics. Our growing knowledge of theories postulating unobservable entities, especially the micro-entities of physics, has uncovered subtle epistemic principles, yet to be adequately described. This development shows that questions about beings that are the focal point of much religion are unanswered. This question is as momentous as it ever was, at least for those of us for whom the heavy draughts of agnosticism or atheism have become impossible to swallow. The rationality of religion is linked to the recognized sciences, the study of which is celebrated universally. Out of this scrutiny will come the principles concerning Religious Experience that will put religion on a satisfactory epistemological footing.

### References

Anselm of Canterbury, St. *Proslogion*, www.stanselminstitute.org/files/AnselmProslogion.pdf (Accessed June 4, 2018).

Aquinas, St Thomas. *Summa Theologiae*, www.newadvent.org/summa/1002.htm#article1 (Accessed June 4, 2018).

Aristotle. "On Prophesying by Dreams" (trans. J. I. Beare) in *The Basic Works of Aristotle*. Edited by Richard McKeon. New York: Random House, 1966.

Augustine of Hippo, St, *On the Trinity*, www.newadvent.org/fathers/130109.htm (Accessed July 11, 2018).

Ayer, Alfred J. *Language, Truth, and Logic*, 2nd ed. New York: Dover Publications, 1946.

Berkeley, George. "A Treatise Concerning the Principles of Human Knowledge," in *The Empiricists*. New York: Anchor Books, 1974 [orig. 1710].

Brasic, James R. "Hallucinations," *Perceptual and Motor Skills* 86 (1998): 851–77.

Buchler, Justus. *Philosophical Writings of Peirce*. New York: Dover Publications, 1955.

Carroll, Michael P. *The Cult of the Virgin Mary: Psychological Origins*. Princeton: Princeton University Press, 1986.

Close, Frank, Michael Marten, and Christine Sutton. *The Particle Explosion*. Oxford: Oxford University Press, 1987.

Davis, Wayne. "Implicature," *The Stanford Encyclopedia of Philosophy* (Fall 2014 ed), Edward N. Zalta (ed.), https://plato.stanford.edu/archives/fall2014/entries/implicature/ (Accessed June 5, 2018).

Decaen, Christopher A. "Aristotle's Aether and Contemporary Science," *The Thomist* 68 (2004): 375–429.

Dennett, Daniel C. "The Self as a Center of Narrative Gravity," in F. Kessel, P. Cole, and D. Johnson (eds.), *Self and Consciousness: Multiple Perspectives*. Hillsdale, NJ: Erlbaum, 1992.

Evans, C. Stephen, "Moral Arguments for the Existence of God," *The Stanford Encyclopedia of Philosophy* (Winter 2016 ed), Edward N. Zalta (ed.), https://plato.stanford.edu/archives/win2016/entries/moral-arguments-god/ (Accessed June 6, 2018).

Feigl, Herbert. "The 'Orthodox' View of Theories: Remarks in Defense as well as Critique," in Michael Rudner and Stephen Winokur (eds.), *Minnesota Studies in the Philosophy of Science: Analysis of Theories and Methods of Physics and Psychology, vol. IV*, pp. 3–15. Minneapolis: University of Minnesota Press, 1970.

Flew, Antony, and Alasdair MacIntyre (eds.). *New Essays in Philosophical Theology*. London: SCM, 1955.

Friederich, Simon. "Fine-Tuning," *The Stanford Encyclopedia of Philosophy* (Spring 2018 Edition), Edward N. Zalta (ed.), https://plato.stanford.edu/archives/spr2018/entries/fine-tuning/ (Accessed June 5, 2018).

Fulford, Kenneth W. M. *Moral Theory and Medical Practice*. New York: Cambridge University Press, 1991.

Hempel, Carl. "Problems and Changes in the Empiricist Criterion of Meaning," *Revue Internationale de Philosophie* 4 (1950): 41–63.

Hume, David. *A Treatise of Human Nature*. Edited by L. A. Selby-Bigge. Oxford: Clarendon Press, 1967 [orig. 1738–40].
   *Dialogues concerning Natural Religion*. Edited with commentary by Nelson Pike. Indianapolis: Bobbs-Merrill, 1970 [orig. 1779].

Jaynes, Julian. *The Origins of Consciousness in the Breakdown of the Bicameral Mind*. Toronto: University of Toronto Press, 1976.

Kant, Immanuel. *Critique of Practical Reason*. Translated by Lewis White Beck. Indianapolis, IN: Bobbs-Merrill, 1956 [orig. 1788].

Mayr, Ernst. "The Autonomy of Biology: The Position of Biology among the Sciences," *The Quarterly Review of Biology* 71 (1996): 97–106.

Mill, John Stuart. *A System of Logic, Ratiocinative and Inductive*. https://en.wikisource.org/wiki/A_System_of_Logic,_Ratiocinative_and_Inductive [orig. 1843] (Accessed June 5, 2018).

Moore, Sebastian. "The Resurrection: A Confusing Paradigm Shift," *The Downside Review* 98 (1980): 257–66.

Nielsen, Kai. *Philosophy and Atheism: In Defense of Atheism*. Buffalo, NY: Prometheus Books, 1985.

Paley, William. *Natural Theology: Or, Evidences of the Existence and Attributes of the Deity, Collected from the Appearances of Nature*. Edited by Matthew Eddy and David Knight. Oxford: Oxford University Press, 2006 [orig. 1802].

Pals, Daniel. *Nine Theories of Religion*, 3rd ed. Oxford: Oxford University Press, 2015.

"Perceptual release theory of hallucinations," http://hallucinations.enacademic.com/1415/perceptual_release_theory_of_hallucinations (Accessed July 2, 2018).

Plantinga, Alvin (ed.). *The Ontological Argument*. New York: Doubleday, 1965.
   *Warranted Christian Belief*. New York: Oxford University Press, 2000.

Plato. *The Dialogues of Plato*. Translated by B. Jowett. New York: Random House, 1937.

Popper, Karl. *The Logic of Scientific Discovery*. London: Routledge, 1959.

Quine, Willard Van Orman. *From a Logical Point of View*, 2nd ed. New York: Harper & Row, 1963.

Quine, Willard Van Orman, and Joseph S. Ullian. *The Web of Belief.* http:// socialistica.lenin.ru/analytic/txt/q/quine_1.htm (Accessed June 5, 2018).

Rorty, Richard, and Gianni Vattimo. *The Future of Religion*. Edited by Santiago Zabala. New York: Columbia University Press, 2004.

Searle, John. *The Rediscovery of the Mind*. Cambridge, MA: Massachusetts Institute of Technology, 1992.

Smart, John (Jack) Jamieson Carswell, and John Haldane. *Atheism and Theism*, 2nd ed. Oxford: Blackwell Publishing, 2003.

Smart, Ninian. *The World's Religions*, 2nd ed. Cambridge: Cambridge University Press, 1998.

Smith, Quentin. "The Metaphilosophy of Naturalism," *Philo: A Journal of Philosophy* 4 (2001): 195–215.

Swinburne, Richard. *The Existence of God*, 2nd. ed. Oxford: Clarendon Press, 2004.

Tulodziecki, Dana. "Shattering the Myth of Semmelweis," *Philosophy of Science* 80 (2013): 1065–75.

Uebel, Thomas. "Vienna Circle," *The Stanford Encyclopedia of Philosophy* (Spring 2016 ed), Edward N. Zalta (ed.), https://plato.stanford.edu/archives/spr2016/entries/vienna-circle/ (Accessed June 5, 2018).

Wiebe, Phillip H. *Visions of Jesus: Direct Encounters from the New Testament to Today*. Oxford: Oxford University Press, 1997.

Wittgenstein, Ludwig. *Philosophical Investigations*. Translated by G. E. M. Anscombe. London: MacMillan, 1968.

## 3 Theology, Religious Diversity, and Religious Experience

### GWEN GRIFFITH-DICKSON

It's an old joke: A theologian was standing at a bar when a philosopher came in. 'The trouble with you philosophers', maintained the theologian, 'is that you are like a blindfolded person in a pitch-black room, groping for a cat which isn't there'. 'That may be so', rejoindered the philosopher, 'but you theologians *find* the cat'.

Psychology of religion, philosophy of religion, and theology might ordinarily be seen as tackling the same subject matter with separate methodologies: psychology is working with empirical data and its own social-scientific methodology; philosophy is working with reasoning and seeking (or rejecting) a rational ground or foundation for belief; and theology is working with revelation, sacred texts, and various religious authoritative traditions to produce articulations of doctrine and dogma – and thus, in the eyes of some, conjuring up a cat that doesn't exist.

Theology, on this account, is constrained by orthodoxy, and is delimited by a specific faith tradition; 'tradition-specific'.[1] Philosophers often claim that they, in contrast, are free from an *allegiance* or a *loyalty*, some commitment other than to follow where reason and evidence take them.[2]

Theology approaches religious experience differently from philosophy or psychology; and, even within the same discipline, different theological approaches diverge in how they handle the topic. There are differing perspectives of what 'experience' means and what the term 'religious' should signify, as well as conflicting accounts of the role that experience plays in theology. Finally, in recent years there have been a variety of different takes on how theology should respond to the phenomenon of religious diversity. This is not merely a question of

---

[1] D'Costa, *Christianity and World Religions*, p. 3.
[2] Although I would argue that philosophies are just as 'situated' in a culture as theology can be. See Griffith-Dickson, *Philosophy of Religion*, chapter 2.

different opinions – but different disciplinary approaches altogether. This chapter will consider first how theology handles the two key phenomena: religion and religious experience. It then considers how theology has responded to the fact of religious diversity by generating different kinds of academic activity, before turning to the question of how it affects the study of religious experience in a theological way.

## THEOLOGY AND 'RELIGION'

As distinguished from psychology of religion and philosophy of religion, theology – it could be said – is not the study of 'religion'.

The word 'religion' is a European word. Some languages and language families, including those from cultures suffused by prayer, worship, and piety – such as Sanskrit and Hawai'ian – do not have a corresponding term. In recent times 'religion' has proved a very difficult word to define, which is evident not only when social sciences have to employ it, but even more so when courts and laws and tax regulations have to deal with it. It is surprisingly difficult to draw a boundary that includes all the traditions one wants to include, while excluding other ideologies, belief systems, or affinity groups on which some do not want to confer the same privileges or rights. The deeper lesson in this is that religion is not a stable, culture-free term. We might imagine there to be a thing we call religion that exists in different cultural varieties, but this obscures a messier reality. There are different manifestations of spirituality and prayer, communal life, meaning, texts, challenge, identity, beliefs and authority arising in different patterns around the world; and, moreover, they are not readily separable from culture.[3]

Historically, when Christianity or Islam has deployed the generic term 'religion' – often to contrast with their *own* religious teaching and practice – it is because there is a political or ideological need to identify the majority faith against all the others. Thus, the concept of 'religion' and how it has been deployed has carried an ideological or political function for much of its history. An example in our time would be Samuel Huntingdon's construction of an account of a 'clash of civilizations', where his list of 'seven or eight' civilizations ('Western, Confucian, Japanese, Islamic, Hindu, Slavic-Orthodox, Latin American, and possibly African') contains four described by their religion, as opposed to others designated by geography or culture-region ('Western').

---

[3] Griffith-Dickson, "Religion", and *Philosophy of Religion*; Barnes, *Interreligious Learning*, pp. 32–47.

Huntingdon argues that 'the survival of the West' depends on 'Americans reaffirming their Western identity and Westerners accepting their civilization as unique not universal and uniting to renew and preserve it against challenges from non-Western societies'.[4] More recently, Elizabeth Shakman Hurd has analysed the way 'religion' is constructed and manipulated to achieve foreign policy goals.[5] The construction of complex phenomena as 'religious' therefore can serve a political objective. Defining religion – or denying the religious roots of one's own standpoint – is not always a dispassionate, disinterested affair.

Even when it is not politically manipulated, the term cannot free itself from cultural baggage and the risk of imposing a perceptual grid from one's own cultural preoccupations. An uncritical deployment of the word 'religion', then, is a treacherous starting point for understanding the faiths of the world. Through obscuring its assumptions, it encourages one to engage with other 'religions' by expecting them to be analogous to one's own 'religion'. Christians, for example, often expect to understand what other religions are about by examining their doctrines, yet this is a flawed approach even for Christianity's closest relative, Judaism, let alone Taoism, Confucian traditions, or many indigenous religions: faith traditions might define themselves primarily not by doctrinal beliefs, but on right living or practices that unite and support the community. Such fundamental differences in outlook can persist even after conversion: John Charlot observes that Hawai'ian Christians often emphasise God the Father more than God the Son in their worship, as the theology of creation is more deeply congenial to their cultural and spiritual heritage than is the theology of redemption.[6]

Even without these sociological and political concerns, there is a straightforward justification lying behind the claim that theology is not simply the study of religion. The word applies to all or most of the different varieties of faith and spiritual belief. Christian theology, however, has traditionally seen itself as dealing with the doctrines, beliefs, and practices of its own tradition: the subject matter of Christian Theology is not religion but Christianity; and the same can be applied with suitable modifications to other faith traditions that contain a historical

[4] Huntington, *Clash*, chapter 1. As I wrote in 2003, "Whether Western culture is really under threat of extinction by other cultures, or whether in fact it is truer to say that other cultures, especially indigenous ones, are under threat from the spread and domination of American or Western culture is of course open to dispute". Griffith-Dickson, "Religion", p. 15.

[5] Shakman Hurd, *Beyond Religious Freedom*.

[6] Charlot, "Contemporary Polynesian Thinking".

practice of disciplined reflection on their texts, traditions, and beliefs. How a theological practice deals with *other* religions, however, is another matter entirely from its explication of its own beliefs and texts. Thus, the discussion of mainstream topics of 'Theology' is not the same as the theological treatment of the issue of 'religion' as a general, universal phenomenon – or the issue of religions in the plural, all claiming to be true: the undeniable fact of religious diversity.

Therefore, if we are considering a *theological* approach, it is not trivial to recognise that theology is not, naively put, the study of religion; and not only because religion is a constructed concept that functions as a Trojan horse to smuggle in cultural assumptions. Another reason is that theology, as tradition-specific, is itself not religiously neutral but is an approach that creates understanding and meaning for those *within its own faith community*. It is not meeting a demand for acceptance and validity from everyone in the academy, regardless of belief or outlook. This is a significant difference, therefore, from philosophy or the social sciences not only in its methods, but also in how the object of study itself is constituted. Since theology does not claim to work from a neutral standpoint, the way a philosopher would, '*whose* religious experience?' is a question that must be asked in order to create boundaries for defining the object of study. If Christian theology is the explication of Christianity, not the study of *religion*, when Christian theology considers religious experience, does it only study the religious experience of Christians?

## THEOLOGY AND RELIGIOUS EXPERIENCE

If the word 'religion' is unstable, the term 'religious experience' is notoriously vague, and researchers – especially psychologists – need to spend considerable time and space defining it and setting a boundary and scope to their investigation. In philosophical and psychological treatments, it most often refers to specific events in someone's life that were particularly striking, and which they would mark out from ordinary moments in their everyday lives. What makes it religious, and whether it is narrowly defined or broad, is part of the difficulty in conducting the investigation.

However, unlike philosophy of religion or the social sciences of psychology, sociology, and anthropology, theology does not investigate discrete events experienced by persons and seek to quarry out knowledge, insight or data using specific analytic tools. The relationship of theology to religious experience, or the significance of religious experience to theological production, is not that of a phenomenon and data to be analysed and interpreted using methodologies and processes.

In addition to a specific extraordinary event, the term 'religious experience' can also mean something much more diffuse, with a dividing line as hazy as the horizon at sea in a rainstorm. Handled by theologians such as Bernard Lonergan, religious experience is not simply a term for an unusual striking moment, but is itself a 'realm of meaning', or indeed 'an unrestricted state of love'.[7] For those who understand themselves as spiritual, religious experience is indeed the whole of life viewed as spiritually significant: setbacks and triumphs interpreted as trials and blessings, or perceptions of natural beauty leading to praise of a Creator. It is most often this broader understanding – experiencing the whole of life as an encounter with a loving God – that characterizes a theological approach to understanding the significance of religious experience.

What role experience plays in theology generally is a complex historical question beyond the scope of this chapter. Briefly, one view is that theology's starting point is God's revelation in Scripture, and in some views (characteristically Catholic) also from the tradition of Church teaching. This position is often described as pre-modern, or scholastic. With the humanism of the Renaissance period, accelerating in the nineteenth century with Friedrich Schleiermacher, theology has been described as taking a more subjective turn and therefore focusing on the phenomenon of human, lived experience.

This focus on religious experience, however, is not exclusively 'Protestant', and need not be opposed to an interest in doctrine, orthodoxy, or objectivity, as the twentieth-century Catholic examples of Bernard Lonergan, Karl Rahner, and Hans Urs von Balthasar all show. Nor does it divide neatly into pre-modern, modern, and indeed post-modern, as contemporary theologians all reflect differing patterns in how they consider experience to be the stuff of theological activity. Keith Ward, when grounding his own understanding of 'Comparative Theology', writes:

> It is important that it is a disciplined intellectual exercise which gives knowledge of objective reality. It is not some sort of imaginative fantasizing on personal experiences, in which logic gives way to rhetoric. Nor is it the expression of some socially relative form of thought which lives alongside many others

---

[7] Lonergan, *Method in Theology*.

without disputing their claims to truth. The discipline of theology claims rigorous intellectual thought and it claims truth about God.[8]

Thus many theologians, both Catholic and Protestant, would say that the task of theology, for most Christian systematic theologians, is not to use ever-advancing empirical, experiential knowledge to build out a fully-fleshed academic understanding of the human person. As Pope argues, theology is not constructed on the religious experiences of its founders or its adherents, but (with reference to Christianity) on Jesus, his fate, and what Christians believe about him: 'theology is not the introspective exploration of the human condition, but the attempt to understand what it means to have been subject to God's address in the history of a particular nation (Israel) and the life, teaching, death, and resurrection of a particular person (Jesus)'.[9] As a consequence, in the Christian tradition, 'religious experience must have a place, but interpreting apart from the categories developed by Christian theology appears to place personal experience over divine revelation leading to the charge that to give too much emphasis to the former results in speaking about the self rather than God'.[10]

At the same time, some contemporary theologians see theology precisely as a process of reflection on experience, citing Anselm of Canterbury, who spoke of 'faith seeking understanding', and thus consider experience to be essentially one of the sources with which theology engages. Lonergan and Rahner are two substantial contributors. Alan Race argues that, given the task of theology is to reflect on experience, we need to consider what that experience consists of: it is not only the legacy of Christian history, but also our present world of religious diversity. Thus, religious diversity itself is precisely a topic for Christian theology.[11]

Theologians of these diverging camps would agree, in the end, that theological reflection does not simply collect unusual experiences, extract data from them, and create new theory or knowledge or build a case or argument. Theological reflection on 'real life' is natural, a normal activity for thinking people of faith, and the relation between experience and reflection, thinking, and action is a dynamic interaction often described as 'the hermeneutical circle'.

---

[8] Ward, *Religion and Revelation*, pp. 5–6.
[9] Pope, "Immediate Revelation", p. 109.
[10] Ibid., p. 113.
[11] Race and Hedges, *Christian Approaches*, p. 9.

The upshot is that asking for a 'theological' approach to investigating religious experience risks receiving a highly subversive answer, one that wreaks havoc on the necessarily tidy definitions of social scientists and philosophers of religion. For empirical or analytic enquiry, clear boundaries and transparent definitions are necessary to make sense of the phenomenon studied. But theology is disruptive, challenging the significance of the boundaries being set and the very activity of setting them. Further, the more that theological thinking seeks to be in dialogue with 'real life' and undertakes its enquiry precisely in order to create real-world impact, the more unstable the definitions and categories need to be as this real-world experience changes.

Given that experience is a starting point for theological reflection, the most overwhelming development in Christian theology in recent decades has been a revolution in what counts as the experience *relevant* for theological reflection – or more specifically, as we asked earlier, *whose* experience counts. Liberation theology, begun in Latin America in the 1970s, inaugurated a change of methodological tools from European philosophy (once deemed 'the handmaid of theology' in the eyes of Western Christian theologians) to Marxist economic-sociological interpretive categories and methods. Once these were applied to the lived experience of Latin Americans, questions about poverty, disadvantage, marginalisation, the disparity of wealth, the use of power, and Christian rhetoric to justify inequality all came to the fore as the proper subject of theology. This yields strikingly different understandings of how to understand core Christian concepts of grace and salvation: is it something that we experience in this world, in our actual daily lives and material circumstances, or only in the next world? Black theology and theological treatments of race were not far behind, along with feminist theology and the consideration of sex and gender. The differing experiences yielded by what some bodies can and can't do has more recently become a topic for theological analysis as theology considers disability. The insight that our identities are 'intersectional' – that various characteristics such as our gender, our race, and our social class all intersect and have an impact both on our experience and our treatment by others – has also yielded new approaches, such as Womanist Theology, the theology of African-American women.

One such account gives an example of how theology, using an expanded awareness of what constitutes 'experience' and 'theology', can create a profound body of insights. In *Stand Your Ground: Black Bodies and the Justice of God*, Kelly Douglas Brown takes as her theological starting point the murder of seventeen-year-old Trayvon Martin, and other young African Americans. From the standpoint of the mother of a son who could have been Trayvon, she interrogates and challenges the cultural and political landscape of the US, where violence against and killing of African Americans repeatedly occurs with impunity, thereafter to derive the theological meaning of God and the message for black faith through the cross and resurrection of Jesus.

> In the stand-your-ground war today, crucifixion comes in the form of gun violence. The Matthean question today might be, 'But Lord, when did we see you dying and on the cross?' And Jesus would answer, 'On a Florida sidewalk, at a Florida gas station, on a Michigan porch, on a street in North Carolina. As you did it to one of these young black bodies, you did it to me'. The tragedy of the cross is the tragedy of stand-your-ground war. It is in the face of Trayvon dying on a sidewalk that we see the face of Jesus dying on the cross. To know the extent of God's love, one must recognize the face of Jesus in the face of Trayvon.[12]

A typical analytic philosopher of religion would not likely consider this a 'religious experience', and deem this passage inappropriate for this book. But this is precisely the challenge that theology has to offer to this debate: what counts as an experience which claims to reveal God, to impart religious or spiritual meaning? To view the work of a theologian like Kelly Brown Douglas as a valid contribution to reflection on religious experience is precisely pushing at the boundaries of experience in the subversive, disruptive way that contemporary theology does. The murder of a young man might not be a numinous religious encounter with God – but as the shocking, all-too-real experience of people of colour it demands a theological response; and, as such, it counts as theological reflection on human experience that has religious importance.

The philosopher of religion at the bar, then, could reasonably object that the theologian was expanding the concept of 'religious experience' into something so broad that it becomes vacuous. 'If even murder can count as a "religious experience"', he might say, waving his drink, 'then the whole of human existence counts as something you theologians might have to reflect on theologically'.

And the theologian might well respond, 'Yes – *exactly*'.

---

[12] Douglas Brown, *Stand Your Ground*, p. 179–80.

## THEOLOGY MEETS RELIGIOUS DIVERSITY: THE
## THEOLOGY OF RELIGIONS

So whilst philosophy of religion requires a clearly defined sub-category of experience to examine, called *'religious* experience', theology rejects this: it would mean that our relationship to the divine or ultimate is a mere subset of the experiences of our lives, rather than the ground of our being and purpose – even in moments of tragedy or evil. Theologians thus accept that they cannot examine a narrow class of individual personal experiences to evidence theological claims; this activity is simply not a part of their repertoire.

As we have seen, there is increasing appreciation amongst theologians of the diversity of Christian experience: including race and ethnicity, gender, inequality, and ability. But even if theologians only consider the experience of their own faith tradition, in today's world our everyday experience includes the experience of a 'religious other': people who believe and practice their faith differently. Even Western Christian experience must therefore acknowledge an increasing recognition of the reality and impact of religious diversity that surrounds the Western Christian. (Religious diversity has always been more visible in the Middle East, South Asia, and Africa, and it has always been clearer for those who live their lives as a religious minority *anywhere*. The term 'religious diversity' here refers to the fact that there are many manifestations of spiritual beliefs and practices in the world. 'Religious pluralism' is often used for this phenomenon, but in this chapter the term pluralism describes a particular theological stance.)

Once again, philosophy and theology have responded to religious diversity differently. For Western philosophers of religion, the religious diversity found in religious experience prompted a quandary as old as Hume's skeptical critique: spiritual experiences from different religious traditions substantiate conflicting religious claims, which cannot all be correct. Thus, the ostensible task for philosophers of religion was to examine specific classes of experience called 'religious', but now arising from different religions, and to address the problem of adjudicating between conflicting truth claims.

On the theological frontier, as 'religious experience' potentially embraces the whole field of religious life, theology faced a much more substantial task than just examining the impact of religious diversity on the understanding of discrete numinous life-events. Rather, theology must take on board the significance of the religious *life* of other traditions. In a much-cited passage from 1972, William Cantwell Smith stated that, from now on, any 'serious intellectual statement of the Christian faith must include a doctrinal account of the existence of other faiths'.[13]

John Hick was one of the first and most influential to respond to Cantwell Smith's call, and his theory of religions has become foundational for modern notions of religious pluralism. Hick utilises Kant's distinction between 'things as we perceive them' and 'things as they are in themselves', to distinguish 'Ultimate Reality as it really is in itself' from 'Ultimate Reality as we perceive it'. The various different religions are thus 'different human responses to the one divine Reality', yet this divine reality transcends all human description. Each religious tradition therefore provides an authentic conception of this one reality, whilst lacking direct access or a *uniquely* correct account.[14] For philosophy of religion a key question is whether religious experience genuinely responds to a reality beyond ourselves if it is embodied in our own concepts and imagery. If so, then you must construct your interpretation of religion 'in its world-wide and history-long variety of forms'.[15] Thus, for Hick, in dealing with the question of religious experience the philosopher is immediately confronted with the fact of religious diversity. As a philosopher it is impossible to privilege one tradition over another as having a monopoly on truth, and thus the challenge is to make sense of the plurality of faith traditions, giving rise to their different kinds of religious experience.[16]

Following on from Hick, Alan Race developed a three-fold paradigm to articulate the possible stances towards non-Christian faiths, in what was to become the emergent discipline of the theology of religions.[17]

*Exclusivism* is often taken to be the traditional or the conservative view. The believer considers his faith to be true; for the Christian, the Bible and Christian faith are true and normative. Faith traditions can be seen to be 'exclusive', insofar as their claims might conflict with other claims, and, when in conflict with another religion, they maintain that their tradition is true. For the Christian, Jesus Christ is the only way to salvation. Other faiths can, of course, hold exclusivist views.

*Inclusivism* takes its starting-point as the truth of one's own tradition; thus, for the Christian, that Jesus Christ represents the unique

---

[13] Cantwell Smith, *The Faith*, p. 133.
[14] See Hick, *Interpretation*, and *God and the Universe of Faiths*.
[15] Hick, "Theology of Religions", p. 26.
[16] Ibid., p. 27.
[17] Race, *Christians*.

path to salvation. However, it holds this claim together with the belief that God wills all to be saved, and the sheer historical fact that much of humankind has never had the opportunity to hear the Christian testimony. Thus, it often offers some account of how saving grace is uniquely tied to Jesus Christ, yet God's offer of grace and salvation can be mediated through other traditions. It is often seen to be a particularly Catholic position, because its exponent Karl Rahner was a Catholic theologian. Rahner deployed the concept of the 'anonymous Christian': that someone who lives a good and holy life without being in a position to hear and accept the Gospel can nevertheless be saved. This understandably has been found condescending, and there are contemporary versions of inclusivism that are more subtle. It is also not a uniquely Christian phenomenon; Kirstin Kiblinger, for example, sets out Buddhist examples that she analyses as inclusivist.[18]

*Pluralism* is a response to perceived drawbacks of the first two positions identified by Race. Existing in different forms with different methods, in the version based on Hick's account it sees truth, salvation, liberation, or enlightenment in all religions. In a late statement of his position, Hick argued that philosophy of religions – note the plural – rests on three premises, two epistemological and one empirical. The first epistemological premise is that it is as rational to base religious beliefs on religious experience as on sensory experience (except when there is good reason not to); and the second is the critical realist principle, that there is a world outside our experience existing independently of our awareness of it, but that our awareness of it is mediated through our own concepts and cognition. His third claim, which he describes as empirical, is that 'the moral and spiritual fruits in human lives of the different great world faiths seem, so far as we can tell, to be of more or less equal value'.[19] For Hick, this points us to a pluralistic interpretation of religion as it is implausible to privilege one particular religious tradition over the others, and the task is to make sense of this plurality of traditions. 'And so the pluralist hypothesis, as I see it, is that there is an ultimate transcendent reality which is differently conceived, and therefore differently experienced, and therefore differently responded to in life within the different great religious traditions'.[20] (Many criticisms of Hick specifically, and pluralism generally, rest on a critique of his Kantianism, and criticism of pluralism can rest on an

---

[18]  Kiblinger, "Relating Theology of Religions", p. 32 and *Buddhist Inclusivism.*
[19]  Hick, "Theology of Religions", p. 26.
[20]  Ibid., p. 27.

assumption that it is ultimately a relativist position. Peter Byrne, however, has argued persuasively that in fact pluralism only makes sense as a critically realist position which eschews Kantian idealism, and is not relativist.[21])

All of these three positions are broad outlooks, capable of various shades of opinion and appearing in both naïve and sophisticated versions. The three-fold typology itself is all-pervasive in the literature, finding both broad acceptance and plentiful criticism, both of the individual positions as well as the idea of the schema. Some have felt its original presentation to be loaded, with the implication that it is evolutionary, with exclusivist and inclusivist positions seen as inadequate and the pluralist as the most evolved and the most satisfactory. Others have argued that 'pluralism' is not ultimately a different, third position as it is really either a disguised exclusivism (since it claims the pluralist view is uniquely true) or a disguised inclusivism (since, while accepting the validity of other faiths, it inevitably understands them as included within its own theological framework, whether consciously or not).[22] Others have sought to add a fourth position, sometimes while renaming the first three.[23]

Perry Schmidt-Leukel, however, defends the three-fold typology against all comers on strictly logical grounds; once naturalism, the rejection of religious claims, is added, there are four positions which are logically comprehensive and thus logically there really are only three religious stances possible:

- The religious claims of teaching a path of salvation are either all false (*naturalism*) or they are not all false.
- If they are not all false, then either only one of them is true (*exclusivism*) or more than one is true.
- If more than one is true, then there is either one singular maximum of that truth (*inclusivism*) or there is no singular maximum, so that at least some are equally true (*pluralism*).[24]

Strictly speaking, these three positions are dealing with two fundamental issues: truth-claims or which revelation is true and correct; and salvation, enlightenment, liberation – who is to be 'saved' and how.

[21] Byrne, *Prolegomena*.
[22] See Hedges, "Reflection", *passim*, for an overview.
[23] Expansions to a fourfold model can be found in Panikkar, *The Intrareligious Dialogue* and Knitter, *Introducing Theology of Religions*.
[24] Schmidt-Leukel, *Religious Pluralism*, p. 4.

The second question, in fact, is dependent on the first, as the wording of Schmidt-Leukel's first bullet point indicates. In practice, however, there are many issues that intertwine when we come to consider other faiths – their beliefs, their texts, their practices; but also the concrete human individuals we meet, live next door to, fight, marry, or campaign with. Therefore, our personal attitudes towards religious diversity, in practice, bundle together a number of contrasting issues that might pull an individual in different directions: truth, salvation-enlightenment-liberation, loyalty, 'do we all believe in the same God?', personal goodness or holiness and its role in redemption and our fate in the afterlife, God's compassion for all, personal identity, respect and friendliness in interpersonal conduct, and compatibility or clash when living together in the same communities or societies. As such, many believers in practice feel tensions between the three options as applied to the truth of their own tradition, as compared to what their natural inclinations or their personal ethics require when interacting with others. At the end of the day, for those who are in direct contact with people from other faith traditions, the issue of truth might not be their most compelling question. 'How should I interact with my neighbour?' might be a more urgent matter.

One could see the work of theology of religions, then, as responding to the new task of making sense of religious diversity *from within* one faith experience. What does the existence of many faiths mean for Christian witness and Christian truth? Equally, what does Buddhism or Islam make of Christian claims for Christ? Through making sense of this experience theologically, it makes sense of our faith experience of the existence of a religious other. When returning to the question of 'Whose religious experience counts?' for theological enquiry, then, on a theology of religions approach this remains the Christian's experience, or the Jewish experience, and so on: what Christians make of the existence of other faiths. What is transformative is that our experience includes the experience of a religious other, but the theology is not *representing* the viewpoint of the other and exploring its meaning within their own religious framework.

## THEOLOGY INTERACTS WITH RELIGIOUS DIVERSITY: COMPARATIVE THEOLOGY

The theology of religions is but one academic endeavour responding to the fascinating phenomenon of religious diversity; Comparative Theology is another. Keith Ward was one of the first in recent times to conduct an extensive project under this methodological banner; he unfolds his project in a series of works examining core theological topics such as revelation and creation. In his first, he establishes the intellectual foundation on which this endeavour is based. He asserts that there is a proper intellectual study, a form of theology which explores religious beliefs and practices with regard to their truth and rationality – thus distinguishing it, as theology, from 'religious studies' – but which is undertaken with reference to more than one faith-community and is not committed in advance to that tradition. The study of revelation cannot be taken out of history; it is no longer tenable to consider the views of a particular religious tradition in isolation from the others. Indeed, one can conceive of Divine communication being addressed to different communities at different times in the frameworks, interests, and values that make sense to them. Ultimately, *theology is a pluralistic discipline. In it, people of differing beliefs can co-operate, discuss, argue, and converse*'.[25] As theology consists of reflection on ultimate reality and the goal of human existence, it can be done from the perspective of many faiths. 'It is better undertaken in knowledge of and in conversation with those of beliefs other than one's own'.[26]

There is a different scholarly endeavour underway in the United States, recently called 'the new Comparative Theology'. This Comparative Theology undertakes the interpretation of one's own faith by investigating others.[27] Its practitioners are not given to sweeping theological assertions so much as to careful textual studies, deeply informed and expert in the other tradition and aspiring to read the text like an insider to that faith. As Francis Clooney writes, theology 'is a mode of inquiry that engages a wide range of issues with full intellectual force, but within the constraints of a tradition'.[28] Comparative Theology consists of acts of faith seeking understanding which are rooted in a particular faith tradition but which, from that foundation, venture into learning from one or more other faith traditions; those acts are sought for the sake of fresh theological insights that are indebted to the newly encountered traditions as well as the home tradition.[29] As described by Catherine Cornille, Comparative Theology 'engages different religious

[25] Ward, *Religion and Revelation*, p. 45.
[26] Ibid., p. 46.
[27] Clooney, *New Comparative Theology*.
[28] Clooney, *Comparative Theology*, p. 9.
[29] Ibid., p. 10.

traditions around common questions, each tradition contributing to a deeper or higher understanding of the particular quest'.[30]

There are important differences between Ward's approach and that of Clooney, James Fredericks, or Cornille, in my view. Broadly speaking, Ward is undertaking a constructive work, drawing on the resources and materials to construct a theological investigation of a concept or theme just as Christian theologians normally do, but with a wider range of sources and a new layer of intellectual challenges that arise from the interaction of the faiths themselves and the impact on truth-questions. The 'new' Comparative Theology most often undertakes very precise, detailed textual study, but abstains from the task of constructing a composite answer to the bigger theological questions of revelation, creation, and other key theological concepts.

Inevitably, disagreements have broken out between the advocates of the theology of religions as a practice and comparative theology, and this differing conception of what Comparative Theology consists underlies these differing preferences. Clooney, Fredericks, and others have argued that, with the threefold paradigm, theology of religions has reached an impasse.[31] Whether it is viewed as a dead end or whether it is seen as just too soon to answer such big questions without a century of detailed textual studies, some proponents of Comparative Theology maintain that the theoretical task of theology of religions should be abandoned in favour of studies in Comparative Theology and on-the-ground interfaith dialogue.

Challengers to this view argue instead that Comparative Theology itself presupposes a theology of religion, even if tacitly. Noting that Clooney for example has indicated that he is a form of inclusivist, Schmidt-Leukel and Kiblinger argue in different ways that the activity of Comparative Theology necessarily goes forward based on certain presuppositions that cannot be avoided. Kiblinger argues that theology of religions is properly prior, in that it consists in 'getting clarity on our theological presuppositions' and contains 'reading strategies' that are necessary to Comparative Theology. Without that clarity as a foundation, we might well be reading texts differently.[32] Schmidt-Leukel lays down the significant charge that it is the bigger questions that make such an enterprise *theological*; if one abstains from them merely to

---

[30] Cornille, *Impossibility*, p. 14.
[31] Clooney, *New Comparative Theology, passim.*
[32] Kiblinger, "Relating Theology of Religions", p. 29.

engage in comparative textual study, the vaunted Comparative Theology is really none other than the old Comparative Religions.[33]

As an apparently new third approach – but arguably deeply indebted to Ward's earlier practice – Schmidt-Leukel has recently proposed a conception of 'interreligious theology' as the natural progression for theology from the acceptance of the stance of religious pluralism. No longer is the religious other simply the boundary that marks out one's own religious identity; no longer is truth and theological reflection confined only to the sources of one's own tradition. Instead, theology will become 'interreligious'; it will draw on other religions and their sources in order to formulate its answers.[34] This responds not only to religious developments, but to the sociological religious pluralization experienced globally. While any given theologian will still be based primarily in one tradition, 'Interreligious theology is possible only if it proceeds from the assumption that theologically relevant truth is not confined to one's own religious tradition but also found in other religions'.[35] Its starting points are trust, the unity of reality, interreligious discourse, and openness; and it is to be perspectival, imaginative, comparative, and constructive.[36]

Comparative Theology can be seen as providing a different implicit answer to our test question: *whose* religious experience is under consideration? With this theological practice, the religious other is no longer simply the object of Christian or Hindu or Jewish experience. Rather, the experience of other faiths speaking for themselves, particularly as embodied in religious texts, are placed side-by-side, with insights for one's own faith tradition coming from each of the texts as well as from the juxtaposition.

## THEOLOGY EMBRACING RELIGIOUS DIVERSITY: THEOLOGY OF INTERRELIGIOUS DIALOGUE

Meanwhile, some theologians in the field have also focused on dialogue itself or the sharing of religious experience itself as the subject matter for theological reflection, a fundamentally different approach to Theology of Religions and Comparative Theology. The theology of interreligious dialogue theologizes not about truth and salvation, but

---

[33] Schmidt-Leukel, *Religious Pluralism*, pp. 29–30.
[34] Ibid.
[35] Ibid., p. 130.
[36] Ibid., chapter 9.

precisely on the experience of being confronted by one who is irreducibly different, who is my neighbour or friend, but who challenges and enriches me by her difference. John Friday writes:

> The element of relationship in theology of interreligious dialogue is crucial and requires taking the religions seriously enough to actually engage with, and learn from them. Such learning not only includes learning about the 'other', but also learning about ourselves, and more specifically, our religious selves, that is, as people who have some degree of commitment to the doctrines and practices of a particular religious tradition. On this view, encountering religious difference provides an opportunity for self-discovery, and indeed, more profound understanding.[37]

Michael Barnes has produced a substantial body of work on this project. Unlike a detailed interreligious textual exegesis, as characterises many essays in Comparative Theology, Barnes' project is about a human Other; for him, interreligious learning begins with the meeting of persons, not the reading of texts. Nor does Barnes frame theology's task, when confronted by religious difference, as a matter of deciding on the truth or prospects for salvation of the manifold of religious witnesses in comparison to the Christian one. Rejecting the 'normative pluralism' of the threefold paradigm's third option, and acknowledging that the task is one undertaken from a position of faith, he calls for a theology of dialogue, 'a theology which would seek to reflect on the Christian experience of existing in relationship with the other'.[38]

The task for Barnes then is not to deal with the 'problem' of religious diversity, nor is it to create theory, but to create a Christian understanding of what it means to be in a relationship with other communities of faith. 'An open engagement with people of other faiths is itself deeply theological – and specifically Christological – because it is informed by a vision of the Trinitarian God who acts as both host and guest – the source of the gift by which Christians presume to communicate to others and the means by which the gift is shared'.[39] Turning his thinking subsequently to the idea of interreligious *learning*, and seeking to develop a *spirituality* of dialogue, Barnes seeks 'a more self-reflective account of Christianity in dialogue, a school of faith that responds to God's imperative to give and receive love by forever moving across

[37] Friday, "Discerning", p. 95.
[38] Barnes, *Theology*, pp. 23–24.
[39] Ibid., p. 239.

boundaries and translating its faith into forms that others can understand'.[40] Ultimately then his work aims to shift our attention from who possesses the truth to what one does to *realise* the truth,[41] and that can only be found in relationship with others.

Arguably this moves a thinker such as Barnes beyond the threefold paradigm; a theological decision does not need to be made on who possesses the truth, but rather a personal journey must be made in order to respond with integrity, humility, and joy towards mutual openness to the truth in response to those who are different.

A theology of religious dialogue thus moves further when embracing the religious experiences of other religions. Religious experience now includes the experience of dialogue: thus my experience of the religious other and their experience of me, which I discover through dialogue, but moving beyond this to include our experience of a *relationship*.

CONCLUSION

It is clear from this survey that there are many ways that the theological thinker can engage with the phenomenon of religious diversity that reveals itself when we contemplate religious experience. The variation that exists is not merely between different positions on a spectrum from 'liberal' to 'conservative'; the point is that the response to religious diversity has spawned different sub-disciplines altogether, and how one proceeds depends on which kind of work one aspires to. The thinker therefore needs to ask oneself, what is it I am trying to achieve? What questions do I want to answer? Is it a question about validity, truth, and which traditions most closely embody it? Or is it a question of gaining richer insights, whatever the source?

The starting-point, methods, and approach must necessarily follow a prior commitment to that question. But these initial questions will follow from your deeper philosophical or theological commitments: whether you believe truth or correctness resides in one cultural-religious context, and whether it does so exclusively, principally, or equally with others.

However, it should be recalled that the exclusivist-inclusivist-pluralist question pertains to questions about truth claims and final human destiny. This is not the only set of questions to be asked; and, in

---

[40] Barnes, *Interreligious Learning*, p. 261.
[41] Ibid., p. 266.

particular when we attend to interpreting and understanding religious *experience*, it is less likely that this is the most urgent direction of enquiry. Instead, questions such as meaning, self-understanding, and seeking a window – or a mirror – on human experience might acquire more significance; the phenomenon of religious experience generally, or the impact of individual religious experiences specifically, is less frequently a soteriological enterprise.

Here it should be noted that thinkers can acknowledge their personal origins in a faith stance, or a cultural secular stance; they can also accept that this will have a profound effect on how they perceive and interpret the objects of their study. Moreover, they can feel that an integral part of their identity springs from this dimension of their experience. They can feel profoundly committed to their community and value a sense of belonging to *this* tradition and *these* people. All of these are possible *without* taking truth-claims or theories of salvation as the object of inquiry. And, as long as this is so, identifying strongly with one particular tradition does not entail holding an exclusivist or inclusivist position. Nor does a pluralist stance on truth and salvation have a monopoly on openness and respect towards others who embrace different beliefs and practices. Thus, it is possible to understand oneself as fully immersed and faithful to your tradition, fully open and respectful towards others, without needing to commit to one of the positions in the threefold paradigm.

A critical question, then, deserves an answer in order to study religious experience from a theological angle. *Whose* religious experience is under consideration, and how are we to engage with it? While this in not in the foreground of a social scientific or philosophical methodology, as I have argued here it *is* the determining factor, however tacit, in choosing your theological practice. Is it your role to articulate Christian experience, now expanded to include the fact that we experience religious diversity and must make theological sense of it? Is it rather to compare and contrast different traditions in religious experience? Or is it to understand our experience to be disclosed to us through the experience of the other? All of these are valid approaches, but require clarity about their differing aims and claims.

As we have seen, a key difference between a theological orientation and other disciplines to the question of religious experience is found first of all in the concept of experience itself. For the theologian, religious experience does not uniquely designate an exceptional moment with unusual features; rather, it is our lived experience, puzzling, threatening, awe-inspiring, or love-generating, whose ultimate sense and meaning believers seek in relation to their spiritual tradition.

Meanwhile, religious experience in our world is an experience of religious diversity. While it is valid to focus on a single tradition as an area of enquiry, any enquiry that seeks to understand the significance of the experience as a whole – most of all, any that understands itself as a theological one – must engage with the reality of religious difference.

### References

Barnes, M. *Theology and the Dialogue of Religions*. Cambridge: Cambridge University Press, 2002.

    *Interreligious Learning. Dialogue, Spirituality and the Christian Imagination*. Cambridge: Cambridge University Press, 2012.

Byrne, P. *Prolegomena to Religious Pluralism: Reference and Realism in Religion*. London: St Martin's Press, 1995.

Cantwell Smith, W. *The Faith of Other Men*. New York: Harper Torchbooks, 1972.

Charlot, J. "Contemporary Polynesian Thinking," in Eliot Deutsch and Ron Bontekoe (eds.), *A Companion to World Philosophies*. Oxford: Blackwell, 1991.

Clooney, F. X. *Comparative Theology: Deep Learning across Religious Borders*. Boston: Wiley, 2010.

    (ed.). *The New Comparative Theology: Interreligious Insights from the Next Generation*. Edinburgh: T & T Clark, 2010.

Cornille, C. *The Impossibility of Interreligious Dialogue*. New York: The Crossroad Publishing Company, 2008.

D'Costa, G. *Christianity and World Religions: Disputed Questions in the Theology of Religions*. Boston: Wiley-Blackwell, 2009.

Douglas, K. B. *Stand Your Ground: Black Bodies and the Justice of God*. New York: Orbis Books, 2015.

Friday, J. "Discerning Criteria of Religious Experience in Theology of Interreligious Dialogue," in T. Merrigan and J. Friday (eds.), *The Past, Present, and Future of Theologies of Interreligious Dialogue*. Oxford: Oxford University Press, 2017.

Griffith-Dickson, G. "Religion – A Western Invention?," in H. Haring, J. Martin, and F. Wilfred (eds.), *Concilium Learning from Other Faiths*. London: SCM Press, 2003.

    *Philosophy of Religion*. London: SCM Press, 2007, chapter 2.

Hedges, P. "A Reflection on Typologies: Negotiating a Fast-Moving Discussion," in A. Race and P. Hedges (eds.), *Christian Approaches to Other Faiths*. London: SCM Press, 2008.

Hick, J. *God and the Universe of Faiths: Essays in the Philosophy of Religion*. London: Macmillan, 1973.

    *An Interpretation of Religion: Humanity's Varied Response to the Transcendent*. London: Palgrave Macmillan, 1989.

    "Theology of Religions versus Philosophy of Religions," in T. Bartel (ed.), *Comparative Theology – Essays for Keith Ward*. London: SPCK, 2003.

Huntingdon, S. *The Clash of Civilizations*. New York: Simon and Schuster, 1996.

Kiblinger, K. *Buddhist Inclusivism: Attitudes towards Religious Others*. London: Ashgate, 2005.

"Relating Theology of Religions and Comparative Theology," in F. X. Clooney, (ed.), *The New Comparative Theology: Interreligious Insights from the Next Generation*. Edinburgh: T & T Clark, 2010.

Knitter, P. *Introducing Theologies of Religions*. New York: Maryknoll, 2002.

Lonergan, B. *Method in Theology*. Evanston, IL: Seabury, 1972.

Panikkar, R. *The Intrareligious Dialogue*. New York: Paulist Press, 1984.

Pope, R. "Immediate Revelation or the Basest Idolatry? Theology and Religious Experience," in B. Schmidt (ed.), *The Study of Religious Experience: Approaches and Methodologies*. Sheffield, England: Equinox Publishing, 2016.

Race, A. *Christians and Religious Pluralism: Patterns in the Christian Theology of Religions*. London: SCM Press, 1983.

Race A., and P. Hedges (eds.). *Christian Approaches to Other Faiths*. London: SCM Press, 2008.

Schmidt-Leukel, P. *Religious Pluralism and Interreligious Theology*. New York: Orbis Books, 2017.

Shakman Hurd, E. *Beyond Religious Freedom: The New Global Politics of Religion*. Princeton: Princeton University Press, 2015.

Ward, K. *Religion and Revelation: A Theology of Revelation in the World's Religions*. Oxford: Oxford University Press, 1994.

# Part II

*Religious Experience in Traditional Monotheism*

# 4  Illumined by Meaning: Religious Experience in the Book of Job

HOWARD WETTSTEIN

Foreign to what we might call the religious imagination of the Hebrew Bible are concepts like *belief, religious experience,* even *religious imagination.* In the biblical idiom, one cannot so much as formulate the thought that one believes that God exists.[1] This is in part because *belief* is, as I say, foreign, and in part because it would be a bit like saying that one believes that the weather is real. God, part of the furniture of the universe, goes without saying. While *belief* is not, so to speak, on the table, *emunah*, roughly *faith* – aspects of which are loyalty, steadfastness, even intimacy, and, as Buber adds, walking in God's tempo – such things are central to a life with God.

Of course, it makes perfectly good sense to inquire about the religious beliefs of a contemporary practitioner of traditional Judaism. But the conceptual repertoire of the biblical text matters. It lingers in Jewish tradition even where it no longer dominates. It explains, for example, the more than central roles of practice and affect: love, awe, and gratitude. All of this by contrast to the role of the doxastic.[2]

Utilizing an appropriately light touch, we can also apply *our* concepts to the biblical narrative. My focus, in what follows, is what one might call Job's religious experience, his encounter with God, as God presents Himself and His creation in God's speech "from the Whirlwind." God's address represents nature, and God's relation to nature, in what was for Job – as it is for many of us – a new key, one that may have occasioned in Job a more mature view of God and of the world.

The Book of Job represents a distinctive, even unconventional, treatment of its subject. This is hardly *the* Jewish approach, for there

---

[1] I speak here about propositional belief, belief "that *p*." There are biblical contexts in which believing a person is in play.

[2] As Jewish religious ways have developed, certainly since medieval times, concepts like *belief* have come to play a more central role. For many nowadays, *belief* is, as in the other Abrahamic faiths, the *sine qua non*. Still, the centrality of practice and affect is unchallenged.

is no such thing. Jewish ways are various, from the rationalism of Maimonides to the mysticism of *kabbalah;* from the sense of intense engagement with the Talmud as a religious pinnacle to Maimonides's idea of an individual's contemplation of the *active intellect* to the *Chassidic* sense of affective intimacy with God. And the Hebrew bible itself is a bit like a library, not a theoretically unified presentation.

The Whirlwind vision goes deep. It resonates with – anticipates, one might say – later philosophic developments like Spinoza's ideal of viewing the world *sub specie aeternitatis,* under the aspect of eternity. Job, diseased, bereft, sitting alone on a pile of ash, is stunned, lifted up by God's words, again filled with awe. Job remains but dust and ashes – but illumined by meaning.

## JOB, PRE-WHIRLWIND

> Did you notice my servant, Job. There is no one on earth like him: a man of perfect integrity, who fears God and avoids evil.[3]

So speaks God to the skeptical heavenly Accuser,[4] almost bragging. "God-fearing" is sometimes used generically, to characterize a person of faith. So perhaps it's not only fear that characterizes Job's piety; it seems plausible (although unstated in the text) that Job's stated attention to God bespeaks his love. And God returns the favor with gifts of family and fortune. God is Job's touchstone, his rock, and his redeemer. Living without God is inconceivable.

And then it happens. Job's children are killed; his wife leaves; his fortune is lost; his body is diseased. How does this happen, and why? The text explains: the Accuser suggested to God that perhaps Job's loyalty was superficial, a consequence of God's favoring Job with a life of abundance. And God allowed the Accuser to test Job. That's the

---

[3] *The Book of Job,* p. 6. I am grateful to Stephen Mitchell's translation and his eye-opening "Introduction." Albeit abridged and at times far from a word-for-word translation, Mitchell's Job seems to me to capture the spirit of the book. His notes on translation, both in the "Introduction" and the notes section, are important, especially with regard to pivotal sentences, such as 42:6. I will quote some of Mitchell's most helpful remarks throughout this chapter.

In the sentence just quoted in the text, the translation "servant" seems not quite right to me. One who acts in the service of God; that's the idea. "Service," as when we say that someone's remarks were in the service of truth. Servitude is not in question.

[4] The Accuser, called "Satan," is not to be identified with Satan of later understanding. As I say below, Jung suggests that Job's Satan represents God's insecurity. In any case, Satan here should be seen on the analogy of a heavenly special counsel, keeping his eye out for actionable breaches.

explanation at the beginning of the book. C. G. Jung comments that the Accuser represents God's insecurity; that Job's being tested is a matter of "Does he really love me?"[5] Some commentators maintain that the first two (prose) chapters – the story of God and the Accuser – are a later addition or an earlier saga, a way of framing a classic parable, the story told in the poetic innards of the book.[6]

Stephen Mitchell comments:

> ... the world of the prologue [the story of God and the Accuser] is two-dimensional, and its divinities are very small potatoes. It is like a puppet show. The author first brings out the patient Job, his untrusting god, and the chief spy/prosecutor, and has the figurines enact the ancient story in the puppet theater of his prose. Then behind them, the larger curtain rises, and flesh and blood actors begin to voice their passions on life-sized stage. Finally, the vast, unnamable God appears.[7]

Why-questions aside, this wondrous book tells an archetypal story of devastating loss and spiritual restoration. Particularly notable are Job's transformations. Until the catastrophe, Job lives in harmony with the universe and God. The rupture could not have been more complete or more radical. Job must be thinking – some of his remarks to the Comforters suggest this – "How naïve I've been about God's justice, and about the goodness and sweetness of life; there is bitterness to life, and despite my loyalty to God it has found me." That's the first of Job's transforming insights, a recognition of life's wide-ranging injustice. I'll return in the next section to the second; it is occasioned by God's Whirlwind speech.

Job's awakening resonates. The contented sense that all (or pretty much all, or at least enough) is well with the universe – that things are more or less in their right order – is easy to come by when one's life is going well. How quickly, suddenly, that can change. We all know about the dark; we see it all around us. But until it hits home, we often persist content with God and His world. And then we become incensed. How strange our reaction! As if we know that it rains from time to time and place to place, but when it rains on us we are outraged, incredulous,

---

[5] Jung, *Answer to Job*.

[6] In what reads like a prose postscript, Job is restored not only spiritually (as in the prior poetry) but is returned to an even more wondrous life than the one with which he began, more children, more riches, etc. The prose at the beginning and end, even if added on, may represent even older folk stories.

[7] Mitchell, "Introduction," *The Book of Job*, pp xi–xii.

asking "Why?" as if it makes no sense. Christopher Hitchens, dying of cancer, was asked whether he ever wonders, "Why me?" He responded, "Why not me?" But he was a New Atheist. Until the very end.[8]

Many see such bad fortune as God hiding his face, raising questions about why God would do this and whether such doings are compatible with God's goodness. Job feels these questions, not as a matter of theory, but of life and death. Job desperately needs to make sense of his plight; he longs for what was his life, to feel awe for and love towards God, others, the world. It's not only the pain – physical pain and the anguish of loss. The universe seems robbed of its coherence, its solidity. What's going on? And where is God in all this awfulness? Why doesn't He speak? What might His silence mean? One who loses a friend, lover, or even a child, may still sense God's arm around one. Indeed, a couple who loses a child may emerge greatly diminished but with a strengthened bond. Similarly, one's intimacy with God can grow from hardship. But Job's loss is more devastating; God is lost to him.

Imagine Job's prayer life, rich and satisfying early on. Even after the devastating loss of his children, he feels, or so the text suggests, God's touch. "God gives and God takes, blessed be the name of God." Later, sitting in the dust, covered with boils "from his scalp to the soles of his feet," he remains with God. "Curse God and die," cries his wife. He demurs: "We have accepted good fortune from God; surely we can accept bad fortune too." His friends, the Comforters, come to mourn with him. They sit with him for seven days and seven nights. They cry, they mourn Job's losses, tearing their clothing, sprinkling dust on their heads. Then Job explodes, "God damn the day I was born."[9]

The friends are shocked, offended. Job's alienation, his rage, these do not sit well with their conventional piety. They rebuke Job: God is good; God is just; Job must somehow deserve his fate; he should ask for forgiveness. We readers, having read the first two chapters, know about God and the Accuser.[10] We sympathize with Job's fury at their suggestion of Job's guilt. The Bible's less-than-positive portrayal of the Comforters and their conventional piety is striking. Not to speak of God's

---

[8] Stephen Mitchell comments (pp. xv–xvi), with an eye to what's to come: "There is no answer [to 'Why me?'] because it is the wrong question. [One who asks it] will have to struggle with it until he is exhausted, like a child crying itself to sleep."

[9] Job 3:3; Mitchell, *The Book of Job*, p. 13; or "Annul the day I was born . . .," Alter, *The Wisdom Books*, p. 8.

[10] Even without the first two chapters, it seems implausible to connect the slings and arrows of life with sin. There are, it goes without saying, too many awful people who flourish and too many horrors experienced by the virtuous.

rejection of their prayer at the end of the book. The Book of Job is a radical, surprising addition to the biblical corpus.

The confrontation between Job and his friends grows in intensity: they hurl accusations, Job returns fire to them and indeed to God. Job, as Mitchell says, becomes God's Accuser, outraged at injustice. Mitchell incisively adds:[11]

> All this bewilderment and outrage couldn't be so intense if Job didn't truly love God. He senses that in spite of appearances there is somewhere an ultimate justice, but he doesn't know where. He is like a nobler Othello who has been brought conclusive evidence that his wife has betrayed him: his honesty won't allow him to disbelieve it, but his love won't allow him to believe it. On the spikes of this dilemma he must remain impaled. That is what makes his cry so profoundly moving.

Job's words of prayer, if there are any, must now feel like words scattered into the void. His children lost, his wife gone, his friends betraying him, God altogether inaccessible; Job is utterly alone. God's face is truly hidden. What was at the heart of the relationship between Job and God – something approaching intimacy – is no more. Job can barely remember it. And it's not only God that is lost to Job. It's as if nothing means anything. So goes God; so goes life's meaning.

## THE WHIRLWIND VISION: GOD'S RESPONSE TO JOB

"[The Book of Job's] astounding poetry eclipses all other biblical poetry ..." The poet, having given Job such vividly powerful language for the articulation of his outrage and his anguish, now fashions still greater poetry for God. The wide-ranging panorama of creation in the Voice from the Whirlwind shows a sublimity of expression, a plasticity of description, an ability to evoke the complex and dynamic interplay of beauty and violence in the natural world and even an originality of metaphoric inventiveness that surpasses all poetry, great as it is, that Job has spoken.[12]

Even in translation – Alter's or the Mitchell translation that I've been quoting – God's speech astounds. And poetry seems an apt genre for the content, as I'll explain.

---

[11] Mitchell, *The Book of Job*, p. xvii.
[12] Alter, *The Wisdom Books*, p. 3.

God's first words, in almost every paragraph/stanza,[13] are critical of
Job, even (perhaps) angry. God begins:

Where were you when I planned the earth?
Tell me, if you are so wise.
Do you know who took its dimensions,
measuring its length with a cord?
What were its pillars built on?
Who laid down its cornerstone,
while the morning stars burst out singing
and the angels shouted for joy![14]

Here there seems a disconnect. If God allowed the Accuser to bring
such misery on Job, Job's hurt and anger make good sense. "What is
going on?" Job wants to know. "What has become of our bond, our
intimacy?" God, we might suppose, would be understanding of such
questioning, as He was, say, with Abraham's probing about Sodom and
Gomorrah.[15] Instead, God upbraids Job: "Where were you ...?" As if to
say, "Who are you to question me?"

But that can't be what God's critical stance means, for then God
would join the ranks of the Comforters. Indeed, God later tells the
Comforters that they got Him wrong, this as opposed to Job who spoke
the truth. (We are never quite told what truth that was.)[16] "My servant
Job will pray for you, and for his sake I will overlook your sin."[17]

God's pointed questions remain a subject for speculation. Perhaps
He is reacting to what may seem like arrogance on the part of Job, that
Job presumes to know how it all works, or should work. Perhaps there is
at least a tinge of frustration in His response, an unspoken acknowledge-
ment of the chaos He has wrought. Or, to me most likely, perhaps there
is no anger; God's questions simply emphasize and underscore that Job
does not know whereof he speaks. In speaking of God, justice, and
injustice, Job is over his head.

---

[13] The stanzas are the work of the translator. It seems likely that it's his way of
displaying the fact that it is poetry that we are seeing and that Job heard.

[14] Job: 38:4; Mitchell, *The Book of Job*, p. 79

[15] Cf. Genesis 18: 16–33.

[16] Mitchell's suggestion, *The Book of Job*, pp. xvi–xvii: "Job's straightforwardness [as in
'He hands the earth to the wicked ...'] is itself a kind of innocence, and is what the
god of the epilogue refers to when he tells the friends, 'You have not spoken the truth
about me, as my servant Job has'." Job blasphemes, but speaks innocently and
sincerely.

[17] Job: 42:7–8; Mitchell: "The Epilogue," *The Book of Job*, p. 79.

In their volume and insistence, these questions acquire a peculiar quality. They sound in our ears as a ground bass to the melody of their content, and eventually function as a kind of benign subliminal message, asking a fundamental question that will dissolve everything Job thought he knew.[18]

It is as if God responds to Job's questions: "Why, you ask, do such things happen? The question is the wrong one; it emerges from your small, constricted picture of my world and of my relation to it." A very different way of thinking about these things is, I suggest, the real point of God's speech, something that emerges not from God's questions but from their continuation. Each question introduces something very different, in tone and affect. "Where were you ...?" leads to the angel's shouts of joy.

The Whirlwind passage, unique in biblical literature, has God speaking as a poet. God sings! And what He sings about is not sin, or justice, or anything doctrinal but rather the wonders of the creation. Moreover, God speaks in his own voice, in the first person. As opposed to say, the Genesis account of creation – there God is spoken of in the third person, as if by a narrator.

The opportunity for Job – derivatively for us – is one of a kind: to hear God characterize the creation in his own voice, revealing something of what it means to Him.[19] I imagine Job, bereft, still sitting in ashes, in great pain, but now stunned, hanging on every word. Here is a selection from what follows the stanza quoted above:

Were you there when I stopped the waters,
as they issued gushing from the womb?
When I wrapped the ocean in clouds
and swaddled the sea in shadows?
When I closed it in with barriers
and set its boundaries, saying,
"Here you may come, but no farther;
here shall your proud waves break."
Have you ever commanded morning
or guided dawn to its place –
To hold the corners of the sky
and shake off the last few stars?

---

[18] Mitchell, "Introduction," *The Book of Job*, p. xix.

[19] I speak here as if the book is a history rather than a parable. Still, the *Book of Job* reveals a view of God's outlook that is part of the canon.

All things are touched with color;
the whole world is changed.
Have you walked through the depths of the ocean
or dived to the floor of the sea?
Have you stood at the gates of doom
or looked through the gates of death?
Have you seen to the edge of the universe
Speak up, if you have such knowledge.
. . . . . . . . . . . . . . . . . . . . . . . . . . . .
Do you hunt game for the lioness
and feed her ravenous cubs,
when they crouch in their den, impatient,
or lie in ambush in the thicket?
Who finds her prey at nightfall,
when her cubs are aching with hunger?
Do you tell the antelope to calve
or ease her when she is in labor?
Do you count the months of her fullness
and know when her time has come?
She kneels; she tightens her womb;
she pants, she presses, gives birth.
Her little ones grow up;
they leave and never return.
. . . . . . . . . . . . . . . . . . . . . . . . . . . . . . . . . . . . . . .
Do you show the hawk how to fly,
stretching his wings on the wind?
Do you teach the vulture to soar
and build his nest in the clouds?
He makes his home on the mountaintop,
on the unapproachable crag.
He sits and scans for prey;
from far off his eyes can spot it;
his little ones drink its blood.
Where the unburied are, he is.

Discussions of the Whirlwind speech often seem almost exclusively focused on God's "Where were you" questions, on God's critique of Job. As if the wonders of which God speaks are simply ways of emphasizing Job's ignorance. God's words and indeed the book may then be seen as advancing a religious view that is hardly radical, something in the spirit of theodicy: God rebukes Job for his impertinence; there is justice, a divine plan, but it remains inaccessible to humankind. Job's return to God, his spiritual recovery, is then announced in 42:6, "Therefore do I recant, and I repent in dust and ashes."[20] Job has been defeated.

This has always seemed to me a misreading of the book and of its spirit. And perhaps not even the most natural reading of the pivotal passage, 42:6. My alternative: It is as if God takes Job to the top of the mountain: "Here is my world, as I see it." It is a world of joy-inducing beauty and jaw-dropping coldness. God's relation to the world is intimate, even maternal/paternal, the oceans gushing from Her womb, God fathering the rain. God seems awed, takes pride in all of it, a parental pride as it were: the angels singing for joy at the creation; the wonders of the birth of the day; the maternal lioness, hunting other animals to feed her children, and the vulture, who nurtures his little ones on the blood of his prey. Even death induces awe, if one can peer through its gates.

> Job – astonished, elevated, overwhelmed – is almost speechless:
> I had heard of you with my ears
> but now my eyes have seen you.
> Therefore I will be quiet,
> comforted that I am dust.
>
> (Job: 42:6)[21]

As Spinoza saw, there is both elevation and comfort in viewing the world under the aspect of eternity, *sub specie aeternitatis*. The text emphasizes comfort (on Mitchell's reading). But if it's comfort that Job experiences, it is a comfort born of elevation. Merely reading God's words, as we have, has great power. One can only imagine Job's experience. Or one cannot. This is Job's second epiphany; he is disabused of his original and originally comfortable ways of thinking and graced with a glimpse of what Mitchell calls the sabbath vision, the world as "very good."

---

[20] Alter translation. This translation does not quite commit one to the religious view articulated in the present paragraph. It may be compatible with the view I prefer, the one about to be articulated.

[21] The pivotal Hebrew word is *nichamti*, which can be read as "comforted" or "repentant." How strange; these two readings are so very different! I follow Mitchell's reading, "comforted." He points out that the verb occurs several other times in Job, all meaning "comforted." Still, one doesn't differ with Alter lightly. And, as I say in fn. 20, Alter's translation, "repentant," while it fits well with the approach to the Whirlwind speech that I reject, it may be compatible with my preferred view. That is, the recanting and repenting may be a matter of coming to see that he, Job, was far out of his depth in questioning the reason for his tragic losses. Reasons are hardly the point.

For Job to observe the world from God's vantage point, to see it as very good, perhaps magical, is to be lifted from Job's time and place and to be liberated from the inevitable self-obsession induced by suffering. Job's alienation recedes; he can now see the world – with its wonders and with its slings and arrows – as home. As with one's mother's home, one's family home, one belongs. The safety provided is only safety in a sense; all sorts of adversity may still be present or may come at one from unknown quarters. But even in Job's condition and situation, one can almost feel God's touch, as if God's arm is around one, come what may. The day after Donald Trump's election victory, President Obama remarked to an aide, "There are more stars in the heavens than grains of sand on earth."

There is here a strangely dual condition that is quietly at the heart of Whirlwind vision and near the heart of one sort of religious life and perhaps even of the human condition. We are incarnate, mortal, live in the real world, go about our human ways. Yet we are little lower than the angels, able to view the world as a god would.

Here's the duality in the context of, amazingly, basketball; from the biography of Bill Russell:

> Every so often a Celtic game would heat up so that it became more than a physical or even mental game, and would be magical. That feeling is difficult to describe, and I certainly never talked about it when I was playing. When it happened, I could feel my play rise to a new level. It came rarely and would last anywhere from five minutes to a whole quarter or more. It would surround not only me and the other Celtics but also the players on the other team, and even the referees. To me, the key was that *both* teams had to be playing at their peaks, and they had to be competitive.
>
> That mystical feeling ... never started with a hot streak by a single player, or with a breakdown of one team's defense. It usually began when three or four of the ten guys on the floor would heat up; they would be the catalysts ... The feeling would spread to the other guys, and we'd all levitate. Then the game would just take off, and there'd be a natural ebb and flow that reminded you of how rhythmic and musical basketball is supposed to be. I'd find myself thinking, "This is it. I want this to keep going." I'd be out there talking to the other Celtics, encouraging them and pushing myself harder, but at the same time part of me would be pulling for the other players too.
>
> At that special level all sorts of odd things happened. The game would be in a white heat of competition, and yet somehow

I wouldn't feel competitive – which is a miracle in itself. I'd be putting out the maximum effort, straining, coughing up parts of my lungs as we ran, and yet I never felt the pain. The game would move so quickly that every fake, cut and pass would be surprising, and yet nothing could surprise me. It was almost as if we were playing in slow motion.

There have been many times in my career when I felt moved or joyful, but these were the moments when I had chills pulsing up and down my spine. Sometimes the feeling would last all the way to the end of the game, and when that happened I never cared who won. If we lost, I'd still be as free and high as a sky hawk ... [These moments] were sweet when they came, and the hope that one would come was one of my strongest motivations for walking out there.[22]

What Russell tasted was indeed magical, transformative. Needless to say, he needed to be playing basketball – engaged in the real world, playing his heart out – for the transcendent[23] perspective to be available to him, and then only rarely. But once he experienced the pulsing chills, the "mystical feeling," the game took on new meaning; the mere possibility of such moments became one of his strongest motivations for playing.

Russell writes that basketball has aspects of art and war. As a warrior, Russell was fierce, almost brutal. Levitating, alive to the sport's "rhythmic and musical" quality, he was indifferent to victory, "pulling also for the other [team's] players." Who was Bill Russell? How might he have been both warrior and seer at once? But he was.

In the same way we are, need to be, rooted in the world. But an opening to the world *sub specie aeternitatis* can transform. Perhaps the moments of the vision are rare and don't occur in the midst of an ordinary Tuesday. And, for some, the vision remains just a momentary thing. But if one is sufficiently taken with it, or by it, it can become a background condition of one's life, always potentially present to consciousness. A. J. Heschel speaks this way of awe. For many of us, awe is strictly a sometime occurrence. But for the sufficiently spiritually developed, it constitutes a background condition of everyday life, coming to the foreground with some frequency. As one in my seventies,

---

[22] Russell and Branch, *Second Wind*.

[23] The word has resonances of the supernatural; perhaps this very human phenomenon partakes of those resonances. It is what Russell speaks of as levitating. More on transcendence in the section entitled "Varieties of Religious Experience."

it sometimes does not take much more than a look at the early morning sky, or the face of a child, to activate a sense of awe and even a hint of the Whirlwind vision. Perhaps experiences of awe are or can become suggestions of such a vision.

Were one to live exclusively *sub specie aeternitatis*, one would not be human. One would not be so deeply angered by injustice, or evil more generally. One would not be fighting the good fight, laboring mightily to improve the human condition, outraged at injustice and all the rest. Just as Bill Russell would not be engaged in his own good fight, straining to win with all his being. And one could and many do live their lives without benefit of the Sabbath vision. But as Russell suggests a mere glimpse of the transcendent perspective is a game-changer.[24]

The book of Job is, as noted, a bold treatment of its subject. First, God's candidate for most righteous is not an Israelite: Job is "from the east" and his friends' names are not Israelite names. Then there is the cruelty attributed to God in the first chapters, including killing innocents and all manner of incredible suffering imposed on Job. But there is perhaps nothing more bold than the speech from the Whirlwind. God does not merely speak with Job as He speaks with other prophets. God, moved to poetry, shares[25] with Job expressions of awe and love for, and pride in, His creation. God is intimate with His/our world, clapping, as Mitchell has it, for bolts of lightning.[26] He sings of its astounding beauty, its vitality, its awfulness; in short, its magic. What Job is witnessing – and this puts into relief all the other aspects of boldness – might well be described as God's own religious experience. This is a staggering thought.[27]

In the end, even before the final restoration of Job's good fortune,[28] Job is chastened, wiser; transformed first by the tragedy and then by

---

[24] The details of this sabbath vision are another thing; I hope to return to it elsewhere. It is related to but not the same as Thomas Nagel's "view from nowhere," since values remain very much with one. God, speaking to Job, is taken with the world's beauty. And Job's enlightenment hardly leaves him with Nagel's skepticism. Cf. Nagel, *The View from Nowhere.*

[25] Despite the overuse of the term in our culture, here it is serious.

[26] Whose response is, like that of Abraham, "Here we are." Mitchell here takes poetic license. Alter (p. 567) translates 38:34–35: "Can you lift your voice to the cloud ... Can you send lightning bolts on their way, and they will say to you, 'Here we are'."

[27] Alan Zeitchik points out that, in the Book of Hosea, we get a glimpse into what is another side of God's emotional life, His longing – almost aching – for and anger with His people. God, it seems, does not always view things under the aspect of eternity, another staggering thought.

[28] In chapter 42, v. 7–17.

these moments with God. His still limited understanding of God's ways now incorporates the dark along with the light, the wonders of the creation including its cruelty, its horrors. Meaning has returned; God is no longer a vague memory. Prayer life is again possible. It is significant that Job's salvation does not await his finally being materially restored.

I will conclude this section with brief discussions of three matters, each of which is worthy of extended attention, all of which further illuminate the Whirlwind vision. First, it is a curiosity of God's poetic vision that we humans fail to get so much as a mention. As if we were minor players in God's world, almost an afterthought. That's very strange in light of the Genesis creation narrative which seems to place us at the apex of the creation. At the same time the Book of Job seems to strike out on its own in many respects. Why, though, in this way? Where do we figure in?

It remains the case that, although we don't get any mention in the speech, Job is the addressee. It is only with us that God can share His vision. Here we have another reverberation of God's "Where were you?" questions. Those questions constitute a corrective to a natural reading – misreading – of the Genesis creation story. We seem to be the pinnacle of creation, the prize of the sixth day. But if so, how can it be that the universe seems unconcerned with us, unconcerned with justice. "What's going on here?" we ask. God's rebuke puts Job is his and we in our place: God's creation is hardly all about us. At the same time, we are a – not *the* – pinnacle of creation, without which the universe would be inarticulate, without which God's vision would never be understood.

A second topic, certainly worthy of extended discussion elsewhere: At the end of the book, God remarks that Job – but not the Comforters – spoke the truth about Him. What truth is that? Mitchell suggests that God here shows appreciation for Job's sincerity, his innocence.[29] Significant here may be another of God's difficult-to-translate utterances to Job, 40:8. Mitchell's translation:

Do you dare deny my judgment?
Am I wrong because you are right?

The idea seems to be that Job's being right is compatible with God's being without blame. Being right about what? Being right, I suppose, about Job's innocence, about his having done nothing to warrant his fate.

---

[29] Mitchell, *The Book of Job*, pp. xvi–xvii.

But then how is God blameless? The answer was suggested by God's speech from the Whirlwind: the world, wondrous as it is, is not morally ordered. Morality, deep as it goes in us, endorsed by God in another context, is not written into the atoms. Job is entirely right about his plight being entirely undeserved. We would do well, though, to relinquish our anger at cosmic injustice, perhaps to allow, as did Christopher Hitchens,[30] a sense of irony to stand in its place.[31] Hitchens, no doubt with a twinkle in his eye – and perhaps a tear – was reflecting on what, although altogether shockingly unexpected, is hardly unexpected in the larger scheme of the universe.

A final point concerns doctrine, specifically that God articulates no new doctrine by way of His speech. At the same time Job learns something, something he did not know before, indeed something of the greatest importance. But how do we say what that is?

Hubert Dreyfus, in a lecture on existentialism, raised the question of why the existentialist philosophers so often wrote novels rather than philosophical treatises. He answered by way of the medieval distinction between reason and revelation. Philosophy is traditionally the domain of reason: propositions are formulated with an eye to clarity; arguments are given and evaluated. Camus and Sartre, pondering deep questions about life that do not lend themselves to traditional philosophical techniques, instead sought to take the reader on a journey. The engaged reader vicariously experiences situations that make vivid a distinctive sense of life and its significance. Certainly, these authors make remarks along the journey that direct attention and yield insight. But such remarks are hardly articulated propositions about life's meaning. Nevertheless, the reader may emerge with a new window on life and its challenges, even a new way in the world. This is the way of revelation.

Perhaps, and this is difficult to make out in detail, what Job learns is related to the distinction between *learning how* and *learning that*. The issue is usually formulated in terms of *knowing how* versus *knowing that*. The question is whether know-how is in the end a matter of knowledge of propositions, or whether, as I am inclined to suppose, there is something primitive about know-how, something not to be reduced to propositional knowledge.

---

[30] As noted on p. 5, Hitchens was asked whether he ever wonders, "Why me?" "Why not me?" was his answer.

[31] Thanks to Larry Wright for the profound suggestion about the virtues of irony in place of anger.

It seems plausible that *understanding*, as well as *wisdom*, are similarly not reducible to knowledge of propositions. Job, taken to the top of the mountain, is transformed. His enlarged understanding, while it may involve propositional knowledge, is surely not reducible to such.

## VARIETIES OF RELIGIOUS EXPERIENCE

Religious experience, as William James reminds us, is of many varieties. Job's penultimate remark

> I had heard of you with my ears;
> But now my eyes have seen you[32]

is presumably not a reference to a visual experience. No such experience – nothing like a burning bush – is reported in the text. Instead, God speaks to him. So far, no surprise: religious experience surely includes auditory experience. But just how expansive is the category of religious experience?

Let's distinguish two varieties of transcendence,[33] a distinction that the Whirlwind episode encourages (quietly) or at least illustrates. First, there is Job's experience of God's presence. Second, there is his vision of the world as God sees it, his moment of seeing the world through God's eyes. The two come together in the episode but we may tease them apart: Imagine one at the low point of one's life, alone, without resources, struggling with illness. Imagine further that she, a poet, is gifted with great imagination. Let her be seized by a vision like that of the Whirlwind, albeit not spoken by God – an epiphany without a revelation. Her reaction, we may suppose, is similar to Job's: awestruck, elevated, and humbled all at once, her own troubles – previously preoccupying – are replaced in the foreground by the majesty of God's creation. Is this not a religious experience? Indeed, given that the Book of Job is a parable – as it is widely seen – Job's Whirlwind vision is in fact the product of human wisdom and poetic imagination. It remains, or so it seems to me, a religious vision, and not only when spoken by God.

To so proceed is to take the category of religious experience to be expansive. Why not also include powerful moments of prayer, in which

---

[32] Mitchell, *The Book of Job*, p. 88; 42:5.
[33] I owe this way of putting it to Yitzchak Blau.

one pours out her heart to God and feels that she has made contact? Or a stunning moment with another person, prompting a sense of deep meaning, perhaps awe? Indeed, the more religiously engaged a person, the more she will experience a wide range of everyday happenings as religiously significant. The heavens declare God's glory to one sufficiently religiously sensitive.

A question now arises about the extent of the God-consciousness necessary for the experience to count as a religious experience. Surely – or very plausibly – one doesn't need to be thinking explicitly about God. The phenomenology here is subtle. One who knows a great deal about Van Gogh – his work, his life, his relationships – may feel all sorts of resonances of those things when viewing one of his works. His experience of the art is infused with the person of Van Gogh, including the aspects just mentioned. Similarly for the religiously accomplished; her experience of God's wonders are infused with God.

A remark of Robert M. Adams suggests an even more expansive way of thinking about religious experience. Adams, in conversation, remarked that religious outlooks are those that give a central place in life and in life's meaning to awe and love. Adams, a devout Christian, may have meant that even a secularist may connect with God whether or not she so realizes. Or perhaps Adams simply meant to broaden the category of the religious, to see deep points of connection with what one might call a secular religiosity. Either way, the category of religious experience is broadened significantly.

Imagine now a Job figure from our own times, one entirely secular, perhaps allergic to God-talk. He too might experience a species of Whirlwind vision, this time not only not presented by God, but not even mentioning God, not even implicitly. On the view suggested by Adam's remark, we may count this a religious experience. Adams's sense of these things has great resonance for some, me included. Long ago, at my first experience of a performance of Handel's *Messiah*, I, then an atheist, commented to my wife, "A problem with atheism is that it cuts down on one's religious experiences." Engaged with Handel's oratorio, one tastes love and awe and wondrousness. One also tastes God, even if one takes the term to be, one might say, purely metaphorical.

We need not legislate about the range of the expression, "religious experience." Intuitions about the term may well vary. Some will want to save "religious experiences" for cases in which God is experienced, or at least more or less explicitly in the picture. But a God-intoxicated person may well see the experiences of non-believers as religiously significant. To quote my late friend and teacher, Rabbi Mickey Rosen, "Never mind about belief, come sing with me."[34,35]

### References

Alter, Robert. *The Wisdom Books: A Translation with Commentary*. London: W.W. Norton and Company, 2010, p. 8.

Jung, Carl Gustav. *Answer to Job*. Princeton, NJ: Princeton University Press, 1958. Translated by R. F. C. Hull. Extracted from Vol. 11 of *Collected Works of C. G. Jung*.

Nagel, Thomas. *The View from Nowhere*. Oxford: Oxford University Press, 1986.

Russell, Bill, and Taylor Branch. *Second Wind*. New York: Random House, 1979.

*The Book of Job*. Translated by Stephen Mitchell (abridged). New York: Harper-Perennial, 1992.

[34] Rosen saw engagement with song to be a more reliable indication of the state of one's soul than assent to propositions. Robert M. Adams, in communication (lightly edited): "The British composer Ralph Vaughn Williams was the son of an Anglican parish priest. He had lost any propositional religious belief, but was hugely invested in religious music, wrote it wonderfully, and served on committees that edited hymnals. Though I didn't know him personally, I might say he could sing religion though he couldn't speak it."

[35] I am grateful to many – friends, colleagues, students, audience members – for comments on and reactions to various incarnations of this paper. For comments on the last versions, I am grateful to Robert M. Adams, Yitzchak Blau, Herb Morris, Paul K. Moser, David Shatz, and Alan Zaitchik. I am more than grateful for discussions of these matters over the years with Yuval Avnur, Jeff Helmreich, and Harry Frankfurt.

JAMES D. G. DUNN

## INTRODUCTION

It is important to realize that religious experience played an important part in the beginnings of Christianity. Christianity, like any religion, can easily be focused on and even reduced to statements of faith, creedal formulae, religious practice, and ceremonial hierarchy. All too easily religious experience can be simply identified with what happened in revivals of the past – individuals swooning, or "slain in the Spirit," or speaking in ecstasy. Such experiences were certainly a feature, for example, in the ministries of the Wesleys, of Jonathan Edwards, and of early Pentecostalism. But to limit "religious experience" to such uninhibited emotional events would be as unfair and unjustified as limiting "joy" to "ecstasy" or "singing" to "crying out." There are experiences too deep for words, experiences which consist of thoughtful reflection rather than ecstatic utterance, experiences of being loved and valued without spoken expression, and so on.

So it is the range of religious experience in the beginnings of Christianity on which we will focus, starting with Jesus himself, and then the earliest days of Christianity as represented by Luke's history, by Paul's letters, and by the other writings which became the New Testament.

## JESUS

The story of Jesus really begins where Mark began his Gospel – with Jesus' baptism by John the Baptist. Before that event we know too little of Jesus to speak with any great confidence of his religious experience – the one possible exception being Luke 2.49. But Mark's account begins with a bang. Jesus had come to be baptized by the Baptist in the river Jordan, and as he came up out of the water, he immediately saw the heavens opened and the Spirit of God descending on him like a dove. And he heard a voice from heaven: "You are my beloved Son, with you

I am well pleased" (Mark 1.10–11). Notably Mark narrates the event as the personal experience of Jesus ("he saw the heavens opened"). Matthew follows Mark here (Matt. 3.16–17), though Luke suggests it was a more public spectacle: "the Holy Spirit descended upon him in bodily form as a dove" (Luke 3.22).

The two central features of Jesus' baptism indicate the principal features of the experience which motivated and empowered his ministry – his sense of sonship and of empowerment by the Spirit.

### Jesus' Sense of Sonship

Jesus is remembered as praying to God as "Father" (particularly Matt. 11.25–26/Luke 10.21; Mark 14.36 pars.), and as addressing God as "*abba*," a word expressive of a family relationship of some intimacy. This memory is recalled explicitly in only one Gospel passage (Mark 14.36), but presumably underlies the more common *pater*. A rather striking confirmation is the fact that Jesus taught his disciples to pray in the same way (Luke 11.2/Matt. 6.9); and still more striking that the first Christians rejoiced in being able to pray in the same way, and to rejoice in the implication, or better, assurance that they shared in Christ's own sonship (Rom. 8.15–17; Gal. 4.6–7). This sense of intimate sonship which Jesus experienced is expressed in several other Gospel passages: notably the somewhat exceptional Matt. 11.27/Luke 10.22 – "No one knows the Son except the Father, and no one knows the Father except the Son, and anyone to whom the Son chooses to reveal him"; and the parable of the wicked tenants, climaxing in the murder of the estate owner's son (Mark 12.1–9 pars.); also Mark 13.32/Matt. 24.36. So there are no grounds to dispute this remembered insight into Jesus' own experience.

### Jesus' Sense of Being Empowered by the Spirit

There is little question that Jesus was also remembered as a notable exorcist, and that he attributed his success to the Spirit of God. The most striking evidence is the variously combined sayings in Mark 3.22–26 pars., Matt. 12.27–28/Luke 11.19–29, and Mark 3.28-29 pars. Noteworthy is the fact that Jesus saw such exorcisms as evidence of the presence of the kingdom of God, which was his principal message (Matt. 12.28/Luke 11.20). Indeed, to refuse to acknowledge the role of the Spirit in such cases was for Jesus unforgiveable (Matt. 12.32/Luke 12.10)! According to Luke 4.18, Jesus made explicit claim to have been anointed with the Spirit and commissioned particularly to preach good news to the poor. Since he clearly saw his mission to the poor as a high priority (Luke 6.20/Matt. 5.3; Matt. 11.5/Luke 7.22), it is natural to conclude that Jesus saw himself as the one in whom Isa. 61.1 found fulfillment.

### EARLY DISCIPLES

There were clearly two foundational sets of experiences which effectively launched Christianity – appearances of Jesus after his death, and the Pentecost experience of the first disciples.

### The Resurrection Appearances

One of the most striking features of Christianity's beginnings is what appears to be the lack of interest as to where Jesus had been buried. The tradition of Jesus' tomb being found empty on the Sunday after his crucifixion is fundamental to understanding how Christianity began. It dominates the final chapters of the New Testament Gospels, and who can doubt that if there had been any uncertainty on the subject, the search for where Jesus' body had been taken to and laid to rest would have been a strong motivation which few if any of the first disciples could have resisted. Such a lack of interest as to "where Jesus' body really lay" is one of the most striking and unshakeable facts of the beginnings of Christianity. That Jesus' tomb was empty is one of the best established "givens" in the origins of Christianity.

A striking feature of the tradition here is the range of appearances claimed. In 1 Cor. 15.3–7, Paul recalls the testimony which he received when he was converted, that is, within two or three years of Jesus' crucifixion. Not just appearances to individuals such as Cephas (Peter) and James, Jesus' brother. But also to "the twelve," the number twelve maintained for obviously "twelve tribes of Israel" reasons. And also large groups – "more than five hundred," and "all the apostles." Were they all (merely) visionary in character? The Acts accounts of the appearance to Paul can certainly be understood in these terms (Acts 9.3–8; 22.6–11; 26.13–18,19 – "the heavenly vision"). But few if any in the Gospels can be understood in that way. And Luke makes a point of emphasizing the physicality of Jesus' resurrected body (Luke 24.36–43). How that fits with Paul's exposition regarding the resurrection body of believers (1 Cor. 15.42–49) is unclear, but the appearance tradition is clear and consistent in itself.

A not unimportant question is whether the resurrection appearances took place only over a limited period. Luke's account in Acts 1 clearly implies that the period of appearances lasted for only forty days and ended with Jesus' ascension to heaven (1.3–11) – perhaps simply to indicate that the subsequent experiences of the Spirit were different from the resurrection appearances. Luke restricts his account of such appearances to the Jerusalem area, though Matthew narrates the final appearance as taking place in Galilee (Matt. 28.16–20), which is still conceivable within Luke's forty days. More important is the fact that Paul includes the converting appearance to himself, some two years later, in the 1 Cor. 15 list of appearances. It is presumably because of his awareness of the more limited time period recalled by Luke that Paul makes a point of introducing the appearance to himself as "last of all" – a recognition, perhaps, that the appearance to himself was exceptional (he calls it an "abortion," 1 Cor. 15.8) – which may also explain why the appearance to Paul was understood as more "visionary" than the others.

### Experiences of the Spirit

According to Acts, the other most striking feature of Christianity's beginnings was the sequence of vivid experiences of the Holy Spirit. A characteristic and distinctive phrase in Acts is Luke's talk of individuals being "filled with the Spirit" (Acts 2.4; 4.8, 31; 9.17; 13.9, 32) or "full of the Spirit" (6.3, 5; 7.55; 11.24).

The most striking case is Pentecost, when the disciples "were filled with the Holy Spirit and began to speak in other languages, as the Spirit gave them utterance" (2.4). The effect was such that a crowd gathered and had to be assured that the disciples were not drunk (2.15). In his following speech Peter referred the crowd to the prophecy of Joel 2.28–32 as having been fulfilled before them. Subsequently Peter is again said to have been "filled with the Holy Spirit" (Acts 4.8), and the disciples as a group are "filled with the Spirit and spoke the word of God with boldness" (4.31). And Paul too, having been filled by the Spirit through the ministry of Ananias (9.17–18), is again "filled with the Holy Spirit" for his denunciation of Elymas, the false prophet in Cyprus (13.9). And again the disciples in Pisidian Antioch are "filled with joy and the Holy Spirit" (13.52). So Luke appears to be content to use the phrase "filled with the Spirit" for both an initial/initiating or renewed experience and for an anointing for a special ministry of word or action.

"Full of the Spirit" describes a qualification looked for in those to be chosen to engage in diaconal ministry (6.3) and of Stephen in particular (6.5). This seems to envisage a more constant state, which Stephen displayed in the climax of his trial (7.55), and Barnabas displayed in his review of the breakthrough in the mission to Syrian Antioch (11.24). It is equally striking how careful Luke is to attribute to the

Spirit both the decisive development in Paul's mission (to extend his mission to Europe) and his determination to make his final return to Jerusalem (16.6–10; 19.21; 20.22).

The "gift" of the Holy Spirit is referred to a number of times as the decisive factor in becoming a Christian (2.38; 5.32; 8.18–20; 11.17; 15.8). The most striking phrase, however, is "baptized with the Holy Spirit." Luke makes a point of beginning his second volume by recalling a prediction of the risen Jesus, that as John (the Baptist) had baptized with water, so his (Jesus') disciples would very soon be baptized with the Holy Spirit (Acts 1.5). The reference forward to the disciples' experience at Pentecost is clear (1.8). Evidently, it was not enough that the disciples had been with Jesus during the latter's ministry. It was not even enough that they had been witnesses of his resurrection. They needed to be equipped for the ministry, which Acts goes on to relate. And the anointing of the Spirit at Pentecost, narrated in Acts 2, constituted precisely that equipping for mission. Interestingly, Luke does not refer to the phrase itself very much. So it is particularly interesting that he makes a point of telling how Peter justified the breakthrough of his exceptional baptizing of the Roman centurion, Cornelius, and his household, by recalling the prediction of Jesus that as John had baptized with water, so his disciples would be baptized with the Holy Spirit (11.16). The implication is clear: that what happened at Caesarea with the Gentile Cornelius was as decisive a breakthrough in the earliest Christian understanding of mission as was Pentecost itself. The good news was for all, and those responsible to spread the good news were well equipped for the task.

Equally striking is the fact that Luke clearly saw the gift of the Spirit as the crucial element in becoming a Christian. If the act of "believing in the Lord Jesus Christ" is a way of describing the commitment of conversion (9.42; 10.43; 14.23; 16.31), then it is striking that Peter recalls the Pentecost experience as happening "when we believed in the Lord Jesus Christ" (11.17). The implication is clear: that the central element in becoming a Christian is the reception of the Spirit.

This indeed is a point which Luke goes out of his way to emphasize. In chapter 8 he narrates how Philip's mission to Samaria was incomplete, despite its success in many believing and being baptized. Why? The converted Samaritans had not received the Spirit, and Peter and John had to hasten to Samaria to complete Philip's work (8.14–17). In chapter 10 the Spirit evidently had to take the initiative, and come upon the Gentile centurion Cornelius and his close circle of friends, prior to any of them being baptized. In the event, baptism was the corollary to their receiving the Spirit, not the other way round (10.44–48). And in chapter 19 those already baptized with John (the Baptist's) baptism have to go through the whole process of initiation – baptism in the name of the Lord Jesus, laying on of hands, and the reception of the Holy Spirit (19.4–6). For Paul there could be no real commitment of belief without those who make the commitment receiving the Spirit (19.2–3).

### Enthusiastic Beginnings

According to Acts there were several other distinctive features which marked out the earliest days of the Jesus movement after Pentecost. Most striking were the "wonders and signs" (2.19, 22, 43; 4.30; 5.12; 7.36; 8.13; 14.3). Examples of the more "ordinary" healings are the lame man at the "Beautiful Gate" of the temple (3.1–10), Paul's blindness when converted (9.18), Aeneas' paralysis (9.33–34), and the cripple in Lystra (14.8–10), as well as the healings performed by Philip in Samaria (8.7) and by Paul in Malta (28.8–9). More striking are the restorations from death of Tabitha by Peter (9.36–41) and of Eutychus by Paul (20.9–12). Still more striking are the healings brought about by Peter's shadow (5.15–16) and by handkerchiefs or scarves touched by Paul (19.11–12). Most striking of all are the miracles of judgment – the death of Ananias and Sapphira (5.1–11) and the blinding of Elymas (13.8–11) – and the miracles of liberation from prison of Peter (5.19–24; 12.6–11) and of Paul (16.26). That there were such events readily to be understood as miracles is affirmed firsthand by Paul (Rom. 15.19; 1 Cor. 12.10, 28–29; 2 Cor. 12.12; Gal. 3.5) and by the writer to the Hebrews (Heb. 2.4).

We should also mention the visions, also predicted by Joel (Acts 2.17), which were regularly experienced according to Luke's account, most of those recalled by Luke proving to be crucial in the development of the Christian mission. I refer particularly to Stephen's vision of the Son of Man standing at the right hand of God which enraged his listeners (7.55–56), the visions which converted Saul/Paul on the road to Damascus (9.3–8, 10–16; 26.19), the sequence of visions which led to the conversion of the Gentile centurion Cornelius (10.3–6, 11–16, 19), Paul's vision of "a man of Macedonia" pleading with him to cross over to Macedonia to proclaim the good news there (16.9–10), and Paul's vision of Jesus when he was praying in the Jerusalem temple which he recalls in 22.17–21.

Similarly, Luke had no hesitation in recalling occasions when the Spirit was heard speaking (10.19–20; 11.12; 13.2), presumably in words of prophecy as in 11.28 and 21.4. The restoration of the Spirit of prophecy as longed for by Moses (Num. 11.29) and predicted by Joel (2.28–32), is given particular emphasis by Luke in his account of Pentecost (Acts 2.17–18) and is taken as demonstrating the reception of the Spirit in 10.46 and 19.6. Prophets played an important role subsequently in determining the actions of the first disciples (11.28–29; 13.2; 15.32; 21.10–11). Interestingly, Luke includes reference to the four unmarried daughters of Philip the evangelist who had the gift of prophecy (21.9). And he had no hesitation in portraying speaking in tongues/(unknown) languages as the outcome or an indication of the Spirit's reception (2.4; 10.46; 19.6), though only in the first occasion (Pentecost) are the recipients portrayed as speaking in known foreign languages. Finally, it would be appropriate to note the "joy" which seems to have been a feature of the early successful mission (8.8; 13.52; 15.3).

In short, the Acts of the Apostles is often renamed as "the Acts of the Holy Spirit." The justification for that title is sufficiently evident in what has just been reviewed.

PAUL

We learn more about religious experience within earliest Christianity from Paul than from any other of the NT writers. Particularly fascinating is his own experience, but also the role of experience in what he presents as characteristic discipleship, and the advice and exhortation on the subject which he gives generously in his letters.

**Paul's Own Experience**
We have already noted Paul's insistence that his own experience of conversion should be included in the list of Jesus' resurrection appearances, albeit "last of all" (1 Cor. 15.8). The same passage shows how conscious he was that his claim, the foundational claim for his whole status within the new movement, would be found by many of the first believers in Jesus to be audacious. For he at once adds that he was "the least of the apostles" and "unfit to be called an apostle, because I persecuted the church of God" (15.9). But he goes on: "Yet by the grace of God I am what I am, and his grace toward me has not been in vain. On the contrary, I worked harder than any of them – though it was not I, but the grace of God that is with me" (15.10).

This comes after Paul's initial self-introduction – "Paul, called to be an apostle of Christ Jesus ..." (1.1) – and his self-conscious reference to "us apostles" as playing a critical role in the final stages of God's purpose in the world (4.9). His sensitivity on the subject is expressed most clearly in his first letter to the Corinthians, 9.1–2: "Am I not free?

Am I not an apostle? Have I not seen Jesus our Lord? If I am not an apostle to others, at least I am to you, for you are the seal of my apostleship in the Lord." Clearly, and understandably, Paul's claim to have been appointed an apostle by the exalted Christ was regarded as audacious and unacceptable by some or many of the earliest believers, not surprising since many of the first believers had suffered from his pre-conversion persecution of the first Christians. Paul recognized and understood such doubting concerns, but felt sufficiently confident in the success of his mission among the Gentiles to cherish the confidence that his claim and status as an apostle of Jesus Christ should and would be recognized, and not only among his own converts.

Ironically, he had to defend himself from attacks from the opposite direction – from "super-apostles" who undermined his work by proclaiming a different gospel (2 Cor. 11.5, 13). His response was to recall the Corinthians to the "signs and wonders and mighty works" which had been performed among them, "the signs of a true apostle" – himself, of course (12.11–12). The challenge to his apostolic authority which emerged particularly from the Corinthian assembly was particularly painful for Paul, but thankfully it does not seem to have been repeated in his other churches. However, we should note the evidence in what was probably his first (preserved) letter (Gal. 1.13–19) regarding the sensitivities among the original disciples of Jesus over his claim to be an apostle set apart by God and called by his grace to proclaim Christ among the Gentiles.

We should pause longer over 2 Cor. 10–13, for this contains some of Paul's most personal accounts in defending his work from opponents whose criticism was penetrating and wounding. In one of the most moving passages that Paul ever wrote, he evidently found it necessary to "boast" of his own experience of privilege and suffering (11.21–33). This boasting climaxes in his personal experience of being "caught up to the third heaven," "into Paradise" when he "heard things that are not to be told, that no mortal is permitted to repeat" (12.1–4). More moving still is his confession that "a thorn in the flesh" was given to him to keep him from being too elated (12.7) – what ailment he was referring to we do not know. Most memorable is the Lord's response when Paul pleaded to be relieved of this thorn: "my grace is sufficient for you, for my power is made perfect in weakness." No sequence of passages takes us more deeply into the religious experience of the first Christians.

We should add, however, Paul's particularly moving response to criticism from the committed circumcision faction which sought to counteract (they would say, complete) his mission to Gentiles by having the Gentile converts circumcised, in Phil. 3. He stresses that he himself had every ground for confidence in his Jewish heritage (3.4–6) but goes on to insist that the privilege of "knowing Christ Jesus" as his Lord far outweighed what he had previously valued so highly. He even counts it as "rubbish" (3.8) and in contrast stresses that his ambition now was "to know Christ and the power of his resurrection," while recognizing that the way to resurrection of the dead was through suffering (3.9–11). The way he elaborates this ambition (3.12–14) shows that Paul's sense of "knowing Christ" was the heart and driving force of his mission.

Finally, we should not fail to note that fundamental for Paul was his experience of *liberty*. The transition from the sobering reality of his own sinfulness in Rom. 7.7–25 is described in precisely these terms: "the law of the Spirit of life in Christ Jesus has set you free from the law of sin and death" (8.2). Similarly, in reflecting on how the old covenant had been abused and misunderstood, Paul appended to the description of his own conversion: "where the Spirit of the Lord is, there is freedom" (2 Cor. 3.17). There can hardly be any clearer reminder that the Spirit was experienced, not least by Paul, as a liberating power.

### Christ-Shaped Experience

Often missed or neglected in Paul's theology are his many phrases focused on Christ. They all reflect what could be called a basic presupposition of his life's mission, and often with a semi-explicit experiential dimension. "In Christ" occurs over 80 times in the Pauline corpus, not counting the equivalent "in him/in whom" phrases (e.g. Rom. 6.11; 12.5; 16.7; 1 Cor. 1.30; 2 Cor. 5.17; 12.2; 3.26; Gal. 2.4). "In the Lord" occurs some 26 times – most frequently in Philippians: for example, Paul rejoices that brothers have been "made confident in the Lord" to speak the word with boldness (Phil. 1.14); he "hopes in the Lord" and "trusts in the Lord" regarding future activities (2.19, 24); he calls them to "rejoice in the Lord" (3.1), to "stand firm in the Lord" (4.1), to "agree in the Lord" (4.2), and to "rejoice in the Lord always" (4.4). Less frequently Paul speaks of Christ indwelling the believer, where a similar sense of inner resource is implied. Particularly poignant is Gal. 2.19–20: "I have been crucified with Christ; and it is no longer I that live, but Christ lives in me." In Col. 1.27 "Christ in you" is "the hope of glory," and Col. 3.4 can also speak of the future revelation of "Christ who is our life." Clearly there was a deep-rooted experience which often welled up in the explicit joy and boldness of Paul's ministry. Not least, we should note, this was expressed in *hope* – "eagerly awaiting the hope of righteousness by the Spirit from faith" (Gal. 5.5; see also Rom. 8.24–25).

An equally striking feature of Paul's theology is his "with Christ" motif. Typically he uses the phrase with future reference: to be with Christ in heaven (Phil. 1.23; 1 Thes. 4.17; 5.10); to appear with Christ in glory or at the parousia (Col. 3.4; 1 Thes 4.14). Most eye-catching, however, is Col. 2.13, where Paul speaks of believers as having *already* been "made alive together with him." Moreover, Paul also makes regular use of *syn*-(with)-compounds, notably here, to describe a sharing in Christ's death and life. Most notable is Rom. 6.4–8: "So then we were buried with him through baptism into death … For if we have become knit together with the very likeness of his death, we shall certainly also be knit together with the very likeness of his resurrection. Knowing this, that our old nature has been crucified with him … But if we have died with Christ, we believe that we shall also live with him" (see also e.g. Rom. 8.17 and Col. 2.12–13). Here too we see evidence of a strong sense of bound-upness-with-Christ which must have sustained Paul strongly, even and not least in the darkest moments of his ministry.

A notable feature is that Paul does not hesitate to indicate the strong emotional character of his experiences of the Spirit. Rom. 5.5 – "the love of God poured out in your hearts," as though from an upended pitcher. 1 Cor. 12.13 – "all irrigated with/drenched in the one Spirit," like the coming of the monsoon rains. 1 Thess. 1.6 – the gospel received "with joy of the Holy Spirit." Nor should we miss the implication of the verb Paul uses when he characterizes the distinctive prayer of the first Christians: "When we cry out (*krazein*), 'Abba! Father!' it is that very Spirit bearing witness with our spirits that we are children of God" (Rom. 8.15–16).

That this prayer was remembered by the first Christians as distinctive of Jesus' own prayer life underlines the important fact that, for Paul and the first Christians, the Spirit they experienced and rejoiced in was precisely the Spirit of Jesus. They were sharing not just in Jesus' own prayer of sonship, but in Jesus' own sonship itself (8.17). This was one of the key ways in which they were being shaped in accordance with the image of God in Christ (2 Cor. 3.18). All this underlines what Luke had no inhibition in recalling: that in earliest Christianity reception of the Spirit was not simply an article of faith to be affirmed, but an experience, evidently a rich and enriching experience, enjoyed by the first believers.

### The Body of Christ

One of the most striking features of Paul's theology is the degree to which he regarded the spiritual experience of his churches as shared experiences, as experiences which bound them together, not isolating them in some distinctive hierarchy – the "shared experience (*koinōnia*) of the Spirit" as the basis of their common life in Christ. "In the one Spirit we were all baptized into one body ... and we were all made to drink of one Spirit" (1 Cor. 12.13). A notable feature of his letters is the amount of his teaching which he devotes to instructing those listening to his letters being read on their corporate identity and how they should function as a charismatic community. It is the first element in his exhortation in Rom. 12.4–8, following the intensive theology of the preceding chapters. And in 1 Corinthians the teaching and exhortation absorbs three chapters (1 Cor. 12–14; see also Eph. 4.7–16).

The key word in these two passages is *charisma*, "charism." Since the word is hardly attested before Paul, it is worth remembering that it is a concept we owe almost entirely to Paul. *Charisma* is an expression of *charis* ("grace"), of God's gracious act, or as Paul also describes it in 1 Cor. 12, "the manifestation of the Spirit for the common good" (12.7). For Paul, it is important to notice, the body of Christ functioned as a charismatic community. The list of charisms in the two passages are basically charisms of speech – prophecy, teaching, encouraging (Rom. 12.6–7), "utterances of wisdom and knowledge," prophecy and tongues (1 Cor. 12.8–10, 28–30); and charisms of action – service, sharing, caring, acts of mercy (Rom. 12.7–8), charisms of healing and miraculous activities (1 Cor. 12.9–10, 28–30), "helpful deeds" and "giving guidance" (12.28).

It is worth noting that Paul's lists include both the eye-catching and the more humdrum activities. As also the degree of integration in the lists: prophecy must be accompanied by discernment – 12.10; 14.29 (was it genuine inspiration?). And tongues must be accompanied by "interpretation" – 12.10; 14.27–28 (so that any message is conveyed in intelligible speech). And not least that every member of the worshipping community should have a part to play in the worship: "to each is given the manifestation of the Spirit for the common good" (12.7). Paul emphasizes the point by noting that no human body consists solely of an eye or solely of an ear (12.17–20), and that no member of the body can dismiss the other functions as unnecessary or less valuable (12.21–26).

This was a very idealistic vision of how the church, any local church, should live out its role as the body of Christ in a particular place. Is it any wonder that the vision did not provide an enduring model for even the early churches established by Paul? In the Pastoral letters *charisma* no longer seems to denote a great variety of ministries and services. The term is used only with reference to Timothy (1 Tim. 4.14;

2 Tim. 1.6) and seems to denote his power of office. It seems to have lost its dynamic character and to refer to a power or ability which Timothy possesses, which he has within himself, a gift given once for all through an act of ordination. It would appear, then, that the Pauline vision of charismatic community has faded, and *charisma* has become in effect subordinate to office. Thus, we might justifiably conclude, the dynamism of shared experience, presumably regarded as too threatening to good organization, was increasingly lost to view. Is this always what happens when a second generation attempts to formalize the enthusiasms of a founding generation?

In any case, Paul himself would no doubt have affirmed that the "fruit of the Spirit" (Gal. 5.22–23) were more important than the "gifts of the Spirit." It is certainly no accident that his exaltation of love as the supreme mark of spirituality comes smack in the middle of his treatment of the charismatic community of Christ's body (1 Cor. 13).

JOHN

Writing at about the same time as the Pastoral Epistles, the Johannine writings demonstrate that in the 80s and 90s of the first century there were Christians and Christian communities where the flame still burned brightly and experience of the Spirit was deeply cherished.

**The Vitality of Religious Experience**
This is demonstrated, for example, by the fact that words like "life," "loving," "knowing," and "believing" all appear with great regularity in both John's Gospel and the Johannine letters, indeed more frequently than in Paul's letters. It is noteworthy that John draws on rich experiential imagery. Characteristic is Jesus' elaboration to Nicodemus of his counsel that "no one can see the kingdom of God without being born from above." Jesus explains: "The wind blows where it chooses, and you hear the sound of it, but you do not know where it comes from or where it goes. So it is with everyone who is born of the Spirit" (John 3.3–8). Similarly in Jesus' response to the Samaritan woman who is puzzled by Jesus' request for a drink. Jesus again draws powerfully on everyday experience: "Everyone who drinks of this water will be thirsty again, but those who drink of the water that I will give them will never be thirsty. The water that I give will become in them a spring of water gushing up to eternal life" (4.7–14). And in Jerusalem, on the last, the great day of the Feast of Tabernacles, Jesus cries out: "Let anyone who is thirsty come to me, and let the one who believes in me drink. As the

scripture has said, 'Out of the believer's heart shall flow rivers of living water'." John adds the explanation: "Now he said this about the Spirit, which believers in him were to receive" (7.37–39). It is hard to doubt that such writing recalled profound experiences which were understood as expressions of the Spirit.

Similarly with 1 John. For example, "The anointing that you received from him (the Son) abides in you, and so you do not need anyone to teach you. But as his anointing teaches you about all things ... abide in him" (2.27). "By this we know that he abides in us, by the Spirit that he has given us" (3.24; repeated in 4.13). "The Spirit is the one that testifies, for the Spirit is the truth. There are three that testify: the Spirit and the water and the blood ... Those who believe in the Son of God have the testimony in their hearts ... And this is the testimony: God gave us eternal life, and this life is in his Son" (5.6–11). Who can doubt that such was indeed the testimony of all or most of those to and for whom John was writing?

## The Spirit Is Experienced as the Spirit of Jesus

This identification of the Holy Spirit as the Spirit of Jesus is nowhere so clearly marked as in John's Gospel. Note the implication of John 1.32–33: the Spirit descended on Jesus and "remained on him." The implication is clear, that the union of Jesus and the Spirit continued throughout his ministry and after his exaltation. And the implication becomes clearer thereafter. In 6.62–63 and 7.37–39 the imagery of eating the body/flesh of Jesus and drinking the water from Jesus symbolizes the reception of the life-giving Spirit. It is implied in the "tandem" relationship between the ministry of Jesus and that of the "Paraclete." For example, both come forth from the Father (15.26; 16.27–28); both are given and sent by the Father (3.16–17; 14.16, 26); both teach the disciples (6.59; 7.14, 28; 8.20; 14.26); and both are unrecognized by the world (14.17; 16.3). In 19.30 (probably) and 20.22 (certainly) the Spirit is depicted as the spirit/breath of Jesus. Above all this is indicated in the explicit description of the Spirit as the *"other* Paraclete/Counsellor" (14.26), where Jesus is clearly understood to be the *first* Paraclete/Advocate (1 John 2.1). As also in the fact that the coming of the Spirit evidently fulfils the promise of Jesus to come again and dwell in his disciples (John 14.15–26). In other words, John assures his readers that the experience of the Spirit is the experience of the risen and exalted Jesus.

Two comments are appropriate here. First, in relating the Spirit to Jesus in this way John is doing what Paul did: John's "other Paraclete" is

Paul's "Spirit of Jesus." For John, as for Paul, the Spirit has ceased to be
an impersonal divine power; the experience of new life in itself (3.5–8;
4.10–14; 6.63; 7.37–39; 20.22) does not sufficiently characterize the
activity of the Spirit. The Spirit has in effect taken on a fuller or more
precise character, which is the character of Jesus himself. The personality of Jesus, we may say, has become the personality of the Spirit. As the
Logos and Wisdom of divine revelation has been identified with Jesus
and with his character (1.1–18), so the Spirit of revelation is to be
recognized as having that very same character.

Second, the importance of this equation is the recognition that
experience of the Spirit affords an immediate and direct continuity
between believers and Jesus. The lengthening time gap between John
and the historical Jesus, and the continuing delay of the parousia, do not
mean a steadily increasing distance between successive generations of
Christians and Christ. On the contrary, each generation is as close to
Christ as the last, and the first, because the Paraclete is the immediate
link between Jesus and his disciples in every generation. In other words,
and of central importance for John, the link and continuity between
Christ and his followers of successive generations is provided not by
sacraments or offices or human figures, but directly by the Spirit. This is
one of John's central points: the vitality of Christian experience does not
cease because the Jesus of history has faded into the past and the coming
again of Jesus has faded into the future. On the contrary, Christian
experience retains its vitality because the Spirit of Jesus is at work here
and now as the other Paraclete.

### The Spirit and the Gospel

It is one of John's most positive contributions to Christianity that he
brings the dialectic between present Spirit and original gospel into sharp
focus. In his Gospel this comes to clearest expression in the role attributed to the Paraclete in 14.26 and 16.12–14. Worth noting here is the
balance achieved in these verses between the continuing revelatory work
of the Spirit and the revelation already given. So, 14.26: "he will teach
you everything," which must include teaching which Jesus had not (yet)
been able to give his disciples while with them (cf. 16.12); "and will keep
you in mind of all that I have said to you" (cf. 15.15) – the new revelation
in direct continuity with the original revelation (16.12–14): "he will
guide you into/in all truth" (new revelation – v.12), which is balanced
by "he will not speak on his own authority . . ." – Jesus himself is the truth
(14.6). Again, "he will declare to you the things that are coming," which
is balanced by, "he will glorify me, for he will take what is mine and

declare it to you." Clearly implied is that the new revelation will in effect be drawn out of the old by way of interpretation. In these passages both present inspiration and interpretation of the past are bound together in the dynamic of religious inspiration and experience.

If we are in doubt as to what John had in mind, we need look no further than his Gospel itself. For John would undoubtedly have regarded his own Gospel as the product of this inspiring Spirit. In effect, these words constitute an implicit apologia for his Gospel. And the way John carries this out becomes a model for how the good news of Jesus may be retold. The teaching function of the Spirit is *not* limited to recalling the *ipsissima verba* of the historical Jesus. But neither does it claim new revelation which effectively ignores the Jesus tradition. There is both freedom and control – liberty to reinterpret and remould the original kerygma, while at the same time the original kerygma remains as a check and restraint. The more freedom we recognize in John's handling of the kerygmatic tradition, the more striking his concept of inspired reinterpretation becomes.

The same dynamic is evident in John's concept of worship. The key verse is John 4.23–24: "God is Spirit, and those who worship him must worship in Spirit and truth." "In Spirit" must imply "by the Spirit's inspiration," that is, what we might characterize simply as charismatic worship. For in the immediate context, worship in Spirit is set in pointed contrast to worship through temple and sacred place. The worship that God seeks is a worship not frozen to a sacred building or by conformity to a static tradition, but a worship which is living, the constantly renewed response to God who is Spirit as prompted and enabled by the Spirit of God. "In truth," the truth revealed in Jesus, confirms that for John true worship is determined by the same balance between Gospel tradition and inspiring Spirit – inspired by the Spirit of Jesus and according to the truth revealed in Jesus. If truth be told, John's is a concept of worship too challenging, and perhaps too scary, for most present-day traditions of Christian worship to rise to.

## THE REST OF THE NEW TESTAMENT

It is noticeable that interest in and concern about religious experience become much less prominent in the other letters which make up the New Testament. Why this should be is unclear. Was it that respect for tradition and desire for good order constrained the earlier enthusiastic tendencies, or simply the transition from the spontaneity of the first generation to the safeguarding concerns of their successors?

## Hebrews

This book draws its initial warnings from the failure of the Israelites wandering in the wilderness to enter the promised land (Heb. 3.11–4.11). The writer speaks of "the word of God" as "living and active, sharper than any two-edged sword," dividing soul from spirit – presumably attesting experience of penetrating readings or sermons. Likewise the talk of "approaching the throne of grace with boldness ... to receive mercy and grace in time of need" (4.15). He refers to "those who have been enlightened, and tasted the heavenly gift, and have shared in the Holy Spirit" (6.4), and encourages those who have "the full assurance of hope" (6.11). In turn, he assures them that the blood of Christ will "purify your conscience from dead works" (9.14) and encourages them to enter the heavenly sanctuary, the very presence of God, which Christ has opened to them (10.19–22). His meditation on the history of faith (11) climaxes in the thought of "looking to Jesus" (12.2), the need for spiritual discipline (12.3–11), and the assurance that those for whom the letter has been written have come to "the heavenly Jerusalem" (12.22) to "worship with reverence and awe" (12.28; echoed again in 13.14–15).

## James

This has remarkably little about religious experience. He talks about joy in trials (Jas. 1.2), advocates the prayer of faith for wisdom (1.5–8), reassures those who "endure temptation" (1.12), and encourages meekness in welcoming "the implanted word" (1.21). He warns against empty faith (2.14–26), promotes the search for "wisdom from above" (3.12–18), and urges humility (4.13–16) and endurance (5.11). Somewhat oddly, love of God is expected more than experienced (1.12; 2.5).

## 1 Peter

Peter begins by reminding its recipients that they had been "given a new birth into a living hope" (1 Pet. 1.3) enabling them to "rejoice with an indescribable and glorious joy" (1.8). They are encouraged to "live in reverent fear" (1.17), as having been "born anew" (1.23), and to "long for the pure spiritual milk" by which they "may grow into salvation" (2.2), for they have been "called out of darkness into his marvelous light" (2.9). Slaves are appealed to as "being aware of God" (2.19), and wives are encouraged by reference to "the holy women who hoped in God" (3.5), a hope for which they too should be ready to give an account (3.15). Interestingly, baptism is described as "an appeal to God for a good conscience" (3.21), and the audience is appealed to as "good stewards of the manifold grace of God" (4.10). They are assured that "the Spirit of

God is resting on you" (4.14), and exhorted to clothe themselves with humility (5.4–6).

## 2 Peter
This letter makes a number of references to what in other New Testament writings would have rich experiential overtones, but here seem rather formal – the hope for abundant 'grace and peace in the knowledge of God' (2 Pet. 1.2; similarly 1.3, 8, 2.20, and 3.18); the divine power giving "everything needed for life and godliness" (1.3); the talk of "supporting your faith with goodness" (1.5); even the formal echo of the transfiguration (1.16–18); and the talk of "waiting for the coming of the day of God" (3.12). The richest experiential note, perhaps significantly, is the affirmation that "no prophecy ever came by human will, but individuals moved by the Holy Spirit spoke from God" (1.21).

## Jude
In Jude the only noteworthy passage is the contrast between "these worldly people, devoid of the Spirit" and those encouraged to "pray in the Holy Spirit" (Jude 19–20).

## The Revelation to John
This apocalypse stands out in this outline of what appears to be a diminishing interest in religious experience as such in the second generation of Christianity (apart from the other Johannine writings). For John's Revelation is, as the title indicates, the account of a sustained apocalypse or series of revelations. It presents itself as the record of what someone called John (another John?) was given to see regarding "what must soon take place" (Rev. 1.1). The claim is exceptional within the biblical record. There are not a few "revelations" in the biblical accounts, notably in Daniel. But a revelation, or unbroken series of revelations, taking up twenty-two chapters is unparalleled in the Bible. And though the overlap period between the first and second centuries gave rise to several apocalypses, the visionary ecstasy of John's apocalypse makes it stand out.

Much of Revelation, to say bluntly, is pretty horrific, in particular what the seven trumpets seem to portend in chapters 8 and 9, and the seven plagues in chapters 15 and 16. It is important, then, to remember that it was written at a time when the young Christian movement in Asia Minor was in expectation of and perhaps already experiencing tremendous persecution. And the rejoicing in the fall of Babylon, the symbol of all persecution in Jewish tradition is entirely understandable (chaper 18). As is the rejoicing in the marriage of the Lamb to the persecuted bride, "clothed with fine linen," which is "the righteous deeds of the saints" (19.8), and the hope for "the new Jerusalem" into which only those will enter "who are written in the Lamb's book of life" (21.27). Altogether a sobering prospect to hold before a persecuted church.

### Further Reading

Dunn, James D. G. *Baptism in the Holy Spirit*. London: SCM, 1970.
   *Jesus and the Spirit: A Study of the Religious and Charismatic Experience of Jesus and the First Christians*. London: SCM, 1975.
   *The Theology of Paul the Apostle*. Grand Rapids: Eerdmans, 1998.
   *Jesus Remembered*. Grand Rapids: Eerdmans, 2003.
   *The New Perspective on Paul*. WUNT 185; Tübingen: Mohr Siebeck, 2005; revised, Grand Rapids: Eerdmans, 2007.

# 6 Religious Experience in Traditional Islam

WILLIAM C. CHITTICK

Numerous terms were employed in Islamic languages to designate the ways in which people perceive and experience ordinary and extra-ordinary phenomena pointing back to God, though the words used nowadays to translate the modern notion of experience (e.g., *tajriba*) were not among them. Anyone acquainted with Islam will be aware that what is commonly called "Sufism" or "Islamic mysticism" addresses the issue of experiencing God's presence in voluminous detail. Given Sufism's prominence over history, this means that the path of finding and perceiving God has been a preoccupation of countless Muslims. Carl Ernst is expressing the consensus of specialists when he says, "Islamic mysticism is one of the most extensive traditions of spiritual-ity in the history of religions. From its origins in the Prophet Muham-mad and the Qur'anic revelation, the mystical trend among Muslims has played an extraordinary role in the public and private development of the Islamic faith."[1] Here I will highlight a few themes in the primary literature.

Let me begin by explaining why Sufism rather than any other form of Islamic learning provides the most detailed expositions and analyses of the soul's awareness and perception of God. From earliest times it was clear to Muslims that the Quran addresses a great variety of issues that can be subsumed under the word "religion" (*dīn*), a term that was com-monly used to designate Islam as a whole or, with a modifier, other traditions such as Judaism and Christianity. Before the nineteenth century *al-dīn*, "the religion," was used in Arabic more commonly than *al-islām*, "the submission." How the word was understood is encapsulated in a famous saying of Muhammad explaining that the religion brought by the Quran differentiates three dimensions of human engagement with

---

[1] From the preface to Sells, *Early Islamic Mysticism*, p. 1. For the best survey of the field, though far from comprehensive, see Knysh, *Sufism*. For a fine appreciation of Sufi literature, see Schimmel, *Mystical Dimensions of Islam*.

God: practice and ritual, faith and understanding, and beautification of character.[2]

Islam has no priesthood, so the transmission of the religion was the task of the *'ulamâ'*, the "knowers" or "learned," that is, scholars recognized by their communities as having the competence to speak with authority. These ulama gradually developed several fields of learning, each field focusing on one of the religion's three dimensions; only the most outstanding scholars were able to integrate all three dimensions into a coherent vision of the whole. Setting down the details of right practice became the specialty of experts in jurisprudence (*fiqh*). They devoted their efforts to codifying the Shariah (literally, "the broad path"), a word that was commonly employed for the instructions about do's and don'ts found in the Quran and the Hadith. Because the jurists dealt with law, they tended to form links with the ruling powers of the day, and other scholars often criticized them for their worldly inclinations. Given the political orientation of modern institutions, it should come as no surprise that most ulama who play prominent roles in contemporary Islam have little religious knowledge other than jurisprudence.

The religion's second dimension, faith and understanding, became the specialty of three groups. Scholars of Kalam (dogmatic theology) used the tools of intellect or reason (*'aql*) to clarify the Quranic depiction of God and explain his exact relationship with his human servants. Scholars of philosophy (*falsafa*) also stressed the importance of intellect, but they followed in the tracks of Aristotle and Plotinus in order to delve into the mysteries of the Necessary Being and the human soul. Although the secondary literature has usually portrayed the philosophers as scientific types with little patience for religion, their impatience was not with faith and understanding, but rather with the strident efforts of both jurists and theologians to impose their own versions of orthopraxy and orthodoxy on everyone else.

As for scholars of Sufism, they left the codification of the Shariah to the jurists, the delineation of dogma to the Kalam experts, and the appropriation of ancient wisdom to the philosophers. They focused instead on becoming truly human, that is, on discovering and actualizing the divine beauty within oneself. Like the philosophers, Sufis aimed explicitly at overcoming the forgetfulness endemic to the human "soul"

---

[2] I am referring to the Hadith of Gabriel, often cited by Muslim scholars to delineate the three realms of engagement with God. For an analysis of "the religion" in these terms, see Murata and Chittick, *The Vision of Islam*.

or "self" (the same word *nafs* is used in both senses). Like them they offered broad overviews of reality rooted in metaphysics (*ilāhiyyāt*, "the divine things") while describing the human soul as a microcosm, created in the "form" (*ṣūra*) of God. God, as the possessor of "the most beautiful names" (Quran 7:180), is "the most beautiful Creator" (Quran 23:14) who "formed you and made your forms beautiful" (Quran 40:64, 64:3). Both Sufis and philosophers held that the soul's original divine form, created in the "most beautiful stature" (Quran 95:4), corresponded perfectly with God and the macrocosm. The soul, however, had fallen out of balance because of forgetfulness and the misuse of free will, so it needed purification and rectification. In contrast to the early philosophers, Sufi teachers did not neglect the religious rules and theological dogma. They considered them instead prerequisites for beautifying the soul.[3]

Both philosophers and Sufis differentiated between two basic sorts of knowledge, using the generic word *'ilm*. The first sort is "transmitted" (*naqlī*), that is, handed down by society; it includes practically everything we know or think we know – language, culture, scripture, dogma, law, science. The second sort is "intellectual" (*'aqlī*). It can only be actualized by discovering it within oneself, even if it can be described in transmitted terms; examples include mathematics and metaphysics. Once acquired, intellectual knowledge is self-evident, which is to say that knowers cannot deny the truth that they find in their own souls. Sufi teachers often distinguished between these two sorts of knowledge by calling the first *'ilm* in the sense of learning acquired from others and the second *ma'rifa* or "recognition." In the standard descriptions, learning is acquired by hearsay and imitation (*taqlīd*), while recognition is gained by realization (*taḥqīq*), which is actualization of the soul's potential by perceiving the truth (*ḥaqq*) and reality (*ḥaqīqa*) of the self, the universe, and the Real (*al-ḥaqq*).[4]

When the Quran is read with attention to the second and third dimensions of the religion – faith and beautification of the soul – it is obvious that the book highlights perception of the world and the soul. These two – world and self, or macrocosm and microcosm – display what the Quran calls the "signs" (*āyāt*) of God, all of which signify the reality of their Creator. Repeatedly the Quran asks its readers to heed

---

[3] On the common goals of philosophy and Sufism, see, for example, Zargar, *The Polished Mirror*.
[4] On the interplay between the two sorts of knowing, see Chittick, *Science of the Cosmos*.

the signs. "In the earth are signs for those with certainty, and in your souls. What, do you not see?" (51:20–21). It rebukes them for not employing their seeing, hearing, understanding, and witnessing to perceive the signs: "They have hearts but do not understand with them, they have eyes but do not see with them, they have ears but do not hear with them" (7:179). It pays close attention to the soul's diverse attributes and character traits (akhlāq), praising the beautiful and condemning the ugly. Some forms of Quran commentary – an activity undertaken by specialists in every school of thought – interpreted many verses as allusions (ishārāt) to the manner in which the soul experiences the divine presence while climbing the ladder toward realization.[5]

The Quran's frequent mention of the soul's qualities and attributes contributed to the development of an extensive literature on what can be called "spiritual psychology," the goal of which was to provide a roadmap for beautification and realization. Philosophers like Avicenna (d. 1037) followed Greek models in writing books on *ʿilm al-nafs*, "the knowledge of the soul," and *akhlāq*, "ethics," though the literal meaning of this latter word is "character traits." The philosophers considered the soul a potential intellect in need of training and discipline so that it could find its innate intellectual light and act accordingly.[6] Many of them held that their final goal was achieving "similarity to God" (al-tashabbuh bi'l-ilāh) or "deiformity" (ta'alluh, from the same root as Allāh). Sufis agreed with the philosophers in their general evaluation of the soul's need for transformation, but they drew most of their terminology and practical instructions from the Quran, the Hadith, and the lives and sayings of the saintly forbears.

Many important works by Sufi teachers have been translated into European languages. Readers will quickly see that these works focus on the achievement of first-hand, realized knowledge rather than the explanation of dogma or law. Their authors often criticized other scholars for not understanding that transmitted knowledge is a means to an end. They reminded their readers that the legal nitpicking of the jurists, the dogmatic assertions of the Kalam experts, and the logical analyses of the philosophers too often distracted people from the goal of knowledge, which is to actualize the beautiful divine form within the

---

[5] For three examples of commentaries that investigate spiritual psychology (all available for free download at altafsir.com), see al-Qushayrī (d. 1072), *Laṭāʾif al-ishārāt: Subtle Allusions*; Maybudī (twelfth century), *Kashf al-asrār*; and al-Kāshānī (d. ca. 1330), *Tafsīr al-Kāshānī*.

[6] For an Aristotelian who insisted that the goal of philosophy was actualizing one's true self, see Chittick, *The Heart of Islamic Philosophy*.

soul. Shams-i Tabrīzī, the famous teacher of Rūmī (d. 1273), summed up their perspective with these words:

> Why do you study knowledge for the sake of worldly mouthfuls? This rope is for people to come out of the well, not for them to go from this well into that well.
>
> You must bind yourself to knowing this: "Who am I? What substance am I? Why have I come? Where am I going? From whence is my root? At this time what am I doing? Toward what have I turned my face?"[7]

John Renard has provided a long anthology of important early texts delving into the nature of religious experience in *Knowledge of God in Classical Sufism*. He writes in his introduction that Sufi teachers always made a distinction between *'ilm* and *ma'rifa*. Trying to catch the connotations of the latter word, he explains that the standard translation as gnosis is misleading. He chooses instead to render the word variously as experiential knowledge, infused knowledge, intimate knowledge, and mystical knowledge. It seems, however, that the best way to catch the sense of *ma'rifa* is to translate it consistently as recognition, which is its Quranic and everyday meaning. Translating it in a variety of ways obscures the fact that one sort of knowing is at issue. Translating it as gnosis, which has no verbal form in English, has led many scholars to ignore the word's frequent use in the earliest sources. Its *locus classicus* is a famous saying ascribed to the Prophet: "He who *recognizes* himself *recognizes* his Lord." Constantly quoted and glossed by Sufi teachers, this saying asserts that one will never perceive God without perceiving one's own soul. Given the soul's potential omniscience because of its divine form, in coming to know itself the soul "re-cognizes" what it already knows. After all, Sufi teachers like to remind us, God taught Adam "all the names" (Quran 2:30), and every one of us is Adam (="human" in Arabic).

It should also be noted that the meaning of the important Quranic term *dhikr*, "remembrance," overlaps with that of *ma'rifa*. When our father Adam "forgot" (Quran 20:115), God reminded him and he remembered, and then God forgave him and appointed him vicegerent in the earth. The Quran describes "reminder" (*dhikrā*) as the primary function of the prophets, who were traditionally numbered at 124,000, beginning with Adam and ending with Muhammad. Remembrance is

---

[7] Chittick, *Me & Rumi*, p. 51.

then the proper human response to a prophetic message. The book frequently encourages *dhikr*, specifically *dhikr Allāh*, "the remembrance of God," as the cure for forgetfulness. Practically all Sufi teachers inculcated the methodical practice of *dhikr*.

The most famous and influential of the numerous early books differentiating between knowledge and recognition while detailing the theory and practice of actualizing true human nature is the forty-volume work of the renowned scholar Abū Ḥāmid al-Ghazālī (d. 1111), *Bringing to Life the Sciences of the Religion* (*Iḥyā' 'ulūm al-dīn*). The title of this book, like the title of his Persian reworking of the text, *The Alchemy of Felicity* (*Kīmiyā-yi sa 'ādat*), points to self-recognition and God-recognition as the raison d'être of the transmitted sciences. "Recognition," as one of the early Sufi teachers put it, "is the heart's life with God."[8]

## THE WORLDVIEW

The Islamic worldview was presented mythically in the Quran and Hadith and elaborated upon by generations of scholars. It was typically explained in terms of three principles: the assertion of divine unity (*tawḥīd*), prophecy (*nubuwwa*), and the return to God (*ma 'ād*). Most Muslims went no further in their knowledge of these principles than memorized catechisms. The predominant methodologies of Kalam meant that students of theology were trained in rational argumentation rather than self-reflection and self-understanding. In a typical passage from *The Alchemy of Felicity*, Ghazālī differentiates among various levels of understanding *tawḥīd*, putting the dogmatic theologians in the same category as the common people. He describes the higher stages of asserting God's unity using the words witnessing (*mushāhada*), togetherness (*jam '*), and annihilation (*fanā '*), all three of which were much discussed in Sufi literature.

> The first degree of *tawḥīd* is that someone says with the tongue, "There is no god but God," but he does not believe it in the heart. This is the *tawḥīd* of the hypocrite.

---

[8] Muḥammad ibn al-Faḍl (d. 931), as quoted by Qushayrī, *al-Risāla*; for a slightly different translation, see Knysh, *Al-Qushayri's Epistle on Sufism*, p. 325. On the importance of the heart in the Quran and Islamic psychology generally, see Murata, *The Tao of Islam*, chapter 10.

The second degree is that someone believes its meaning in the heart on the basis of imitation, like the common man; or on the basis of some sort of evidence, like the Kalam expert.

The third degree is that someone sees by way of witnessing that everything comes forth from one root, that there is no more than one actor, and that no one else has any activity. This is a light that appears in the heart, and witnessing is gained through this light. This is not like the belief of the common person or the Kalam expert, for belief [*i'tiqād*] is a knot [*'uqda*] tied in the heart by means of imitation or evidence. But witnessing is an expansion of the heart that unties all knots.

There are differences between these three: one person convinces himself to believe that the master is in the house because so-and-so said he is in the house. This is the imitation of the common man, who heard it from his mother and father. Another person infers that the master is in the house because the horse and servants are standing by the doorway. This is like the belief of the Kalam expert. The third person sees him inside the house by way of witnessing. This is like the *tawḥīd* of the recognizers. Although this third *tawḥīd* is great in degree, its possessor still sees creation along with seeing and knowing the Creator, and he knows that creation comes from the Creator. So in this there is multiplicity and manyness. As long as he sees two, he stays in dispersion and does not have togetherness.

The perfection of *tawḥīd* is the fourth degree. The person sees nothing but one. He sees and recognizes that all are one. Dispersion has no way into this witnessing. This is what the Sufis call "annihilation in *tawḥīd*."[9]

In short, *tawḥīd* is the assertion that there is nothing truly real but the Real (*al-ḥaqq*) – a word that the Quran uses to designate not only God himself, but also true, appropriate, and right along with the corresponding nouns. In several verses the Quran juxtaposes *ḥaqq* with *bāṭil*, "unreal," such as "The real comes, and the unreal vanishes away" (Quran 17:81). Avicenna explains the theological meanings of *ḥaqq* and *bāṭil* in his *Metaphysics*: "By Its essence the Necessary Existence is the Real constantly, and the possible existence is real through something else, but unreal in itself. Hence everything other than the One

---

[9] Cited in Chittick, *Divine Love*, pp. 416–17.

Necessary Existence is unreal in itself."[10] In *al-Maqṣad al-asnā* ("The furthest goal"), a commentary on the divine names, Ghazālī follows the same line of reasoning:

> Everything about which a report may be given is either absolutely unreal, absolutely real, or real in one respect and unreal in another respect. That which is impossible by essence is the absolutely unreal. That which is necessary by essence is the absolutely real. That which is possible by essence ... is real in one respect and unreal in another ... By this you will recognize that the absolutely real is the true existence by its essence, and every real thing takes its reality from it.[11]

If I stress the notion of *tawḥīd* – the assertion of the unique reality of the Real – it is because the vast Islamic literature on the cultivation of the inner life and the clarification of inner experience cannot be contextualized unless we grasp that the authors had no doubt whatsoever that the Real alone is real. When Sufi teachers contrast imitation with "realization" – literally, the actualization of the Real – they are declaring that the human soul can be completed and perfected only by establishing a firmly rooted awareness of the presence of the Real, not simply by blindly following in the footsteps of those who have gone before. They recognized that everything other than the Real per se is unreal, including all human perception and experience. They understood that those who have "mystical experience" may indeed imagine that they are seeing or tasting or witnessing or contemplating God per se, and certainly Sufi poetry can often be read in such terms. But careful attention to the metaphysics and theology behind such statements shows that Muslim scholars were perfectly aware of the caveats.

Rūmī explains the point toward the beginning of his great epic of love, the *Mathnawī*: "If you pour the ocean into a pot, // how much will it hold? One day's store."[12] Junayd of Baghdad (d. 910), often considered the founder of the explicitly Sufi movement, put it this way: "The water takes on the color of the cup."[13] Aḥmad Samʿānī (d. 1140), author of a masterful Persian commentary on the divine names that investigates the diverse implications of finding God in the self and the world, clarifies the issue while explaining why Moses was denied the vision

---

[10] Avicenna, *al-Shifāʾ*, pp. 38–39 (my translation).
[11] *al-Maqṣad al-asnā*, ed. Fadlou Shehadi, p. 137.
[12] *The Mathnawī*, ed. R. A. Nicholson, book I, verse 20.
[13] Ibn al-ʿArabī often explains the meaning of this sentence in terms of the soul's experience of the Real. See, for example, Chittick, *Sufi Path of Knowledge*, pp. 341, 344, 368 (hereafter SPK).

of God at Mount Sinai (Quran 7:143): "When He bestows on you vision of Himself, He will give it in the measure of your eyes' capacity, not in the measure of His majesty and beauty. This is why it has been said, *'He spoke to Moses in respect of Moses. Had He spoken to Moses in respect of His tremendousness, Moses would have melted'.*"[14]

The other two principles of faith – prophecy and the return to God – also play major roles in describing the human situation and bringing home the necessity of beautifying the soul. The principle of prophecy asserts that God in his mercy sent prophets to remind people of their true nature and guide them to their ultimate felicity (*sa'āda*). The third principle then explains the necessity of preparing for death and resurrection, events which pertain to the "compulsory return" undergone by everyone. The Tariqah (*ṭarīqa*) – the "narrow path" followed by the Sufis – was often called the "voluntary return," for its goal was to return to God before death.

Sufi teachers modeled their descriptions of the Tariqah on accounts of the *mi'rāj* or "ladder" of Muhammad, that is, his "night journey" (*isrā'*), during which he ascended up through the seven heavens, then on to hell, paradise, and finally into the Divine Presence (commentators find reference to the event in Quran 17:1 and 53:1ff.).[15] In some accounts of the path, like the famous poem of Farīd al-Dīn 'Aṭṭār (d. 1221), *Manṭiq al-ṭayr* ("The language of the birds"), there are seven preliminary stages corresponding to the seven heavens traversed by Muhammad. 'Aṭṭār describes them as seven mountains that the birds must fly over in order to reach their king, the *Sīmurgh* or "phoenix." Of the many birds that undertake the journey, only "thirty birds" – *sī murgh* – reach the end, discovering that they themselves are identical with the *Sīmurgh*. 'Aṭṭār explains the mountains as character traits of the perfected soul, namely seeking, love, recognition, unneediness, *tawḥīd*, bewilderment, and poverty.[16]

Most descriptions of the ascent to God provide a larger number of stages, such as 40, 100, or even 1,001. In each case the author's goal is to guide seekers in navigating the uncharted realms of their own souls. People need such guidance because, as remarked by the Andalusian sage Ibn 'Arabī (d. 1240) – called the "greatest teacher" by the Sufi tradition –

---

[14] Chittick, *Repose of the Spirits*, p. 19. Original emphasis.
[15] The possible influence of the detailed Islamic accounts of this journey on Dante's *Divine Comedy* has been discussed by historians since the 1919 book of Palacios, *La Escatología musulmana en la Divina Comedia*.
[16] The book has been translated into English partly or wholly several times, beginning with Edward Fitzgerald in 1889.

"The soul is an ocean without shore, so knowledge of it has no end."[17] In *Bringing to Life the Sciences of the Religion*, Ghazālī discusses the ascending stages of the Tariqah as beautiful character traits (*maḥāsin al-akhlāq*) that are innate to the soul's divine form but concealed by forgetfulness. In his commentary on the divine names he points out that seekers of God should strive "to become characterized by the character traits of God" (al-*takhalluq bi-akhlāq Allāh*), traits that are designated by God's most beautiful names. Ibn ʿArabī says that becoming characterized by God's character traits is equivalent to the philosophical goal of similarity to God and provides a nutshell description of Sufism.[18]

The best known of the early accounts of the Tariqah is the *Risāla* or "treatise" by Abu'l-Qāsim al-Qushayrī (d. 1072) from Nishapur.[19] He devotes a good deal of the book to delineating the "states" (*aḥwāl*) and "stations" (*maqāmāt*) experienced by travelers on the path. States are temporary alterations of awareness that should be accepted as divine gifts but otherwise ignored, lest they divert seekers from the goal. Like most authors, he depicts them in pairs because of their constantly changing, yin-yang nature: contraction and expansion, awe and intimacy, gathering and dispersion, annihilation and subsistence, absence and presence, sobriety and drunkenness, variegation and stability, proximity and distance. Their complementarity reflects the two basic modes of perceiving the Real: God as transcendent and God as immanent. These two perceptions were commonly described in terms of the contrasting divine attributes of wrath and mercy, or majesty and beauty, or severity and gentleness, or justice and bounty, always with the understanding that, as the Prophet put it, "God's mercy takes precedence over His wrath."[20]

As for the "stations," these were understood as permanent character traits actualized by the soul during its climb on the ladder of realization. Qushayrī offers forty brief chapters describing them in roughly ascending order. Among them he lists repentance, striving, seclusion, scrupulosity, renunciation, silence, fear, hope, sadness, humility,

---

[17] *al-Futūḥāt al-makkiyya*, vol. III, p. 121, line 25 (quoted in SPK 345).
[18] SPK 283.
[19] The best of the three available translations into English is that of Knysh, *Al-Qushayrī's Epistle*.
[20] In *The Tao of Islam* Murata quotes many Sufis and philosophers to show how they understood this divine complementarity as reflected in the soul and the universe. For a 500-page twelfth-century text that describes the soul's engagement with God in terms of divine complementarity, see Chittick, *Repose of the Spirits*.

contentment, trust, gratitude, certainty, patience, watchfulness, approval, sincerity, truthfulness, shame, and chivalry. His contemporary in Herat, ʿAbdallāh Anṣārī (d. 1088), wrote two classic depictions of one hundred stations on the path, one in Arabic and one in Persian. Adding a good deal of subtlety to his books, he explained that each of the character traits he describes has three ascending levels, a tripartite scheme that correlates with the distinction drawn by Sufi teachers among three basic types of wayfarers: the common, the elect, and the elect of the elect.

Philosophy and Kalam always remained elite enterprises, but Sufism attracted people from all walks of life and became by far the most popular form of learning. It made available to all Muslims the means of intensifying their engagement with God on the basis of the prophetic model. As noted, the most prominent of the practices stressed by the Sufi teachers was *dhikr*, the remembrance, mention, or invocation of God's names, a practice firmly grounded in the Quran, the Hadith, and the developed Islamic worldview.[21] Historians and anthropologists have often remarked on Sufism's use of invocation and other techniques to provide the general populace with religious experience, though they have sometimes missed the fact that such activities give us a better picture of mainstream Islam than do the writings of the jurists and theologians, a point that Shahab Ahmed stresses in his book *What is Islam?* He writes, for example,

> The historical preoccupation of Muslims with the exploration of the meaningful is evidenced by the prolific social practice of the Sufi *samāʿ* – literally, "audition" – those personal and collective exercises of Sufi existential experience that were performed at any time, but especially in public on Thursday evenings in *khānqāh*s and at Sufi shrines throughout the Balkans-to-Bengal complex (the most well-known example of which, today, is the whirling of the dervishes of the order of Mawlānā Jalāl-ud-Dīn Rūmī), and through which the Muslim sought direct, personal, subjective somatic taste (*dhawq*) of the Divine in a private domain of knowledge beyond the prescribed forms of correctness.[22]

Many Western scholars have associated Sufism with folk religion, often forgetting that it also provided the most elite and sophisticated teachings of the tradition. Ibn ʿArabī was called the "greatest teacher"

[21] See Chittick, "On the Cosmology of *Dhikr*."
[22] Ahmed, *What Is Islam?*, p. 286.

precisely because of his unparalleled mastery and synthesis of metaphysics, theology, cosmology, spiritual psychology, principles of jurisprudence, and jurisprudence. Drawing from the most erudite expressions of the developed schools of learning, he tied everything back to specific Quranic verses and hadiths. Indeed, though he does not have a separate commentary on the Quran (unlike hundreds of other scholars), the depth and profundity of his explanations of the sacred text were unprecedented. The fact that his tomb in Damascus is still a place of pilgrimage for people from all walks of life reminds us of his saintly reputation.

One of the qualities that set Ibn 'Arabī apart from most other teachers was his analysis of religious experience, both in terms of his own personal unveilings (*kashf*), witnessings (*shuhūd*), tastings (*dhawq*), findings (*wujūd*), and visions (*ru'ya*), and in terms of the theoretical explanation of the status of the non-ordinary cognitions called by such names. In his voluminous and non-repetitive works, he remarks in passing or describes in detail many experiences that he underwent, beginning with a massive opening (*futūḥ*) when he was barely into his teens. By his own account, as reported to a disciple,

> I began my retreat at the first light and reached opening before sunrise. After that I entered the "shining of the full moon" and other stations, one after another. I stayed in my place for fourteen months. Through that I gained all the mysteries that I put down in writing after the opening. My opening was a single attraction at that moment.[23]

In one of his many references to this opening, he writes, "Everything I have mentioned after it in all my speech is simply the differentiation of the all-inclusive reality that was contained in that look at the One Reality."[24] He called his magnum opus "The Meccan Openings" (*al-Futūḥāt al-makkiyya*) precisely because it describes knowledge that was opened up to him, without any exertion or seeking on his part, during his pilgrimage to Mecca in the year 1202. He explains this in the book's preface, where he also provides the full title (notice the use of the word *ma'rifa*): *The Treatise of the Meccan Openings: On Recognizing the Secrets of the Master and the Kingdom.*[25]

---

[23] SPK, p. xiii.
[24] *Futūḥāt* II 548.14 (SPK, xiv).
[25] One of Ibn 'Arabī's contemporaries, Rūzbihān Baqlī from Shiraz, describes his own remarkable visions of God's presence in *Kāshif al-asrār*, translated by Carl Ernst as *The Unveiling of Secrets: Diary of a Sufi Master.*

## IMAGINATION'S OMNIPRESENCE

The orientalist Henry Corbin (d. 1978) performed a great service to Islamic studies by bringing to light the importance of a number of philosophers and Sufis who had been relatively ignored by Western scholarship. In *Creative Imagination in the Sufism of Ibn ʿArabī* and other books, Corbin used the tools of phenomenology to stress the importance of imagination and to analyze encounters with the unseen worlds described by Ibn ʿArabī and others.[26] In doing so, however, he tended to extract the teachings from their metaphysical and cosmological context. More interesting, perhaps, is Ibn ʿArabī's own analysis of imagination's role in human cognition, a role that can help us understand the necessarily ambiguous nature of all experience, religious or otherwise.

In Islamic thought everything that exists in any respect whatsoever can be divided into two sorts: God and other than God, or the Real and the unreal. In explaining these two, Ibn ʿArabī often has recourse to the notion of "self-disclosure" (*tajallī*), a term drawn from the Quran's account of Moses at Mount Sinai (7:143), where God "disclosed himself" not to Moses, but to the mountain, shattering it to dust. Many teachers before Ibn ʿArabī had used the term to designate the contingent reality of the universe. Even Avicenna, who preferred abstract, non-Quranic terms when discussing the Necessary and the possible, found the term "self-disclosure" congenial in his explanation of the divine love that drives all existent things to their final goals:

> Each of the existent things loves the Absolute Good with an innate love, and the Absolute Good discloses Itself to Its lovers. Their receptions of Its self-disclosure and their conjunctions with It, however, are disparate. The furthest limit of proximity to It is the reception of Its self-disclosure in reality, I mean, as perfectly as possible. This is what the Sufis call "unification." In Its munificence, the Good loves that Its self-disclosure be received. Then the things come into existence by means of Its self-disclosure.[27]

Ibn ʿArabī often explains why "the existent things" – which are Rūmī's "pots" and Junayd's "cups" – have disparate receptions of the Absolute Good's self-disclosure. The multiplicity of the things goes

---

[26] Corbin, *Creative Imagination in the Sufism of Ibn ʿArabī*.
[27] From the last chapter of *Risāla fiʾl-ʿishq*, translated in Chittick, *Divine Love*, p. 284.

back to the Necessary Being, whose self-awareness comprehends all beings and all becoming. Given that God in his eternity "knows all things," as the Quran says repeatedly, he plays no role in determining their quiddities – they are what he knows them to be, always and forever. He simply issues the command "Be!" to their fixed thingness: "His only command, when He desires a thing, is to say to it 'Be!' and it comes to be" (Quran 36:82).[28] In respect of their inherent nonexistence the things known eternally by God are unreal, but in respect of their God-given existence in the world, they are real. It follows that each thing is *huwa lā huwa*, "He/not He" or "it/not it." Each is itself inasmuch as it negates the Real, but other than itself inasmuch as it affirms the Real.

Ambiguity – the state of being it/not it – pertains to everything other than God. It is a characteristic of *khayāl*, a word that designates both external images and internal imagination. Whether we see an image in a mirror or in our own minds, it is it/not it, which is to say that it is itself in one respect and not itself in another. Hence the entire cosmos can be called imagination, for it is the sum total of the possible things, which are images hanging between the Necessary Existence and absolute nonexistence. As Ibn 'Arabī puts it in one passage,

> Everything other than the Essence of the Real is in the station of transmutation, speedy and slow. Everything other than the Essence of the Real is intervening imagination and vanishing shadow. No created thing remains in this world, the hereafter, and what is between the two, neither spirit, nor soul, nor anything other than God – I mean the Essence of God – upon a single state; rather, it undergoes continual change from form to form constantly and forever. And imagination is nothing but this ... So the cosmos only became manifest within imagination. It is imagined in itself. So it is it, and it is not it.[29]

Following in the line of the Quran and Muslim thought generally, Ibn 'Arabī subdivides this realm of divine self-disclosure, which he sometimes calls "nondelimited imagination," into three worlds. Most intense in divine attributes and intelligible luminosity is "heaven" or the spiritual world, home of angels and disengaged intellects. Least intense is "earth" or the realm of corporeality and sense perception.

---

[28] On the immutable fixity of things, see, for example SPK, 83–89, 297–301.
[29] *Futūḥāt* 2:313.17 (SPK, 118).

Standing between heaven and earth is the World of Imagination, a realm that is both spiritual and bodily, or neither one nor the other.

The human microcosm, created in the form of God per se, mirrors the macrocosm, so each individual human being has a three-level structure: luminous spirit, dark body, and in-between soul. The spirit is characterized by an intensity of divine attributes, for it is the direct manifestation of the divine light. The body is qualified by exceedingly weak reverberations of the same attributes, so weak that they can be called by the names of their opposites. The spirit is alive, knowing, desiring, powerful, speaking, hearing, seeing, and so on down the list of God's ninety-nine names, while the body is dead, ignorant, apathetic, weak, mute, deaf, and blind. The body's life does not belong to the clay substratum, but to the intermediate level of soul. The soul is then an image of both spirit and body, a never repeating self-disclosure of the Real hanging between light and darkness. It remains in a constant state of flux, pulled upward by the light of the spirit and downward by the darkness of clay. To use Rūmī's imagery, the soul is an angel's wing stuck to a donkey's tail, its destiny to be determined by which of the two sides predominates.[30]

In terms of the cosmology and psychology formulated by philosophers and Sufis, the first two dimensions of the religion – practice and faith – prepare the ground for the third dimension, beautifying the soul. In other words, the goal of life is to intensify the light of the spirit and overcome the darkness of the body, always with God's help. Once the soul becomes aware of itself, it experiences the ongoing self-disclosures of the Real, but these self-disclosures are shaped and colored by the soul's cup. Eventually the soul's dependence on the body will disappear, for only at a relatively early stage of its development does it need eyes to see and ears to hear, as we witness already in dreams. The great philosopher Mullā Ṣadrā (d. 1640) provides extensive analyses of the soul's experiences as it ascends in the stages of recognition and realization. He summarizes his position in one of his favorite aphorisms: "The soul is bodily in origination and spiritual in subsistence" (*al-nafs jismāniyyat al-ḥudūth rūḥāniyyat al-baqā*').[31]

In one explanation of the meaning of He/not He, Ibn ʿArabī says that "He" designates light or existence, for "God is the light of the heavens

[30]  Chittick, *Sufi Path of Love*, p. 87.
[31]  See, for example, the fourth volume of Mullā Ṣadrā's magnum opus, al-Asfār al-arbaʿa ("The Four Journeys"), translated by L. Peervani as *Spiritual Psychology: The Fourth Intellectual Journey*.

and the earth" (Quran 24:35). "Not He" then designates darkness or nonexistence. All perception (*idrāk*) takes place through the presence of light in darkness, for neither light nor darkness can be perceived in itself.

> Were it not for light, nothing whatsoever would be perceived, neither object of knowledge, nor sensory object, nor imagined object. The names of light are diverse in keeping with the names set down for the faculties. The common people see these as names of the faculties, but the recognizers see them as names of the light through which perception takes place. When you perceive sounds, you call that light "hearing." When you perceive sights, you call that light "seeing." When you perceive objects of touch, you call that light "touch." So also is the case with objects of imagination. Hence the faculty of touch is nothing but light. Smell, taste, imagination, memory, reason, reflection, conceptualization, and everything through which perception takes place are nothing but light.
>
> As for perceived things, if they did not have the preparedness to receive the perception of the one who perceives them, they would not be perceived. First they possess manifestation to the perceiver, and then they are perceived. Manifestation is light. Hence every perceived thing must have a relationship with light through which it gains the preparedness to be perceived, so every known thing has a relationship with the Real, and the Real is Light.[32]

### PERCEIVING THE REAL

To perceive anything at all is to perceive the Real's self-disclosure, for there is nothing else to perceive. As Ghazālī often says, "There is nothing in existence but God." Why people perceive and experience God in endlessly diverse ways goes back to a host of factors. One is that "Self-disclosure never repeats itself," which means that the manifestation of the One is always one and unique. As Avicenna put it, the things' have disparate receptions of the Absolute Good when it discloses itself. In other words, the Infinite One gives rise to an infinity of ones. If we imagine a boundless sphere whose center is the One, every point

---

[32] *Futūḥāt* III 276.32 (SPK, 214).

within the sphere will be the center's reflection, but different from every other point because of its coordinates.

The ability to recognize what we actually perceive goes back to our cups' receptivity, the importance of which Ibn ʿArabī often explains. In one long passage he uses the analogy of a king to suggest why ignorance prevents people from seeing God, despite the fact that, "Wherever you turn, there is the face of God" (Quran 2:115).

> God proportioned the human configuration ..., then "He blew into him of His spirit" [Quran 32:9]. At that there became manifest within him a soul governing the frame. It became manifest through the form of the frame's constitution, so the souls became ranked in excellence, just as the constitutions are ranked in excellence. In the same way, sunlight strikes diverse colors in glass and gives forth lights that are diverse in color, whether red, yellow, blue, or something else, in keeping with the color of the glass in the view of the eye. The diversity that arrives newly in the light derives only from the locus ... The frames receive governance from these souls only in the measure of their preparedness ... Among the souls are the clever and the dull, in keeping with the frame's constitution ...
>
> For example, when we see that a king takes on the form of the commoners and walks among the people in the market such that they do not recognize him as the king, he has no weight in their souls. However, when someone who recognizes him encounters him in that state, the magnificence and measure of the king come to abide in his soul. Hence his knowledge of the king leaves a trace in him, so he honors him, shows courtesy, and prostrates himself before him.[33]

In short, the soul's preparedness for perception and understanding determines what it experiences. Few people have enough recognition of their own souls to differentiate among the three basic levels of perception – the sensory, the imaginal, and the intellectual (or spiritual). Except in rare instances, exemplified by the prophets and the friends of God (*awliyāʾ*), all "significant" perceptions fall short of the spiritual realm and pertain rather to the imaginal realm, which is neither spiritual nor bodily.

---

[33] *Futūḥāt* 3:554.6. For the whole passage, see Chittick, *The Self-Disclosure of God*, pp. 325–26.

A good deal of Sufi literature addresses how to discern light from darkness in the ambiguous, imaginal realm of perception. Most mystical experiences – unveilings, contemplations, visions, tastings, recognitions – take place in the soul, the microcosmic world of imagination. On the macrocosmic level, the World of Imagination is the realm of intermediary beings that are neither angels nor human, beings that are generally called "jinn." The Quran asserts that they were created from "fire," which combines the spirit's light with clay's darkness. Satan himself is a jinn, which explains in Islamic terms how he could have disobeyed God, given that the Quran says that angels – who are created of light – cannot disobey the divine command. Since the soul is intermediate and "fiery" by nature, it is innately inclined to receive the deceptive and flickering luminosity of the imaginal realms. A saying of the Prophet points out that the jinn have access to human souls: "Satan runs in the blood of every child of Adam." About Satan the Quran says, "He sees you – he and his tribe – from where you see them not" (7:27). So no one should be surprised that the texts frequently stress the dangers of attempting to navigate the ocean of the soul without a qualified guide, who is traditionally called the "shaykh," that is, the elder or teacher. His authority derives from having had his advancement on the path ritually confirmed by his own shaykh. In all formalized Sufi orders – of which there have been and still are hundreds – the chain of transmitted authority goes back to the Prophet, who embodies the divine guidance revealed in the Quran.

Sufi literature often warns about thinking that "mystical experience" is by definition a good thing, or, far worse, that it delivers its recipient from the obligation to follow the Quran and the Prophet. Some authors wrote books describing the perils faced by those who allow their visions to hold sway. The great twelfth-century master Rūzbihān Baqlī (d. 1209), for example, wrote a Persian treatise called *Ghalaṭāt al-sālikīn*, "The errors of the wayfarers." He notes that among the errors of the weak is that "They enter the world of imagination and see images, but they fancy that this is unveiling."[34] Ibn ʿArabī frequently discusses the perils faced by the soul when it is exposed to the unseen realms.[35] A Persian treatise attributed to his disciple Ṣadr al-Dīn Qūnawī (d. 1274) puts the issue in a nutshell:

---

[34] *Risālat al-quds wa Risāla-yi ghalaṭāt al-sālikīn*, ed. Nurbakhsh, p. 94.
[35] See, for example, chapter 17 of SPK, "The Pitfalls of the Path."

Whenever a recognizer and traveler finds something shining down from the horizon of Heaven's Kingdom on the tablet of his heart, he must compare it with the Book of God. If it agrees with the Book, he should accept it; if not, he should pay no heed. Then he should compare it with the Sunnah of the Messenger. If it corresponds to it, he should judge it to be true; if not, he should take no further action. In the same way he should also compare it with the consensus of the ulama and the shaykhs of the Community ... For, the errors of this path have no end, because the signs on the horizons and in the souls become confused in formal and supraformal unveilings. No one is saved from the clashing waves of the oceans of the signs except the masters among His sincere servants – and how few they are! Hence, except in rare and exceptional cases, one cannot avoid the need for a shaykh who is a wayfarer, a truth-teller, and a realizer. "He who has no shaykh has Satan for his shaykh" is the allusion of the king of the recognizers, Abū Yazīd Basṭāmī.[36]

To summarize, both Sufism and philosophy pay a great deal of attention to human experience of the Real, whether this takes place by means of the external senses in the signs of the outside world, or by means of the internal senses and intellect in the signs of the inside world. People can and do experience the Real, but they will not be able to understand what it is that they are actually experiencing without the discipline of the path. Ibn ʿArabī reminds his readers of the Quranic statement that God is "with you wherever you are" (57:4). But, he remarks, "God did not say, 'And you are with Him,' since the manner in which He accompanies us is unknown. He knows how He accompanies us, but we do not know how He accompanies us. So witness is affirmed for Him in relation to us, but it is negated from us in relation to Him."[37]

The Quran suggests that nearness (*qurb*) to God is the goal of the human quest. Ibn ʿArabī explains what nearness has to do with the divine witness.

God says, "We are nearer to him than the jugular vein" (50:16), thereby describing Himself as being near to His servants. But what is desired from "nearness" is that it be the attribute of the servant. The servant should be qualified as being near to the Real exactly as the Real is qualified as being near to him. He says, "He is with you wherever you are" (57:4). The Men of God seek to be with the Real

---

[36] Chittick, *Faith and Practice of Islam*, p. 55.
[37] *Futūḥāt* II 582.10 (SPK, 364).

forever in whatever form He discloses Himself. He never ceases disclosing Himself in the forms of His servants continuously, so the servant is with Him wherever He discloses Himself continuously ... The recognizers never cease witnessing nearness continuously, since they never cease witnessing forms within themselves and outside of themselves, and that is nothing but the self-disclosure of the Real.[38]

## THE PATH OF LOVE

Most Sufi masters have taught that love provides the motive force for recognizing oneself and finding God's self-disclosure in the soul and the world. They commonly contrasted the cold abstraction of rationality with love's transforming fire. As Rūmī put it, when a philosopher like Avicenna tried to delve into the divine mysteries, he became "an ass on ice." As for love, it "burns away everything except the everlasting Beloved."[39] Many Sufi teachers held that poetry and song – by far the most popular forms of literature in traditional Muslim societies – provided the ideal vehicle for conveying love's transformative power. Love's object, after all, is always beauty, and, as the Prophet put it, "God is beautiful, and He loves beauty." The imagery and symbolism of the poets provided the most effective means of describing the beauty of the divine Beloved and stirring up love in the hearts of seekers. The rational abstractions of Kalam and philosophy tended rather to stress the indifference of the Supreme, Transcendent Reality to puny human aspirations.

The goal of lovers is union (*wiṣāl*), a point obvious from the everyday experience of "metaphorical love" (*'ishq-i majāzī*), which is love for anything other than the Real. Not that metaphorical love is a bad thing, for, as the well-known Arabic proverb puts it, "The metaphor is the bridge to the reality," and the reality is God. All metaphorical love prepares the way for loving God and achieving union with him. Jurists and Kalam experts found the idea that people could obtain union with God repellant and condemned such talk, but their objections never prevented Sufi teachers from holding it up as their goal. Ibn 'Arabī explains what they meant by the term:

The Real is perpetually in a state of union with created existence. Through this He is a God ... What takes place for the people of

---

[38] *Futūḥāt* II 558.27 (SPK, 365–66).
[39] Cited in Chittick, *Sufi Path of Love*, pp. 264, 215.

solicitude, the Folk of God, is that God gives them vision and unveils their insights until they witness this withness. This – that is, the recognizer's witnessing – is what is called "union," for the recognizer has become joined to a witnessing of the actual situation.[40]

The historical role of Sufism has everything to do with the fact that it brought the experience of God's presence into everyday life, an experience that was implicitly denied by the juridical and theological interpretations of the religion, both of which stressed obedience to the Shariah and blind adherence to the creed. The Sufi teachers turned their attention instead to the divine love that infuses the universe and tends to be forgotten by calculating intellects. They read the Quran as a "love letter," as Shams-i Tabrīzī put it.[41] They saw that it affirms two basic sorts of divine love, thereby providing the groundwork for all theory and practice. The first sort is unqualified, for it asserts the reality of *tawḥīd*: there is nothing real but the Real, so there is no beloved but God, no lover but God, and no love but God. The Quran voices this love in the verse, "He loves them, and they love Him" (Quran 5:54). God's love is unqualified because he loves human beings eternally, and people's love for God is unqualified because they love God innately, whether or not they are aware of the fact.

The second sort of love takes into account free will and the role of the prophetic reminders. It invites people to turn away from metaphorical love and recognize their true Beloved. The king is walking among them in the bazaar, but they have no way to recognize him unless they follow the path of those who witness his presence – God's prophets and friends. The path of following is summed up in the verse, "Say [O Muhammad!]: 'If you love God, follow me; God will love you'" (Quran 3:31). When people follow the Prophet and when God comes to love them with this second kind of love, the fruit will be "union." An explicit early statement of this union is found in the most authoritative collection of Hadith and is constantly quoted in Sufi literature. The Prophet narrated from God that he says, "So much does My servant seek nearness to Me through supererogatory works that I love him. When I love him, I am his hearing, so he hears through Me; his eyesight, so he sees through Me; his tongue, so he speaks through Me; his feet, so he walks through Me; his hands, so he takes through Me; his heart, so he knows through Me."[42]

---

[40] *Futūḥāt* II 480.12 (SPK, 365).
[41] Chittick, *Me & Rumi*, p. 156.
[42] See Chittick, *Divine Love*, p. 427.

## References

Ahmed, Shahab. *What Is Islam? The Importance of Being Islamic.* Princeton: Princeton University Press, 2016.
Avicenna. *al-Shifā': The Metaphysics of the Healing.* Edited and translated by Michael Marmura. Provo, UT: Brigham Young University Press, 2005.
Baqlī, Rūzbihān. *Risālat al-quds wa Risāla-yi ghalaṭāt al-sālikīn.* Edited by J. Nurbakhsh. Tehran: Khānqāh-i Niʿmatullāhī, 1351/1972.
*Kāshif al-asrār.* Translated by Carl Ernst as *The Unveiling of Secrets: Diary of a Sufi Master.* Chapel Hill: Parvardigar, 1997.
Chittick, William C. *The Sufi Path of Love: The Spiritual Teachings of Rumi.* Albany: State University of New York Press, 1983.
*The Sufi Path of Knowledge: Ibn al-ʿArabī's Metaphysics of Imagination.* Albany: State University of New York Press, 1989.
*Faith and Practice of Islam: Three Thirteenth-Century Sufi Texts.* Albany: State University of New York Press, 1992.
*The Self-Disclosure of God: Principles of Ibn al-ʿArabī's Cosmology.* Albany: State University of New York Press, 1998.
*The Heart of Islamic Philosophy: The Quest for Self-Knowledge in the Teachings of Afḍal al-Dīn Kāshānī.* Oxford: Oxford University Press, 2001.
"On the Cosmology of Dhikr," in James S. Cutsinger (ed.), *Paths to the Heart: Sufism and the Christian East.* Bloomington: World Wisdom Books, 2002, pp. 48–63.
*Me & Rumi: The Autobiography of Shams-i Tabrizi.* Louisville: Fons Vitae, 2004.
*Science of the Cosmos, Science of the Soul: The Pertinence of Islamic Cosmology in the Modern World.* Oxford: Oneworld, 2007.
*Divine Love: Islamic Literature and the Path to God.* New Haven: Yale University Press, 2013.
*The Repose of the Spirits: A Sufi Commentary on the Divine Names.* Albany: State University of New York Press, 2019.
Corbin, Henry. *Creative Imagination in the Sufism of Ibn ʿArabī.* Princeton: Princeton University Press, 1969. Reissued as *Alone with the Alone,* 1998.
Ghazālī, Abū Ḥāmid al-. *al-Maqṣad al-asnā.* Edited by Fadlou Shehadi. Beirut: Dār al-Mashriq, 1971.
*Iḥyāʾ ʿulūm al-dīn.* Beirut: Dār al-Hādī, 1993.
*Kīmiyā-yi saʿādat.* Translated by Jay R. Crook as *The Alchemy of Happiness.* Chicago: Kazi Publications, 2002.
Kāshānī, ʿAbd al-Razzāq al-. *Tafsīr al-Kāshānī.* Translated by Feras Hamza. www.altafsir.com/Books/kashani.pdf.
Knysh, Alexander. *Sufism: A New History of Islamic Mysticism.* Princeton: Princeton University Press, 2017.
Maybudī, Rashīd al-Dīn. *Kashf al-asrār: The Unveiling of the Mysteries.* Translated by W. C. Chittick. Louisville: Fons Vitae, 2015.
Murata, Sachiko. *The Tao of Islam: A Sourcebook on Gender Relationships in Islamic Thought.* Albany: State University of New York Press, 1992.
Murata, Sachiko, and William C. Chittick, *The Vision of Islam.* New York: Paragon House, 1994.

Palacios, Miguel Asín. *La Escatología musulmana en la Divina Comedia.* Abridged translation as *Islam and the Divine Comedy.* London: Routledge, 1968.

Qushayrī, Abu'l-Qāsim al-. *al-Risāla.* Translated by A. Knysh. *Al-Qushayri's Epistle on Sufism.* Reading, UK: Garnet Publishing, 2007.

   *Laṭā'if al-ishārāt: Subtle Allusions.* Translated by K. Z. Sands. Louisville: Fons Vitae, 2017.

Rūmī, Jalāl al-Dīn. *The Mathnawī.* Edited and translated by R. A. Nicholson. London: Luzac, 1925–40.

Sadrā Shīrāzī, Mullā. *al-Asfār al-arbaʿa.* Vol. 4. Translated by L. Peervani as *Spiritual Psychology: The Fourth Intellectual Journey.* London: ICAS Press, 2008.

Schimmel, Annemarie. *Mystical Dimensions of Islam.* Chapel Hill: The University of North Carolina Press, 1975.

Sells, Michael. *Early Islamic Mysticism.* New York: Paulist Press, 1996.

Zargar, Cyrus Ali. *The Polished Mirror: Storytelling and the Pursuit of Virtue in Islamic Philosophy and Sufism.* Oxford: Oneworld, 2017.

# Part III

*Religious Experience Outside Traditional Monotheism*

# 7 Religious Experience in Ancient Confucianism and Daoism

## XINZHONG YAO

Although the term 'religious experience' was not coined till the beginning of the twentieth century by William James,[1] experiences of a religious nature have been closely associated with human awareness of their own existence and its relations with the 'Other' since the very beginning of recorded human consciousness. It has been argued that 'Religious experience is one of the central facts of religion. Without it there would be no religions'[2], and Frederic J. Streng further claims that 'Religion was first experienced as rapture before natural phenomena, for example in the experience of day break'.[3] Due to civilizational divergences, however, perceptions and manifestations of religious experience differ from culture to culture, and from religion to religion. Religious experiences in Chinese traditions are characterized not only by the interconnection between the spiritual and the human but also by the interaction between the transcendent and the immanent and the interdependence between the religious other and the secular experient.

### RELIGIOUS EXPERIENCE IN EARLY CHINA

Religion started as early as the Chinese civilization came into shape. Almost all excavated burial sites in ancient China were religion-related where a clear sign of beliefs in the interaction between the living and the dead was intentionally marked, and measures to ensure the good life after death were abundantly visible. However, the earliest records of experiences of a religious nature were not clearly made until the time of oracle bone inscriptions dated to the Shang Dynasty (c.1600–c.1045 BCE), which are commonly agreed to be the first writing system of Chinese language known today. A kind of pyromancy was engaged

---

[1] James, *The Varieties of Religious Experience*, p. 489.
[2] Argyle, *Psychology and Religion*, p. 46.
[3] Streng, *Understanding Religious Life*, 2nd ed., p. 26.

consistently by applying fire to bones such as turtle plastrons and cattle scapulas for the purpose of divination, seeking answers to questions arising from personal, political, and religious experiences. Such practices started 'from the late fourth millennium B.C.', and 'reached its height by Shang times, with the widespread use of tortoise shells ("plastromancy") in addition to shoulder blades'.[4] 'Approximately 150,000 fragments of inscribed Shang oracle bones have now been recovered from near Anyang, in the northern panhandle. This was evidently the site of a major cult center where the Late Shang (ca. 1200–1045 B.C.E.) worshiped their ancestors and buried their last nine kings in large cruciform pit burials in the royal cemetery situated at Xibeigang'.[5]

Oracle bone inscriptions show that divination (*bu*, 卜) was the main tool to build up an effective communicative channel between the Shang kings and their ancestors or other spiritual powers, in order to obtain approval or blessing from the latter, implying that they were eager to seek harmony or unity between the human and the spiritual world. Through reading the cracks of the shells or bones, the diviners came to decipher 'responses' from their ancestors or spiritual powers concerning such matters and issues as 'sickness, childbirth, the good fortune of the night, the day, or the coming ten-day week, disaster, distress, trouble, dreams, troop mobilization, military campaigns, meteorological and celestial phenomena, agriculture, settlement building, administrative orders, hunting expeditions and excursions'; in other words, 'the king submitted virtually all aspects of his life to the pyromantic shell or bone for spiritual guidance'.[6] While most of these divinatory questions are concerned with seemingly secular matters (for example, 'about averting disasters, about the weather, and about the hunt'), some are explicitly related to religious belief and experience such as how to interpret a particular encounter with the deceased ancestor or spiritual power in dreams, whether or not a particular sickness was caused by the deceased father or grandfather of the incumbent king, through the way 'to communicate with the dead ancestors upon whose blessings the continued success of the dynasty depended'.[7]

Having launched a collected rebellion war that eventually led to the overthrowing of the powerful Shang dynasty around 1045 BCE, early Zhou rulers continued their search for spiritual guidance *via* divination

---

[4] Kung and Ching, *Christianity and Chinese Religions*, p.11.
[5] de Bary and Bloom, *Sources of Chinese Tradition*, p. 4.
[6] Ibid., pp. 5, 21.
[7] Ibid., p. 20.

and worship. Their teachings, activities, and religious practices are supposed to have been partially recorded in the texts that are later labelled as 'ancient Chinese classics', including the *Book of History* (*shu*, 書), the *Book of Poetry* (*shi*, 詩), the *Book of Rites* (*li*, 禮), and the *Book of Changes* (*yi*, 易). The last one, in particular, became recognized as the 'common roots' in late Confucianism and Daoism, and is often claimed to have shed 'new light on many a secret hidden in the often puzzling modes of thought of that mysterious sage, Lao-tse [Laozi], and of his pupils, as well as on many ideas that appear in the Confucian tradition as axioms'.[8] This book was in fact a collection compiled over a long period, initially as a kind of handbook for diviners to engage yet another major way of divination (*shi*, 筮) based on eight trigrams (three-line symbolic diagrams) and sixty-four hexagrams. By casting milfoil stalks the diviners would get different diagrams which were taken as indications of good or bad fortune for a particular situation, and how to read the diagrams was closely associated with personal experiences. This is interpreted by C. G. Jung as 'synchronicity' that shows 'a particular interdependence of objective events among themselves as well as with the subjective (psychic) states of the observer or observers'; Jung further claims that '[t]he method of the *I Ching* does indeed take into account the hidden individual quality in things and men, and in one's own unconscious self as well'.[9]

Whether termed 'religious' or 'psychological', experiences as such were clearly inherited in, or more precisely were moulded into, the culture in which ancient Confucianism and Daoism were brought forward and transmitted from generation to generation. They will be taken as the background on which we come to discuss how religious experience was embraced, perceived, and envisaged by early Confucian and Daoist masters and scholars. The fact that there are no terms in Chinese classics equivalent to 'religious experience' does not mean that the Chinese did not have religious experience or religious experience was not important for them. From Confucian and Daoist texts we find abundant evidence for occasions when people felt the influence or control of mystical power, had emotional communication with a spiritual being, were enlightened by a new view of life and death, had a dream that was extraordinary but was believed to be true, went through mysterious feelings such as hearing, seeing, smelling something inexplainable, had a visionary experience either alone or together with others, or

[8] *I Ching or Book of Changes*, p. xlvii.
[9] Ibid., pp. xxiv, xxviii.

experienced the union with the universe or cosmic power, in which one came to become one body with the universe.

The reason why religious experience received so much attention in ancient China can be found in the particular spirituality of its traditions. The Chinese in general placed more emphasis on the experiential than on the rational, in which the ultimate truth was experienced before being accepted and taken as the norm for personal life. Cultivated in such religiosity and mentality, no attempts were made to draw lines between experience and rationality or between facts and values; instead attention was paid to questions of how to get the same truth from different kinds of experiences and how to lead from one's experiential particulars to the universal principle. Thus, syncretism became the underlying colour of most religious perceptions and experiences in China. In their experiences many people of different spiritual orientations came to believe that all spiritual powers, no matter what origins they came from, must be held in awe, and that both reverence and sincerity were needed in order to initiate interaction between the spiritual and the human, from which religious experiences of different kinds were brought into the fore.

## CONFUCIANISM AND DAOISM

It is difficult to set up clear historical and practical boundaries for what we call ancient 'Confucianism' and 'Daoism'. In popular literature Confucianism is generally said to start with Confucius (Kongzi, 孔子, Master Kong 551–479 BCE) and Daoism with Laozi (老子, the Old Master c. 600–? BCE). However, there are scholarly arguments that, as philosophical and religious traditions, 'Confucianism' and 'Daoism' predated these two so-called founders. For example, it has been suggested that ideas and practices in ritual and education by ritual masters in the Shang dynasty whose teachings and practices were carried into the Zhou period gave rise to the school that was later labelled as the *ru*, 儒, or *literati* tradition[10]. In a similar way, some scholars have put forward arguments that Daoism came from indigenous religious beliefs and practices in early China[11] or started from the Yellow Emperor (Huangdi, 黄帝)[12], a legendary figure or cultural hero in the third millennium BCE. The close relation between Daoist practices and the

---

[10]  Yao, *Introduction to Confucianism*, pp. 18–20.
[11]  Jiyu, *Zhongguo Daojiao Shi*, p. 6.
[12]  Ching, *Chinese Religions*, p. 103.

Yellow Emperor's teachings was once singled out to form a particularly popular Daoism school called Huang-Lao (Huangdi and Laozi) during the Han Dynasty (221 BCE–220 CE).

The names 'Confucianism' and 'Daoism' are even more problematic than the time of their formation. Many people have noted that '*ru*' is more than what the term 'Confucianism' literally reveals, and some of them have even proposed to replace 'Confucianism' with 'Ruism'.[13] Different opinions are put forward about the role Confucius played in forming and shaping what was to become the *literati* tradition. There had already been a long tradition before Confucius that was substantiated as moral-religious-political teachings by the politicians and thinkers of the Western Zhou (c.1045–771 BCE), which Confucius fully embraced and was determined to transmit. The transmitted teachings were then further developed and expanded by such great masters as Mengzi (Meng Ke, 孟柯, 372–289 BCE) and Xunzi (Xun Qing, 荀卿, c.313–238 BCE) in the Warring States period (475–221 BCE). Although suffering persecution in the hands of Legalists and the First Emperor of Qin (r. 221–210 BCE), Confucianism was revived and further developed through the debates between the New Script School and the Old Script School during the Western Han Dynasty (206 BCE–8 CE). Following the advice by Han Confucian masters, in particular, Dong Zhongshu (董仲舒, c.179–104 BCE), the Emperor Wu of the Han (r. 140–87 BCE) took the final step and established the Confucian classics as the textbooks for state education and the worship of Confucius as the state cult. While overshadowed by Buddhism and Daoism after the collapse of the Han, Confucianism came to revival during the Song Dynasty (960–1273) and was even termed 'Neo-Confucianism' in the form of the Principle Learning (*lixue*, 理学) and the Heart-mind Learning (*xinxue*, 心学) that dominated the ideological world of China and East Asia until the beginning of the twentieth century.[14]

'Daoism' also has multiple meanings, and it covers at least two interrelated and yet distinguishable dimensions of a tradition, *dao jia*, 道家, philosophical Daoism, and *dao jiao*, 道教, religious Daoism. The earlier form of Daoism refers to the teachings by the recluses who were unsatisfied with the political and social situations in the Spring and Autumn period (770–476 BCE), and elevated 'following the natural way'

---

[13] Jensen, *Manufacturing Confucianism*.

[14] For how Confucianism became a world religion in the nineteenth century and continues to be central to the debate of its religious nature, see Sun, *Confucianism as a World Religion*.

as the model for humans. These recluses gave up hopes for saving the world from chaos and destruction, and advocated either complete withdrawal from the world or a kind of apathy that was contrary to any positive intervention. Apart from the close relation to the early Daoist teachings, religious Daoism also has its roots, however, in other features of ancient Chinese culture, such as the practices of two kinds of religious figures called *wu* (巫, shamans or spirit mediums) and *fangshi* (方士, ritual specialists who served as medical doctors and magicians).[15] Drawing upon the teachings of the Daoist classics, the *Daode jing* and the *Zhuangzi*, parts of such extant texts as *Guanzi* and *Liezi*, religious Daoism expanded itself in the form of Huang-Lao school in the Western Han Dynasty, and then in the form of political movements in the Eastern Han in the second century CE. Revolutionary leaders were 'inspired by direct contact with the divine who claimed to have the perfect solution to the world's problems and to lead the people into the new age of Great Peace', and two of them were claimed to have 'received their powers – including the ability to heal, make rain, and create social harmony – from a deity understood as the personification of the Dao and called ... Lord Lao. They founded the first organized Daoist community'.[16] These founders are known as the Heavenly Masters (*tianshi*, 天師) heading the long tradition within Daoism called 'Heavenly Masters Daoism'. Religious Daoist teachings and experiences were further developed and enriched by many Daoist followers, such as ritual master Wei Huacun (魏华存, 251–334), alchemist Ge Hong (葛洪, 283–343), immortality practitioner Tao Hongjing (陶弘景, 456–536), and, later, the eccentric ascetic Wang Chongyang (王重阳, 1112–1170) into various schools, sects, traditions, and popular cultures, representing different stages of Daoist history, different dimensions of philosophical and religious teachings, and different forms of syncretic Daoism as well as intensive interaction between them.

Confucianism and Daoism became two main streams of Chinese thought after a long evolution.[17] According to the *Records of the Grand Historian* (*shiji*, 史記, the first proper history book in China recording legendary and actual historical figures and events supported by comparatively reliable materials as well as by comments of the author Sima Qian (c.145–87 BCE), the historian during the reign of the Emperor Wu of the Western Han Dynasty), Confucius was a junior contemporary of

[15] Jochim, *Chinese Religions*, p. 9.
[16] Kohn, *Introducing Daoism*, p. 86.
[17] Fung, *A Short History of Chinese Philosophy*, p. 30.

Laozi who was the librarian of the Zhou Empire. Confucius went to the capital to learn from Laozi on ritual, probably when he was 34 years old. Of the many stories that surrounded the meeting of the two 'founders', the most famous recorded that Confucius told his students that Laozi could only be regarded as the mysterious dragon. Stories about the encounters and significant differences between Confucius and 'Daoist' recluses were also recorded in the *Analects*, for example, the Keeper of the Stone Gate, the Mad Carriage Driver of Chu, and the Farmers at the Ford. On these occasions Confucius and his disciples were ridiculed or scorned by the latter and Confucius remarked in disagreement with Daoist ideas and ideals.[18]

## TYPES OF CONFUCIAN AND DAOIST EXPERIENCES

'Religious experience' has been used to refer to a variety of experiences that are common to human spirituality. Its diversity of references can be seen from the fact that a number of such terms are in use interchangeably with it as 'spiritual experience', 'mystical experience', 'cosmic consciousness', 'paranormal experience', or 'psychological experience'. As far as the references of religious experience are concerned, we can find two broad categories. On the one hand, religious experience is said to be the same or similar to individuals' daily experience. William James was particularly concerned with 'the feelings, acts, and experiences of individual men in their solitude, so far as they apprehend themselves to stand in relation to whatever they may consider the divine'.[19] From this, Peggy Morgan comes to suggest that religious experience is none other than 'ordinary, everyday experience in depth'.[20] On the other hand, religious experience is associated with the mystic realm or exists in the transmission between the visible and the invisible world. Ninian Smart confirms that 'A religious experience involves some kind of "perception" of the *invisible* world, or involves a perception that some visible person or thing is a manifestation of the invisible world',[21] and that religious experience is 'a deep awareness of a benevolent non-physical power which appears to be partly or wholly beyond, and far greater than, the individual self'.[22] For other scholars, to be qualified as

---

[18] *The Analects of Confucius*, p. 150.
[19] James, *The Varieties of Religious Experience*, pp. 29–30.
[20] Morgan, "Continuing the Work," p. 20.
[21] Ninian Smart, *The Religious Experience of Mankind*, New York: Charles Scribner's Sons, third edition, 1984, p. 15.
[22] Hardy, *The Spiritual Nature of Man*, p. 1.

'religious experience', it must be associated with the mystical, the numinous, or the transcendental[23].

In the context of ancient Confucianism and Daoism, there is a central theme running through most religious experiences, namely, the unity between the human and the spiritual, between the secular and the sacred, or between the immanent and the transcendent, typically expressed as the harmony of Heaven and Humans (*tianren heyi*, 天人合一), although Confucianism and Daoism interpret what Heaven and humans are in quite different terms. Following this theme, we can classify the major forms of religious experience into three types, respectively centred on three kinds of relationships. The first type of religious experience is of a metaphysical nature, aiming at the ontological security through apprehending the unity between what is high (the fundamental law of Heaven or the Way) and what is low (learning or practices), to smooth out their tension, and to gain or regain harmony between the ontological power and human activities. The second type is of an existentialistic nature, derived from early ancestor worship and aiming at the continuity between the past and the present, to enable the experients to make sense of seemingly irrational or unpredictable realities. The third type is of a mystic nature aiming at the harmony between the internal and the external, through cultivating the human heart-mind (*xin*, 心) and/or body, either to realize the virtue within, to make the vital force (*qi*, 氣) grow, or to strengthen the vital essence (*jing*, 精) in which the perfect unity of the external world and the internal world, the mind and the body, and the material and the spiritual would be reached.

With all these three types of religious experiences in Confucianism and Daoism, we can identify a strong tendency towards moderate anthropocentrism. The experiences recorded or implied in the classics are often concerned with immanent issues of secular importance, involving either moral questions (as seen in the *Analects*) or mystical issues (as observed in the *Daode jing*). Due to the mundane contents of Confucian experiences, some scholars have suggested that Confucianism is no more a religion than Platonism or Aristotelianism.[24] It is observed that 'Great Western Sinologues such as Legge and Giles have emphasized the agnostic character of Confucianism,' and people like Derk Bodde even suggested that 'The Chinese have been less concerned with the supernatural than with the worlds of nature and man. They are

---

[23]  Maxwell and Tschudin, *Seeing the Invisible*, p. 15.
[24]  Fung, *Short History of Chinese Philosophy*, p. 1.

not a people for whom religious ideas and activities constitute an all-important and absorbing part of life'.[25] Confucius was sometimes seen as completely indifferent to religious issues, since it is recorded in the *Analects* that the Master never talked about four things, namely prodigies, miraculous powers, disorders, and spirits. If religious experience were to be defined in terms of involving these powers, then we would have to conclude that Confucian experiences can hardly be said to be religious. However, there are many other occasions on which Confucius demonstrated ultimate concerns about human life and destiny. Although his emphasis was on how to serve humans and not on how to serve the spirits, he took the understanding of human affairs as the necessary path leading to the understanding of the spiritual world. For example, when his disciple asked what wisdom was, he confirmed that wisdom was to 'devote yourself earnestly to man's duties, and respect spiritual beings, but keep them at a distance'.[26]

Are such attitudes and experiences religious? De Vos correctly points out that 'a system of thought can be considered a religion only if something is held sacred within this system', but he then proceeds to conclude, controversially, that since in Confucianism one has to look to some source other than the supernatural for the embodiment of the sacred, it is impossible to identify it as a religion.[27] The Confucian experience of the sacred is less concerned with the supernatural than with humanity, but it is not simply humanistic. It is rooted in the unity between the human and what we deem as the sacred. Involving spirits but not being confined to it, Confucian experience demonstrates a unique feature of spiritual humanism.[28]

The sacred nature of Daoist experiences equally challenges our perception of religious experiences. Early Daoist texts are not concerned solely with religious matters, as Livia Kohn put it: 'The *Daode jing* can be read as a religious, political, military, or naturalistic treatise, dealing with psychology, the natural world, or society ... while there is an

[25] Yang, *Religion in Chinese Society*, p. 4.
[26] *The Analects of Confucius*, trans. Lau, pp. 84, 107. Arthur Waley seems to be more enthusiastic about the religious nature of Confucius' attitude. He translates this paragraph as 'The master said, he who devotes himself to securing for his subjects what it is right they should have, who by respect for the spirits keeps them at a distance, may be termed wise'. He further explains: 'When the Spirits of hills and streams do not receive their proper share of ritual and sacrifice, they do not "keep their distance" but "possess" human beings, causing madness, sickness, pestilence etc.' (*The Analects of Confucius*, trans. Waley, p. 120, fn 2).
[27] Tu et al., *The Confucianism World Observed*, p. 12.
[28] Tu, "A Spiritual Turn in Philosophy."

obvious relation of Dao to the absolute of mystics in general, it is not clear whether it is immanent or transcendent'.[29] Many people have seen Daoist maxims or poetic verses as philosophically oriented and concerned only with how to lead a natural way of life. The key for our understanding Daoist experiences is the word of Dao, which Julia Ching believes to be 'an equivalent of both the Greek word *logos*, the Word, and the other Greek word *hodos*'.[30] It is usually translated as the Way, although on many occasions it is simply left untranslated as 'Dao' in pinyin or 'Tao' in the Wade-Giles transliteration system. It is the Dao rather than spirits per se or religion in a normal sense that characterizes Daoist experiences. For example, in chapter 60 of the *Daode jing*, we read that

> If Tao [Dao] is employed to rule the empire,
> Spiritual beings will lose their supernatural power.
> Not that they lose their spiritual power,
> But their spiritual power can no longer harm people.[31]

Different from other traditions where conquering or possessing underlies all kinds of religious experiences, in Daoism it is submission, yielding, or giving away that characterizes Dao. Dao is thus compared to water because water 'benefits all things and does not compete with them. It dwells in (lowly) places that all disdain'.[32] It is the Dao rather than anything else that determines what we are and what we will become. Life and death are for Daoists merely different stages of natural transformation, as Zhuangzi put it that 'I received life because the time had come; I will lose it because the order of things passes on. Be content with this time and dwell in this order and then neither sorrow nor joy can touch you'.[33]

However, this does not mean that Daoist texts have nothing to do with sacred experiences. In the *Daode jing* we read the experience of the sage who becomes equivalent to Dao and enters eternity by embracing the one:

> Therefore the sage, by embracing the One becomes a model for the world.
> By not showing himself, he becomes illustrious.

[29] Kohn, *Introducing Daoism*, p. 25.
[30] Ching, *Chinese Religions*, p. 87.
[31] Chan, *A Source Book in Chinese Philosophy*, p. 168.
[32] Ibid., p. 143.
[33] de Bary and Bloom, *Sources of Chinese Tradition*, p. 109.

By not being important, he becomes prominent.
By not being given to self-praise, he is given credit.
By not promoting himself, he endures for long.[34]

Religious experiences in Confucianism and Daoism involve both the secular and the sacred, the core of which is to seek the harmony between them rather than to separate them. To be more precise, religious experience in a Confucian and Daoist context often arises when an individual is aware of something that is both above us and within us and whose action or intention has had or will have a direct impact on our life. Confucians and Daoists are consciously engaged in the interaction between the sacred and the human. On the one hand, what enables humans to be human is not by their animal qualities but by their spiritual longing for moral excellence (*de*, 德), or eternity (*jiu*, 久), or immortality (*bu xiu*, 不朽). This longing is closely related to their views on the extra-human power that is represented, respectively, by *tian* (天, Heaven) or Dao (道, the Way), and that is understood as determining human experience of life and destiny. This kind of experience is often involved with the process of how to overcome human finitude, and can therefore be termed as 'transcending experience'. On the other hand, attention is directed to human matters dealing with ethical, political, communal, familial, and personal dimensions of life, through cultivating the heart-mind, human nature (*xing*, 性), the vital power (*qi*, 氣), the vital essence (*jing*, 精), and the spirit (*shen*, 神) within to enable the inborn potential to be fully manifested, developed, or to enable humans to be one with the cosmic power (*qi*, 氣). As this kind of experience is dependent on human efforts and consciousness, we call it 'human-centred experience'.

## TRANSCENDING EXPERIENCES

Despite a clear focus on how to lead a moral or natural life in the human world, Confucian and Daoist experiences demonstrate characteristics of transcending secularity by consciously attaching themselves to the ultimate power. Of the embodiments of the transcendent, *tian* is the most frequently used term to which a sense of 'the absolute dependence' is present. In the long history *tian* was indeed the gravity centre for a great proportion of religious experiences among ancient Confucian and Daoist practitioners. Although adopting 'Heaven' as a convenient

---

[34] Ibid., p. 85.

English translation in this chapter, *tian* is in fact a very difficult word to define, and its meaning is stretched between the supernatural power or the sublime 'law' that governs all the world, to the natural sky that hangs above the earth, while ambiguous among the vast areas in between. However, compared with the meaning it is perceived of in modern times, it was much more religious and spiritual in ancient China. From the Shang and Zhou periods onwards, Heaven was claimed to be the patron deity of the royal house to whom only the king or emperor was legitimately entitled to make sacrifices on behalf of his subjects. This is evidenced in many passages of the *Book of History* and the *Book of Poetry*, two of the oldest extant texts recording ideas and experiences in early China. Heaven, the Decree or Will or Mandate of Heaven (*tian ming*, 天命) was portrayed as the ultimate being that determined success or failure in the human world, placing a particular responsibility on the shoulders of the head of the state: 'Heaven loves the people, and the sovereign should reverently carry out (this mind) of Heaven'.[35] This perception was later gradually absorbed into popular religions and folklores and Heaven became the supreme Lord (*huang tian*, 皇天 or *tian di*, 天帝) who ruled the spiritual as well as human world: 'The Monarch of Heaven has general control of the six paths, and he is the divine authority'.[36]

In the *Analects of Confucius*, *tian* appears forty-nine times. Apart from twenty-three times when it is used as part of the phrase for the world or empire (*tian xia*, 天下), the rest are mainly used as the spiritual or transcendental being or power. For example, it is associated with *ming* as the decree of Heaven, as Confucius taught that a gentleman must stand in awe of three things, the first of which was the Decree of Heaven. When used alone, Heaven represents the Transcendent of the Confucian world: 'Life and death are a matter of Destiny; wealth and honor depend on Heaven'.[37] When Confucius was not understood appropriately and his students asked for a reason, Confucius loudly pronounced that he did not complain against Heaven, nor did he blame other people. What he wanted to do was simply to study from below through to what was up. He was confident that if he was ever understood thoroughly, that could be by Heaven only.[38] Heaven was also

[35] "Shu King (The Book of History)," p. 127.
[36] Dudbridge, *Religious Experience and Lay Society in T'ang China*, p. 50.
[37] *The Analects of Confucius*, trans. Lau, pp. 113, 140.
[38] 'The Master said, 'There is no one who knows me'. Zigong said, 'How could it be that no one knows you?' The Master said, 'I bear neither a grievance against Heaven nor a

employed as the power that was believed to sanction, approve, or condemn a particular behaviour. When Confucius was under the suspicion of doing something inappropriate, he swore in the name of Heaven: 'If I have done anything improper, may Heaven's curse be on me, may Heaven's curse be on me!'[39] It seems clear that on these occasions Heaven functions in the same way as God in other religious and cultural traditions, who is regarded as the only guarantor for human affairs.[40] Transcendent as Heaven is, individual human beings take its blessing or mandate as an assurance of success.[41] It was this teaching that became the basic tenet of Confucian doctrines on politics and education.

From what has been said in the last paragraphs about the cases of Confucius, we can see that the transcending nature of Confucian experiences is evident in three respects, involving three kinds of belief and experience that are closely related to Heaven. First, Confucians hold a firm faith in Heaven as the divine order or as the Supreme Lord, to whom or which individual Confucians devote themselves entirely and sincerely. Secondly, Confucians have an unquestionable belief in human destiny, the course of which depends upon both Heaven as the transcendent power and human fulfilment of what is decreed. Thirdly, Confucians uphold a strong commitment to the Principles or Law of Heaven, which is believed not only to be the absolute rules for human life, but also to be knowable through divination, observation, the teachings of the sage and self-cultivation.

Religious experience in Confucianism is often identical with moral experience.[42] In Confucian ethics, Heaven is located as the sole source

---

grudge against men. And as learning here below penetrates to what is above, it must be Heaven that knows me!' *Sources of Chinese Tradition*, p. 58.

[39] *The Analects of Confucius*, trans. Lau, p. 85.

[40] In a way similar to monotheism where people exclaim in such words as 'My God'! or 'Jesus Christ'! 'Heaven' is often used in interjections, when the Chinese express their amazement or unbelievable surprise by exclaiming 'My Heaven!'.

[41] In the 2005 religious experience survey in Mainland China, we found that belief in Heaven or the Will of Heaven both intensify people's religious consciousness, and account for 25.7 per cent of the total reported experiences. Yao and Badham, *Religious Experience in Contemporary China*.

[42] Chung-ying Cheng claims, for example, that religious experience in Confucianism is concerned with the ultimate and the total reality, 'in which the moral consciousness of the human person becomes a specific manifestation of the human person's consciousness of the ultimate and the total, and the consciousness of the ultimate and the total in the human person becomes also a specific moral fulfilment of the human person's nature and its ultimate goodness. Furthermore, morality is where the relation of the individual to the ultimate and the total and its significance are realized simultaneously'. Cheng, *New Dimensions*, p. 454.

of virtue from which all moral norms and good character spring, and as the criterion by which all human behaviours are measured or evaluated. Confucius claimed that his virtue was produced (*sheng*, 生) by Heaven, and he committed himself to learning when he was 15 years old, and by 50 he already understood the decree of Heaven. In a typical Confucian context, *ming*, 命 refers both to human destiny (*ming*) and to the decree of Heaven (*tian ming*), and the two are often interchangeably used for the predetermined realm to be understood. In the words of Mengzi, Heaven has the power to determine who should rule the world: 'If Heaven wishes to give the Empire to a good and wise man, then it should be given to a good and wise man'; however, using 'wishes to give' here does not necessarily mean that Heaven is really a personal god, as we can see from Mengzi that 'When a thing is done though by no one, then it is the work of Heaven; when a thing comes about though no one brings it about, then it is destiny'.[43] Kwong-Loi Shun is convinced that this sentence has clearly revealed that destiny and Heaven are associated with each other, but with different emphases: 'the difference between "*t'ien*" and "*ming*" is probably that the former emphasizes the source of such things and the latter the outcome'.[44]

Apart from the spiritual and ethical applications, Confucian experience also relies on Heaven as the metaphysical entity responsible for what the world is and what it will become. While an ordinary person cannot know Heaven directly, he can know his own nature, and then the nature of other people, beings, and things by which he may be able to experience the power of Heaven indirectly. It is believed that all are produced by Heaven from which the common nature has been formed: 'Heaven gives birth to all things in such a way that they have one root' (*yiben*, 一本).[45] Taken as the ultimate source of beings, things, and events and the laws of all movement and quietude, the Confucian Heaven was gradually interpreted as 'Nature'. Heaven reveals the secrets of the universe through the way of changes. Both Confucius and Mengzi insisted that 'Heaven does not speak but reveals itself through its acts and deeds',[46] and Xunzi directly defined Heaven as Nature and denied any favour or disfavour Heaven could inflict on humans: 'The course of Nature [Heaven] is consistent ... If you respond to the constancy of Nature's course with good government, there will be

---

[43] *The Analects of Confucius*, trans. Lau, p. 145.
[44] Shun, *Mencius and Early Chinese Thought*, p. 77.
[45] *The Analects of Confucius*, trans. Lau, p. 105.
[46] Ibid., p. 143.

good fortune; if you respond to it with disorder, there will be misfortune'.[47] This way, the transcending Heaven is successfully transformed to the mundane politics and ethics which is best illustrated by the poetic verses quoted in Mengzi: 'Heaven sees with the eyes of the people; Heaven hears with the ears of the people'.[48] This has also paved the way for a Confucian basic doctrine that the human experiencing of Heaven or the Way of Heaven must be made through ordinary matters and things at hand.

Compared with Confucians, early Daoist philosophers tend not to take Heaven as a moral or spiritual power or entity. In the *Daode jing*, although *tian* is used ninety-two times, it appears in the phrase for the world (*tian xia*) sixty times, and in the phrase of *tian di* (天地, the world or Nature) ten times. In the remaining twenty-two times when *tian* is used alone, it mostly refers to the metaphysical entity existing before the birth of humans. However, questions might be raised concerning the true nature of Heaven when we read in chapter 59 that 'To rule people and to serve Heaven there is nothing better than to be frugal', and in chapter 67 that 'When Heaven is to save a person, Heaven will protect him through deep love'.[49] What does it mean by 'serving Heaven'? How can Heaven, if being a natural entity only, come to protect humans through deep love? These cases provide evidence that even in the most agnostic texts, the Daoist experience of Heaven is more than phenomenological and naturalistic; it may also point to something spiritual, ethical, or mysterious.

Central to the transcending experiences of Daoism is not Heaven but the Way (Dao/Tao). The Way is mystic by nature and is therefore beyond human language. In the *Daode jing* we read that 'The Way that can be spoken of is not the constant Way'; the Way is equated with the 'Spirit of Valley', and is likened to be the 'mysterious female', the gate of which is called 'the root of Heaven and Earth'.[50] Sublime and subtle, the Daoist Way is not always appreciated by all the people. People of different intelligence and spirit would experience it differently:

> When the highest type of men hear Tao,
> They diligently practice it.
> When the average type of men hear Tao,
> They half believe in it.

---

[47] *Xunzi*, p. 533.
[48] *The Analects of Confucius*, trans. Lau, p. 144.
[49] Chan, *A Source Book in Chinese Philosophy*, pp. 167, 171.
[50] de Bary and Bloom, *Sources of Chinese Tradition*, pp. 79, 82.

When the lowest type of men hear Tao,
They laugh heartily at it ...
The Tao which is bright appears to be dark.
The Tao which goes forward appears to fall backward ...
Tao is hidden and nameless.
Yet it is Tao alone that skillfully provides for all and brings them to
    perfection.[51]

On the other hand, although the Way is transcending, Daoist experience is not to depart totally from the human; rather it is said to return to one's origin. Chapter 16 states unambiguously that

To return to destiny is called the eternal.
To know the eternal is called Enlightenment.
Not to know the eternal is to act blindly to result in disaster.
He who knows the eternal is all-embracing.
Being all-embracing, he is impartial.
Being impartial, he is kingly (universal).
Being kingly, he is one with Nature.
Being one with Nature, he is in accord with Tao.
Being in accord with Tao, he is everlasting,
And is free from danger throughout his lifetime.[52]

The concept of the Way is not exclusively used by Daoists; it is in fact universal to all Chinese philosophies and religions. Experiences of the Way are widely observable in Confucian and Mohist practices as well. Taking the Way as a central concept, Confucians use it nonetheless differently from early Daoist philosophers. For Confucians, the Way is not as mystic an entity as in Daoism that is taken as the mysterious origin of the world; the divine nature of the Way is manifested by being associated with Heaven that is taken as the guide for the way of humans. The Way of Heaven is not secular, however; its spiritual depth is not easily apprehensible to an ordinary mind. The Way is one of the key concepts in the *Analects*, where it appears eighty-nine times. In all these usages it is embedded in human experiences on the ultimate principle or norm. Confucius was fully aware of the subtlety and profoundness of the Way of Heaven so much so that he seldom talked about it, but at the same time he pronounced that 'In the morning, hear the Way; in the evening, die content!'[53]

[51] Chan, *A Source Book in Chinese Philosophy*, p. 160.
[52] Ibid., pp. 147–48.
[53] Ibid., p. 26.

Mysterious as the Daoist Way is, it seems that early Daoists did not simply place it outside of human well-being. On the contrary, only in the interaction between the Way and human heart-mind can we truly experience its power and nature. In the chapter on 'Inward Training' in the *Book of Guanzi*[54] it is said that:

Tao has no fixed residence, and it only stays inside the benevolent heart of human beings. If the heart is tranquil, and the vitality is in order, Tao will stop and stay there. Tao is not far away from us, and life of human beings can be generated if it has inherited there ... If one cultivates his mind and remains serene, Tao could be reached.[55]

Similar to Daoists, Confucians also considered the Way not to be grasped by intelligence but by experience, and can be either taken or abandoned. In an ideal society, those who follow the Way would be promoted to the position of ruling, while those who abuse it should be demoted or even executed; as the right way of life, the Way is taken as the righteous goal of life that must be realized by practicing what is right. Confucians see the Way as part of human life experiences: 'The Way cannot be separated from [humans] for a moment. What can be separated [from humans] is not the Way'.[56] The reason why the Way is part of our life but is difficult grasp fully is said to be that we often deviate from the Middle Way (*zhong dao*, 中道): 'I know why the Way is not understood. The Worthy go beyond it and the unworthy do not come up to it'.[57] Imminence and immanence in Confucianism are therefore perfectly combined in their experiences of the Way, and the transcending experience is successfully placed in personal and communal daily life. From his own experience Confucius taught his students:

Have the firm faith to devote yourself to learning, and abide to the death in the good Way. Enter not a state that is in peril; stay not in a state that is in danger. Show yourself when the Way prevails in the Empire, but hide yourself when it does not. It is a shameful matter

[54] The chapter entitled 'Inward Training' (*neiye*, 內業) is called by A. C. Graham 'probably the oldest mystical text in China', and is regarded as representing the earliest and original Daoism by Harold David Roth. Roth argues that 'One of the distinctive contributions to the discussion of Daoist origins is that it represents the earliest extant presentations of a mystical practice in all early sources of Taoist thought'. *Original Tao-Inward Training and the Foundations of Taoist Mysticism*, p. 2.

[55] *Guanzi*, p. 989.

[56] Chan, *A Source Book in Chinese Philosophy*, p. 98.

[57] Ibid., p. 99.

to be poor and humble when the Way prevails in the state. Equally, it is a shameful matter to be rich and noble when the Way falls in disuse in the state.[58]

Focusing on the transcending values hidden in ethical matters, Confucians do not venture to any extra-human events for spiritual experience. The only instance we find in the *Analects* that is close to a spiritual encounter is perhaps Confucius' dreaming of the Duke of Zhou, the chief designer of the ritual and music culture and the representative of the 'Way of Former Kings'.[59] This pales in comparison with those claimed by Daoists, the most frequently quoted of which is the first Heavenly Master, Zhang Daoling's, 张道陵 reception of the Supreme Lord Lao[60], and the deified Laozi, who 'on the first day of the fifth moon', met Zhang 'in the cave of the Quting mountain in the district of Shu', and 'appointed him Master of the Three Heavens, of the One Correct qi-energy of Peace of the Great Mysterious Capital'.[61]

### HUMAN-CENTRED EXPERIENCES

Full of the sense of 'the numinous' that is evoked or awakened through transcending experiences, the majority of Confucians and early Daoists are nevertheless leaned to secular life, enriched by various experiences involving human nature and destiny often in the connection with the family and social networks. It is natural for them to invigorate religious experiences concerning *zu* (祖, ancestor), *li* (禮, ritual), *xin* (the heart-mind), and *qi* (氣, the vital energy).

From the earliest recorded history down to today, religious experiences in China have been under heavy influences of ancestor worship, and presented in the form of encounters with the spirits of ancestors.[62] This demonstrates the importance of the family for religious experience to which Confucianism is primarily associated. One of the key

---

[58] *The Analects of Confucius*, trans. Lau, p. 94.
[59] Confucius deplored the decline of his physical and psychological conditions when for a long time he did not have a dream in which he consulted his sage, the Duke of Zhou. *The Analects of Confucius*, trans. Lau, p. 86.
[60] Fabrizio, *The Encyclopedia of Taoism*, II, p. 1222.
[61] de Bary and Bloom, *Sources of Chinese Tradition*, p. 402.
[62] In the survey of 2005 on religious experience in Mainland China, it has been reported that 'in the experiences of religious or spiritual powers, 20.8% of the interviewees reported that they were once or frequently influenced by their ancestors, which ranks the fourth highest among all the eight options'. Yao and Badham, *Religious Experience in Contemporary China*, p. 61.

teachings the *Book of History* left to later Confucians is that Heaven and ancestors are closely related, and the mandate of Heaven would be lost if the royal descendent did not manifest the brilliant virtues of their ancestors: 'The Mandate of Heaven is not easily [preserved]. Heaven is hard to depend on. Those who have lost the mandate did so because they could not practice and carry on the reverence and the brilliant virtue of their forefathers'.[63] Confucianism carried on 'the Way of the former kings', and placed an emphasis on consulting the spirits of the dead, making sacrifices to forefathers and praising the great achievements of the past. In this tradition, ancestors were believed to be not only alive but also powerful in determining the destiny and welfare of the living community. The spirits of departed ancestors were viewed as guarantors and protectors of living human beings, and the living were regarded as supporters and assistants for the departed. It was believed that if not provided with proper sacrifices and if not informed periodically about the state of the family's affairs, ancestors would be upset and could return to punish their descendants.[64] Confucius, who believed that the intimate relationship between the ancestor and the descendant was the foundation of the human world, accepted and developed this tradition, stressing that descendants should give the three years' mourning to their deceased parents not only for the repaying of their care and love but also to magnify their glorious virtues.[65] He required that services to ancestors be given as if they were alive, and sacrifices to spiritual beings be performed as if these beings were in front of us.[66] From this we can see that Confucius did not bluntly reject the other world; rather, he regarded the connection between the past and the present as the most important part of human experiences. He stressed the importance of filial piety (*xiao*, 孝), and used this concept to characterise not only the proper rituals of sacrifice to the ancestors but also

[63] Chan, *A Source Book in Chinese Philosophy*, p. 7.
[64] In the *Book of Rites*, we read a conversation between Confucius and his disciple. The disciple asked about the meaning of spirits and ghosts, and Confucius explained that when the intellectual spirit is in its fullest station it is called the vital power, and when the animal soul is in its fullest station it is called a ghost. It is the union of spirits and ghosts that forms the highest exhibition of doctrine. All the living must die, and dying, return to the ground; this is what is called 'ghost'. *Sacred Books of China*, p. 220, with my moderations.
[65] 'The noble person, while (his parents) are still alive, reverently nourishes them; and when they are dead, he reverently sacrifices to them; his thought is how to the end of life not to disgrace them'. de Bary and Bloom, *Sources of Chinese Tradition*, p. 342.
[66] de Bary and Bloom, *Sources of Chinese Tradition*, p. 48.

the proper attitude and behaviour towards living parents.[67] Later Confucians further developed and propagated this idea, so that filial piety acquired a high profile on the Confucian agenda.

Ancestor worship also explains why ritual is so important for Confucianism. Furthering the original ritual as part of 'sacrificial rites', Confucians elaborated on the moral contents and purpose of rites and rituals, as it is stated in the *Book of Rites* that it was necessary for ritual experiences to be accompanied by 'sincerity and gravity in presenting the offerings to spiritual Beings on occasions of supplication, thanksgiving, and various sacrifices'.[68] Interpreted as such, rites were intended to harmonize the beginning and the end, the living and the dead, and the cosmos and the human, facilitating the transmission from the spiritual world to the human world, as confirmed in the *Book of Rites* that:

> The rites to be observed by all under heaven were intended to promote the return to the beginning; to promote spiritual beings; to promote the harmonious use of all resources and appliances of government; to promote righteousness; and to promote humility ... Let these five things be united through the rites for the regulation of all under heaven, and though there may be some extravagant and perverse who are not kept in order, they will be few.[69]

With ancestor worship came the issues about life and death. Both Confucians and Daoists tend to regard life and death as natural matters, but their experiences reveal different spiritual orientations. For early Confucians, life and death are a matter predetermined by one's destiny, while for Daoist philosophers, one's life and death depend on the Way: being close to the Way is to live, while departing from the Way is to die[70]. Therefore, having a long and meaningful life is regarded as good fortune, and the *Book of History* lists five blessings for all people, most of them concerned with what a good and long life is: 'of the five happinesses, the first is long life; the second is riches; the third is soundness of body and serenity of mind; the fourth is the love of virtue; the fifth is an end

---

[67] Arthur Waley notices that in the *Book of Poetry*, filial piety refers almost exclusively to piety towards the dead, while in the *Analects*, it is used for both piety to the dead and love of the living parents. *The Analects of Confucius*, trans. Waley, p. 38.
[68] *Sacred Books of China*, p. 64.
[69] Ibid., pp. 219–20 (with moderations).
[70] 'When man is born, he is tender and weak. At death, he is stiff and hard. All things, the grass as well as trees, are tender and supple while alive. When dead, they are withered and dried' (chapter 76). Chan, *A Source Book in Chinese Philosophy*, p. 174.

crowning one's life'.[71] Both Confucians and Daoists tend to highlight the importance of self-cultivation for a good life, and the majority of their experiences are associated with various kinds of practices in nourishing the life, which is considered not only one of the duties to Heaven but also parallel to the burial of the dead and services to the ancestors.[72]

Daoist philosophy in general rejects any unnatural means to prolonging one's physical life, but the *Daode jing* considers '*jiu*', 久 (eternality) and '*changsheng*', 长生 (long life or immortality) the necessary quality of the Dao: 'Heaven is eternal and Earth everlasting. They can be eternal and everlasting because they do not exist for themselves, and for this reason can exist forever'.[73] Zhuangzi uses one of his dreams to make a claim that our experience of being human might merely have been an illusory image.[74] While claiming that a 'true person' (*zhen ren*, 真人) would neither fear death nor be over joyful in life, Zhuangzi nevertheless taught his disciples that 'Follow the middle, go by what is constant, and you can stay in one piece, keep yourself alive, look after your parents, and live out your years'.[75] In 'Immortality Daoism' that was developed later, cultivating longevity is not only a moral duty to the self but also one of the strongest religious aspirations. For this reason, they adopted a variety of ways to cultivate immortality, generating a large amount of experiences in practicing herb medicine, meditation, *qigong*, dietetic or sexual practices, and alchemy. The so-called external alchemy (*wai dan*, 外丹) was to produce an 'immortal elixir' by heating and mixing various chemicals such as mercury.[76] However, its popularity gradually faded, not only because it failed to prolong life, but also because the poisonous chemicals often shortened life or killed the people. Later Daoists developed what is called 'internal alchemy' (*nei dan*, 内丹) as a new way to gain immortality, producing the 'elixir' by cultivating the vital power within one's body.[77] Daoist experiences of

[71] de Bary and Bloom, *Sources of Chinese Tradition*, p. 32.
[72] 'This great mutual consideration and harmony would ensure the constant nourishment of the living, the burial of the dead, and the service of the spirits (of the departed)'. The Treatise on Li Yun of the *Book of Rites*, see *Sacred Books of China*, p. 391.
[73] Chan, *A Source Book in Chinese Philosophy*, pp. 142–43.
[74] *Zhuangzi*, p. 47.
[75] de Bary and Bloom, *Sources of Chinese Tradition*, p. 103.
[76] Ge Hong, *Baopuzi*, 抱朴子 (*Master Embracing Simplicity*), particularly the chapter of 'Xianyao', 仙藥 (Transcendent Medicines) of the Inner Volume (neipian, 内篇). See Wang, *Baopuzi neipian jiaoshi* 抱樸子校釋.
[77] 'Many Taoist texts of the Song dynasty (960–1279 C.E.) onward set forth as their highest ideal the immortality and heavenly ascension of the "internal elixir"

cultivating the vital power have significantly enriched the sources of Chinese medicine, martial arts, and physical education.

Confucianism places an emphasis on cultivating life too, but their experiences are mostly in the moral field. Idealists such as Mengzi started with their particular views on the heart-mind. For Mengzi, the heart-mind is what we get from Heaven, and is originally good. Due to environmental contamination and human negligence, however, this originally good heart-mind is frequently spoiled or even totally lost. Confucian learning for him is therefore nothing but making efforts to find the astray heart-mind (*qiu fang xin*, 求放心). Mengzi deplored that when losing chickens and dogs people all knew to look for them; but when losing the heart-mind they were indifferent. Looking for the lost heart-mind is understood as an inward journey the noble person (*junzi*, 君子) must pursue, and it is also called 'preserving' (*cun*, 存) or 'nourishing' (*yang*, 養) the heart-mind because goodness is not imposed upon us from outside. Morally nourishing is to cultivate virtues that are believed to be innate to the heart/mind and to encourage growth of a moral character through cultivating one's nature (*yang xin*, 養性), nourishing the vital power and following the righteous course. The nourishing of the heart-mind and the vital power is presented in a mystical process of moral experience that enables one to nourish and possess the 'vast and flowing power' (*yang haoran zhi qi*, 養浩然之气). If nourished with uprightness and not injured, this vast and flowing power is believed to be able to 'fill the space between Heaven and Earth'.[78] A noble person nourishes his heart-mind by virtues, and such a heart-mind would not be subject to the swing of external and material achievements or failures. This is what Mengzi described as the 'unmoved heart-mind' (*bu dong xin*, 不动心), which he said he had achieved when he was forty years old. A noble person is noble, not in the sense that he has the originally good heart-mind while others do not, but in that the noble person preserves or retains his heart-mind. A small person (*xiao ren*, 小人) is morally degenerated not because he was born evil but because he did not look after his heart-mind properly.

To Mengzi, a noble person has no other worries but is anxious to be an equal of the sage. He believes that everybody is able to be a sage

---

(*nei dan*), a divine, internal entity concocted from the pure, subtle forces latent in the body. When it ascends, this entity, which is also known as the "yang spirit" (*yang shen*) or the "body outside of the body" (*shenwai zhi shen*), is said to leave the mortal body behind'. Eskildsen, *Asceticism in Early Taoist Religion*, p. 8.

[78] de Bary and Bloom, *Sources of Chinese Tradition*, p. 127.

because they already have the same heart-mind as that of the sage. According to Mengzi, the whole life is an organic experience that starts from preserving this heart-mind, taking care of it and not allowing it to be lost, and continues to develop and expand it in the way of doing nothing that is not benevolent and acting in no other way except in full accordance with the rites. The ultimate end of the process is to know Heaven and to serve Heaven: 'For a man to give full realization to his heart is for him to understand his nature, and a man who knows his own nature will know Heaven'.[79] This experience must not be simply understood as an epistemological event, but a spiritual process in which one would be totally transformed and enlightened; or in other words, it is the experiential path to be a sage. This point can be best illustrated by the experience of Wang Yangming (王阳明, 1472–1529), a Confucian idealist master of the Ming dynasty (1368–1644) who said that he gained this 'enlightenment' when he was thirty-six years old during exile in a remote area, whereby he came to fully realize that human nature was where sagehood truly lay and we should look into our own mind for the ultimate truth: 'The one night, in the year 1508, he awoke and shouted so loudly that people living nearby were startled. What caused his excitement was that upon awakening he had suddenly discovered that so-called things are not entities in the external world but objects of consciousness'.[80]

In Daoism, cultivating the heart-mind is also important for the connection between the temporary and the eternal. The *Daode jing* advocates that the 'emptied heart-mind' is the necessary path to eternity:

> To know harmony means to be in accord with the eternal.
> To be in accord with the eternal means to be enlightened.
> To force the growth of life means ill omen. For the mind to employ
>   the vital force without restraint means violence . . .
> Which means being contrary to Tao.
> Whatever is contrary to Tao will soon perish'.[81]

Zhuangzi advocates the 'fasting of the mind', which is explained as:

> Maintaining the unity of your will, listen not with your ears but with your mind. Listen not with your mind but with your primal breath. The ears are limited to listening, the mind is limited to

---

[79] *The Analects of Confucius*, trans. Lau, p. 182.
[80] Chang, *Wang Yang-ming*, p. 5.
[81] Chan, *A Source Book in Chinese Philosophy*, p. 166.

tallying. The primal breath, however, awaits things emptily. It is only through the Way that one can gather emptiness, and emptiness is the fasting of the mind.[82]

Daoist experience is taken as an effective tool for the realization of the ultimate truth and for sagehood or immortality. Daoist texts elaborate on the interconnection between *qi*, 氣, the vital power, *shen*, 神, spirits, and *jing*, 精, the vital essence, which are believed to be the three most essential cosmic powers not only for human transformation from the mortal to the immortal but also for the whole universe to keep in balance. For the experience of the last one, for instance, we read in the chapter on 'Internal Training' in the *Book of Guanzi*:

This is what makes life come into being:
Below, it generates the five grains,
Above, it brings about the constellated stars.
When it flows in the interstices of Heaven and Earth,
It is called 'spiritual beings';
When it is stored up inside [a person's] chest,
It is called 'sageliness'.[83]

CONCLUSION

Religious experience in ancient Confucianism and Daoism is manifested in diversified ways to reveal extensive interactions between the human and the spiritual realms. Due to the fact that the spiritual has been understood in such different terms as godly beings, divine powers, fundamental laws, sublime qualities, mysterious animals,[84] extraordinary scenarios,[85] the experiences perceived and engaged were inevitably multidimensional and multi-layered. It takes a variety of forms such as particular messages or secrets delivered by a sage or an immortal, the enlightened awareness of the ultimate truth, the deep insight into the true nature and heart-mind of humans, the encounter with mysterious figures, the seeing of extraordinary images, awakening revelations in dreams, etc.

[82] *Wandering on the Way*, p. 32.
[83] Kirkland, *Taoism – The Enduring Tradition*, p. 43.
[84] For example, dragon, phoenix, fish, or snake, which symbolise an auspicious or inauspicious sign.
[85] For example, good or bad *fengshui*, auspicious or inauspicious encounters.

Roughly divided into two categories, the transcendent-centred and the human-centred, Confucian and Daoist experiences are nonetheless converged in the common pursuits for human well-being and in the interconnection between the past, the present, and the future. Deeply embedded in all kinds of religious experience is the ultimate concern about human life and destiny which is manifested in personal, familial, political, and educational matters. The interdependence between the spiritual and the experient is the key to understanding ancient Confucian and Daoist experiences. Their relationship is initiated in mutual reliance, is sustained by the interaction between the spiritual and the person(s) concerned, and often ends up with mutual transformation. There are two kinds of action the spiritual would take to affect an experient. On the one hand, the spiritual could 'exercise restraint and control, working negatively through fear or positively as commitment, devotion, duty and love (agape)',[86] by which the spiritual functions as an inspiration for the person who is involved in a particular experience. On the other hand, the experient longs for the higher realm, either through self-cultivation, or learning, or practicing, by which he or she is physically, morally, and/or spiritually enhanced or transformed. The higher realm is not necessarily in contradiction with the lower realm, but represents a new dimension of life, a new insight into the phenomenal world, a new step in the ladder of self-empowerment, or a new experience of the old way of living. It is often experienced that the higher realm cannot be reached unless the experient works hard in the lower through his or her own efforts.

In fact, the 'higher' and the 'lower' are not appropriate words for Confucian and Daoist experiences, as they could cause misunderstandings of the so-called two stages. Religious experiences in ancient Confucianism and Daoism are not in general divided into two irrelevant realms, just as the spiritual and the human are not separated as the two opposite worlds but the two interconnected dimensions of the same world. Combined, the two dimensions become the whole of life experience while, separated, they mutually affect and transform each other. The spiritual in Confucian and Daoist experiences is both the Other power that stands above human existence and the intrinsic power that is innate to every individual's own self. The two seemingly contradicting powers are often placed to work together in the same direction. This point has been vividly illustrated by a well quoted poem from the

---

[86] Brown, *The Psychology of Religious Belief*, p. 118.

*Book of Poetry*: 'Heaven in giving birth to humankind, created for each thing its own rule. The people's common disposition is to love this admirable virtue'.[87] While the first sentence indicates that humans are subject to heavenly law, the second illustrates that the people have an innate power to initiate their love of heavenly virtue to manifest the unity between the transcendent and the immanent. No matter whatever terms are employed for Heaven and the people, this kind of interconnection, interdependence, and inter-transformation is always there, either implicitly or explicitly, in the religious experiences of ancient Confucianism and Daoism.

## References

*The Analects of Confucius*. Translated by Arthur Waley. London: George Allen & Unwin, 1938.

*The Analects of Confucius*. Translated by D. C. Lau. London: Penguin Classics, 1979.

Argyle, Michael. *Psychology and Religion: An Introduction*. London: Routledge, 2000.

Brown, Laurence Binet. *The Psychology of Religious Belief*. Cambridge, MA: Academic Press, 1987.

Chan, Wing-tsit. *A Source Book in Chinese Philosophy*. Princeton: Princeton University Press, 1963.

Chang, Carsun. *Wang Yang-ming: Idealist Philosopher of Sixteenth-century China*. New York: St. John's University Press, 1962.

Cheng, Chung-ying. *New Dimensions of Confucian and Neo-Confucian Philosophy*. Albany: State University of New York Press, 1991.

Ching, Julia. *Chinese Religions*. London: MacMillan, 1993.

De Bary, William Theodore, and Irene Bloom (eds.). *Sources of Chinese Tradition*, 2nd ed., vol. 1. New York: Columbia University Press, 1999.

Dudbridge, Glen. *Religious Experience and Lay Society in T'ang China – A Reading of Tai Fu's Kuang-i chi*. Cambridge: Cambridge University Press, 1995.

Eskildsen, Stephen. *Asceticism in Early Taoist Religion*. New York: SUNY Press, 1998.

Fung, Yu-lan. *A Short History of Chinese Philosophy: A Systematic Account of Chinese Philosophy from Its Origins to the Present Day*. Edited by Derk Bodde. New York: The Free Press, 1966.

*Guanzi*, vol. III. Nanning: Guangxi Normal University Press, 2005.

Hardy, Alister. *The Spiritual Nature of Man: A Study of Contemporary Religious Experience*. Oxford: Oxford University Press, 1979.

---

[87] de Bary and Bloom, *Sources of Chinese Tradition*, pp. 149–50.

*I Ching or Book of Changes*. Translated by Richard Wilhelm, rendered into English by Cary F. Baynes, with a foreword by C. G. Jung. London: Penguin Books, 1989.

James, William. *The Varieties of Religious Experience*. New York: Routledge, 2002.

Jensen, Lionel M. *Manufacturing Confucianism: Chinese Traditions and Universal Civilization*. Durham, NC: Duke University Press, 1998.

Jiyu, Ren (ed.). *Zhongguo Daojiao Shi*, vol. 1. Beijing: Zhongguo shehui kexue chubanshe, 2001.

Jochim, Christian. *Chinese Religions – A Cultural Perspective*. Englewood Cliffs, NJ: Prentice Hall, 1986.

Kirkland, Russell. *Taoism – The Enduring Tradition*. London: Routledge, 2004.

Kohn, Livia. *Introducing Daoism*. New York: Routledge, 2003.

Kung, Hans, and Julia Ching. *Christianity and Chinese Religions*. London: SCM Press Ltd., 1993.

Maxwell, Meg, and Verena Tschudin (eds.). *Seeing the Invisible – Modern Religious and Other Transcendent Experiences*. Harmondsworth: Penguin Books, 1990.

Morgan, Peggy. "Continuing the Work," *De Numine* 35 (2004): 20.

Pregadio, Fabrizio (ed.). *The Encyclopedia of Taoism*, II. London: Routledge, 2008.

Roth, Harold D. *Original Tao-Inward Training and the Foundations of Taoist Mysticism*. New York: Columbia University Press, 2004.

*Sacred Books of China, The Texts of Confucianism*, Part III, *The Li Ki*, I–X. Translated by James Legge. Oxford: Clarendon Press, 1885.

"Shu King (The Book of History)." Translated by James Legge, in F. Max Müller (ed.), *The Sacred Books of China*, Part I, in *The Sacred Books of the East*, vol. III. Delhi: Motilal Banarsidass, 1970.

Shun, Kwong-Loi. *Mencius and Early Chinese Thought*. Palo Alto, CA: Stanford University Press, 1997.

Smart, Ninian. *The Religious Experience of Mankind*, 3rd ed. New York: Charles Scribner's Sons, 1984.

*Sources of Chinese Tradition – From Earliest Times to 1600*, 2nd ed., vol. 1. Compiled by W. M. Theodore de Bary and Irene Bloom. New York: Columbia University Press, 1999.

Streng, Frederick J. *Understanding Religious Life*, 2nd ed., Belmont, CA: Wadsworth Publishing Company, 1976.

Sun, Anna. *Confucianism as a World Religion: Contested Histories and Contemporary Realities*. Princeton, NJ: Princeton University Press, 2013.

Tu, Wei-ming. "A Spiritual Turn in Philosophy: Rethinking the Global Significance of Confucian Humanism," *Journal of Philosophical Research* 37 (Suppl) (2012): 389–401.

Tu, Wei-ming, Milan Hejtmanek, and Alan Wachman (eds.). *The Confucianism World Observed – A Contemporary Discussion of Confucian Humanism in East Asia*. Honolulu, Hawaii: The East-West Centre, 1992.

*Wandering on the Way – Early Taoist Tales and Parables of Chuang Tzu*. Translated with an Introduction and Commentary by Victor H. Mair. New York: Bantam Books, 1994.

Wang, Ming, 王明 (coll. and annot.). Baopuzi neipian jiaoshi 抱樸子校釋. Beijing: Zhonghua shuju 中華書局, 1985.

*Xunzi*. Translated by John Knoblock. Changsha: Hunan Renmin Publishing House, 1999.

Yang, C. K. *Religion in Chinese Society: A Study of Contemporary Social Functions of Religion and Some of Their Historical Factors*. Berkeley: University of California Press, 1961.

Yao, Xinzhong. *An Introduction to Confucianism*. Cambridge: Cambridge University Press, 2000.

Yao, Xinzhong and Paul Badham. *Religious Experience in Contemporary China*. Cardiff: University of Wales Press, 2007.

*Zhuangzi*. Translated by Wang Rongpei and Ren Xiuhua. Changsha: Hunan People's Publishing House, 1997.

# 8 Religious Experience in Buddhism

DAVID BURTON

Religious experience is foundational to Buddhism, according to many accounts. Buddhism is rooted in the Buddha's Enlightenment or Awakening (*bodhi*) experience that followers of his teaching aspire to replicate. Buddhists believe that the Buddha's Enlightenment experience eradicated his suffering and ended the cycle of rebirths for him. Buddhist teachings prescribe ethical and meditative practices that are intended to reproduce this radical transformation of experience for practitioners, permanently replacing their ignorance, hatred, and greed with compassion and wisdom. Buddhist texts devote much attention to descriptions of the negative, unwholesome (Pāli: *akusala*; Sanskrit: *akuśala*) psychological states that unenlightened people experience, and the positive, wholesome (Pāli: *kusala*; Sanskrit: *kuśala*) mental states that arise, and grow progressively stronger, as the practitioner traverses the various stages on the path to Enlightenment. Buddhists are encouraged to seek experiential confirmation that the Buddha's teaching is true, rather than simply relying on faith and the testimony of others. Buddhist philosophical views are not mere intellectual exercises but are intended to be incorporated into Buddhist practitioners' experience. The efficacy of the Buddha's teachings to transform experience can be tested and confirmed by putting into practice the Buddha's ethical and meditative techniques.

However, this generalized and brief explanation of Buddhist attitudes to religious experience masks a great deal of complexity. Buddhism is extremely diverse; it includes numerous traditions that have developed over long periods of time and in many different cultures. The nature of religious experiences that Buddhists recount are varied and are relative to their specific historical, philosophical, and ritual contexts. An examination of accounts of Buddhist religious experiences reveals the wide range of insights and visions that are reported in different cultures, time periods, and Buddhist traditions.

Enlightenment is a minority pursuit in Buddhism; it is often thought to be out of reach for most Buddhists. There is a widespread Buddhist belief that we live in an age of moral and cognitive degeneracy in which Enlightenment is an unrealistic goal. Many Buddhist traditions view the pursuit of Enlightenment as a long and arduous endeavour, taking many lifetimes. Ethnographic and historical studies of monastic Buddhism demonstrate that the cultivation of Enlightened experience through meditation is less common than is often believed; ritual activities, academic study, administrative and teaching duties, menial labour and so forth take up far more time and energy for many Buddhist monastics. A few religious virtuosos may engage in meditation in a more focused manner (Sharf 1995: 241–46; Gyatso 1999: 116–17). Even when Enlightenment is the aim to which a Buddhist aspires, there is considerable heterogeneity in the descriptions of the experience, and the techniques that are said to bring it about.

For most Buddhists, including the laity and many monastics, less exalted experiences through good actions (Pāli: *kamma*; Sanskrit: *karma*) are often the objective, such as the experience of fortunate rebirths and wellbeing in this life. In the pursuit of these goals, Buddhist teachings such as impermanence, nonattachment, and generosity often inform the way Buddhists live their lives. In addition, Buddhists commonly believe that favorable effects can occur in their lived experience through the protective presence of spirits and the numinous power of amulets. Auspicious rituals such as chanting and the worship of relics and Buddha images are also commonly believed to have beneficial consequences.

Western preconceptions have often led to accounts of Buddhism that overemphasize the role of personal experience for Buddhists. This produces a simplified picture that neglects aspects of Buddhism – such as the ritual, scriptural, institutional, sociological, and political – that are also of central importance.

These features of Buddhism also interact with the experiential dimension in important ways. For instance, Buddhist teachers may claim to have religious experiences – insights into reality, visions of Buddhas, and so forth – that are used to legitimize authority, leadership roles, and the authenticity of the sects to which these teachers belong. Scriptural and commentarial teachings inform, and are arguably informed by, meditation experiences. Ritual observances can have experiential effects – such as focusing and calming the mind and the production of religiously significant visions – that blur the distinction between ritual and meditation. To treat the experiential dimension in isolation from these other factors leads to a distorted, partial view of Buddhism.

Robert Sharf (1995: 228) claims that "the role of experience in the history of Buddhism has been greatly exaggerated in contemporary scholarship." He contends that the significance of meditation, supposedly the quintessential Buddhist experience, has been overplayed due to romantic projections about Buddhism by Western scholars and enthusiasts. In addition, some popular Asian Buddhist modernist reformers, who have influenced and been influenced by Western interpretations of Buddhism, construe Buddhism as fundamentally about meditation practices and the transformative personal experiences that they are said to produce (Sharf 1995: 241–59).

Sharf contends that autobiographical writing about personal experiences is rare in pre-modern Buddhism and that it is naïve to assume that abstruse philosophical manuals – such as Buddhaghosa's *Visuddhimagga*, Asaṅga's *Bodhisattvabhūmi*, Kamalaśīla's *Bhāvanākramas*, and many others – that describe in detail the stages of the Buddhist path are reports of the actual meditation experiences of their scholastic authors or anyone else. Instead, he regards them as "prescriptive systematizations of scriptural materials" (Sharf 1995: 236) and not necessarily based on personal experiences. He also casts doubt on the view that these treatises were commonly used as guidebooks for successful meditation. Historical and ethnographic evidence indicates that "they functioned more as sacred talismans than as practical guides. Texts on meditation were venerated as invaluable spiritual treasures to be copied, memorized, chanted, and otherwise revered" rather than as productive of inner experiences (241). He does not deny that there may have been Buddhist meditators who had transformative experiences and altered states of consciousness but that "the actual practice of what we would call meditation rarely played a major role in Buddhist monastic life" (241). He claims that the social, political, and ideological effects of Buddhist reports and representations of religious experiences are the proper topics of academic study. These phenomena are available for public scrutiny, unlike the private, subjective, and indeterminate mental episodes to which the reports purportedly refer (Sharf 1998: 110–14; Bush 2012: 207–10).

Sharf's skepticism is a useful corrective to the romantic, idealized misperception that Buddhists in general devote their lives to the cultivation of transformative meditative experiences and the pursuit of Enlightenment. It is also a reminder not to assume that the doctrines of various Buddhist traditions are necessarily derived from the personal experience of the authors of the doctrinal texts; nor are they definitely reports by these authors of the experiences of other Buddhists. The modern emphasis on individual experiences has tended to produce a subjectivized view of Buddhism at the expense of other features of Buddhist traditions such as the institutional and the ritual. Sharf also rightly emphasizes the political function that descriptions of Buddhist religious experiences often have; they bestow power and authority on those who claim to have had them and sometimes marginalize those who have not.

However, Janet Gyatso (1999: 116) rightly warns that "this important revision of western presumptions about Buddhist practice should not be taken to the extreme, to suggest that Buddhists do not also sometimes seek what they take to be religiously salvific experience through meditation and other practices." She focuses on various forms of Tibetan Buddhism in which there is an indigenous tradition of interest in religious experience, prior to any Western influence. Tibetan Buddhism often emphasizes that effective teachers need to have meditation experiences, there are meditation retreats to enable lay and monastic practitioners to have such experiences, and a small minority of Buddhist virtuosos specialize in this pursuit (Gyatso 1999: 116–17). She points to pre-modern Tibetan Buddhist autobiographical accounts that provide first-person reports of "dreams, meditative sensations, visions, and insights" (116). We will see later that such autobiographical records of significant religious experiences also occur in various other Buddhist traditions.

The experiential dimension of Buddhism has often been overemphasized; however, it should not be dismissed. Buddhist reports of religious experiences continue to be an important area of academic study and controversy. The remainder of this chapter will examine some further important facets of these Buddhist accounts and the philosophical questions that they stimulate.

## MEDITATIVE EXPERIENCE AND DOCTRINAL INNOVATION

A much-debated question is whether meditative experiences that Buddhists report simply conform to pre-existing doctrines or can be the source of new insights and some of the doctrinal innovations that have characterized Buddhism throughout its history.

Perhaps Buddhists simply get the meditative experiences for which they have been trained. Robert Gimello (1978: 193) contends that

Buddhist meditative practices produce experiences that confirm already established doctrines. He claims that these experiences are "deliberately contrived exemplifications of Buddhist doctrine" rather than doctrines being derived from these experiences.

It is true that Buddhist meditative experiences often conform to accepted tenets. This is ordinarily the case for practitioners who follow well-rehearsed training procedures for inducing experiences that are thought to validate the doctrines of their specific Buddhist tradition. Furthermore, doctrinal innovations can precede and condition meditative experiences rather than being discovered through meditation. "Philosophical beliefs shape meditative techniques, provide specific expectations, and thus have a formative influence on the kinds of experience which are actually produced, as well as on the philosophical conclusions which are drawn from these experiences" (Griffiths 1990: xiv).

Nevertheless, meditative experiences can arguably lead to the formulation of new doctrines, or modifications of old ones, even if these experiences always occur in a doctrinal context which informs them. While such experiences do not occur in an intellectual vacuum, they need not always simply reiterate the established teachings. Most notably, Buddhists believe this to have been the case when the Buddha gained Enlightenment in a state of profound meditative absorption and subsequently propounded his teaching based on that experience. No doubt his purported Enlightenment experience was only possible given the ancient Indian religious and cultural context in which ideas about suffering, renunciation, liberation, karma, and rebirth, and so forth were already current; nevertheless, his meditative experience, according to the scriptural accounts, led to teachings that were genuinely new.

Gyatso (1999: 116) shows that, in Tibetan Buddhism, some personal religious meditative visions and insights are claimed to be the basis for "theoretical and systematic discussions of the Buddhist path." Lambert Schmithausen (2005: 246–47) argues that the Indian Yogācāra teaching of mind-only (*cittamātra*) was historically possible because of pre-existing Mahāyāna notions about the illusory nature of phenomena; however, the further development of these ideas "primarily resulted" from generalizations to non-meditative life from the experience of meditative objects as products of the mind. "The results of meditative practice inform the philosophical views of practicing Buddhists with new experiences, and thus suggest new ways in which the philosophical system can be modified and developed" (Griffiths 1990: xiv).

## TRANQUILITY AND INSIGHT

'*Bhāvanā*' is a Buddhist term that can be translated as meditative cultivation or development and is important in discussions of Buddhist religious experience. It refers to the development of higher states of consciousness and realization that Buddhist meditative techniques are intended to facilitate. In many Buddhist traditions, meditation is categorized into two types: the cultivation of tranquility (Pāli: *samathabhāvanā*; Sanskrit: *śamathabhāvanā*) and the cultivation of insight (Pāli: *vipassanābhāvanā*; Sanskrit: *vipaśyanābhāvanā*). Both forms of meditation are often regarded as necessary; however, the development of tranquility is commonly considered to be preparatory to insight meditation.

Techniques of tranquility meditation make the mind still and highly concentrated with the capacity to remain continuously focused on one object, such as the breath or a colored disk (Harvey 2013: 325–27). They involve withdrawal from the external world and the overcoming of various psychological obstructions that inhibit mental absorption. There is a stock list of five hindrances that impede progress in tranquility meditation: sensual desire, ill-will, sloth and torpor, restlessness and worry, and doubt. By removing them, the mind is said to enter eight ascending higher states of consciousness (Pāli: *jhāna*; Sanskrit: *dhyāna*). The characteristics of each of these are mapped out with some precision and detail; however, the basic point is that each is more rarified and calm than the preceding one. The normally incessant and turbulent flow of emotions and thoughts is pacified, so that by the fourth of these altered states of consciousness, it is said that only the experience of equanimity remains; pleasure, pain, and all emotional responses are superseded (Harvey 2013: 329–31).

The mind that achieves these states of consciousness is reputed to be powerful so that the meditator develops paranormal abilities including clairaudience, clairvoyance, telepathy, knowledge of one's and others' past rebirths in accordance with their karma, and magical powers such as flying, walking on water, being in several locations at once, and so forth (Harvey 2013: 332). These supernormal powers are useful for the Enlightened, allowing them to enact their compassion more effectively. In addition, the perception of past lives provides experiential confirmation of the key Buddhist teachings of karma and rebirth. Nevertheless, they are not considered to be the final Buddhist objective. On the contrary, these powers and the states of calm absorption that accompany them, if treated as ends in themselves, would be a distraction for meditators whose aim is Enlightenment. These higher states of consciousness need to be coupled with insight meditation.

Accounts vary about precisely how much concentration and tranquility is required, and the precise relationship between tranquility and insight meditation practices is a matter of debate (Gethin 1998: 198–200; Harvey 2013: 332–39). However, a common view is that, with the mind in a potent and focused state, the Buddhist meditator can engage in the cultivation of insight, which entails reflection on fundamental Buddhist doctrines and their application to one's experience. Through attainment of the *jhānas*, "consciousness is purified and made ready to see the Truth with great clarity of vision" (Barnes 1978: 66). The meditator who then cultivates insight penetrates deeply into the ultimate truth with an undistracted mind, free from agitation; it is focused and its energies undispersed. Through insight meditation combined with tranquility meditation, the Buddhist teachings about reality are interiorized and experienced directly rather than simply intellectually. When in such a heightened state of consciousness, analysis of the ultimate truth and its applicability to one's experiences is believed to have profound effects; it is thought to be the means of removing greed, hatred, and delusion, the deep-rooted emotional and cognitive impediments to Enlightenment.

There is considerable diversity in Buddhist accounts of the ultimate truth that is said to be experienced as the result of insight. Non-Mahāyāna Indian Buddhist schools viewed insight as requiring the analysis of conventional entities such as trees, tables, and persons into their fundamental constituents (Pāli: *dhammas*; Sanskrit: *dharmas*), which were regarded as ultimately real; however, these schools disagreed about the number and characteristics of these *dharmas*. Moreover, Sautrāntika Buddhists focused on the momentary nature of the ultimately real fundamental constituents. Yet the Sarvāstivādins attributed a type of permanent existence to these *dharmas* (Williams, Tribe, and Wynne 2012: 83–92).

Many Mahāyāna Buddhists claim that emptiness (*śūnyatā*) is the ultimate truth that is experienced in insight meditation. However, Mahāyāna Buddhists construe emptiness in different ways, depending on their tradition. Mādhyamikas think emptiness is the absence of intrinsic existence of all phenomena, and that they all exist merely conventionally, including the *dharmas* that the non-Mahāyāna Buddhists think are ultimately real. Yogācārins understand emptiness as the absence of the subject-object duality; only the mind has intrinsic existence. The influence of *tathāgatagarbha* ideas led to the view that emptiness is the absence of all cognitive and affective defilements in one's intrinsically pure Buddha nature. Hua yan Buddhists see emptiness in terms of the mutual interpenetration of all phenomena (Williams 2009: 63–148).

More examples of doctrinal diversity could be given. This leads to complex hermeneutical issues about how, and whether, these different descriptions of the ultimate truth said to be experienced in Enlightenment are reconcilable.

## TRANQUILITY WITHOUT INSIGHT

The explanation of the relationship between tranquility and insight meditation discussed in the previous section sees them as compatible. However, Paul Griffiths has suggested that the goals of the two forms of meditation are actually in conflict. This is because insight meditation is about honing one's analytical, rational skills to gain a clear understanding of the way things really are, as expressed in Buddhist doctrines. In contrast, tranquility meditation is about withdrawing the mind from rational thinking, which falls away as the mind progresses through the *jhānas*. After the first *jhāna*, discursive thought is said to cease, so it is hard to understand how insight meditation could occur beyond this heightened state of consciousness. Griffiths argues that the cultivation of insight and the cultivation of tranquility originally represented two distinct soteriological goals, brought into an uneasy alliance by the later Buddhist tradition (Griffiths 1986: 14–16).

He focuses on the meditative state called the cessation of sensation and conceptualization (*saññāvedayitanirodha*), which is identified by early Buddhist sources. This is tranquility meditation taken to its logical conclusion; the meditator withdraws completely from all external stimulation and all internal mental activity. The mind is tranquil because it has entirely shut down. Mental functions of sensation, perception, and conceptualization are said to be entirely absent so that the mind becomes blank for as long as this frame of mind (or no mind) persists. This is not a state of insight into the way things really are. On the contrary, the cessation of sensation and conceptualization has no epistemic (or other) content at all and seems to be indistinguishable from unconsciousness. Many later Buddhist commentators marginalize the soteriological significance of the cessation of sensation and conceptualization; for them, Buddhist Enlightenment requires insight into the way things really are, which is evidently not possible for a mind which has temporarily ceased to operate. Indeed, "it quickly became orthodoxy for Indian Buddhist intellectuals that salvation must involve some degree of intellectual appropriation of doctrine" (Griffiths 1986: 23) which is not achievable in this state of (un)consciousness. However, some early Pāli texts attribute great value to the attainment of the cessation of sensation and conceptualization; they equate it with *nibbāna* itself. For them, the final aim of Buddhist practice is the total stilling of the mind, which ends the craving that causes suffering, rather than the achievement of penetrating insight into reality. "There appears to be some tension between a view which regards dispassionate knowledge of the way things are as a *sine qua non* and constituent factor of Enlightenment, and a view which sees complete unconsciousness, the cessation of all mental functions, as essential to, or even identical with, enlightenment" (Griffiths 1986: xvi).

This tension foreshadows a controversy in the later history of Buddhism. Many teachings and traditions give a prominent soteriological role to rational analysis and systematic reflection on the way things really are; others focus more on the removal from the mind of such discursive thinking, which is considered an obstacle, rather than an aid, to the realization of Enlightenment. These divergent approaches to Buddhist practice are exemplified by the Indian and Chinese sides in the reports of the eighth century bSam yas debates in Tibet between Kamalaśīla and Heshang Moheyan. The Indian scholar monk Kamalaśīla advocated an approach to meditation that combined attainment of tranquility with systematic reflection on the nature of reality to achieve wisdom that eradicates the cognitive and emotional obstacles to Enlightenment. According to Kamalaśīla, tranquility and insight meditation are compatible; the cultivation of tranquility stabilizes the mind to facilitate successful insight meditation, and a direct perception of the way things really are, so that the meditator's reflections have a transformational impact on their personality rather than being a merely intellectual endeavour. However, tranquility meditation without the cultivation of insight will not lead to Enlightenment because Enlightenment is a state of experiential knowledge that requires correct analysis of reality. It occurs gradually as the result of a long process of ethical and meditative training. By contrast, the Chan monk Heshang Moheyan reportedly claimed that Enlightenment occurs suddenly and requires only the experience of meditative absorption, in which all mental activity, including reflection on the nature of reality, is counterproductive. Enlightenment requires only stilling of the mind; rational thinking about the nature of reality is an obscuration which needs to be removed. According to Tibetan accounts, the debates were won by Kamalaśīla

(Williams 2009: 191–94). However, Heshang Moheyan also expressed a persistent strand of thinking in Buddhism with deep historical roots.

## NON-CONCEPTUALITY AND INEFFABILITY

Buddhist Enlightenment is often described as a non-conceptual insight into the ultimate truth, even by those Buddhist traditions that value rational thinking and conceptualization of the ultimate truth as a means to gain Enlightenment. This is different from the aforementioned cessation of perception and conceptualization that entails the complete absence of all mental activity and is best described as a non-experience in which consciousness is temporarily suspended. By contrast, if Enlightenment is a non-conceptual insight, then it has epistemic content; it is an experience of knowing the way things really are that is not mediated by concepts and language (Griffiths 1990: 85–90).

This presents a challenge to the influential constructivist epistemology, influenced by Immanuel Kant, which views all experiences as necessarily mediated by concepts rather than direct, undistorted encounters with reality (King 1999: 175–86). While many Buddhists would agree that experience prior to Enlightenment is mediated by concepts, they claim that the experience of Enlightenment is different; no concepts stand between the meditator and the ultimate truth that they perceive. Conceptualization falls away as the meditator becomes absorbed in the direct experience of the way things really are.

The post-Kantian constructivist may object that there must be conceptualization going on in the supposedly unmediated experience of the ultimate truth, even if it is at a subconscious level of which the meditator is unaware. There is no such thing as an unmediated experience; we cannot get behind the veil of concepts to see things as they really are, independent of the interpretations that our minds place upon them.

But many Buddhists would reject this view. This is not to say that conceptualization of the ultimate truth is unnecessary prior to this Enlightenment; we have seen that, for many Buddhists, proper reflection on the way things really are is vital to bring about the unmediated Enlightened experience. Correct concepts about the ultimate truth are a necessary precursor to Enlightenment. Nor is it the case that the ultimate truth that is experienced in an unmediated way is later completely unamenable to conceptualization. On the contrary, it may be possible to communicate in concepts and words what was experienced – for example, emptiness, mind only, non-duality, the Buddha nature, the radical impermanence of all phenomena, the bliss of *nirvāṇa* and so forth – in post-meditative reports. Indeed, the Buddhists' commitment to the claim that the Enlightened experience of ultimate truth transcends concepts and words does not prevent them from presenting often highly divergent descriptions of the truth which is experienced.

What is the relationship between descriptions of the non-conceptual experience of the ultimate truth and the actual experience? Most Buddhist traditions claim that the Enlightened experience of the ultimate truth is in some sense inexpressible; however, modest and stronger forms of ineffability can be found in Buddhism (Burton 2017: 135–57).

If ineffability is modest, then the relationship between words that describe the ultimate truth and the inexpressible experience of ultimate truth is relatively close and continuous. Descriptions communicate what is experienced, but lack the impact of the direct, fully immersive experience, much like the description of a tiger is different from the encounter face-to-face with a tiger in which one may be 'lost for words' and unable to conceptualize the experience when it is happening. This does not, of course, preclude a description of what the encounter with the tiger would be, or was, like; however, the description is no substitute for the actual experience. The ultimate truth really is correctly described as impermanence, emptiness, Buddha nature, or mind only and so forth, but the description needs to be distinguished from the direct perception of this ultimate truth.

If ineffability is stronger, then there is greater discontinuity between the descriptions of Enlightened experience and the actual experience. Literal ineffability is paradoxical and incoherent (Yandell 1993: 62). Nevertheless, Buddhists can claim that concepts of the Enlightened experience fail to do justice to its extraordinary nature; descriptions can, at best, be metaphors which are suggestive of the Enlightened knowledge that is largely beyond the purview of concepts and words. The ineffable Enlightened experience is not devoid of epistemic content; on the contrary, something is known, but words or concepts can only provide hints of its character.

## INTROSPECTION AND NOT-SELF

Buddhists often claim that religious experience – in the form of the mindful, analytical introspection that occurs in insight meditation – plays a crucial role in the justification of key Buddhist doctrines. These teachings are proved to be true because the meditator has a confirming experience of them while in a heightened state of consciousness, as the Buddha is said to have done on the night of his Enlightenment.

This can be illustrated by reference to the Buddhist doctrine that there is no enduring, unchanging self. The not-self teaching is an implication of the Buddhist teaching of universal impermanence. The Buddhists claim, what we conventionally call the 'self' is really a conglomeration of numerous psychological, and, for many Buddhists, physical events. They are all transient and interact through complex causal connections. The individual is a composite of these events and is nothing more than the totality of these events. The 'I' is a process rather than a substance. There is no abiding, let alone permanent, self that possesses the vast number of changing mental and physical states that together constitute the person.

Buddhists are encouraged to develop an introspective awareness, often in the context of meditation, of the absence of a self. Mindful analysis of the contents of one's experiences is said to reveal only a flow of changing events – bodily processes, feelings, perceptions, volitions, and moments of consciousness – with no evidence of an abiding self. The realization through careful introspection that there is no such self is said to be fundamental to Buddhist Enlightenment. Conversely, attachment to the wrong view that there is a self is thought to be a basic form of ignorance and cause of suffering.

How successful is this Buddhist appeal to introspective experience to justify the not-self doctrine? Its simplicity, directness, and empiricism may seem attractive; simply look within and carefully observe what is happening. Perceptions, feelings, volitions, and so forth come and go, but there is no unchanging self that can be observed. Therefore, such a self does not exist. Such direct, experiential insights are sometimes regarded in Buddhism as indubitable in a manner that views reached through reasoning are not. However, there are problems with this approach.

One difficulty is that some non-Buddhist religious traditions rely on introspective experience to support, rather than deny, the existence of the self. For instance, Jains claim that meditation reveals the existence of a permanent, independent soul (*jīva*); the realization that this soul is one's fundamental nature is central to Jain spiritual progress and Enlightenment. How is one to adjudicate between these two contradictory introspective experiences? It seems that the different accounts of introspective experience reflect the doctrinal assumptions that Buddhists and Jains bring to these experiences. Buddhists have the view that there is no self and their introspective experiences confirm this view. Jains have the view that there is a self and their introspective experiences confirm this view. Experience follows and conforms to pre-established doctrine, rather than the truth of doctrine being established by experience. The Buddhists may claim that their report of introspective experience is accurate, and that the Jains – and others who find a self when they introspect – are mistaken and have not paid sufficient attention to the truth that introspection reveals; however, the Jains can make the same objection to Buddhists' claim. It seems impossible to rely on evidence gained through introspection to determine which view is true. Introspective experience, therefore, does not prove whether there is or is not a self; it just demonstrates that it *appears* to Buddhists that there is no self and it *appears* to others, such as Jains, that there is a self (Yandell 1993: 280–98).

Even within Buddhism there are disagreements about what introspection reveals. Although many Buddhists do accept the not-self doctrine, some adherents of the Mahāyāna *tathāgatagarbha* teaching contend that the Buddha nature is one's permanent luminous consciousness, concealed in unenlightened experience by adventitious defilements such as greed, hatred, and delusion (Williams 2009: 103–12). This seems perilously close to claiming that there is a self after all, even if some of these Buddhists are reluctant to use this terminology. Such Buddhists often believe that the existence of this permanent, luminous consciousness is revealed through Enlightened, introspective meditation experience. This implies that those Buddhists who see only impermanent mental and physical phenomena, and do not discern this Buddha nature within them when they introspect, have not seen deeply enough into their own being, or have misinterpreted what introspection has revealed to them.

Even if those Buddhists who adhere to the not-self teachings were right that introspection yields no evidence of a self, this would not prove that there is no self. This is because the self may be the type of entity that is not accessible to introspection. The self may be the witness, the observer, of experiences. It may be the subject who has the experiences that are available to introspection without itself being observable through introspection. Arguably, this self unifies diverse sensations into coherent experiences and enables the recollection of past experiences as being one's own, without itself being a possible object of experience. The Buddhist appeal to introspection only works on the unproven assumption that all existent mental phenomena, including the self, must be potentially detectable via introspection.

Buddhists present other arguments that do not rely directly on introspective experience in support of the not-self doctrine and to refute the view that a substantial self exists (Gethin 1998: 136–38). Whether they are persuasive is debatable and not the topic of discussion here. What seems clear is that introspective experiences cannot provide an objective justification for the Buddhist not-self teaching, or other Buddhist doctrines, even if Buddhists may sometimes claim otherwise. These experiences may convince the Buddhists themselves of the truth of Buddhist teachings, but there will always be others who claim to have contradictory introspective experiences – of the self, God, and so forth – and those who claim that the way things really are is not necessarily accessible to introspection anyway. For the Buddhists to be convincing to those who are not predisposed to accept Buddhist views, they need to demonstrate that their meditative experience of not-self, and other Buddhist teachings, is indeed the way things really are, rather than simply the way things appear to them. To do that, they must appeal to criteria other than personal religious experience.

## RELIGIOUS VISIONS

The metaphors of sight and vision are pervasive in Buddhist traditions. The Buddha is said to have the extraordinary power to *see* the workings of karma in his and others' past lives and the entire process of dependent origination throughout the universe. Enlightened knowledge is described as *insight* into the ultimate truth and *seeing* things as they really are. This experience of Enlightened vision "suggests incisive knowledge that penetrates delusions and conceptual fabrications apprehending the truth as it is" (McMahan 2010). Unlike theoretical knowledge, this seeing is a direct perception or knowledge by acquaintance which has immediacy and transformative impact, removing engrained ignorance that stands in the way of Enlightenment.

Visual experiences are important in Buddhism. In the Theravāda tradition, there are some meditation practices that employ visualization. For example, we have seen that one technique uses a colored disk as the focus for concentration. Another imagines the decomposition of a corpse as a means of reflecting on the impermanence of the body. In the *mettābhāvanā* meditation, the practitioner visualizes friends, strangers, and enemies with the aim of cultivating impartial loving kindness toward everyone (Harvey 2013: 326–27).

In Mahāyāna and Vajrayāna Buddhism, visionary experiences of Buddhas and Bodhisattvas have a prominent place. A function of some art and iconography from these traditions is to assist the Buddhist practitioner to have such visions and to represent what is purportedly seen. There are numerous meditation and devotional practices in which the practitioner envisions a Buddha or Bodhisattva as a focus of worship. These experiences are commonly regarded as resulting in actual encounters with the holy being who is visualized, rather than being simply products of the Buddhist's imagination. The practitioner enters into a relationship with the visualized Buddha or Bodhisattva who can bestow blessings and teachings. There is evidence that, from the inception of Mahāyāna Buddhism, visionary experiences of Buddhas may have been a "particularly potent impetus to religious practice" (Williams 2009: 28). These visions were also one way in which Mahāyāna Buddhists sought to authenticate their *sūtras* as genuinely the word of Buddha. The teachings in these texts were sometimes believed to be communicated via encounters in meditations and dreams with Buddhas who reside in celestial realms known as Buddha Fields or Pure Lands (Harrison 2003). Mahāyāna Buddhists could regard these teachings as further revelations, superior to those transmitted to non-Mahāyāna traditions by the historical Buddha.

An early Mahāyāna visualization occurs in the *Pratyutpanna Sūtra*, a scripture that prescribes the 'recollection of the Buddha' meditation. The practitioner is instructed to concentrate on the Buddha Amitāyus teaching the Buddhist doctrine in his Buddha Field. Concentration on this task is said to last for seven days and nights, resulting in a direct encounter with this Buddha in his celestial realm (Williams 2009: 212).

Perhaps this sustained focus on the image of a Buddha in his Buddha Field results in an elaborate and powerful hallucination where imagination becomes confused with reality. It would be unsurprising that Buddhist meditators produced visions of Buddhas, and mistook them as real, if the Buddhists were already predisposed to believe in the reality of these Buddhas and have spent a prolonged period in meditation trying to visualize them. One tends to get the experiences for which one's mind has been conditioned.

Nevertheless, the view of the devout practitioner is that such a vision need not be a figment of the imagination; on the contrary, it can be a conduit to a higher reality, that of the Buddha in his Buddha Field, where the practitioner performs meritorious acts of worship and receives teachings that can then be imparted to others after emerging from the religious experience. A dismissive attitude to such visions as mere hallucinations may be rooted in an unproven assumption that the material world is more real than the visionary world.

The Chinese Buddhist monk Fazhao (d c. 820 CE), a patriarch of the Mahāyāna Pure Land tradition, was a prominent proponent of the visualization practice of recollecting the Buddha Amitābha. He devoted his annual summer retreat to the continual circumambulation of a shrine to Amitābha Buddha while visualizing the Buddha's form and chanting his name. A vivid account of his experiences describes how, after two weeks of this practice, he entered a state of meditative absorption in which he was transported to Amitābha's Pure Land where Amitābha entrusted him with the five-tempo recitation of the Buddha's name, which became a hallmark of Fazhao's practice and teaching (Stevenson 1996: 207, 220–22) .

There are also vivid reports of Fazhao's visions during his visit to the sacred mountain, Wutai, said to be the earthly residence of the Bodhisattva Mañjuśrī. His spirit was transported into the presence of Mañjuśrī in his magical Bamboo Monastery and Diamond Grotto. Mañjuśrī predicts Fazhao's future Buddhahood and teaches him that recollection, through visualization, of Amitābha Buddha and the invocation of Amitābha's name are the supreme Buddhist practices. Mañjuśrī also assures him that devout practitioners will be reborn in Amitābha's Pure Land (Stevenson 1996: 213–18).

These accounts are interesting from several perspectives. Mañjuśrī, in the report of Fazhao's vision of him, confirms the soteriological value of having visions of the Buddha. The records of Fazhao's visions of Amitābha and Mañjuśrī also demonstrate that Buddhist religious visions often have a shamanistic character, where the devout practitioner is transported in spirit to the domain of a Buddha or Bodhisattva with whom personal communication ensues. Furthermore, this communication can include new teachings, prophecies, and confirmations of the practitioner's legitimacy as a leader of the Buddhist community. In addition, when Fazhao relates his experiences to his monks, some of them subsequently have collective miraculous visions of Mañjuśrī and so forth (Stevenson 1996: 219). Buddhist religious visions can be communal and not simply individual in character.

There are numerous other reports of Chinese and Japanese Buddhists who practiced meditation to gain visions of the Pure Land. Great significance is often attributed to such visions, especially when death is impending. Buddhists often believe that near death states of mind are a big influence on one's future rebirth; Pure Land Buddhists believe that if consciousness visualizes the Pure Land at death, this can bring about rebirth there. Records of deathbed experiences are a feature of this tradition, including experiences of the Pure Land's bright clouds and golden mountains, the Buddha coming from the Pure Land to welcome a dying monk, visions of hell prompting a dying man to chant the name of

Amitābha, and so forth (Becker 1984: 140–47). The widespread nature of these accounts, and the similarities between them, persuaded many of these Buddhists that they were not imaginary. They were empirically verifiable in the sense that they had been observed to be experienced by many different people (Becker 1984: 147). A skeptic may object that it is likely that people who have received similar religious conditioning about what will occur as death nears would construct similar experiences that conform to their expectations.

Dreams are also an important form of religious experience in various Buddhist traditions. A striking example is the Sōtō Zen patriarch, Keizan Jōkin (1268–1325), who made detailed reports of his dreams and attributed great significance to them. Bernard Faure (1996: 115) observed that "Keizan was an inveterate dreamer who made dreams into a veritable way of life: they supplied a criterion for truth, but also an instrument of power." In other words, his dreams contained revelations of doctrinal teachings but also provided legitimacy for his leadership of the Sōtō tradition and the worldly decisions that he made, such as when a detailed dream convinced him to establish the Yōkōji temple. And "he acquired through his dreams and visions a feeling that he had a supernatural mission" (Faure 1996: 115). This was typical of various Buddhists of the period for whom dreams had considerable importance, validating political authority and power, providing access to the higher reality of transcendent Buddhas and Bodhisattvas, and having a transformative influence on the practitioner. Such dreams were believed to be responses from these holy beings to ritual worship, signs of spiritual progress, and to have the auspicious power to remove karmic, cognitive, and moral faults that prevent Enlightenment (Faure 1996: 122–32).

It is uncertain whether Buddhists such as Keizan really had the dreams that they purported to have had, especially given the social, political, and economic benefits that such claims could afford (Faure 1996: 138–43). In addition, commonly "dreams in Mahāyāna Buddhism play essentially the role of a negative metaphor, serving to reveal the lack of reality of this world" (118). Mahāyāna texts often say that this world is like a dream; it is empty, illusory, and merely a mental creation. "Dreams were nothing but the product of false ideas and … the entire universe is only a dream that must be categorically rejected" (118). Dreams and visualizations are as illusory as everyday reality rather than containing higher revelations. Moreover, in theory, Zen Buddhists reject the soteriological significance of dreams and other visions because they emphasize that Enlightenment (*satori*) is unmediated by concepts and images. However, in practice many Mahāyāna

Buddhists, including Zen Buddhists such as Keizan, did value dreams. It was recognized that some dreams may mislead rather than reveal truth, but the theoretical disapproval of dreams in general is largely rhetorical (117–21).

Religious visions are also central to Indian and Tibetan tantric traditions which make use of *sādhanas*, instructions for the structured visualization of a Bodhisattva or Buddha, or group of Buddhas and/or Bodhisattvas. These are "intended as a guide for the practice of invoking, and mentally creating and retaining the visual image of, a sacred figure" (Gomez 1995: 318). These *sādhanas* often include elaborate ritual performances and detailed descriptions of the holy beings who are being invoked through the visualization process and who bestow teachings and remove sufferings. The benefits of such visionary encounters are said to include protection from worldly misfortunes, the mastery of magical powers, and, ultimately, the attainment of Enlightenment (Gomez 1995: 319, 327).

## ALTRUISTIC EXPERIENCE

Buddhist traditions are united in extolling other-regarding attitudes as virtues, and the cultivation of altruistic emotions is a vital part of Buddhist religious experience. The Buddha is thought to be the paragon of altruism, who devoted his life to founding a Buddhist community teaching the Dharma to others so that they too could become Enlightened. Those who gain Enlightenment are believed to possess unmitigated compassion. In pursuit of this high-minded ethical ideal, Buddhist practitioners are encouraged to develop concern for others and to overcome their selfish proclivities. The Theravāda *Karaṇīyamettā Sutta* (1994) proclaims that "even as a mother protects with her life her child, her only child, so with a boundless heart should one cherish all living beings, radiating kindness over the entire world." This is not just about a change in behaviour; primarily it requires a shift in motivation, so that one acts out of a desire for the welfare of others rather than self-oriented intentions. This transformation in experience is supported by Buddhist ethical precepts that encourage generosity, empathy, and respect for others.

There are also contemplative techniques that develop altruistic attitudes and to counteract entrenched selfish tendencies. The four *brahmavihāra* meditations possibly have a pre-Buddhist origin but are adopted in early Buddhist texts. They are the cultivation of loving kindness, compassion for those who are suffering, sympathetic joy for those who are happy, and equanimity, which is steadfastness in the face of the vicissitudes of life. The latter enables one to feel and express the altruistic mental states without wavering and with impartiality. The Theravāda position is that attainment of these meditative states leads to a rarefied rebirth in the abode (*vihāra*) of the god Brahmā, a heavenly realm at the upper reaches of *samsāra*, rather than *nirvāṇa*. These beneficial practices do not alone lead to Enlightenment, even if they develop altruistic attitudes that characterize the Enlightened mind. The latter requires insight into the nature of reality by following the Buddhist Eightfold Path (Dīghanikāya 1987: II.251). Enlightenment requires wisdom as well as selfless concern for others.

However, Richard Gombrich analyzes two *suttas* from the Pāli Canon to demonstrate that they consider the attainment of the *brahmavihāras* to be equivalent to Enlightenment itself. The cultivation of impartial kindness for all sentient beings would have been a way to salvation: "To be totally benevolent is to be liberated." He contends that these *suttas* were misconstrued by later commentators and the orthodox Theravāda view developed that the cultivation of altruistic emotions is not sufficient for Enlightenment (Gombrich 2006: 57–64).

In Mahāyāna Buddhism, the experience of compassion is central to the Bodhisattva ideal, to which Mahāyāna Buddhists are encouraged to aspire. The Bodhisattvas vow to assist all suffering sentient beings and to work for their welfare and salvation. They pledge to remain in the cycle of rebirths to help all others gain Enlightenment. To become a Bodhisattva requires a genuinely altruistic motivation, which is referred to as the generation of the *bodhicitta*, the Enlightenment mind. The *bodhicitta* is the yearning to assist all sentient beings which motivates the Bodhisattvas to embark on the long and arduous path to omniscient Buddhahood, where they will have the wisdom, compassion, and power to help others most effectively. The arising of the *bodhicitta* is regarded as a life-transforming experience and a reorientation of the Buddhist's motivation, in which the Buddhist's normally selfish inclinations are replaced by compassion. However, this compassion must be coupled with wisdom, which, in the Mahāyāna context, means insight into emptiness. Without wisdom, the Bodhisattva's other virtues are blind (Williams, Tribe, and Wynne 2012: 100). The Bodhisattva experiences compassion for all sentient beings but also develops profound understanding of the way things really are.

Śāntideva (c. seventh to eighth century) and later Tibetan commentators describe meditative practices that are designed to lead to the arising of the *bodhicitta* by stimulating the practitioner's compassion.

They involve deep reflection on the fact that all sentient beings are the same as oneself in wanting happiness and being averse to suffering. One should regard others as oneself, seeking always to alleviate their suffering. Moreover, one should reflect that a selfish preoccupation with one's own happiness only leads to one's own suffering, whereas authentic concern for the well-being of others is the source of genuine happiness and fulfilment for oneself (Edelglass 2009: 390–91; Williams 2009: 197–98).

Becoming an advanced Bodhisattva or Buddha, whose mind is infused with wisdom and compassion, is surely far removed from the everyday lives of many Buddhists. We have already seen that this is true in general of idealized depictions of Buddhism as focused on the pursuit of Enlightened experience, the life of meditation and so forth. And yet these ideals can be sources of inspiration and guidance for Buddhists. They are exemplars of Buddhist values that can – if only in an incomplete and approximate manner – be developed in ordinary experience.

## References

Barnes, Michael. "Religious Experience in Buddhism," *The Way* 18 (1978): 59–66.

Becker, Carl B. "Religious Visions: Experiential Grounds for the Pure Land Tradition," *The Eastern Buddhist* 17 (1984): 138–53.

Burton, David. *Buddhist: A Contemporary Philosophical Investigation*. Abingdon: Routledge, 2017.

Bush, Stephen S. "Are Religious Experiences too Private to Study?," *The Journal of Religion* 92 (2012): 199–223.

*Dīghanikāya. Thus Have I Heard. The Long Discourses of the Buddha*. Translated by Maurice Walshe. Boston: Wisdom Publications, 1987.

Edelglass, William. "The Bodhisattva Path: Śāntideva's *Bodhicaryāvatāra*," in William Edelglass and Jay L. Garfield (eds.), *Buddhist Philosophy: Essential Readings*, pp. 388–99. Oxford: Oxford University Press, 2009.

Faure, Bernard. *Visions of Power: Imagining Medieval Japanese Buddhism*. Princeton: Princeton University Press, 1996.

Gethin, Rupert. *The Foundations of Buddhism*. Oxford: Oxford University Press, 1998.

Gimello, Robert M. 1978. "Mysticism and Meditation," in Steven T. Katz (ed.), *Mysticism and Philosophical Analysis*, pp. 170–99. Oxford: Oxford University Press.

Gombrich, Richard. *How Buddhism Began: The Conditioned Genesis of the Early Teachings*, 2nd ed. London: Routledge, 2006.

Gomez, Luis O. "Two Tantric Meditations: Visualizing the Deity," in Donald S. Lopez, Jr (ed.), *Buddhism in Practice*, pp. 318–27. Princeton, NJ: Princeton University Press, 1995.

Griffiths, Paul J. *On Being Mindless: Buddhist Meditation and the Mind-Body Problem*. La Salle, IL: Open Court, 1986.

"Pure Consciousness and Indian Buddhism," in Robert K. C. Forman (ed.), *The Problem of Pure Consciousness*, pp. 71–97. Oxford: Oxford University Press, 1990.

Gyatso, Janet. "Healing Burns with Fire: The Facilitations of Experience in Tibetan Buddhism," *Journal of the American Academy of Religion* 67 (1) (1999): 113–47.

Harrison, Paul. "Mediums and Messages: Reflections on the Production of Mahāyāna," *The Eastern Buddhist* 35 (2003): 115–51.

Harvey, Peter. *An Introduction to Buddhism: Teachings, History and Practices*, 2nd ed. Cambridge: Cambridge University Press, 2013.

*Karaṇīyamettā Sutta. Karaniya Metta Sutta: The Buddha's Words on Loving-kindness*. Translated by the Amaravati Sangha, 1994. www.accesstoinsight .org/tipitaka/kn/khp/khp.9.amar.html

King, Richard. *Orientalism and Religion: Postcolonial Theory, India and 'the Mystic East'*. London: Routledge, 1999.

McMahan, David L. "Vision and Visualization," *Oxford Bibliographies* (2010). www.oxfordbibliographies.com

Schmithausen, Lambert . "On the Problem of the Relation of Spiritual Practice and Philosophical Theory in Buddhism," in Paul Williams (ed.), *Buddhism: Critical Concepts in Religious Studies*, pp. 242–54. London: Routledge, 2005. Originally published in Cultural Department of the Embassy of the Federal Republic of Germany (ed.), *German Scholars on India*, pp. 235–50. New Delhi and Varanasi: Chowkhamba, 1973.

Sharf, Robert H. "Buddhist Modernism and the Rhetoric of Meditative Experience," *Numen* 42 (1995): 228–83.

"Experience," in Mark C. Taylor (ed.), *Critical Terms for Religious Studies*, pp. 94–116. Chicago: University of Chicago Press, 1998.

Stevenson, Daniel. "Visions of Mañjuśrī on Mount Wutai," in Donald S. Lopez, Jr. (ed.), *Religions of China in Practice*, pp. 203–22. Princeton, NJ: Princeton University Press, 1996.

Williams, Paul. *Mahāyāna Buddhism: The Doctrinal Foundations*, 2nd ed. London: Routledge, 2009.

Williams, Paul, Anthony Tribe and Alexander Wynne. *Buddhist Thought: A Complete Introduction to the Indian Traditions*, 2nd ed. Abingdon: Routledge, 2012.

Yandell, Keith E. *The Epistemology of Religious Experience*. Cambridge: Cambridge University Press, 1993.

# 9 Rāmānuja's Eleventh Century Hindu Theology of Religious Experience: An Informative, Performative, Transformative Discourse

## FRANCIS X. CLOONEY, SJ

Rāmānuja (1017–1137) was a philosopher and theologian; a saint and mystic, a lover of God; a proponent of the harmony of Tamil and Sanskrit traditions; a premier leader of the south Indian Hindu Śrīvaiṣṇava community and a reformer of its ritual practices. Nine works are attributed to him: *Vedārtha Saṃgraha* (*Summary of the Meaning of the Veda*), on the right interpretation of the Upaniṣads and the right use of them in the theological and spiritual practice of the devotee; the *Gītā Bhāṣya* (*Commentary on the Bhagavad Gītā*); the *Śrī Bhāṣya* (*Auspicious Commentary on the Brahma Sūtras*);[1] the *Vedānta Dīpā* and *Vedānta Sāra* (respectively, the *Light of Vedānta* and the *Essence of Vedānta*, summaries of Rāmānuja's reading of Vedānta in the *Brahma Sūtras*); the *Gadyatrayam* (three long prose prayers of surrender to Nārāyaṇa with the Goddess Śrī): surrender as an interior act, in the *Śaraṇāgatigadyam*; at the great Śrīraṅgam temple, in the *Śrīraṅgagadyam*; and in heaven, in the *Śrīvaikuṇṭagadyam*; and finally, the *Nityam* (the *Manual of Daily Worship*).[2] Rāmānuja is also a larger than life figure in his tradition, revered for his brilliant readings of the Vedāntic tradition, his deep love for the devotional songs of the Tamil poet saints known as the āḻvārs (perhaps, "those immersed [in God]," and for charting the way of life many Śrīvaiṣṇavas still follow today.

Rāmānuja's writings include philosophy and theology, the interpretation of scripture and rules for interpretation, pious prayers and the rules for daily worship. As we shall see, all of this nourishes his program for a life fully given over to love of God. He is therefore an excellent case study when we take up the work of exploring "Hindu religious

---

[1] The Brahma Sūtras are a set of about 550 brief statements summarizing the content and method of the Upaniṣads regarding Brahman.

[2] See Carman, *Theology of Rāmānuja* for an overview of Rāmānuja's oeuvre. In the following pages, I will touch upon all his works excepting the *Vedāntadīpā* and *Vedāntasāra*, taken to be abbreviated forms of the *Śrībhāṣya*. Their constructive contribution requires further study. See van Buitenen, introduction to *Gītābhāṣya*.

experience." At the end of this chapter, I will move briefly from the example of Rāmānuja to a wider circle of figures in the Hindu religious context whose work might similarly yield insights into religious experience in the Hindu context.

Much can be said about religious experience according to Rāmānuja, as we shall see, but what we might say about Rāmānuja's own experience remains conjectural. There is a relative lack of historical data about Rāmānuja,[3] and we are faced also with the unsurprising and typical impersonality of his scholastic, commentarial writings. Conversely, we must notice the plethora of hagiographical detail about him, treating this detail as neither history nor fiction, but a communal memory of him passed down for good cause. Throughout, it will be necessary to distinguish the views of Rāmānuja *on* experience from the experience *of* Rāmānuja, even if in the end it will seem unduly cautious to separate entirely what he writes from what he experienced.

Regarding the kind of experience which I have in mind here, I have found helpful Bernard McGinn's essay, "Mystical Consciousness: A Modest Proposal," wherein he reviews the language of "experience," "mystical experience," and "mysticism."[4] Most pertinently, he points to the danger of a privatization and de-theologization of discourse on mysticism by appeals to pure, personal, and even private experience. Rather,

> If we take *spirituality* as a broad term signifying the whole range of beliefs and practices by which the Christian church strives to live out its commitment to the Spirit present in the Risen Christ (*1 Corinthians* 6:14–20; *2 Corinthians* 3:17), then we can understand *mysticism as the inner and hidden realization of spirituality* through a *transforming consciousness of God's immediate presence.* Mysticism, or more precisely, *the mystical element within Christian spirituality, is the goal to which spiritual practices aim.* It is a *personal appropriation, but not an individualistic* one, because it is rooted in the life of the Christian community and the grace mediated through that community and its sacraments and rituals.[5]

---

[3] See Dutta, *From Hagiographies to Biographies* for a recent reconstruction of what we know about the Rāmānuja of history.

[4] Readers wishing insight into the specifically Indian context may consult Flood, *The Truth Within*, Forsthoefel, *Knowing beyond Knowledge*, and Veliath, *The Mysticism of Rāmānuja*.

[5] McGinn, "Mystical Consciousness," p. 44, emphasis added.

McGinn very well captures the dynamic that suits Rāmānuja as well as the Christian mystics he has in mind. He goes on to say that mystical consciousness subsumes but goes beyond ordinary consciousness:

> Mystical consciousness ... adds another dimension that transforms the usual components. This third element might be called a consciousness-beyond, or "meta-consciousness" as Thomas Merton once described it. Meta-consciousness is the co-presence of God in our inner acts, not as an object to be understood or grasped, but as the transforming Other who is, as Augustine put it, "more intimate to us than we are to ourselves."[6]

Spirituality, mysticism, mystical consciousness, the personal but not the individualistic, and consciousness-beyond: these definitions and distinctions, even if inevitably inexact when applied to Rāmānuja, allow us to think about experience and religious experience, and likewise how to sort out what Rāmānuja means by "experience," "mystical experience," "experience of God," etc.

### RĀMĀNUJA AND HIS TRADITION

Rāmānuja never claimed to be a true innovator or recipient of unprecedented revelations. He spoke for tradition, and is clearly claiming to speak from and for the all-India Sanskrit tradition. Śrīvaiṣṇavas see him also as deeply indebted to and inspired by the vernacular devotional tradition of Tamil Nadu that came to expression in the poetry of the āḷvārs. We can delay for yet another moment our turn to Rāmānuja's own writing, to take note of these background influences. The reading of the Tamil and Sanskrit sources fundamental to Rāmānuja's Śrīvaiṣṇava tradition reinforces the particular balance that characterizes his understanding of experience: the intensification of ordinary experience, by the practical contemplative use of scripture and tradition including ritual practice, for the sake of an ever clearer vision of God, even in this life.

### RĀMĀNUJA'S VEDĀNTIC ROOTS

Like Śaṅkara and other Vedāntins, Rāmānuja was committed to highly refined reasoning that included steadfast arguing of every issue, and, as a

---

[6] Ibid., p. 47.

starting point, a trust in simple perception, what the senses tell us. This is a knowledge that cannot be ignored or contradicted, though one must always be alert to ways in which people are not paying attention to what their senses tell them, have physical disability, or are under the sway of passions and ignorance, such as make them ignore or misinterpret the data coming to them. But like other Vedāntins, he resolutely deferred to the Upaniṣads, to the *Brahma Sūtras* that organize and defend Upaniṣadic teachings, and to texts such as *Bhagavad Gītā*. Such texts are for him rich sources for all necessary knowledge and practice, and much of the time, except in the *Gadya*s and the *Nityam*, he presents himself as a commentator on older writings; and even the prayers and rituals have precedents.[7] And, as Sucharita Adluri[8] has shown, later texts such as the *Viṣṇu Purāṇa*, sometimes neglected on the grounds that they are not authoritative, in fact are decisive for Rāmānuja as he seeks warrants for his views. As a Vedāntin he thus balanced scriptural interpretation, undertaken for the sake of knowledge that could be acquired only from revelation, with respect for perception and reason and, as we shall see, ultimately for experience as well.

For the sake of economy in illumining the Vedāntic background, here I situate Rāmānuja simply with respect to his predecessor, Yāmuna (whom he treated as his guru, though they never met), by citing the concluding ślokas of his *Gītārthasaṃgraha*. His summation regarding the three yogas – action, knowledge, devotion – taught in the *Gītā* stresses their connectedness, and the practicality of the path thus charted:

> Karma yoga is resorting to penance, sacred rivers, almsgiving, performance of sacrifice, etc. Jñāna yoga is establishment in a most purified self by those whose inner selves are subdued. / Bhakti yoga is establishment in meditation, etc., with exclusive pleasure in the highest. But all three yogas are mutually connected. / These three are the means to regular and occasional rites which take the form of worshiping the highest, and to vision of the self by means of yoga. / The person in whom all ignorance has been eradicated, after seeing the self as subordinate to the highest, achieves the highest *bhakti* and by that alone reaches his feet. (nn. 23–26)[9]

---

[7] See for instance Rastelli, "Unaltered Ritual in Transformed Religion" on the indebtedness of the *Nityam* to the *Ahirbudhnya Saṃhita*.

[8] See Adluri, *Textual Authority in Classical Indian Thought*.

[9] My translation of the *Gītārthasaṃgraha*, in consultation with Sampatkumaran.

Realization and practice culminate in an ever more intense focus on God:

> Exclusive focus on the Lord is common to all these eligible persons. If he is desirous of the highest until attaining Him, he will enjoy Him entirely. / The person of knowledge who is focused solely on the highest is such that his life depends entirely on him. His joy and sorrow depend solely on union with or separation from him. He thinks solely of him. (nn. 28–29)

While advance on this path is a gift, nonetheless pious works enhance progress on this path:

> For the person who has gained the self by meditation on the Lord, yoga, speaking, salutations, praise and songs of praise, then the actions of his breath, mind, understanding and senses all pertain to him. / Let him do his own innate karma, etc. for the purpose of *bhakti*, prompted by pleasure alone. Giving up completely all means, let him without fear surrender it to God. As one whose sole pleasure is in complete and exclusive service, let him reach His feet. (nn. 30–32a)[10]

### TAMIL GROUNDING

The other necessary foundation for situating Rāmānuja lies in the Tamil tradition of the āḻvārs. Rāmānuja says nothing about the Tamil tradition of the āḻvārs, but we can respect his tradition by positively situating Rāmānuja as someone who knew the āḻvār poetry well, as a vernacular tradition that prized the cultivation of ever more intensive experience, longing for God.

The āḻvār poetry, collected in the *Divya Prabandham* (*Divine Anthology*), was luxuriant in its Tamil poetic form, full of memorable images and ideas and, everywhere, rich in the language and signs of deep

---

[10] This exposition is probably what Rāmānuja had in mind when he writes, at the start of the *Vaikuntha*, "Having dived into the noble Yāmuna's ocean of ambrosia to the best of my understanding, I make visible the pearl called bhakti-yoga" (my translation). In that *Gadyam*, this yoga of devotion involves a visualization of the entire cosmos, climaxing in a vision of the Lord and surrender to the Lord. This open-ended spiritual journey, ending only in consummation in union with the Lord, a practice, form of meditation, and contemplation that occupies the entirety of a spiritual life. The *Vaikuṇṭha Gadyam* is included in the Rāmānuja's *Gadyatrayam* [1994], but here I am using my own translation.

experiences from which words arise.[11] The tradition of commentators, moreover, always attesting their indebtedness to Rāmānuja, held that the key ālvār work, the *Holy Word of Mouth* (*Tiruvāymoli*) of Śaṭakōpaṉ, is to be read as a work of spiritual pilgrimage, chronicling the ālvār's gradual and turbulent ascent toward vision of God. For instance, in his introduction to his commentary on the *Holy Word*, Nañjīyar, a teacher several generations after Rāmānuja, expounds the necessary dynamics of Śaṭakōpaṉ's experience. The saint is, Nañjīyar explains, overwhelmed by the richness of possible experiences, since

> when he experiences even one of the Lord's qualities, abundant pleasure in that quality begets in him a loss of desire for any inferior objects but also a desire for the Lord's other qualities. His desire increases, so that it becomes impossible to [settle for] grasping these qualities only successively and not all at once. So he grieves, when he loses even a part of what he desires. He likewise is pained when he loses even the smallest part of that experience of the Lord due to factors like memories, etc. connected still to nature and opposed to experience of the Lord ... Because he cannot at the same time experience the pleasurable and painful, these occur successively; but he says that the whole experience happens constantly, when he reflects on it.[12]

Yet when he forgets even part of what he has experienced, he grieves that loss, and he cannot manage to exult in his pleasure in the Lord, and grieve absence at the same time, so he is all the more frustrated. Life without actual, external union with God is intense suffering: "Union of the sort he had with the Lord was *a direct manifestation of knowledge in the same form as perception.* Difference is the confusion arising in his mental experience, when he desired external union but could not obtain it,"[13] which he then expressed indirectly in the voice of a young woman whose beloved has gone away.[14] The entirety of the *Holy Word* is portrayed by the commentators in the tradition of Rāmānuja as the spiritual journey of the ālvār.[15]

---

[11] See Clooney, *His Hiding Place Is Darkness.*
[12] Nañjīyar, *Introduction to His Commentary on Tiruvāymoli,* pp. 64–65. My translation.
[13] Ibid., My emphasis.
[14] Ibid., p. 65.
[15] See Clooney, *Seeing through Texts,* chapter 3, and Clooney, *His Hiding Place Is Darkness.*

As read by Śrīvaiṣṇavas, both the Sanskrit and Tamil traditions tend toward a combination of right knowledge and right practice, which form and then intensify the components of right experience, which itself culminates in direct knowledge of God.

Rāmānuja seems to be inspired by the formative and practical nature of this spirituality, since his works provide ample information and instruction about the pathway to the intensification of experience and, in the *Gadyas* and *Nityam*, paradigmatic examples of that intensified worship. It is arguable that his works as a whole – the commentaries plus devotional prose prayers plus rules for daily worship – offer his community the theological and spiritual/practical frame for the intensification of experience, in particular the experience of encounter with God.

## READING RĀMĀNUJA'S COMMENTARIES

### From Exegesis to Vision in the *Vedārthasaṃgraha*

Rāmānuja's great commentarial works – *Vedārthasaṃgraha*, the *Gītābhāṣya*, and the *Śrībhāṣya* – are impersonal, as is most scholastic writing.[16] As a commentator, Rāmānuja assumes the posture of an instrument of tradition, neither innovator nor dissenter. While his works tell us nothing directly about his own experience or personal history, they set forth in rich and consistent detail a program for religious experience. It is not possible here to delve deeply into any of the texts involved, but some illustrative passages will serve to give a feel for what is at stake regarding the desire for God, experience of God.

The *Vedārthasaṃgraha*, a treatise on scriptural interpretation and the worldview and practice produced by the proper reading of scripture, is taken to be Rāmānuja's first work. But it is sophisticated with respect to the theme of experience, and shows us a dynamic operative in the later *Bhāṣyas* too. At its very start, he explains,

> The only meaning which is to be found in the most important part of the whole body of śrutis, which set forth what is blissful for the entire Universe, is as follows: True knowledge of the individual soul and of the Supreme Spirit, applied to the obligations imposed by the various dharmas pertaining to each stage and station of life, are to precede pious and humble acts of devotion for and meditation on

---

[16] See Cabezon, *Scholasticism in a Comparative Perspective*.

the Supreme Spirit – acts held extremely dear by the devotee – that ultimately result in the attainment of the Supreme Spirit.[17]

He explains then, with several quotations, that the Vedānta statements are undertaken to make known the experience of Brahman in a flawless and abundant bliss preceded by the manifestation of the proper form of the self, a manifestation which is the fruit of meditation on the proper nature and proper forms of the highest self who is the inner controller of it, its proper forms and proper nature which is distinct from the body.

The purpose of this text is to make clear the best methods for interpreting scripture, and the meaning of scripture, such that know-ledge of God is made possible. The goal is practical, that devotion can be purified, cultivated, and intensified over time, growing toward greater and greater immediacy and clarity of insight:

> When he throws himself altogether at the lotus-like feet of the supreme person; when the darkness concealing his innermost self is dispelled by the grace of the supreme person who, supremely compassionate as He is, is pleased with the uninterrupted acts of worship that are dictated by the devotee's *bhakti* in glorification, remembrance, homage, salutation, mortification, exaltation, the listening to the description of His perfections and narrating them himself, meditation, adoration and prostration, etc.; then will he be able to attain the supreme person by virtue of his *bhakti*, which *takes on the form of contemplation in the highest degree of lucid perception, directed to none but Him, uninterrupted, pre-eminent and held preciously dear.*[18]

Later on, Rāmānuja accentuates the possibility of experience, as the refinement of his constructive proposals on exegesis. He summarizes the needed balance of right knowing and right action: "When a person performs the enjoined acts such as the worshipping of the supreme person – which presupposes true knowledge of Him – then, by His favor, he finds happiness culminating in the attainment of Him, and security, according to his qualification."[19] This declaration opens a section of the text that summarizes yet again his way of reading the Upaniṣads as supportive of both nonduality and difference within the reality of God, and in the make-up of the world. Interestingly, the exposition is

---

[17] *Vedārthsaṃgraha*, n. 3, van Buitenen translation.
[18] Ibid., n. 91; my emphasis.
[19] Ibid., n. 126.

punctuated by three increasingly vivid and elaborate portrayals of the Lord, who is the ultimate object of vision.

Immediately after the just cited passage, we have an exposition of the nature of the Lord:

> There are thousands of *śrutis* that declare that this Supreme Brahman Nārāyaṇa has a proper form of undefinable knowledge and beatitude in the purest form; He has immeasurable, innumerable, all-surpassing beautiful qualities, such as knowledge, power, strength, sovereignty, fortitude, glory etc.; the sum-total of spiritual and non-spiritual entities different from Himself are actuated by an act of His will.[20]

The text goes on more intimately to speak of his divine form, divine consort, and heavenly court:

> He possesses one invariable divine form that is in accordance with His pleasure and in harmony with Himself; He has an infinite variety of unsurpassed beautiful ornaments that suit His form, and immeasurable, endless and marvelous weapons of all kinds that are equal to His power; He has a Consort who suits His pleasure and who is in harmony with Him, possessing an immeasurable eminence of proper form, qualities, supernal power, ascendancy and character; He has an infinite entourage of attendants and necessaries, suitable to Him, the knowledge, actions etc. of whom are perfect and whose qualities are limitless; He has an infinite glorious manifestation, such as is fitting to Him, comprising all objects and all means of experience; He has a divine residence, the proper form and nature of which are beyond the ken of thought and the power of expression: all this and so forth is everlasting and irreproachable.[21]

After some intervening arguments on the meaning of debated passages, Rāmānuja elaborates the form of the Lord again, now vividly visualized, even materially.

I cite the whole passage to stress its specificity and vividness, as if God is actually seen:

> He who is always gloriously visible is the preeminent Person who dwells within the orb of the sun. His splendor is like that of a

[20] Ibid., n. 127.
[21] Ibid., n. 127.

colossal mountain of molten gold and His brilliance that of the rays of hundreds of thousands of suns. His long eyes are spotless like the petals of a lotus which, sprouting forth from deep water on a soft stalk, blossoms in the rays of the sun. His eyes and His forehead and His nose are beautiful, His coral-like lips smile graciously, and His soft cheeks are beaming. His neck is as delicately shaped as a conch-shell and His bud-like divine ears, beautifully formed, hang down on His stalwart shoulders. His arms are thick, round and long and He is adorned with fingers that are reddened by nails of a most becoming reddish tinge. His body, with its slender waist and broad chest, is well-proportioned in all parts, and His shape is of an unutterably divine form. His color is pleasing. His feet are as beautiful as budding lotuses. He wears a yellow robe that suits Him and He is adorned with immeasurable, marvelous, endless and divine ornaments –a spotless diadem, earrings, necklaces, the Kaustubha gem, bracelets, anklets, belt etc. and with Conch, Disc, Club, Sword, the Bow Sārṅga, the curl Śrīvatsa and the garland Vanamālā. He attracts eye and thought alike of all by the measureless and boundless beauty that is His. He overflows the entire creation of animate and inanimate beings with the nectar of His comeliness. His youth is exceedingly wonderful, unimaginable and eternal. He is as delicately tender as blossoming flowers. He perfumes the infinite space between the cardinal points with the odor of holiness. His profound majesty is forever encompassing the entire Universe. He looks upon the hosts of His devotees with loving eyes, filled with compassion and affection. His sport is to evolve, sustain and dissolve all the worlds. All evil is foreign to Him. He is the treasury of all beautiful qualities and He is essentially different from all other entities. He is the Supreme Spirit, the Supreme Brahman, Nārāyaṇa.[22]

God is not entirely formless,[23] but can be vividly seen by the readied mind, particularly as instructed and purified in accord with scripture.[24] All of this echoes the *Viṣṇu Purāṇa* VI.7, where the practitioner of devotional yoga constructs an elaborate internal vision of God, so as thereafter, also in meditation, simplifying it more and more.[25]

---

[22] Ibid., n. 134.

[23] Ibid., nn. 222–23.

[24] Ibid., n. 226.

[25] While Rāmānuja's visualizations always end in devotion and worship, in the *Viṣṇu Purāṇa* there seems to be on the one hand a radical nondualism, no difference

Thereafter, vision recurs a third time when Rāmānuja insists that
the scriptures tell us that God can be seen and experienced as if directly.[26] His divine perfections are recollected – "antithetical to all evil,
transcendent and unique. In his substantive nature, he is infinite knowledge and bliss . . ." – as well as his immanence within the world, his
domain: "All sentient and nonsentient entities have their nature, existence, activities and mutual differences controlled by his will. His
supreme glory is infinite and beyond thought in its nature and attributes. He has as the means of his sport, the entire universe, consisting of
multitudinous kinds of countless sentient and non-sentient entities."[27]
After reciting yet again a list of Upaniṣadic texts that speak to the
nature of Brahman, Rāmānuja turns again to the slow but sure process
leading to loving knowledge that is union of the individual self with
Brahman, the Lord:

> We have already declared that the means of attaining Brahman is a
> superior *bhakti* in the form of a meditation approaching extremely
> lucid perception, which is immeasurably and overwhelmingly dear
> to the devotee. It is achieved by complete devotion of *bhakti* which
> is furthered by the performance of one's proper acts preceded by
> knowledge of the orders of reality as learnt from the *śāstra*
> [instructive scriptures]. The word *bhakti* has the sense of a kind of
> love, and this love again that of a certain kind of knowledge.[28]

At the very end of the *Vedārthasaṃgraha*, Rāmānuja again stresses the
immediacy of vision:

> After having realized one's own soul by discrimination, one sees the
> Supreme Spirit by *bhakti*, that is, one has immediate presentation
> of Him, attains Him: this follows because the meaning is the same
> as in the text: ". . . but by exclusive *bhakti* can I (be seen and entered
> into)." Since *bhakti* is taken as a form of cognition, everything is
> established.[29]

Rāmānuja the exegete has a reputation in tradition for being a passion-
ate defender of right interpretation. There is for example the famous
story of *"kapyāsa."* This has to do with the awkward seeming

---

between *ātman* and *brahman*, and, on the other, the ideal of an entirely devotional
life, such as is exemplified by the teacher Khāṇḍikya in the *Viṣṇu Purāṇa* VI.7.

[26] *Vedārthsaṃgraha*, n. 234 ff., van Buitenen translation.

[27] Ibid., n. 234.

[28] Ibid., n. 141, adapted.

[29] Ibid., n. 144, adapted.

comparison of Brahman to the backside of a monkey in the ancient *Chāndogya Upaniṣad*: "... Now, that golden person who is seen within the sun has a golden beard and golden hair. He is exceedingly brilliant, all, even to the tips of his fingernails. His eyes are like a lotus, *kapyāsa* ..." What does *kapyāsa* mean? Is this golden person compared to a lotus and to a monkey's backside? Key is how Rāmānuja's devotion to his teacher Yādavaprakāśa (shown in giving his teacher a massage with oil even while he was teaching) is outdone by his vexation and distress (as testified to by his hot tears) when that teacher (following the older Vedāntin Śaṅkara) interpreted the text to mean that Brahman was in color like the monkey's.[30]

The traditional account was colorfully elaborated by Govindacarya at the beginning of the twentieth century:

> On another day, Rāmānuja – disciple as he was – was anointing his Guru Yādava with oil; when Yādava took into his head to descant on the Vedic verse: *tasya yathā kapyāsaṃ puṇḍarīkam evam akṣiṇi* [*Chāndogya Upaniṣad* I, 6, 7] "Brahman," he said, "(or He who is the Golden-hued in the Sun), has his eyes red like the rear end of a monkey." When Rāmānuja heard this, he felt a pang shooting across his heart to find that he should hear noble Vedic passages thus abused and ill-treated by Yādava. His grief was so keen that a hot tear stole in to his eye, and dropped on the lap of Yādava, as Rāmānuja was bending over him to rub his head with oil. The drop scorched Yādava. He started and looked up. Seeing Rāmānuja troubled, "What ails thee?" asked he. "I am grieved," he said, "that beautiful Vedic lines are so awkwardly construed." "What is thy interpretation, then?" angrily vociferated Yādava. "Sir," cried Rāmānuja, "can you not see that *ka* means water, and *pibati* means to drink. Water-drinker is thus *kapi*, the sun, or the lotus-stalk. *āsa* is to open (*vikasane*) or to rest (*upavasane*). *Puṇḍarīka* is the lotus. And therefore God in the Sun is He whose eyes are like the lotus which blooms under the balmy beams of the sun, or lotus which rests on its stalk below?"[31]

One anecdote does not suffice to authorize a generalization, but it is fair to say that there is a religious energy, purposeful and pointed, operative everywhere in his commentarial writing.

---

[30] Or, more precisely, as the color of a lotus, which in turn is the color of a monkey's rear end.

[31] Govindacarya, *The Life of Rāmānujacharya*, p. 32.

### Delight in Single-Minded Service in the *Gītābhāṣya*

The *Gītābhāṣya* highlights the desire and affective focus of the person who has true knowledge, thus echoing what is arguably the major thrust of the *Gītā* itself. This person is exemplary, says Kṛṣṇa, "because he is ever united with me and single in his devotion."[32] Rāmānuja explains, "To the person of knowledge the attainment of Myself being the only end in view, he is ever with Me. Unlike others who at best focus on the Lord occasionally, the person of knowledge cultivates single-minded devotion to Kṛṣṇa alone." This kind of single-minded, extreme, and unending devotion marks true wisdom, and the Lord himself "is unable to express how much I am dear to the wise person (*jñāni*), since there is no such limit as 'this much' for this love ... I reciprocate his love infinitely."[33]

Rāmānuja returns to the theme in the ninth chapter, describing more amply how true devotees feel and suffer: "Apart from their pleasure in me, without participating in Me, they are unable to attain support for their mind, self and external organs. They have as their sole object their devotion to me."[34] Such people act out their devotion in lives of worship and service, acts charged with emotion manifest in corporeal acts:

> Because of My being very dear to them, without "singing My praises," "striving for My sake," and "bowing to Me in reverence," they are unable to find support for their souls even for a moment. Remembering My names which express my specific attributes, with every part of their body thrilled and their voices made low and indistinct with joy, they give praise constantly, "Rāma!" "Nārāyaṇa!" "Kṛṣṇa!" "Vāsudeva!" etc. Just that way, they engage intently in activities for my sake, such as performing temple worship and offering praise, and doing actions helpful to worship, such as building temples and cultivating temple gardens. They prostrate themselves on the earth like a stick, indifferent to dust, mud and the gravel, with all eight limbs – the mind, understanding, ego, the two feet, two hands, and the head – bowed under the weight of their devotion.[35]

---

[32] *Gītābhāṣya*, at 7.17, Adidevananda translation, adapted.
[33] Ibid.
[34] Ibid., at 9.13.
[35] Ibid., at 9.14.

Such people can live only with God or in yearning for God, otherwise unable to sustain life itself without engaging in worship.[36] At the end of the chapter, this extreme devotion again takes a practical turn, as worship enacted not only by the devotional activities mentioned earlier (and repeated here), but also "secular activities for bodily sustenance and Vedic activities like obligatory and occasional rites," repeated day after day.[37] These are people whose sole interest lies in belonging entirely to the Lord, and who live and worship accordingly.

Such passages – and there are many more in the *Gītābhāṣya* – can be taken as exemplary of Śrīvaiṣṇava life as Rāmānuja conceives of it. He is elaborating the meaning of *Gītā* verses in a way that highlights how the ideal reader might learn from such verses and live similar lives. In this way he commends extreme desire for the Lord, an intensity of soul that is nevertheless also articulated through traditional, orthodox practices.

### Seeing, Remembering, Loving in the *Śrībhāṣya*

The *Śrībhāṣya* is Rāmānuja's most important work. It is largely given over to setting forth his interpretation of the 550 *sūtras* of Bādarayaṇa's *Brahma Sūtras*, a task of commentary the great Vedāntins all took upon themselves, just as theologians in medieval Christian Europe made their way by undertaking the work of interpreting Peter Lombard's *Sentences*. The Sūtras themselves have a practical bent as redacted, interpretation of scripture and philosophical defense of revelation all in preparation for the ordering of meditations, the life of the meditator, with an eye to the results of meditation. In his commentary, Rāmānuja furthers his goal of the intensification and clarification that eventuate in increasing devotion.

This is all clear at the beginning of the *Śrībhāṣya*, in its long introduction. Here we find warrants for Rāmānuja's expectation that knowledge, meditation, and thus too devotion – all of which are inseparable – are rooted in experience and specifically in remembering – perhaps in memories of past intense experiences that are as it were vividly back to life.[38] True knowledge is not a kind of unconsciousness or superconsciousness or merging into the One – as his nondualist competitors might claim – but rather a concerted focusing of the mind on the Lord.

In defending his reading of the Upaniṣads, Rāmānuja says, "When (the Upaniṣad) says, 'The Self, dear, is to be seen,' what is enjoined is the

---

[36] Ibid., at 9.22, 29.
[37] Ibid., at 9.34.
[38] See Clooney, "Uruvelippātu."

meditation having a form the same as seeing," because of the intensity of the remembering that takes place.[39] He adds that "this knowledge, of the form of meditation, and repeated more than once, is of the nature of steady remembrance." This remembrance leads to directness in experience: "Such remembrance has been explained as having the character of 'seeing'; this character of seeing approximates the character of immediate presentation ..."[40] Remembrance – apparently of the Lord's past appearances in one's life – takes on an intense immediacy: "Hence, the one who possesses remembrance, which is marked by the character of immediate presentation, and which itself is dear above all things since the object remembered is such – he, we say, is chosen by the highest Self, and by him the highest Self is gained. Holding steady in this remembrance is what is designated by the word 'devotion,' which has the same meaning as *upāsanā* (meditation)."[41] Devotion thus retains its older meaning, "participation."

Devotion can be practiced, perfected, and intensified through repetition that is supported by devotional ritual practices which also further knowledge of God:

> Sacrifices and the like are enjoined with a view to the origination of knowledge, but it is only knowledge in the form of meditation – daily practised, constantly enhanced by repetition, and continued up to death – that is the means of reaching Brahman. Hence, all the works connected with the different conditions of life are to be performed throughout life only for the purpose of originating such knowledge.[42]

The upshot of this key *Śrībhāṣya* passage is that knowledge is a kind of experience approximating direct vision; this vivid knowledge exists primarily as aroused in the memory of the person who seeks to know and who then lives by knowledge. Given the prominence of this text at the start of the *Śrībhāṣya*, we see it as setting the direction for all that follows in his commentary on the *Sūtras*.

A final passage near the end of the *Śrībhāṣya* merits attention here, if only for the unidentified quotation occurring in it. At IV.1.3, Rāmānuja draws theology and spiritual insight together:

> As the meditating individual soul is the Self of its own body, so the highest Brahman is the Self of the individual soul: this is the proper

---

[39] *Śrībhāṣya*, Thibaut translation, revised.
[40] Ibid.
[41] Ibid.
[42] Ibid.

form of meditation. Why? Because the meditators of old acknowledged this: "Then I am indeed you, holy divinity, and you are me."[43]

There is identity, and yet a language of I-thou contact continues to play a role. Here he draws on his famous analogy, that the world – and all selves – are as it were a body to God, to explain the paradoxical language of unity:

> In the same way therefore as, on the basis of the fact that the individual soul occupies with regard to the body the position of a Self, we reflect, "I am a god – I am a human;" the fact of the individual Self being of the nature of Self justifies us in reflecting, "I belong to the highest Self." On the presupposition of all ideas being finally based on Brahman and hence all words also finally denoting Brahman, the texts therefore make such statements of mutual implication as 'I am you, O holy divinity, and you are me'.[44]

There is a move to intense unity – I am you, you are me – but this identity remains as dialogical as the words describing it. The very end of the *Śrībhāṣya* cites Gītā 7 again, to confirm the final destination of study and all that goes with it:

> As, moreover, the released soul has freed itself from the bondage of karma, has its powers of knowledge fully developed, and has all its being in the supremely blissful intuition of the highest Brahman, it evidently cannot desire anything else nor enter on any other form of activity, and the idea of its returning into the *saṃsāra* therefore is altogether excluded. Nor indeed need we fear that the Supreme Lord when once having taken to himself the Devotee whom he greatly loves will turn him back into the *saṃsāra*. For He himself has said, "To the wise person I am very dear, and dear he is to me. Noble indeed are all these, but the wise person I regard as my very Self. For he, with soul devoted, seeks me only as his highest goal. At the end of many births the wise man goes to me, thinking all is Vāsudeva. Such great-souled men are rarely met with." (*Bhagavad Gītā* 7.17–19)[45]

Both the *Gītābhāṣya* and the *Śrībhāṣya* do the needful with respect to explaining the texts being commented on, and often in a way that

43 Ibid.
44 Ibid.
45 Ibid.

furthers a tradition of attention to scripture already in place. But Rāmānuja is in every case seeking to read the Upaniṣads and *Gītā* and related texts so as to reorient them toward vision of God, cast as an exceedingly pleasurable progress in intimacy with God. In this context, of course, experience is thus not a private experience set apart from tradition, but one that is schooled and disciplined in relation to the great texts that exist precisely to make experience clear and direct.

The *Śrībhāṣya* is highly technical, but an anecdote in Nampiḷḷai's[46] commentary on Śaṭakōpaṉ's *Tiruviruttam* 99 gives a small insight into what Rāmānuja was like during the time of its composition:

> These may be simple words, but:
> In the form of a boar the Lord lifted the whole earth amid the crashing waves:
> For the heaven-dwellers with the *kalpaka* tree, for those who are not, for everyone else, there is no one other than this lord of knowledge.
> Such is the good I've seen.[47]

In Nampiḷḷai's commentary on the verse we are given a series of anecdotes about teachers who are deeply moved in their teaching of the āḻvārs' songs, and thus people "for whom there is no one else." At the end of the list is a scene set in the period when Rāmānuja was writing the *Śrībhāṣya*. He is moved deeply and incessantly by the Tamil verses:

> [Rāmānuja] was all day long immersed in the *Śrībhāṣya*. Having taken his evening meal, he graciously reclined on his bed, and invited Vaṭuka Nampi, "Won't you sing a verse?" When he sang the first verse, Rāmānuja was so very immersed in it that his hair stood on end. When Vaṭuka Nampi sang a second time, Rāmānuja broke down[48] and melted away. Each time Vaṭuka Nampi started, Rāmānuja wept such a flood of tears that he needed to change his upper cloth three or four times.[49]

A passage like this indicates that there is no great split between his intellectual brilliance and affective life. While it would be too much to say that the *Śrībhāṣya* was infused with his tears, the point of this

---

[46] A great teacher, about three generations after Rāmānuja.
[47] Śaṭakōpaṉ, *Tiruviruttam*. My translation.
[48] Literally, burst the tank's boundary.
[49] Nampiḷḷai's *Īṭu* on *Tiruviruttam* 99, p. 333.

anecdote seems to be that Rāmānuja is precisely the person for whom "there is no one else," even when he was writing the *Śrībhāṣya*.

## RĀMĀNUJA'S COMMENTARIAL WRITINGS
## THEMSELVES AS GENERATIVE OF EXPERIENCE

The Śrīvaiṣṇava tradition claims that Rāmānuja's works arise from his own experience – think of the third anecdote at the start of this essay, set as it was in the time when Rāmānuja was composing the *Śrībhāṣya*. The tradition asserts too that his technical commentarial writings are productive of the same experiences in others. In commenting on the *Sri Yatirāja Saptati* (*70 Verses on the King of Ascetics* [Rāmānuja]) of Vedānta Deśika, one of the greatest teachers of the tradition after Rāmānuja, D. Ramaswami Ayyangar comments on the beauty and power of the *Śrībhāṣya*. For example, this is Deśika's verse 29:

> The good word of the lord of ascetics has an essence extolled by great sages. It is the ladder to liberation, the accomplishment of the lasting good fortune of right-hearted persons. It completely banishes all traces of sin, and increases in depth the more one dives into it. May it afford us grace![50]

Here, Ayyangar takes this "good word" to be the *Śrībhāṣya*, the largest and more formidable of Rāmānuja's works, and elaborates on the value of an extended study of it:

> The last excellence is the unfathomable beauty contained in Rāmānuja's works. The meanings of the words employed by Rāmānuja are understood better and better by a repeated study of his works … in some places the meaning lies underground, as it were, and one has to delve and delve to get at them. Employing the analogy or the sea, the deeper a diver dives, the richer is the wealth of pearls and gems that becomes available to him. In the same way as one studies *Śrībhāṣya* again and again, newer and more excellent meanings are obtained by him. And yet the impression left is that there must be many more ideas and meanings to be gathered by further study.[51]

In verse 33, Deśika praises the rich mix of Rāmānuja's writings, such as appeal to the intellect and to the spiritual senses:

---

[50] *Sri Yatirāja Saptati* 29, Ayyangar translation, revised, p. 57.
[51] Ibid., p. 59.

The teaching of Lakṣmaṇārya (Rāmānuja) is the goal for the intellect, and capable of causing the tongues of *rasikas* (those taking delight) to dance, possessed of a pure taste, a rare and unparalleled divine medicine for our ears. Resplendent with thoughts lucid and deep, like a pure sea full of gems, seen as well as unseen, it is a mirror reflecting the husband of Śrī.

Here Ayyangar emphasizes the pleasurable nature of the instruction Rāmānuja gives:

To mouth the several paṅkti or passages of *Śrībhāṣya* and other works of Rāmānuja is by itself productive of pleasure. Even as the lofty sense imbedded in them is the goal or aim of intellect, their pleasant sound is sought after by the tongue. To read aloud or recite the grand and sonorious passages full of ringing rhythm is itself pleasant and enjoyable. This enjoyment is likened to *lāsya līlā* [delight in the play of] dance. The tongue dances in mirth even at the very thought of uttering the passages of Yatirāja's (Rāmānuja's) works.[52]

To study the writings of Rāmānuja is then itself an avenue into deeper, more intense religious experience: words from experience, for experience. This may be taken as paradigmatic for what the point is of Rāmānuja's corpus of writings, the instigation of right reading and right practice, such as lead the practitioner to an ever more complete experience of God.

## RĀMĀNUJA'S DEVOTIONAL WRITINGS

It is customary among scholars to work with the *Vedārthasaṃgraha*, *Gītābhāṣya*, and *Śrībhāṣya*, and we might end our travel through Rāmānuja's works with the preceding. But I wish also to take into account the *Gadya*s and the *Nityam*, where the spiritual nature of Rāmānuja's writing becomes all the more clear.[53]

First, the *Saraṇāgatygadyam*, *Śrīraṅgagadyam*, and *Śrīvaikuṇṭha-gadyam* are altogether rather brief, together comprising fewer than ten

[52] Ibid., p. 68.

[53] In the 1960s, Robert Lester, "Rāmānuja and Śrī-Vaiṣṇavism" drew on linguistic and theological points to support the view that the *Gadya*s and *Nityam* were not composed by Rāmānuja. His view has in fact found little support among scholars thereafter, and provoked fierce opposition from within the community. Nevertheless, most scholars seem inclined not to draw these latter works into their analysis of Rāmānuja's thought. My approach is rather the reverse, thus affording us insight into the 'whole Rāmānuja' who has come down to us over a millennium.

pages of Sanskrit. All three pertain to longing for God and the taking of refuge – fundamentally in the first, at the Śriraṅgam temple in the second, and in heaven, eschatologically we might say, in the third. They can easily be read as works of experience, it would seem, and there are more than fifty "I" statements in the *Gadya*s. In these prayers, Rāmānuja is providing words for his devotees, and it is natural to assume that they are his words too.

Consider these passages from the *Śaraṇāgatigadyam*, beginning with this opening determination, concluding in a prayer to the Goddess Śrī Lakṣmī:

> I have the desire to obtain eternal service of the Lord, service of the nature of finding my only joy in rendering all forms of service appropriate to all states and situations without exception, stimulated by *an unlimited and unsurpassed love* arising from the *boundless and unsurpassed delight in the perfectly full, continuous, enduring and most clear experience of the Lord*, without any other motive, achieved by greater devotion, greater knowledge, and the highest devotion, displayed entirely and solely at the two lotus-like feet of the Lord which are the supreme goal: may my supreme refuge at the lotus feet of the Lord be unending in every situation.[54]

In this prayer too, as in Rāmānuja's other works, that the process is one of intensification that ends in loving service is emphasized, as in this passage near the end of the text:

> My experience of the Lord is perfectly full, continuous, enduring and most clear, without any other motive, achieved by greater devotion, greater knowledge, and the highest devotion. So may I now become an eternal servant of the Lord whose sole joy lies in being entirely dependent without exception in all states without exception, achieved by the infinite and unequalled pleasure born from the experience of the lord in this way.

The Lord responds in kind, promising an eternally increasing state of joy and grace:

> By my grace may you have exclusive and everlasting greater devotion, greater knowledge, and the highest devotion at my two lotus feet, and by my grace alone, may your self have a proper nature

---

[54] My emphasis. My translations, adapted from *Rāmānuja's Gadyatrayam* as translated by V. V. Ramanujam.

and way of being that is solely in service to me, controlled by me, known directly, the expanse of my form in this world, my qualities, forms and proper form, in each state made manifest.

May you experience me alone, and be pleased solely in service to me, may you experience me with a flawless and abundant pleasure, having no other motive, perfectly full, continuous, most enduring and clear, may you be my eternal servant whose sole joy lies in being entirely dependent without exception in all states without exception, achieved by the infinite and unequalled pleasure born from the experience of me in this way.

Here too, we may conjecture that Rāmānuja's experience is behind his words. An anecdote in an old commentary on the *Śaraṇāgatigadyam* is indicative. A key disciple balks at the notion that the Lord has spoken to Rāmānuja with words so encouraging and intimate:

The great Lord (Śrīraṅganātha), out of the great pleasure and love, repeats these words and gladdens the heart of the ācārya by saying, "I am pleased to grant that all your wishes be fulfilled in the fullest measure."

When Rāmānuja's disciple Empār balks at this claim – "How are we to believe that the great Lord was pleased to tell you all this?" – Rāmānuja responds,

These are words which he made me utter after having shown his quality of miscibility (the high mixing with the low) like a fruit in the hand. So, nothing stands in the way of believing that these are His own words. The rest of the *Śaraṇāgatigadyam* are the words expressed by the Lord – the assurance He gave.[55]

Intimacy with the Lord is deeply mutual, and the devotee can expect to hear the voice of the Lord, even as echoed in a repetition of the devotee's own words.

Attention to the other *Gadya*s would serve to give us variations on the theme, to be sure, but here we must limit ourselves to one additional text. Near the end of the third prayer, the *Śrīvaikuṇṭhagadyam*, the repetition of the act of surrender to the Lord opens into an affirmation of devotion, and reaffirmation of the life of devout service of the Lord.

Now the devotee is looked at by the Lord with His glance that is capable of causing one's spiritual rebirth and that is full of

[55] Rāmānuja *Śaraṇāgatigadyam* 17.

overflowing goodness and love, and the devotee is taken by Him into His whole-hearted and loyal service in all places, at all times and in all situations and with His approval. The devotee should then serve Him with great awe and humility and worship Him with folded hands. Experiencing then the unique fervor of emotion and unable, owing to boundless love, to do, to see or to remember anything else, one should again pray for the favor of being the Lord's servant and should remain gazing at Him with the stream of uninterrupted vision.

Meditation on the Lord's cosmic reality in the glory of heaven eventuates in the simple state of being ever seen by the Lord, caught in his glance, and this grace in turn eventuates in a life of service, which is in essence also a mystical state, an uninterrupted vision of God here and in the life to come.

### THE DEEPENING OF EXPERIENCE IN DAILY WORSHIP

I have shown in the preceding pages that Rāmānuja's writing coheres in producing the intellectual conditions for an ever deeper encounter with God, such as leads to face to face encounters, a seeing "as if" that of perception. His writings, read over and over, remove obstacles to the encounter with God and thus keep deepening the experience. Devotional activity follows on the writing, expressive of insights into the nature of the divine-human relationship, and conducive to a further, clear-minded development.

That Rāmānuja has in mind the intensification and extension of experience through practice is made still clearer in the work of his always listed last, the *Nityam*.[56] This is a detailed prescription for the daily morning worship of the devotee, as devotion is disciplined in the frame of regular ritual practice. The text, though short, contains over 250 prescriptions. Yet here, too, we see multiple instances where there is a smooth crossover from mundane detail to devotional intensity:

His hands and feet have been washed well and he has sipped water well. Next then, he chooses ground in a pure and most enchanting place free of noise. He thoroughly purifies it by acts of drying, etc. Through the succession of gurus he approaches the Lord, the supreme guru, and meditates on Him as the goal and the means to

[56] See Rastelli, "Unaltered Ritual in Transformed Religion," and Clooney, "Rāmānuja's Nityam."

the goal, and as the remover of the undesirable and acquirer of the desirable. He meditates on the expanse of the Lord's proper form, forms, qualities, powers, and instruments of sport, all these as specified. Then let him approach the Lord alone as refuge, with the words, "All that is to be avoided ..."[57] (sections III–IV)

A succeeding instruction reminds us of the immediacy of experience and intensity of joy promised in both the *Vedārthasaṃgraha* and in the *Śrībhāṣya*:

> After he has thus come near for refuge, with the movements of his mind enhanced by the Lord's grace, he meditates on that Lord alone, the Lord of all lords, as the Lord of his own self. Let him sit meditating with a meditation *like in form to perception, most clear, uninterrupted, and exceedingly pleasing*. Then let him undertake the worship[58] that has the form of utterly complete service accomplished with immeasurable pleasure born of experiencing Him. (section V)[59]

Consider too this brief passage that gives us a surprising combination of the materially sweet with spiritual delight:

> Then, after placing on the plate cane sugar, honey, melted butter, curd, and milk, he thoroughly purifies them by acts of drying, etc., and sprinkles with the guest-water. *Then, with his head bowed, his eyes wide with delight, his mind delighted, he gives honey-and-milk*. Then let him give water for sipping. (section XVI)[60]

Throughout the *Nityam*, there are also passages that, as in the *Gadya*s, require the practitioner to create an image of the Lord. Consider this small contemplation, which follows the initial purifications and the meditations and mantra recitations that recreate the worshipper so as to make him or her able to approach the Lord. It occurs after the practitioner has ascended in contemplation from the fundamental

---

[57] A quotation from Rāmānuja's *Śaraṇāgatigadyam*, which is thus coordinated with the *Nityam* at this particular point. Clooney, "Rāmānuja's Nityagrantham."

[58] We find *pūjām ārabheta* ('undertake') here and at the end of XIV, and we find *yāgam ārabheta* ('undertake') at the end of VII and IX. *pūjā* and *yāga* might be taken as synonyms, as Sampath, "Daily Routine According to Rāmānuja," 150, suggests, or *yāga* refers to the act that connects heaven and earth, and *pūjā* refers to those more intimate to service of the Lord here on earth.

[59] Sampath, "Daily Routine According to Rāmānuja," my emphasis.

[60] Ibid., my emphasis.

cosmic power up to the very presence of the Lord at the apex of the universe:

> He meditates on the Lord Nārāyaṇa who is seated on the coils of the visualized serpent; his eyes as elongated and pure like petals of the lotus; as adorned with all His adornments, the crowns, bracelets, necklace of pearls, etc., His right leg bent, His left leg forward, His right arm forward and placed on His knee, His left arm placed on the coils of the serpent; as holding the conch and wheel with His two upper hands; as the cause for the creation, preservation and destruction of all; dark in appearance and shines with the kaustubha gem; as the supreme pure being, unprecedented and inconceivable, shining, awake, tall, manifest, His body comprised of the five powers. He does all this with the five upaniṣad mantras. After praying with the root mantra, "Look favorably on my worship," again while reciting the root mantra he falls prostrate like a stick. After rising and offering welcome, let him ask Him to be present up to the completion of the worship. (section IX)

The worshipper then continues the contemplation while descending through the cosmic palaces of the Lord's retinue, with appropriate gestures of honor toward every place and deity met along the way, arriving finally back on the river's edge where the worship began. Then the practitioner can enter into more intimate worship of the Lord. While the details of the image are familiar and can be found in other texts by Rāmānuja, the added point here is the impact of daily repetition, repeated practice in remembering the Lord's appearance in loving detail. Here we have the regulation of experience, its expression in ritual form, and by that means an intensification of it.

Here too we have a clue from the traditional memory of Rāmānuja, such as softens our image of this prescriber of ritual rules. Verse 44 of Poykai Āḻvār's *Mutal Tiruvantāti* opens the door to almost any manner of sincere devotion:

> Whichever form pleases his people, that is his form;
> Whichever name pleases his people, that is his name;
> Whichever way pleases his people who meditate without ceasing,
> That is his way, the one who holds the discus.[61]

The commentator Periyavāccaṉpiḷḷai illustrates the first line with an anecdote about Rāmānuja. He was out walking near the Śrīraṅgam

---

[61] My translation, Clooney, "God for Us," p. 44.

temple, and saw some boys who were playing priests, and for this purpose had outlined in the dust the image of Lord Nārāyaṇa as Raṅganātha. Not only was Rāmānuja not offended by this, but indeed was certain that the Lord was present even in so trivial a form as that produced by playful boys. So he prostrated himself before the image sketched in the dust by the boys, and even took some of that dust as the food offering (*prasādam*) given as a sign of divine favor to one who worships in a temple.

## THE SPIRITUAL PEDAGOGY OF RĀMĀNUJA'S OEUVRE AS A WHOLE

After this brief tour of Rāmānuja's works, it will now be easier to appreciate how the works are purposefully ordered as a useable spiritual architectonic. Vaṭuka Nampi's *Yatirājavaibhavam* presents this logic for the sequence of texts:

> Yatirāja [Rāmānuja] then composed the *Vedārthasaṃgraha*, and the *Vedāntasāra*, *Vedāntadīpā*, and *Śrībhāṣya* for the *Vedānta Sūtras* and a gloss on the *Gītā* and taught them to Vātsyeśa and others.

On the basis of this solid and faithful theological work, Rāmānuja moves into a more experiential mode, for the composition of his prose prayers:

> Then, once on the (day of the) Uttaraphālguni asterism in the Phālguna month, with joy the lord of ascetics (Rāmānuja) took refuge with Raṅganāyikā (Śrī Lakṣmī) and Raṅganātha (Nārāyaṇa) who had been bathed (in the sacred waters), and he uttered the *Gadyatrayam*.

And in turn, all this is given a ritual focus:

> Through his composition called *Nityam*, this lord of ascetics taught the service be undertaken till the end of one's life by one who has understood Reality by his *Śrībhāṣya* and other texts, and has surrendered himself to the Lord of Śrī by the *Gadya*s, and who is leading the life of a person surrendered to the Lord.[62]

This echoes Yāmuna's reading of the *Gītā*, since he likewise called for the "performance of personal duties" and the "cultivation of *bhakti*." By the set of his works, Rāmānuja outlines the cognitive, affective, and

---

[62] Andhrapūrṇa, *Yatirāja-Vaibhavam*, nn. 71, 73–74.

performative steps by which the devout reader is to move toward a complete spiritual existence even in this world.

## GENERALIZING ON AND FROM THE EXPERIENCE OF RĀMĀNUJA

Rāmānuja is representative of his tradition. He adheres to tradition, respecting it, even while re-directing it to his purposes, fusing – entirely in Sanskrit and without referring to the devotional tradition of the ālvārs – the normative texts of Vedānta (Upaniṣads, *Gītā*, *Brahma Sūtras*) with passages from the *Viṣṇu Purāṇa*, and other scriptures that help create a cosmology and a devotional frame. Rāmānuja is a refined intellectual and erudite scholar who knows his sources well, and has worked out a method for reading his sources integrally. He does this without, in his view, giving priority merely to one set of texts or coming up with an interpretation that waters down the intensity of the texts. So too, as we have seen, he consistently uses his readings to create spaces for highly energized and intense experience. His readings are for the intensification of experience, and then serve as a training ground for experience and participation, giving experience a particular shape and focus.

Rāmānuja offers an integral and whole Vedānta. Here we find a balance between nondualist and differentiative dynamics, which creates a formative disposition toward the intensification of experience: the vast gap between the divine and human always being overcome in a realization of a still deeper non-duality of the divine and the human. Rāmānuja is an intellectual who respects ongoing ritual performance and aims at the intensification of experience. He is a scholar who, though immersed in Sanskrit brahminical learning, open (as the tradition testifies) to vernacular culture and tradition: he does not write in Tamil or refer to the literature of the ālvārs, but once one begins to notice those sources, his Sanskrit works are easily read alongside the Tamil. Rāmānuja's intellectually and affectively charged Vedānta is distinctively Śrīvaiṣṇava, to be sure, and thus represents one particular program for religious experience, that ought not be taken as normative even for Vedānta. But the main points I have just highlighted – an integral reading of scriptures in accord with reason and perception, a deeply intellectual approach that nevertheless respects ritual practice and aims toward deep experience, a conception of the intellectual life as formative, and consonance with vernacular language and piety – are consonant with other schools of Vedānta and the array of wider Hindu intellectual practices.

We can therefore learn a great deal about regimes of Hindu religious experience from Rāmānuja, and I hope that I have shown the value of my plan to offer him as this essay's illustrative case study. Nevertheless, other such studies must follow. From Rāmānuja one might move rather easily then to an appreciation of other instances of Hindu scholastic, ritual, and devotional writing that are conducive to deeper religious experience. Within the realm of Vedānta itself, the Advaita path of Śaṅkara offers an obvious partial parallel, and we can see that differing views of words and rites and of Brahman's relation to the world add up to a rather different configuration of religious experience that, as it progresses toward radical nonduality, abandons ritual and then too language, and finally individual consciousness.

We might then also turn to the Kashmir Śaivism of Abhinavagupta, particularly as marked by Abhinavagupta's record of his own experience, or to Gauḍīya Vaiṣṇavism, which was inspired by the ecstatic manifestations of Caitanya – a Bengali devotionalism partially indebted to Rāmānuja, in which we find structured and intensified paths of experience, elaborately explained in commentary and scholastic theological reflection, leading to immediate and intense encounters with God. So too, Yoga taken up as theory and as practice opens another parallel realm. If we attend primarily to the *Yoga Sūtras* (a primary resource, even if not normative for all yoga), we learn that the clarification of states of consciousness leads to a state of consciousness uncluttered by the movements of consciousness – the citta, the consciousness-stuff – that is in utter equilibrium, unmoved by whatever happens. Practice is about maintaining and deepening this state as it approaches its perfection, even in this life.

## References

### Primary Sources in Translation

Andhrapūrṇa. *Yatirāja-Vaibhavam.* Disciple of Rāmānuja. Edited by V. Varadachariar. Madras: M. C. Khrishnan, 1978.

Deśika, Vedānta. *Sri Yatirāja Saptati.* D. Ramaswami Ayyangar edition with commentary. Tirupati: Tirumala Tirupati Devasthanams, 1965.

Nañjīyar. *Introduction to His Commentary on the* Tiruvāymoḻi *of Śaṭakōpaṇ. Bhagavat Viśayam.* Edited by Krishnaswami Ayyangar. Volume 1. Trichi: Books Propagation Society, 1975.

Rāmānuja. *Śrībhāṣya.* Translated by George Thibaut, Sacred Books of the East 48. Oxford: Oxford University Press, 1904.

*Vedārthasaṃgraha.* Translated by S. S. Raghavachar. Mysore: Sri Ramakrishna Ashrama, 1956.

*Vedārthasaṃgraha.* Translated by J. A. B. van Buitenen. Poona: Deccan College Posgratuate and Research Institute, 1956.

*Rāmānuja on the Bhagavadgītā.* Translated by J. A. B. van Buitenen. Delhi: Motilal Banarsidass, 1968.

*The Gītābhāṣya.* Translated by M. R. Sampatkumaran. Madras: Prof. M. Rangacharya Memorial Trust, 1969.

"Le *Nityagrantha* de Rāmānuja," French translation by Anne-Marie Esnoul. *Journal Asiatique* 260 (1–2) (1972), 39–78.

*Śrī Rāmānuja Gītā Bhāṣya.* Translated by Swami Adidevananda. Madras: Sri Ramakrishna Math, 1991.

*Gadyatrayam.* With commentary of Periyavāccaṉpiḷḷai. Translated by V. V. Ramanujam. Chennai: Sri Rangaapriya Pathipakkam, 1994.

Śaṭakōpaṉ. *Tiruviruttam,* with Commentaries (including Naṃpiḷḷai's *Īṭu* and Vātikecari Aḷakīya Manavalacīyar's *Svāpadecam*). Srirangam: Sri Vaisnava Sri, 1996.

Yāmuna. *The Gītārthasaṃgraha.* Translation included in Rāmānuja, *The Gītābhāṣya,* as translated by M. R. Sampatkumaran. Madras: Prof. M. Rangacharya Memorial Trust, 1969.

## Secondary Sources

Adluri, Sucharita. *Textual Authority in Classical Indian Thought: Rāmānuja and the Viṣṇu Purāṇa.* Abingdon: Routledge, 2015.

Cabezon, Jose I. *Scholasticism in a Comparative Perspective.* Albany, NY: State University of New York, 1998.

Carman, John B. *Theology of Rāmānuja: An Essay in Interreligious Understanding.* New Haven, CT: Yale University Press, 1974.

Clooney, Francis X. *Seeing through Texts: Doing Theology among the Srivaisnavas of South India.* Albany, NY: State University of New York, 1996.

"God for Us: Multiple Religious Belonging as Spiritual Practice and Divine Response," in Catherine Cornille (ed.), *Many Mansions? Multiple Religious Belonging and Christian Identity,* pp. 44–60. Maryknoll: Orbis Books, 2002.

"Uruvelippatu: A Tamil Practice of Visualization and Its Significance in Srivaisnavism," *The Journal of Oriental Research (Madras)* 81–82 (2010): 209–24.

*His Hiding Place Is Darkness: An Exercise in Hindu-Catholic Theopoetics.* Palo Alto, CA: Stanford University Press, 2013.

"Rāmānuja's *Nityam*: A Neglected Key to His Theology," *Brahmavidya: The Adyar Library Bulletin* 81–82 (2017–2018): 231–64.

"Meditation in Practice, in Theory: Rāmānuja's Prescriptions on Meditation in the *Nityam* in Light of His Commentarial Works," for a volume of essays marking the 1000th birth anniversary of Rāmānuja. (Forthcoming).

"Rāmānuja's Nityagrantham (Manual of Daily Worship)," *International Journal of Hindu Studies* 24 (3) (2020).

Dutta, Ranjeeta. *From Hagiographies to Biographies: Rāmānuja in Tradition and History.* Oxford: Oxford University Press, 2014.

Flood, Gavin. *The Truth Within: A History of Inwardness in Christianity, Hinduism, and Buddhism.* Oxford: Oxford University Press, 2013.

Forsthoefel, Thomas. *Knowing beyond Knowledge: Epistemologies of Religious Experience in Classical and Modern Advaita.* Farnham: Ashgate, 2002.

Govindacharya, Alkondaville. *The Life of Rāmānujacharya: The Exponent of the Visishtadvaita Philosophy.* Madras: S. Murthy, 1906.

Lester, Robert C. "Rāmānuja and Śrī-Vaiṣṇavism: The Concept of Prapatti or Śaraṇāgati," *History of Religions* 5 (2) (1966): 266–82.

McGinn, Bernard. "Mystical Consciousness: A Modest Proposal," *Spiritus* 8 (1) (2008): 44–63.

Rastelli, Marion. "Unaltered Ritual in Transformed Religion: The Pūjā according to the Ahirbudhnyasaṃhitā 28 and the Nityagrantha," in Jörg Gengnagel, Ute Hüsken, and Śrīlata Raman (eds.), *Words and Deeds: Hindu and Buddhist Rituals in South Asia,* pp 115–52. Wiesbaden: Harrassowitz Verlag, 2005.

Sampath, R. N. "Daily Routine according to Rāmānuja," *Studies in Rāmānuja* (1979): 143–50.

Veliath, Cyril. *The Mysticism of Rāmānuja.* New Delhi: Munshiram Manoharlal Publishers Pvt. Ltd., 1993.

**Part IV**

*Prominent Themes and Challenges*

# 10 Exploring the Nature of Mystical Experience

STEVEN T. KATZ

## INTRODUCTION

The subject matter of this essay will concentrate on the crucial and inescapable interconnection between mystical experience, epistemology, and metaphysics. Its purpose will be to illuminate some of the key epistemological and metaphysical issues that claims regarding mystical experience give rise to.

Mystical experiences in different forms have been known in all the major religious traditions of the world. And these experiences have been the subject of intensive study by theologians and philosophers. In the main, these scholars have concentrated on the mystical experiences as described after the climactic moment(s), by those who have had the experience. Thus, their philosophical interrogations center on issues concerning what mystics, having succeeded in their spiritual quest, report. Accordingly, William James, Rudolf Otto, W. R. Inge, Walter T. Stace, and more recently Ninian Smart ask undeniably significant questions about the content of mystical experiences. For example, James, in his classic *Varieties of Religious Experience* tells his readers: "The Overcoming of the usual barrier between the individual and the Absolute is the great mystic achievement. In mystic states we both become one with the Absolute and we become aware of our oneness."[1] And Inge, in his *Mysticism in Religion*, reports that, "mysticism is the immediate feeling of unity of self with God."[2] Likewise, Rudolf Otto emphasizes that the mystical experiences, based on mystical testimonies, is "a mysterium tremendum et fascinans."[3] And, as recently as 2015, Jason N. Blum has concentrated on "mystical experiential accounts" that he defines "as a report of an encounter between a mystic

---

[1] James, *The Varieties of Religious Experience*, p. 404.
[2] Inge, *Mysticism in Religion*, Appendix.
[3] Otto, *The Idea of the Holy*, chapter IV.

and the ultimate that is more intimate than that afforded by religious practice as performed by the larger, general religious community."[4] This focus on the content of mystical experience, is, of course, legitimate, and we shall return to it. But, at the same time, it must be understood that these reports are not self-explanatory.

## THE IMPORTANCE OF CONTEXT

Therefore, I would like to join this significant conversation about mystical experience but through a decidedly different approach to the material in question. As my first step I would advance a general phenomenological observation based on having read mystical texts from many traditions over many decades. In the course of this reading I have been impressed by the fact – and have had the fact pressed upon me – that the content of mystical experience almost always turns out to be what the mystic wants it to be. As St. Teresa of Avila wrote: "Behold Him whom I seek and Whom I desire."[5] That is, Christian mystics experience God or Jesus, but not *nirvana* and not the *Doa*. Alternatively, Buddhists never experience Jesus or encounter the Virgin Mary, or even God the Father, while *Arjuna* begins with the knowledge of the reality of Krishna and devotes himself to encountering the deity:

> This, my soul's peace, have I heard from Thee,
> The unfolding of the Mystery Supreme
> Named Adhyatman; comprehending which,
> My darkness is dispelled; for now I know –
> O Lotus-eyed! – whence is the bird of men,
> And whence their death, and what the majesties
> Of Thine immortal rule. Fain. would I see,
> As thou Thyself declar'st it, Sovereign Lord!
> The likeness of that glory of thy Form
> Wholly revealed. o Thou Divinest One!
> If this can be, if I may bear the sight,
> Make Thyself visible, Lord of prayers!
> Show me Thy very self, the Eternal God![6]

Now, I am certainly not the first student of mystical texts to note this fundamental circumstance. Since at least the time of William

[4] Blum, *Zen and the Unspeakable God*, p. 5.
[5] Poulain, *Graces of Interior Prayer*, p. 102.
[6] *The Bhagavad Gita, XI*, reprinted in Katz (ed.), *Comparative Mysticism*, p. 351.

James, more than a century ago, scholars have recognized the congruity between the tradition out of which a mystic comes – which sets his or her goals – and the mystical experience that they have. And they have, for more than a century, explained – and this is the essential point I wish to emphasize here – that this similarity, this parallelism, is to be accounted for not by the nature of the experience but by the fact that the mystics, having actually experienced that which is inherently and necessarily ineffable, are forced, when they return from their ecstatic moments, to use the language (or tradition) they know in order to describe the indescribable. Hence the testimony they provide employs the metaphysical, ontological, and doctrinal understandings of their more usual lived context.

Walter T. Stace articulated this crucial claim with paradigmatic clarity: "It is," he wrote, "important as well as possible to make a distinction between a mystical experience itself and the conceptual interpretations that may be put upon it."[7] Stace assumed this hermeneutical position to be correct even though he recognized that "it is probably impossible to isolate 'pure experience'."[8] In response to this important, widely shared, scholarly claim, one needs to consider the following:

1. Mystical experience is not just pure sensation, which is the basic model Stace and others use in thinking about, in conceptualizing, mystical experience. The ultimate realia are known as realia that are either "objects," or beings, or states of being, or altered states of consciousness that require recognition and/or determinations by the mystical experiencer. It is precisely because, for example, God is not a mere "sense-data" to the mystic that he or she is able to know it is God. Note that the vocabulary of mystical reports almost always involves words like love, God's goodness, the fullness of being, unity, spirit. These are not simple sensations like hot and cold. St. Teresa of Avila, for instance, in describing "The Prayer of Quiet," tells her readers that in this state: "He [God] is pleased to grant us some supernatural favor, its coming is accompanied by the greatest peace and quietness and sweetness."[9] Even in the fifth mansion, Teresa describes the fact that in mystical union "love remains alive."[10]

---

[7] Stace, *Mysticism and Philosophy*, p. 7.
[8] Ibid., p. 31.
[9] Saint Teresa of Avila, *The Interior Castle*, p. 81.
[10] Saint Teresa of Avila, *The Life of Teresa of Jesus*, pp. 391–92.

   This paradigm also applies to mystics such as Eckhart and Ruysbroeck, in spite of all their negations and their insistence on the
imageless nature of their experience. Their descriptions of the mystical state employ such terms as "darkness," "silence," "nakedness,"
"barren," "empty," and "desert," all of which are learned terms that
are deeply saturated with meaning(s) and which, in turn, deeply
saturate the mystical consciousness. Furthermore, these sorts of
descriptions are meant by authors like Eckhart to be experiential
terms not just indirect hints made through metaphors. Eckhart, and
later Ruysbroeck, actually stand near the end of a long tradition that
goes back to Plotinus and Pseudo-Dionysius that, while utilizing
apophatic language, nevertheless provides more than the mere raw
itemization of experience. Then, too, one needs to explore the deep
links between apophatic and cataphatic language; the connections
between what mystics say and what they say they cannot say.
2. Stace's own summary of the situation created by mystic experience,
   i.e., of "pure experience" versus the interpretation of this experience, is either irrelevant or self-contradictory as he admits the
   impossibility of "find[ing] sense experience completely free of interpretation." This crucial epistemological concession raises major
   interpretive issues to which we shall return.
3. Stace's position, shared by many other thinkers,[11] puts all the evidential weight on the post-experiential interpretation of the mystical event. It fails altogether to pursue the epistemological issues
   that make the experience the experience it was.
4. The relationship between experience and interpretation is, for Stace
   (and others) always one directional – from experience to the beliefs
   called upon to explain the experience after it occurred. There is no
   recognition that this circumstance contains a two-directional reciprocity. Beliefs shape experiences, just as experience shapes beliefs.
5. In addition, the crucial distinction between experiential immediacy
   and epistemological immediacy goes unrecognized. In the lived
   mystical context this distinction entails the recognition that while
   X, the ultimate objects of concern or the ultimate states of consciousness, are encountered or experienced with an intense immediacy – still, at the same time, this immediacy is already fashioned,
   shaped, influenced by prior conditions of knowing, including a vast

[11] In Zen, and other Asian traditions this is a common view. See, for example, Nishida's
   work in which he referred to "pure experience" as "the state of experience just as it is
   without the least addition of deliberate discrimination," *Inquiry into the God*, p. 3

array of beliefs and associations that the mystic brings to this immediate experience.

6. Stace, wholly on a priori grounds, dismisses all the content in descriptions of mystical experience that do not cohere with his assumption that the only ultimately true mystical experience is a content-less introvertive mystical experience of undifferentiated Oneness. In contradistinction, I would argue for respecting the descriptions of the mystics and for asking the question: Why are these phenomenological reports the way they are?

Put another way, immediate experience, while phenomenologically immediate, is already mediated. That is to say, this mediation vis-à-vis experience is not of the form: "A has an experience of X, X being the ultimate object of concern or ultimate states of consciousness, and then, in a second epistemological operation, knows that X has, for example, properties Alpha, Beta, Delta." Certainly, to decipher the reality of mystical experience as an inference from the phenomenological via the epistemological to form a judgment is altogether misconceived. Rather, the epistemological precedes the phenomenological to create the immediate experience that occurs. In an experience of the sort just described, this would mean that the original phenomenological experience of X is already epistemologically mediated by, for example, Alpha, Beta, Delta. One might well describe this state of epistemological awareness as "mediated immediacy."

Though I focus these critical observations on the influential work of Walter T. Stace, it is apposite to understand that his position was selected for comment because it is representative of the views of so many scholars who have adopted essentially the same erroneous position. This list includes, but is not exhausted by, such luminaries as William James, Evelyn Underhill, Rudolf Otto, Ninian Smart, and more recently, William Wainwright. And it extends to include all those many advocates of the interpretation of mysticism as an undifferentiated *philosophia perennis*. Here one thinks of scholars as different as Aldous Huxley, Frithjof Schuon, and Sayyed Hossein Nasr, and more recently, Robert Forman.

I have chosen to begin with these critical observations because I want to insist that it needs to be recognized, contra James and Stace, and many others, that the scholarly and interpretive concentration on the content of mystical experience – and the post-experiential description of such experience – altogether bypasses a still more fundamental issue, the analysis of which will affect all questions regarding the

content, the *what* of mystical experience. And this is the question of
*how* one experiences, *how* one knows, what one knows in and through
the mystical experience. Which is to say, vis-à-vis mystical experience
and the reports of mystical experience – the reports being the only thing
we know of other people's mystical experiences as we have no direct
access to their experiences as such – that, the first, and major, question
or set of questions that must be thoroughly engaged in the decipher-
ment of mystical sources is epistemological. We need to ask: *how* do
mystics come to experience what they experience?

## NO PURE EXPERIENCE

To raise this philosophical concern is to insist that philosophers and
metaphysicians recognize that the study of mystical experience requires
an investigation of not only the experience per se and the post-
experiential reports of such experiences, but also of what one might call
the consciousness that the mystic brings to, and which, at least in part,
shapes the mystical experience.

To move right to the center of this epistemological issue, I would
now state my basic epistemological assumption that is based on the
totality of the evidence supplied by the world's mystical traditions,
as this evidence is known to me: there is no pure, unmediated experience. Mystical experience, like all experience, is organized by,
processed through, and makes itself available to us in determinate
epistemological ways.

My evidence for this judgment is provided by, and is the result of,
two different sorts of consideration. The first is narrowly philosophical
and emerges out of a reflection on the process of knowing, including
mystical knowing. Here I have been persuaded that, given the sort of
beings we are, *all* knowledge – and here I explicitly include mystical
knowledge – is subject to rules that allow, that make it possible, for
such experience to count as *experience(s)*. Put another way, to decipher
mystical experience we must tie the experience to the conditions of
having such an experience.

In addition, one has to recognize the intentionality of consciousness
and the "meaning carrying" nature of consciousness. Consciousness is
not just confrontation with an object but the giving of meaning to that
confrontation. Even in the ecstatic moment of mystical experience the
mystic is unifying his experiences in a judgment about the *what* of his
or her experience. He or she is synthesizing the mystical manifold into a
unified (not necessarily unitive) awareness. That is, in the mystical

experience we bring our experiences into relationship with concepts that allow us to know the content of such happenings as being more than just sensations. We have an experience not only of sensa, but of God or Christ or *Nirvana*. The "given" is thus known as "something." Accordingly, all experience, including mystical experience, is the end product of activity involving forms of conditioning, and probably of (pre) interpretation.

Here one also needs to consider what role language necessarily plays in the very having of concepts, and, therefore, in experience, even mystical experience. Would one be able, for instance, to experience God as the mystic experiences God, that is God as "loving" and "good," if he or she were like an infant or an animal, having no language? I would go still further and note that even time, which is regularly denied by the mystics as part of their experience – they have, during the mystical experience, a powerful sense of transcending time, of entering a "timeless" reality – is, in actuality, not altogether irrelevant to the mystical experience as the mystic organizes experiences in such a way that the representations, sensations, and experiences that they have are not a simple, unordered, jumble of sensations or representations or experiences. Rather, what is known/experienced is in a certain, meaningful, coherent, temporal order.

Indeed, one always finds that these experiences, however transcendental, are apprehended successively. Which suggests that, in contradistinction to what might be identified as the preferred, that is, most widely accepted, interpretative position vis-à-vis mystical experience, even these extraordinary and remarkable experiences have operative, inescapable, and inexpungable conditions. And that the nature of the self, of human consciousness, provides the ground for these conditions. In consequence, I would insist, *contra* Kant – and without any prior dogmatic conclusions as to the Ultimate Reality or Realities – that we explore the significance of this epistemological circumstance for the possibility, as well as the nature, of transcendental experience.

St. Teresa of Avila in her *Life*,[12] drawing a distinction between Full Union and Rapture, says of Full Union: "For union gives the impression of being just the same at the beginning, in the middle, and at the end, and the effects they produce are both interior and exterior."[13] Alternatively, Rapture develops from its first stage of "being swooped out of the body," then progresses when the soul flies above "all created things"

[12] Saint Teresa of Avila, *The Life of Teresa of Jesus*, chapter 20.
[13] Ibid., p. 189.

until it reaches its "higher point" where it is "submerged in God." Thus, while Rapture develops, Full Union does not. Yet both appear to be sequential in having a beginning, a middle, and an end. Moreover, Teresa is able to identify, and reidentify, that – or who – she encounters from one moment to the next. She not only knows X (Jesus) but, however immediate the "rapture" of "full union," she is able to compare and identify X at time I to X at time II and to identify both as being the same X. And to describe the experience at time II as similar to, and a continuation of, what was encountered at time I.

Mystical reports, in addition, involve spatial notions. For example, God is distinct from the soul and moves toward it. Or God often, though not always, as Angela of Foligno reports, "Comes into the soul."[14] Similarly, Angela writes elsewhere of: "my soul being lifted up."[15] Likewise, Teresa, in *The Interior Castle*[16] tells of an experience in which she "saw" (in a non-bodily way) Jesus "at my right hand ... Jesus seemed to be beside me."[17] And Jesus is also said to walk beside her.[18] Then too, mystics regularly report "seeing" X or Y. This suggests that X or Y is located outside them and is perceived through a spiritual sense of sight. This, of course, is not exactly like seeing ordinary objects in physical space, but it does suggest some form of recognition involving spatial location during mystical experience. However, this is a very complex issue to deconstruct given that neither God nor the soul are corporeal entities. Therefore, for the moment, I will only make this observation with reservation and advance it for consideration.

In this context, I would, to still further complicate the required analysis, call attention to the traditional teaching of Catholic mystics that there are five interior senses, mirroring the five external senses, through which the mystic comes to know God. The seventeenth century French mystic Louis de Pont put this, by then very long standing, teaching very clearly: "the spirit with its faculties of understanding and will, has five interior acts corresponding to the [external] senses, which we call seeing, hearing, smelling, tasting, and touching spiritually, with which it perceives the invisible and detectable things of Almighty God, and makes *experience* of them."[19] This doctrine, that appears to go back

[14] Underhill, *Essentials of Mysticism and Other Essays*, p. 282.
[15] Poulain, *Graces of Interior Prayer*, p. 271.
[16] Saint Teresa of Avila, *The Interior Castle*, chapter 6 and *The Life of Teresa of Jesus*, chapter 27.
[17] Saint Teresa of Avila, *The Life of Teresa of Jesus*, p. 249.
[18] Ibid., p. 180.
[19] Pike, *Mystic Union*, p. 42.

to at least Origen and St. Augustine, was defended by St. Thomas Aquinas, and utilized by, among others, St. Bonaventure, Richard of St. Victor, St. Bernard of Clairvaux, and St. Teresa of Avila. Of course, this doctrine was understood as being only "analogous" to external sense, yet there is a recognition of a process not altogether dissimilar from that operative in acquiring ordinary knowledge. A process that, quoting Luis de Pont again, "*make* mystical experiences."

Though God, as the Catholic tradition has it, "infuses" Himself into the mystical soul, mystical states are acts of, occasions of, grace. Mystics know this experience in specific ways.

This is not, I would immediately add, to argue that the conditions of knowing *cause* the mystical experience. Rather, I am only advancing an argument as to the conditions under which mystical experience occurs, that is when, for other reasons, such an occurrence takes place. These conditions give the mystical experience, whatever the experience may be, and whatever it may be an experience of, its specific form. Thus, to be clear, the account presently being argued for makes *no* claims as to the ontological grounds of mystical experience but, instead, concerns itself only with the shape, the character, of mystical experience when it comes to pass. All that is being asked is that we inquire into the conditions under which, and through which, mystical experiences become the experiences they are. Only once we are aware of the conditions of mystical experience will we be in a position to judge truth claims regarding it. Which is to say, I am not advancing an ontological type argument as has been made by William Alston in his well-known study *Perceiving God*,[20] by Jerome Gellman in his *Mystical Experience of God*, and his prior study, *Experience of God and the Rationality of Theistic Belief*,[21] and earlier by William Wainwright in his study entitled *Mysticism: A Study of Its Nature, Cognitive Value, and Moral Implications*.[22] Instead, I am trying to decipher the unique phenomenology of mystical experience.

I take the foregoing considerations to entail that mystical experiences are conditioned, a phenomenon I describe, as already noted, as "mediated." This fact seems irrefutable. As a result, God or *nirvana*, whatever they might be in *themselves*, are experienced only as we can experience them. To experience them is to have knowledge of them in mediated ways. In advancing this claim it is not my intention to argue

---

[20] Alston, *Perceiving God.*
[21] Gellman, *Experience of God;* and *Mystical Experience of God.*
[22] Wainwright, *Mysticism.*

for the skeptical or negative conclusion that all mystical experiences are only psychological phenomena without ontological correlates.[23] Nor is my view to be misunderstood as being reductionist in character, that is as reducing the ultimate realities with which mystical experience deals, because they are said to be "known" only in mediated ways. Being "mediated" does not reduce the ultimate realities encountered or experienced in mystical moments to being designated as only "appearances." And this because the notion of "mediation" as I here use it, does not refer, is not a reference to, the ontological status of ultimate objects. To describe mystical experience as I do does not lessen the absolute metaphysical status of the ultimate objects or states of consciousness (or being). Instead, it is meant as a formal comment on the status of how these *realia* are known by the mystical self. Furthermore, it needs to be added that while the "mediation" of experience is a universal phenomenon, given the commonality of the mechanisms that facilitate the process of "knowing" (ordinary and mystical) among human beings, the knowledge, the experience that "mediation" produces is distinctive in the case of each tradition because of what an individual brings to the experience as a consequence of his or her rootedness in a particular tradition.

The present argument should, moreover, not be misunderstood as denying the overwhelming immediacy of mystical experience. Instead, what I want to suggest is that the giveness of ultimate realities and ultimate states of consciousness is an admixture of what we bring to experience and what there is to experience.[24] The key epistemic issue is not the *immediacy* of mystical experience but the nature and character of this *immediacy*. And this because, given the sorts of beings we are, there is no avoiding this circumstance – no unmediated access to the given as such.

---

[23] Many readers of my work have mistakenly interpreted it as arguing that mystical experience is *entirely* (i.e., only) a psychological and linguistic-cultural phenomenon. This is altogether incorrect as I have repeatedly noted. See, for instance, my essay, "Language Epistemology and Mysticism," in Katz, *Mysticism and Philosophical Analysis*, p. 64. For examples of this error in interpretation see Robert K. C. Forman, who makes this erroneous claim in his edited volume, *The Problem of Pure Consciousness*, p. 13. Also offering incorrect critical responses are King, "Two Epistemological Models for the Interpretation of Mysticism"; Price, "Mysticism, Meditation and Consciousness"; and Forgie, "Hyper-Kantianism in Recent Discussions of Mysticism." Torben Hammersholt has done an excellent job of analyzing these views in his essay, "Steven T. Katz's 'Philosophy of Mysticism' Revisited."

[24] Here I refer readers back to my comments on mystical experience as being a "mediated immediacy," on p. 7.

## LOGICAL MISTAKES: PARADOX AND INEFFABILITY

In light of what has already been argued, three, oft repeated, repercussive, logical-metaphysical errors need to be exposed.

The first of these has already been considered and is repeated here only for emphasis. It involves the very widespread, very long-standing, very deeply rooted error of recognizing, when analyzing mystical experience, only two steps: (a) mystical experience, and (b) its subsequent interpretation. But the linkage between mystical experience and the language, teachings, and dogmas of the world's religious traditions is *not* only post-experience.

Second, I would call to attention the faulty philosophical argument made by William James in his Gifford lectures in 1901–1902,[25] an argument that has been repeated many times since. James was struck, not surprisingly, by the fact that mystical reports from many traditions across many centuries refer to the mystic's experience as being both "paradoxical" and "ineffable." As a result, he reasoned that these common descriptions could serve as the basis for the comparability and similarity between traditions. But this is a logical error.

The terms "paradox" and "ineffable" do not function as terms that inform us about the specific content of experience, or any given ontological "state of affairs." Rather they function to cloak experience from investigation and to hold mysterious whatever ontological reality the terms are applied to. As a consequence, the use of the terms "paradox" and "ineffable" do not provide data for the comparison of – the comparability of – different experiences. Consider the following example: mystic A claims experience X is paradoxical and ineffable; while mystic B claims experience Y is paradoxical and ineffable. The only logical, permissible conclusion that one can draw in this situation is that both mystic A and mystic B claim their experience is paradoxical: *nothing* can be said about the *content* of their respective experiences X and Y for there is no way, given the limiting nature of claims involving ineffability, to give content to experiences X and Y. X and Y can be anything or nothing. There is simply no legitimate way to learn more about them than that they are unknowable. Furthermore, one apprehends that many different realities and states of being can/could be unknowable. Thus, to assume, as James, Huxley, Stace, and many

---

[25] These were published under the title, *The Varieties of Religious Experience* and became one of the most famous studies of mystical experience in the scholarly literature.

others do, including more recently Robert Forman, that because two mystics, A and B, claim that their experiences are paradoxical they are therefore describing like experiences is a *non sequitur.*

The third logical cum metaphysical error that needs to be avoided is the metaphysical claim that ultimately all mystical experience is the same. This position, which I shall call "the common core argument,"[26] is false given what we know of mystical experience across traditions. These traditions tell us that the "object," the content, and the state(s) of being involved in mystical experience are not univocal. It needs to be comprehended that terms like "God," *nirvana,* etc., are more than names, they are descriptions, or at least disguised descriptions, and carry a meaning relative to some more capacious and comprehensive ontological structure. Thus, the term "God" carries with it ontological characteristics (e.g., all the *omni* predicates we attribute necessarily to God), and again certain predicates relating to what might be called God's personality. For instance, He is said to be "long suffering, forgiving and loving." Alternatively, Christian mystics refer to a Trinitarian God while Sufis and Kabbalists do not. Then, again, *Atman* carries both some of the same as well as considerably different ontic, metaphysical, and "personality" characteristics. And *nirvana* implicates radically different ontological correlates and entails no personality predicates – indeed no God.

Substituting what seem to be more neutral terms such as "Being" for God or *nirvana* also proves less helpful than at first appears, for the term/concept of "Being" is not a free-floating, independent, ontological referent, but part of a (or many) specific meaning-system(s). When Aristotle speaks of "Being," his meaning is different from that intended when the notion finds its way into the philosophical vocabulary of Spinoza and Schelling, or Sartre and Heidegger, to say nothing of Zen or Doaism. W. T. Stace is simply showing his ignorance of Hinduism when he argues that the Self with a capital "S" in the *Advaita Vedanta* is the same thing as the One in his neo-idealist introvertive mysticism. Nor again does the state of *fana* in Sufism represent the introvertive mystical state as Stace claims.[27] Sufis are careful to insist that the state

---

[26] Ninian Smart very clearly represents the older tradition of scholarship and interpretation on this issue of a "common core." He writes: "phenomenologically, mysticism is everywhere the same." "Interpretation and Mystical Experience," p. 91. See here also James, *The Varieties of Religious Experience;* Otto, *The Idea of the Holy;* Zaehner, *Mysticism Sacred and Profane;* Stace, *Mysticism and Philosophy;* and many others.

[27] Stace, *Mysticism and Philosophy,* p. 115.

of *fans fi-Allah*, though it feels like the overcoming of subject and object (i.e., represents a full merging with Allah), is never an authentic ontological state of Unity or Oneness. Again, when Eckhart describes the ultimate mystical state in terms of *Nicht*, "Nothingness," he does not mean to allude to the same "Nothingness" indicated by the notion *Mu* as this concept is used in Chinese thought. Or again in Zen Buddhism. "Nothingness" does not indicate union, absorption, or even oneness as Zen Buddhists deny, a priori, the dualisms to which "oneness" is the antithesis. Likewise, the Sanskrit, Buddhist, notion of *sunyata* implies a "Nothingness" that entails its own "nothingness" or "emptiness." That is to say, *sunyata* entails the denial or affirmation of any metaphysical/ontological existence. It means "letting go" of the idea that "there is something rather than nothing."

For Eckhart, "Nothingness," known and experienced in the Medieval Christian context by a medieval Christian monk, is the "no-thing-ness" that eventuates from the co-mingling of two realities (two forms of being), the Godhead (*die Gottheit*) and the human soul, as these are conceived in the medieval Christian context. This results in what Eckhart labels the *Durchbrechen*, "the breaking through," of the human soul to a sense of oneness, of common being/identity, with the Godhead. The "no-thing-ness" of which Eckhart talks is meant to convey the collapse of the separate "thingness" of God (and the Godhead) and the separate "thingness" of the human soul, and to replace this dualistic circumstance with a "non-dualistic" (or even monistic) one. As Eckhart explains: "God's ground and my ground is the same ground." Thus, ultimately Eckhart's "nothing" – like Mechtild of Magdeburg's "nothing" and Hadewych's "nothing" – is, in actuality, in the medieval Christian context, the greatest "Something." But it is a "Something" to which the language of subject-object, perceiver and perceived, does not apply. Yet, this collapse – or surpassing – of the subject-object distinction, and the transcendence of language (i.e., the apophatic character of the experience in question) does not cancel the fact that this experience receives its phenomenological character and its phenomenological meaning from a specifically conceived metaphysical and Trinitarian context.

Consider one additional, comparative, example by way of illustration of this essential claim for mystical pluralism: Buddhists seek extinction from suffering through elimination of the "self" in a world in which there is no God. *Nirvana* is the absence of all relation, all personality, all love, and the elimination of identity. In comparison, Jewish mystics believe in a self that exists in a world created and providentially cared for by a loving, all-powerful, God. They generally seek the state of *devekuth*, "clinging" to God as their ultimate goal.[28] Given these alternative ontological commitments, there is no intelligible way that anyone can argue that a "no-self" experience of empty calm is the same experience as that of an intense, loving, intimate relationship between two substantial selves, one of whom is the personal God of Judaism. The "extinguishing" of (the illusory) self in a state of being in which there are no selves is not equivalent to the finding of another, especially when this other possesses the predicates attributed to the God of Jewish tradition.

It appears to be the case – in light of the *very* diverse and contradictory evidence supplied by the reports of mystics across traditions – that, even in the mystical moment, human consciousness "knows" ultimate realities in diverse forms. It is this condition of experience that, in turn, causes and produces the diverse noetic elements that are reported in mystical testimonies. It is this multiplicity that mystics bring to their experience that accounts for the varied experiences – and then the divergent reports of experience – that we find in the world's mystical traditions.

There is great specificity in most mystical experiences. So, for example, the early rabbinic sages who ascend to heaven as reported in the *Heichalot* [Palace] (and *Merkavah* [Chariot]) texts – a type of experience shared by St. Paul in his ascent to the third heaven[29] – saw detailed visions of heavenly palaces and the heavenly Temple that mirrored, in a perfect form, the now destroyed Jerusalem Temple.[30] Similarly, Teresa of Avila reports that in the very highest mansion, which is that of Spiritual marriage, the mystical spirit "becomes entangled and is illuminated, as it were, by a cloud of the greatest brightness. It sees these Three Persons [of the Trinity] ... the soul realizes that most certainly and truly all these three persons are one substance and One Power ... and God alone."[31] I call this detail to attention because my contextual explanation makes it possible to explain these very determinate descriptions, while not reducing them to post-experiential epiphenomena.

There is more to say about the methodological and logical issues raised by the mistaken claim for a "common core" to all mystical

---

[28] There are a small minority of Kabbalists who claimed a still more intimate experience. On this group see Idel and McGinn (eds.), *Mystical Union and Monotheistic Faith*.

[29] See 2 *Corinthians* 12:2–3.

[30] They are referenced by Isaiah's vision, ch. 6:1–4.

[31] Saint Teresa of Avila, *The Interior Castle*, pp. 209–10.

experiences. But this must wait for another occasion. However, it is fair to conclude, on the basis of the evidence that has been produced, and the argument regarding it that has been made, that one should *not* assume, a priori, the similarity – and certainty not the sameness – of mystical experience. One should begin with no a priori judgment on this crucial issue and be open, at least as a methodological pre-supposition, to the possibility that the correct paradigm for studying mystical reports and other materials across cultures is *difference*.

## INFLUENCES – RELIGIOUS AND CULTURAL

Mystical experience – in consequence of these and many other aspects of experience – is the result, the outcome, of the unavoidable factors that contribute to, and influence, the knowing/experiencing of mystical consciousness. Furthermore, it must be recognized that the actuality of the mystical experience is inescapably complicated by what I would call the "learned" aspect of mystical experience. These are the many things that the mystical self has been taught in anticipation of – and as part of the search for – the mystical moment and that directly effect how that moment is experienced. First, and perhaps most importantly, he or she has learned an ontology. Thus, to reuse our former example, the Jewish mystic is educated to anticipate, to seek, to find God. The Therevada Buddhist devotee is educated to anticipate, to seek, to realize *nirvana*. (*Nirvana* is not a place or object to be found. Rather, one is nirvanaized.) Therefore, the Therevada Buddhist *never* encounters God while the kabbalist is unfulfilled unless he does have such an encounter.

Extending this accounting of the ontological doctrines of the world's religions – and therefore of their mystical teaching – I note that those Christian mystics, such as Tauler and Suso, schooled on the Neo-Platonic tradition derived from Book VI of the *Enneads*, Dionysius the Areopagite, and Book 9 of Augustine's *Confessions*, have learned of – and therefore anticipated and sought – a unitive, absorptive experience in which, at the climax of the final ascension of the soul in its mystical journey, the soul becomes unified with the Good/God. Alternatively, there are major Christian mystics – for example, the Victorines of the twelfth century, St. Francis as he is known through the mystical experience of the six winged seraph during which he was given the stigmata, the anonymous fourteenth century author of *The Cloud of Unknowing* (sometimes attributed to Walter Hilton), St. John of the Cross, and St. Teresa of Avila – who, predicated on a tradition that goes back to the Bible, most specifically to the *Song of Songs*, seek to have a "loving union" with God, rather than becoming one with Him. In these instances, the mystic draws on a Judaic rather than a Greek metaphysical understanding. Thus, in the Cloud of *Unknowing* we are told:

> Above thyself thou art: because thou attainest to come thither by grace, whither thou mayest not come by nature. This is to say, to be oned to God, in spirit and in love and in accordance of will. Beneath thy God thou art: for although it may be said in a manner that in this time God and thou be not two but one in spirit – insomuch that thou or another that feeleth the perfection of this work may, by reason of that onehead, truly be called a god, as Scripture witnesseth – nevertheless thou art beneath him. For he is God by nature without beginning; and thou sometimes wert nought in substance; and afterwards, when thou wert by his might and his love made aught, thou willfully with sin madest thyself worse than nought. And only by his mercy without thy desert art thou made a god in grace, oned with him in spirit without separation, both here and in the bliss of heaven without any end. So that, although thou be all one with him in grace, yet thou art full far beneath him in nature.[32]

Then, too, while Eckhart's teaching is traditionally associated with the neo-Platonic doctrine of complete loss of self, it should be noted how Christological his mystical writings are. Therefore, it is problematic to employ, to liken, his work, as has often been done,[33] with the unitive experiences reported by Asian mystics. Indeed, it is essential to observe that Eckhart's favorite themes are the Trinity and the Incarnation. Again, one should pay heed to the fact that, for example, Julian of Norwich, in describing her experience, tells her readers:

> And in the same Shewing suddenly the Trinity fulfilled my heart most of joy. And so, I understood, it shall be in heaven without end to all that shall come there. For the Trinity is God: God is the Trinity; the Trinity is our Maker and Keeper, the Trinity is everlasting lover, everlasting joy and bliss, by our Lord Jesus Christ. And this was shewed in the first [shewing] and in all; for where Jesus appeareth, the Blessed Trinity is understood as to my sight.[34]

---

[32] Pp. 89–90.
[33] For example, see Daisetz T. Suzuki's discussion of "Meister Eckhart and Buddhism" which is the title of the opening essay in his *Mysticism: Christian and Buddhist*, pp. 1–31.
[34] Julian of Norwich, *Revelations of Divine Love*, p. 7.

This is a decidedly Christian experience based on what Julian has been taught prior to her experiences, and in anticipation of her mystical encounter. Likewise, the mysticism of St Francis, St. John of the Cross, and St. Teresa of Avila are all dominated by Christological elements. Theirs is not differentiated, unspecific, meta-tradition "mystical experience." It is, rather, an experience of finding the Christ they had been seeking.

Alternatively, compare the radically different experience of the Daoist master Jiang Weiqiao (1870–1955). He reports that: "Every time I sat down to mediate, I would focus my awareness on the cinnabar field in my lower abdomen. I could feel a cloud of hot power there. It came and went, rose and ebbed. I was quite amazed by it." He tells his readers that:

> on the twenty-ninth of the fifth month, during the evening sitting, it happened first: All of a sudden there was this intense rumbling movement in the cinnabar field in my lower abdomen. I had been sitting in quiet meditation as usual, but this was something I really could not control. I was shaken back and forth helplessly. Then an incredibly hot energy began to rise at the bottom of my spine and climbed up further and further until it reached the very top of my head. I was startled and alarmed.[35]

Here mystical experience is inextricably bound to the human body, which is understood as a natural form that grows out of, and is built upon, a repository of flowing energies. At its ultimate stage, for which the Daoist trains, the truth, the ecstatic experience, is about *qi* and the achievement of oneness with the Dao – but remember that the Dao is not God, but the impersonal, primordial universal power.

These different examples, based on the different ontologies of Judaism, Buddhism, Christianity, and Daoism, make clear that the pre-experiential *worldview* learned by the mystic directs and effects the experience he or she seeks, as well as the experience he or she has. Jiang Weiqiao, like all Buddhists, and Hindu mystical masters, does not *experience*, as all the Christian masters do, some variety of God, the Trinity, Jesus, and Mary. This is to emphasize that the Christian masters report *encountering* these transcendental realities, not just using the language and symbols of the Church to describe some "ineffable" happening *ex post facto*.

---

[35] Weiqiao, *Jingzuo fa jiyao*. Cited from Kohn, *Readings in Daoist Mysticism*, p. 108.

1 would also point out that even the so-called pure consciousness experience argued for by Robert K. C. Forman[36] is mediated despite his insistent assertions to the contrary. The fact is that his claims regarding consciousness are, as can be seen on close inspection, based on his long years of study and practice of the decidedly particular tradition of "Transcendental Meditation." This is a form of meditation that incorporates a distinct ontology and psychology within its over-arching metaphysical *Weltanschauung*. Moreover, it may well be, given the ontological presuppositions assumed by the practice of *transcendental meditation*, that the sort of experience produced by *transcendental meditation* should *not* be considered, in light of the nature of the experience it seeks and finds, as a type of mystical experience at all. Not all altered states of consciousness are mystical states of consciousness. So, for instance, drug-induced states of consciousness often associated with LSD and the eating of hallucinogenic mushrooms produce unusual forms of awareness, but they are not mystical forms of awareness. Nor are brain states that, no matter how idiosyncratic, are only states of brain activity. And this because mystical experiences are meetings with, or transformations as a consequence of, experiences with or by way of ultimate realities. They are not just the subjective phenomenon of an altered state of awareness.

## LEARNING TO BE A MYSTIC

In considering the matter of what the mystic learns in advance of his or her supreme experiences, that influences the consummate outcome they seek – and have – I would also call attention, in addition to the matter of ontology, to a number of other factors that it is important to take into account. The first of these is the mystical "role model" of a particular tradition. To take an obvious example, consider the model of Christ that lies at the heart of Christian tradition. Pursuing, this "model" leads to two outcomes – emulating the ideal of suffering, so, for example, the experience of the stigmata most famously connected with St. Francis of Assisi, and the aspiration to embrace Christ as the lover, imaged so erotically by St. Teresa of Avila, based on the love poetry of the *Song of Songs*. In the Islamic mystical tradition, an essential role is played by the model of the Prophet Muhammed. The driving ambition of Sufis is to replicate his *miraj*. In Buddhism, it is, of course, the Buddha's example,

[36] Forman, *Mysticism, Mind, Consciousness.*

the Buddha's actions, that provide the decisive example. As the Buddha renounced worldly attachments and found enlightenment, so the disciples of the Buddha seek their own experience of *nirvana*.

A second formative influence of great importance is one's teacher or guide. Such individuals are central to all mystical traditions, even Zen Buddhism. In this latter tradition, often misrepresented as an anarchic religious teaching, the Zen master is both a paradigm of Zen practice to be followed by his students and the one who, through the setting of seemingly meaningless *koans*, induces the condition of "Zen sickness" in his disciples. It is this state that, in turn, allows them to break through the bonds of ordinary experience and to encounter reality as it really is, in its "suchness." Likewise, Kabbalists have rabbinic teachers, Sufis the Murshid masters, Christian adepts spiritual confessors and mentors, and Hindus gurus. And, not surprisingly, given the diverse traditions in which these teachers are situated (and in some cases create) each of these masters teach different things, even very different things.

Third, mysticism grows in religious communities like sanghas, monasteries, khanegahs, and kabbalistic circles. It does not, contrary to widespread misconceptions, emerge in isolation.

Fourth, mystics learn a language, often a "sacred language" such as Hebrew, Arabic, or Sanskrit. Each of these languages gives words specific meanings in conformity with the ontologies that underlie them. In consequence, words take on meanings that differ from language to language. So, for example, *sunyata*, the "void" of Buddhism, is *not* the "nothingness" of Eckhart; and the concept of "God" in Judaism, Christianity, and Islam is not *Brahman*.

Furthermore, these sacred languages play many roles in mystical traditions and generate many complex issues related to the many-sided relationship of language to mystical experience. Despite the oft-repeated claims that mysticism is ultimately apophatic, it is words, employed in the special way that they are employed by mystics, that makes possible the formation of teachings, of traditions, that pass from one generation to the next.[37]

Fifth, and highly significant in the formation of the pre-experiential and then the experiential consciousness of mystics, is the role played by the sacred scripture of the mystics' tradition. Kabbalah is unintelligible – for all its borrowing from neo-Platonism – outside of the world of the Hebrew

---

[37] I have analyzed in detail how language is utilized by mystics in my essay "Mystical Speech and Mystical Meaning." All the essays in this multi-author collection will repay reading.

Bible and later rabbinic commentaries thereon. Having learned what Isaiah 6.1 saw on his heavenly journey, students of mysticism in the rabbinic era had a blueprint of where they wanted their heavenly ascent to take them and what they wanted to see at the end of their transcendental journey. The most influential book of Kabbalah, the *Zohar*, is a mystical-midrashic exegesis of scripture. Its purpose is to reveal the deepest secrets of the Torah. Sufism is a Qur'an intoxicated mystical practice. Sufis, like Ibn Arabi, ibn Habash Suhrawardi, and Ali Hujwiri, continually cite the Qur'an in order to induce mystical ecstasy. While Sankara's mysticism, for all its creative brilliance is read out of, as well as into, the *Vedas*, his entire mystical project is one rooted in the mysteries of Hindu scripture.

Hindu mystical experience is incomprehensible apart from the *Veda* and the *Bhagavad Gita*, while the experience of kabbalists and Sufis is impenetrable without connecting it to the Torah and the Qur'an, respectively. Likewise, Christian mystics grow up believing that the New Testament is the *Urgrund* for all theological insight and aspiration. Augustine, in his famous description of "seeing" and "touching" God in Book 9 of his *Confessions*, refers to the writings of Paul several times as well as the *Gospel of Matthew* 25:21. Symeon the New Theologian (949–1022), when describing an ecstatic experience, uses Paul's words from 2 *Corinthians* 12:2–3 regarding, "whether he was in the body or outside the body." Bernard of Clairvaux, in a rare report of his own mystical experience, likens it to the *Song of Songs* 2:17 and calls upon numerous texts from Paul. Eckhart, too, was irresistibly and continually engaged in the exploration of scripture – an experience he described as seeking "Christ, the Truth" in the text. Indeed, it was this experiential dimension connected with the study of scripture that led medieval Catholic mystics to describe scripture as "magistra fidei nostrae," "the mistress of our faith."

It should, in addition, be noted that the serious study of scripture inevitably plunges one into such central issues as the hermeneutical rules to be employed in scriptural interpretation, the nature of symbolism and symbolic interpretation, the issues of typology and metonymy, the nature and limits of allegorical interpretation, and, as in Eckhart, the paradoxical formulation and interpretation of biblical teachings. Moreover, it forces one to seek to understand what it means to claim that the Bible, or Qur'an, embodies secrets.

CONCLUSION

To conclude, the methodological and metaphysical claims advanced in this paper are, I recognize, unconventional and provocative – and may upon further examination and reflection be shown to be wrong. But, until then, I would urge that readers take my thesis as to the necessarily "mediated" nature of mystical experience and mystical consciousness seriously and test it for themselves to see if it makes more sense and better explains mystical experience than the more usual accounts that depend on claims regarding a "common core" and which fall back on the notion of "ineffability." In this context, I would remind all students of mysticism that mystical adepts begin their quest by first learning about mystical experience (and the experience had by others), then they seek to have the experience(s) that have been described, and then, if all goes well, they have the experience they have been pursuing, and only then, after their experience has concluded, do they describe their ultimate moments.

### References

Alston, William. *Perceiving God: The Epistemology of Religious Experience.* Ithaca, 1991.

Blum, Jason N. *Zen and the Unspeakable God: Comparative Interpretations of Mystical Experience.* University Park, PA, 2015.

Forgie, William. "Hyper-Kantianism in Recent Discussions of Mysticism," *Religious Studies* 21 (1985): 205–18.

Forman, Robert K. C. (ed.). *The Problem of Pure Consciousness.* New York, 1990.

*Mysticism, Mind, Consciousness.* Albany, 1999.

Gellman, Jerome I. *Experience of God and the Rationality of Theistic Belief.* Ithaca, NY, 1997.

*Mystical Experience of God: A Philosophical Inquiry.* Aldershot, UK, 2001.

Hammersholt, Torben. "Steven T. Katz's 'Philosophy of Mysticism' Revisited," *Journal of the American Academy of Religion* 81 (June 2013): 467–90.

Idel, Moshe, and Bernard McGinn (eds.). *Mystical Union and Monotheistic Faith: An Ecumenical Dialogue.* New York, 1989.

Inge, William R. *Mysticism in Religion.* Chicago, 1948.

James, William. *The Varieties of Religious Experience.* New York, 1902.

Julian of Norwich. *Revelations of Divine Love.* London, 1901.

Katz, Steven T. "Language Epistemology and Mysticism," in Steven T. Katz (ed.), *Mysticism and Philosophical Analysis.* New York, 1978.

"Mystical Speech and Mystical Meaning," in Steven T. Katz (ed.), *Mysticism and Language*, pp. 3–41. New York, 1992.

(ed.). *Comparative Mysticism: An Anthology of Original Sources.* Oxford, 2013.

King, Sally. "Two Epistemological Models for the Interpretation of Mysticism," *Journal of American Academy of Religion* 71 (2) (1988): 257–79.

Kohn, Livia. *Readings in Daoist Mysticism.* St. Petersburg, FL, 2009.

Nishida, Kitaro. *Inquiry into the God.* Translated by Masao Abe and Christopher Ives. New Haven, 1990.

Otto, Rudolf. *The Idea of the Holy: An Inquiry into the Non-Rational Factor in the Idea of the Divine and its Relation to the Rational.* Translated by John W. Harvey. New York, 1958.

Poulain, Augustin. *The Graces of Interior Prayer: A Treatise on Mystical Theology.* St. Louis, 1987.

Pike, Nelson. *Mystic Union: An Essay in the Phenomenology of Mysticism.* Ithaca, 1992.

Price, James R. "Mysticism, Meditation and Consciousness," in Robert K. C. Forman (ed.), *Innate Capacity: Mysticism, Psychology and Philosophy,* pp. 211–222. Oxford, 1998.

Saint Teresa of Avila. *The Life of Teresa of Jesus: The Autobiography of Teresa of Avila.* Translated by E. A. Peers. Garden City, NY, 1960.

    *The Interior Castle.* Translated by E. A. Peers. New York, 1961.

Smart, Ninian. "Interpretation and Mystical Experience," in Richard Woods (ed.), *Understanding Mysticism.* New York, 1980.

Stace, Walter T. *Mysticism and Philosophy.* London, 1961.

Suzuki, Daisetz T. *Mysticism: Christian and Buddhist.* London, 1957.

Underhill, Evelyn. *Essentials of Mysticism and Other Essays.* Oxford, 1999.

Wainwright, William J. *Mysticism: A Study of Its Nature, Cognitive Value, and Moral Implications.* Madison, WI, 1982.

Weiqiao, Jiang. *Jingzuo fa jiyao.* Taipei, 1985.

Zaehner, Robert Charles. *Mysticism Sacred and Profane.* Oxford, 1957.

# 11 Miraculous and Extraordinary Events As Religious Experience

## FIONA BOWIE

> Outdoors we are confronted everywhere with wonders; we see that the miraculous is not extraordinary, but the common mode of existence. It is our daily bread.
>
> (Wendell Berry)

> There are only two ways to live your life. One is as though nothing is a miracle. The other is as though everything is a miracle.
>
> (Albert Einstein)

Both these quotations point to the experience of wonder that is, or can be, part of everyday life. They imply a choice in the way we live our lives, a shift in perspective from a secular view of the world to one of enchantment. Bruno Latour (1993) claimed that we have never stopped having at least the potential for this enchantment. Having studied the way scientific 'facts' are produced in a laboratory setting (Latour and Woolgar 1986), Latour goes on to dismantle the distinction between subject and object, real and fabricated, fact and fetish. 'What we fabricate never possesses, and never loses, its autonomy' (Latour 2010: 21). The secularist and theist are not as far apart as they might suppose, not only because both 'fact' and 'fetish' are constructions which nevertheless influence our lives and possess a degree of autonomy, but because the difference between seeing an event as miraculous or extraordinary on the one hand, or mundane on the other, might only be to view it through a different lens. Some experiences appear to break through any preconceived notions of what is possible or impossible, challenging accepted scientific views of the way the world works. These are often, if not invariably, seen as miracles, suggesting powers beyond the ordinary human capacity for action and creation.

In this essay I start by looking at the notion of experience, and what makes an experience religious, and then at what qualifies an experience deemed as miraculous rather than extraordinary. I use case studies to illustrate the role of experience in extraordinary and miraculous events, and their relation to mystical experience.

## EXPERIENCE AND RELIGION: DEFINITIONS

'Experience', as a noun, describes the process of acquiring knowledge by means of the senses or through performing actions (seeing, feeling, doing). Whether the knowledge is gained actively by seeking the experience, or passively, when something happens to one, it suggests an engagement with and being in the world. We also talk about experience in a verbal sense, its effects on us, how it makes us feel. There is an event or process that took place that alters how we understand or see the world. We seek to actively create certain types of experience for ourselves and others. We weave a narrative of our lives and of who we are from this tapestry of sensuous experience and our reactions to it.

Whether an experience is defined as religious raises questions of definition. For some people 'religion' is synonymous with 'formal, organised communities of faith', for others it refers to a cosmology or way of viewing the world, and the ethical imperatives that follow from that. Anthropologists often fall back on E. B. Tylor's minimal definition of religion as 'the belief in Spiritual Beings' (1958: 8) or on Clifford Geertz's symbolist definition of religion as (1973: 4): "(1) A system of symbols which acts to (2) establish powerful, pervasive, and long-lasting moods and motivations in men by (3) formulating conceptions of a general order of existence and (4) clothing these conceptions with such an aura of factuality that (5) the moods and motivations seem uniquely realistic." Other scholars have emphasised the cultural embeddedness of the whole notion of religion as a separate category and have argued that we should abandon the term altogether.[1] Categories can be useful when we come to compare and describe phenomena, even if we need to be aware of their shortcomings, cultural relativity, or untranslatability. Arthur Lehmann and James Myers (1997: 3) provide a definition that is generous in encompassing miraculous, magical, extraordinary, and mystical events and experiences:

> Expanding the definition of 'religion' beyond the spiritual and superhuman beings to include the extraordinary, the mysterious, and unexplainable allows a more comprehensive view of religious behaviors among the peoples of the world and permits the anthropological investigation of phenomena such as magic, sorcery, curses, and other practices that hold meaning for both preliterate and literate societies.

[1] See for example Timothy Fitzgerald (2007).

Taking a theological perspective, James Mackey is impatient with those who attempt to pre-define 'religion', arguing for a fluid and undogmatic approach. Mackey points out that drawing firm boundaries around what is and is not religious or divine is a feature of both those who most firmly defend their religious boundaries and those who seek to dismiss them altogether (1996: 8–9):

> Of course people who have somehow pre-defined the nature of divinity, and more particularly those who treat the notes of immanence and transcendence in relation to a divine dimension as contraries instead of what they always are in fact, namely, coordinates, can also appear to specify with great accuracy what is to count as religion, as a truly religious dimension of life and knowledge, and what is not. It is interesting to note that this alleged ability is so often shared by those who are most dogmatic about religion and those who, allegedly on scientific grounds, are most dismissive of it.

When looking at extraordinary and miraculous experiences we need a more expansive definition than simply belief in a god or gods. Experiences that are self-described as religious, or which appear to others to fall into that category, vary widely in nature. The focus of this article is on the content of the experiences described and their effects. The boundary between religious and non-religious events can sometimes appear arbitrary and contextual.[2]

## OUT-OF-BODY AND NEAR-DEATH EXPERIENCES: A CASE STUDY

In December 1943 a young American soldier named George Ritchie found himself confined to bed with pneumonia in a hospital barracks at Camp Barkeley, Texas. He had been about to catch a train to Richmond in Virginia to start his medical training, before collapsing and ending up in the hospital. He woke up a short while later and started to look for his clothes. He could see someone lying in the bed from which he had just arisen, but didn't pay too much attention as he was in a hurry to find his clothes and duffle bag so as to catch the train. Passing a sergeant in the corridor, who paid no attention to the young Ritchie and appeared not to see him, he found himself outside the

---

[2] A more detailed discussion of these and other sources is given in Bowie (2006, chapter 1).

hospital. Propelled by his desire, he found himself racing swiftly above the ground in the direction of Richmond, low enough to identify features of the landscape passing beneath him. At a certain point Ritchie lost confidence that he knew the way and decided to stop in order to ask for directions. No sooner had the thought occurred to Ritchie than he found himself slowing down near a town in a big bend in the river, and then hovering fifty feet in the air above a café with a bright neon sign. Ritchie tried asking a passing civilian what town he was in, but the man ignored him. He tried tapping the man on the shoulder, but there was nothing there. Leaning back on the guy wire of a telegraph pole to think things over, Ritchie's body went right through it. Faced with the fact that neither this man nor the hospital sergeant had seen him, Ritchie began to wonder whether, despite everything around him looking normal and solid, it was he who had changed, and he had somehow lost his hardness. If these two people couldn't see him, Ritchie reasoned, what made him think that the people at the medical college in Virginia would be aware of him? If that were the case, his desperate efforts to reach Richmond were in vain. Meanwhile the material part of himself from which he had somehow become separated was still lying in a hospital bed in Texas. On thinking this thought Ritchie found himself hurtling back through the air in the direction from which he had come. Reaching the hospital, he began a desperate search for the room he had rushed away from, and the body still lying in its bed. He realised that he did not have a clear idea what he looked like from the outside and began to search for a young man of his approximate size and age wearing a black onyx oval ring with a golden owl, the symbol of his university Phi Gamma Delta Fraternity. Eventually in the last cubicle he saw a body, with the sheet drawn up over the head, leaving only the arms outside the blankets. On the third finger of the left hand he could see the small gold owl in its black onyx ring (Ritchie 2007).

This is the dramatic beginning to George Ritchie's out-of-body experience as recounted in his book *Return from Tomorrow*. As an experience that deviates from something that is standard, normal, or expected, Ritchie's flight over the southern states without his body was certainly anomalous and extraordinary, at least to his conscious mind at the time. If he had realised that he was in fact dead, or had been familiar with other similar accounts of those who had had an out-of-body experience, he might have regarded the ability to pass through solid objects, his invisibility to the people he addressed, and the use of thought and attention to affect travel as quite normal and even expected.[3] Instead, the young man was so focused on his desire to join his classmates in medical school that it took some time for him to come to terms with the physical changes that had taken place and the event, his death from pneumonia, that had precipitated them.

The experience of being conscious out of the body and the sensation of travelling at great speed according to thought and intention need not be regarded as religious.[4] This first excursion out of his body was, however, only a precursor for Ritchie to a much more profound experience that he certainly did regard as religious. As he sat (mentally at least) on the bed next to the still body under its white sheet, without being able to make contact with it, Ritchie became aware that the light in the room was changing and becoming brighter and brighter, until it would have hurt the retina of his eyes, had he been in his physical body. The light resolved itself into a presence, a man made of light, and the words formed in his mind to stand up. This was followed by what Ritchie described as a 'stupendous certainty' that he was in the presence of the Son of God. This was not a speculation but 'a kind of knowing, immediate and complete' (Ritchie 2007: 58). He knew with absolute certainty that this man loved him and knew everything that there was to know about him, accepting him as he was. Ritchie was also aware that what emanated from this being of light was unconditional love. The man asked Ritchie to show him what he had done with his life, and after struggling to think of achievements of which he could be proud, he realised both that he had done very little, and that the question did not refer to what he might have achieved externally but to how much he had loved.

This discovery of life as a 'school of love' is a classic mystical and religious trope, although not one with which Ritchie had been familiar,

---

[3] Summaries of recent research and thinking on both out-of-body-experiences (Alvarado) and near-death-experiences (Greyson) can be found in Cardeña, Lynn and Krippner (2007). Lawton (2019) details many different accounts of life after death, including George Ritchie's.

[4] Veridical or evidential confirmation that an individual's consciousness is genuinely able to perceive the environment from an alternate perspective to the physical body are relatively rare. In Ritchie's case he recognised the town, Vicksburg, Mississippi, and even the bar, at which he had stopped during his night flight, when returning to Camp Barkeley from Virginia by car the following year, despite never having been to Mississippi before (Ritchie 2007: 110–13). Holden (2009) discusses various veridical perceptions in near-death experiences. There are numerous anecdotal accounts, which together provide a strong basis for concluding that accurate perceptions of the material world from a perspective outside the physical body do occur, but few under controlled experimental conditions.

despite his church upbringing, and he felt rather peeved that no one had told him what this 'final exam' consisted of. Within some Protestant traditions there is suspicion of near-death experiences (NDEs), and the 'being of light' that is so often described is regarded not as Jesus but as Lucifer – Satan the fallen angel, whose name means 'light bringer'. While interpretations of the identity of spiritual beings vary in such accounts, a meeting with a being of light whose nature is unconditional love, and other features of a classic NDE, such as a life review, occur irrespective of the beliefs and expectations of the one who has such an experience (Masumian 2009).

Gregory Shushan (2018), in his comprehensive survey of accounts of NDE in indigenous societies around the world, looks at features of NDEs that appear to be culturally specific. These include the mode of travel towards the light, whether being drawn through a tunnel (as if on a train or by space travel) in most Western accounts, or walking along a road in societies less familiar with tunnels.[5] The physical location of other worlds can also vary, sometimes perceived as an upper realm, in some as contiguous with the earth, and in others perceived as being underground. Other features of the NDE appear to be universal, including the experience of being outside one's body, meeting deceased relatives and beings of light, undergoing a life review, and, in the case of an NDE as opposed to mediumistically related accounts, of reaching a point at which the individual is told to return to his or her body, or chooses to return for a particular purpose.

There are features of a NDE that contradict dogmatic formulations. In the Christian tradition there is an expectation of divine judgement, whereas NDE accounts consistently claim that the loving beings encountered understand, accept, and love people as they are. The element of judgement comes from understanding the consequences of one's actions, and their effect on others, as seen in the life review. Ritchie, for example, realised that his step-mother, who he had kept at an emotional distance, was a loving and courageous woman who had consistently done her best for him. He was mortified by the pain he had caused her and was subsequently able to rebuild the relationship. The element of regret, particularly for those who have taken their own lives, can be much harsher than any externally administered divine punishment. In other instances there is evidence that religious beliefs and ritual practices can be formed as a result of accounts given by those who have had

---

[5] Cross-cultural differences related to tunnels in NDEs are discussed in Athappilly, Greyson and Stevenson (2006).

a NDE, as well as from dreams, shamanistic, mystical, and trance experiences. North America Native American afterlife beliefs, for example, appear to relate to accounts of NDEs. Shamanic journeying can be seen as an attempt to emulate these experiences (Shushan 2018: 85). Shushan concluded that 'Indigenous statements about beliefs often referred to an experience not only as the source and authority of the belief, but also as the actual descriptor of it' (p. 243).[6] Native American revivalist movements appear to have close links to extraordinary or anomalous experiences such as NDEs, and specific rituals are sometimes attempts to follow instructions given while out of the body, or to copy something seen in other realms of existence.

Karlis Osis and Erlendur Haraldsson (2012: 174–75) compared Indian and American experiences of Heaven (although the translation of this term can be culturally problematic), to see whether the Bible or Vedas influenced visionary and near-death experiences. The similarities in accounts between the two countries were far greater than any differences, and where they diverged the differences were slight. Seventeen per cent of Americans in their sample saw threatening environments, mainly related to this world, while none of the Indian sample did, although Indian patients saw threatening apparitions more commonly than American patients. A higher percentage of Indians considered their visions to be religious (67 per cent as opposed to 55 per cent of Americans), and saw places of great beauty and peace (94 per cent and 82 per cent, respectively). Hindus, Christians, and Muslims reported very similar scenes of beautiful gardens, temples, a bright light, and sensations of great peace and of a loving presence. Osis and Haraldsson conclude that (p. 175): 'Indian and American patients saw the same kinds of visions, but Indian emotional reactions were more lively, more positive, and more religious'. The religious background of the person who has a NDE appears to have little influence on the contents of the experience, but negative NDEs and sensations of being lost or alone are more common among sceptics and those with no prior religious belief (Lawson 2019). There appears to be a link between beliefs, values, and expectations while alive and the quality of the immediate post-mortem experience. For those who die convinced that there is nothing beyond the physical body and material existence on earth, the transition to a realm of light can take longer and be less

---

[6] This is an example of what David Hufford (1995) referred to as the 'experiential source hypothesis'.

straightforward than for those who expect life in some form to continue.[7]

Western Abrahamic religious traditions tend to separate the notion of belief from that of experience. Doctrinal and dogmatic religion, ritual activity, and sacred texts come to form a framework that both define the religion and outline the scope of belief. Charismatic individuals who claim a direct experience of the divine are both necessary to breathe new life into these structures and a threat to hierarchical and established authorities. Western religious history is marked by a tension between belief and experience, doctrinal and charismatic authority, tradition and innovation (Weber 2010). While the popularity of books such as George Ritchie's *Return from Tomorrow* testify to a public thirst for knowledge about the afterlife and an appetite for stories of miraculous and extraordinary experiences, these accounts are more likely to be sold in the esoteric than theological sections of bookshops. There is still a cultural taboo in the West around engaging with evidence relating to religious and paranormal phenomena (Hanegraaff 2012), although this does seem to be changing, with authors such as Mario Beauregard, Natalie Trent, and Garry Schwartz talking of a paradigm shift to a 'postmaterialist psychology' (2018).

Western NDEs, such as that recounted by George Ritchie, qualify as a religious experience not simply because of their out-of-body narratives, but because of what happens subsequently. These experiences may not directly influence the doctrines and practices of Christianity or other world religions, but they can have a profound effect on the individual. Ritchie was taken by the being of light, who he identified as Jesus, to various realms, starting with one close to earth populated by people who seemed unaware of the presence of light and love around them, so wrapped up were they in their own vicious thoughts and preoccupied in venting their anger on those around them.[8] He couldn't understand why they didn't simply walk away, but came to see that far from being abandoned they were surrounded and attended by loving presences. For the moment at least they were unable to see them, preferring to remain in the company of people most similar to themselves. Ritchie was then taken to a place of learning where monk-like

---

[7] The journey from scepticism to acceptance of the post-mortem state is vividly described by the Quaker medium Jane Sherwood in her *Post-Mortem Journal* (1991), in which T. E. Lawrence communicates his struggles to come to terms with his attitudes and actions while on earth, and to reach a place of acceptance and growth.

[8] Lawson (2019) gives several examples from a variety of sources describing these zones or planes of existence. These accounts often display a high degree of consistency.

individuals busied themselves with various intellectual projects. It was a zone of thought and Ritchie understood that what was achieved there was central to thought on earth. There are numerous accounts from out-of-body travellers, NDEs, and from mediumistic communications of these planes of learning and invention where discarnate beings continue to work and study, developing prototypes that are received and realised by those on earth who are receptive to their ideas.[9] Ritchie then found himself far from the earth in a vast void, and in the distance glimpsed what looked like a bright, glowing city made of light. As two figures from the city seemed to detach themselves and come towards them, Ritchie found himself hurtling backwards through space to the box-like hospital room he had left in what seemed a lifetime ago (Ritchie 2007: 85).

The language Ritchie used to describe this journey points to a deeply mystical experience of divine presence. While he had started with a desperate hunt for his body and desire to reunite with it, Ritchie found on his return that the thought of being separated from this divine light and love was unbearable. He was still pleading to be allowed to stay with Jesus when he experienced the pain of being back in his body. He didn't have the strength to remove the sheet pulled over his face, but managed to touch the ring on his left hand with his right fingers, and slowly turn it. This was an action that 'saved his life', although that was not how he saw it at the time. The next part of the story has elements that are both extraordinary and miraculous. A ward boy who was to take Ritchie's body to the morgue was sure that the hands were not as he had left them, and suggested to the medical doctor, his senior both in experience and rank, that he should try injecting adrenalin into Ritchie's heart. Medically the idea seemed ridiculous as even if there was a temporary reaction, the rest of the body was already shutting down and had been pronounced dead. Even if he could be revived it was assumed that he would have suffered catastrophic brain damage.[10]

---

[9] There are numerous examples of this in Bruce Moen's 'Voyages' series, in which he describes his out-of-body experiences using techniques developed by Robert Monroe and The Monroe Institute. See, for example, Moen (1997).

[10] Sam Parnia (2013: 219), a medical doctor specialising in resuscitation and researcher into NDEs following cardiac arrest, suggests that a more accurate term in these cases would be an 'actual-death experience', since the patients are not near death, they have actually died. Under optimal conditions, which would include cooling the body to prevent cell decay, a body can be resuscitated up to four hours after clinical death has taken place, although in practice few hospitals have the facilities to do this, and the most likely outcome is a subsequent cardiac arrest or a diminished quality of life rather than a full return to health.

It was only many years later that Ritchie fully appreciated just how unlikely and extraordinary the chain of events that led to his resuscitation had been and how miraculous his gradual return to full health. The commanding officer at the time had written in a notarized statement that Ritchie's was the most amazing medical case he had ever encountered, and that his 'virtual call from death and return to vigorous health has to be explained in terms of other than natural means' (Ritchie 2007: 93).

It was a gradual process for Ritchie to come to terms with and learn the lessons he had been taught the night he died, but it profoundly altered his values and orientation in life. He came to seek out and recognise Jesus in remarkable individuals, and then to look for him in everyone. Whether or not it is cast in a specifically Christian mould, or seen from within another religious tradition, a NDE is almost invariably a 'religious experience' leading to a reorientation of priorities and values, and removing the fear of death. Those who have had an NDE typically say that they do not *believe* in an afterlife, they *know* it exists and what awaits them when they do finally return. 'Religious experience' is here used in a broad sense to include the adoption of ethical imperatives and of a cosmology that includes non-physical planes of existence, divine beings, and a teleology in which life is seen as a school, the purpose of which is to learn how to love others (Morse 1990; Moody 2005). The cultural acceptability of talking about such experiences varies both between and within cultures (Noyes et al. 2009; Shushan 2018).

For some people who feel that they are not believed, or where tales of visiting other realms are pathologised, the experience of return can be quite negative. Life back in a body and the effort of living in a world of resistance and disharmony contrasts starkly with their experience of loving acceptance, and this can be isolating. It is also the case that some NDEs are distressing and their after-effects can be profoundly negative. It has been suggested that these negative NDEs are under-reported and could be more common than the literature suggests (Greyson and Bush 1992). A negative experience may still be framed as religious. If a Christian expects to go to Heaven and to be with Jesus, and instead glimpses the shadow realms of 'Hell', the experience can be terrifying and shameful. Roman Catholic teaching includes a purgatorial realm of cleansing that most people will spend time in before being admitted to Heaven, but Protestant Christians may be unfamiliar with this notion and expect to go straight to what they understand as Heaven (Bush 2007).

The *Bardo Thodol* or *Tibetan Book of the Dead*, traditionally attributed to the Indian mystic Padma-Sambhava who introduced Buddhism to Tibet in the eighth century, is a guide for those who have died to help them reorient themselves in their new life. The translation of *Bardo Thodol* is 'liberation by hearing on after the death plane', and the text was designed to be read to dying and recently departed several times in order to prepare and support them in the different stages and trials they are likely to encounter. A first stage and prerequisite to a good death is the intention of the dying person to act for the good of all sentient beings and to adopt an attitude of love and compassion. This is followed by a reminder to the dead person that he or she needs to see and understand that his or her consciousness is part of the Clear Light, and to unite with it. At the point of death, people may be confused as to whether they are in fact dead, and they can be instructed that if they can see relatives and acquaintances who they know to be dead they have also attained that state. They should then call on a guru or tutelary deity to act as a guide. The body loses its solidity and adopts a shining, illusory form, and thought power takes over as the means of movement and action. There are many other stages that are remarkable for their detail and consistency with experiences from around the globe and across the centuries, despite the specific cultural and Buddhist language and symbology. For example, the *Bardo* instructs the reader to repeat the verse (Padma-Sambhava 1927: 12),

> O nobly-born, when thy body and mind were separating, thou must have experienced a glimpse of the Pure Truth, subtle, sparkling, bright, dazzling, glorious, and radiantly awesome, in appearance like a mirage moving across a landscape in spring-time in one continuous stream of vibrations. Be not daunted thereby, nor terrified, nor awed. That is the radiance of thine own true nature. Recognise it.

This passage from the *Tibetan Book of the Dead* speaks of the early stage of death when the mind and body begin to separate. It is possible to see parallels with George Ritchie's growing awareness of the bright light that he became aware of in his hospital room as he looked at his own dead body, accompanied by the realisation that this light was in fact a wholly good, pure, powerful, loving being. Christianity is reticent about identifying the human with the divine, except in the person of Jesus, but mystics the world over describe a sense of losing oneself in this divine or Pure Truth, and of a sense of identity with it.

Beauregard, Trent, and Schwartz (2018: 31–32) speak of the importance of 'the concilience of inductions' and the 'convergence of evidence' that justify a paradigm shift towards a postmaterialist paradigm.

The term 'consilience of inductions' was taken from the nineteenth century philosopher William Whewell, and quoted in a 2015 issue of *Scientific American* by Michael Shermer. Whewell argued that for a theory to be accepted it must be based on more than one induction, or instance of its occurrence, and that these instances should converge. Shermer used this principle in relation to climate change, but it is equally applicable to miraculous or extraordinary events or to descriptions of the afterlife. Where numerous sources (inductions) speak in similar terms of processes and events (convergence of evidence) they deserve to be taken seriously. A postmaterialist paradigm includes examining evidence from sources that contradict Newtonian physics and avoid the tendency to pathologize any experiences that conflict with it (Beauregard, Trent, and Schwartz 2018).

## MIRACLES AND RELIGIOUS EXPERIENCE

There is no standard agreed definition as to what constitutes a miracle. In common parlance a lucky or surprising event, or a remarkable achievement, is considered a miracle. A standard dictionary definition of a miracle in a religious sense is 'an unusual or mysterious event that is thought to have been caused by a god because it does not follow the usual laws of nature'.[11] In twelfth century usage a miracle is 'a wonderous work of God', from the Latin *miraculum*, an 'object of wonder'. It is cognate in several languages with the word 'to smile' (Greek *meidan*). From the mid-thirteenth century a miracle is 'something that excites wonder or astonishment', 'an extraordinary or remarkable feat', and does not invoke supernatural power. The medieval Miracle Play was 'a dramatic representation of the life of Christ or a saint or other sacred subjects'.[12] The shift in meaning from something that evokes wonder or a representation of the life of Christ to something that is outside the 'laws of nature' and therefore must involve a powerful external intervention is a consequence of a post-Enlightenment understanding of the natural world as ordered and constrained by laws that are predictable and discoverable.[13]

---

[11] Cambridge Dictionary Online: https://dictionary.cambridge.org/dictionary/english/miracle

[12] Online Etymology Dictionary: www.etymonline.com/word/miracle

[13] Biologist Rupert Sheldrake (2012) has argued convincingly that these so-called laws of nature were never as predictable and fixed as the term suggests, and are more habits than laws.

This begs the question as to what is a natural and what is a supernatural event that contravenes natural laws. For a materially minded Western scientist or philosopher this could be anything that cannot be explained according to a strictly physicalist, material view of the universe. For other Westerners who have a more expanded view of what is natural, and in most non-Western societies, the boundaries between what is natural and expected and what is anomalous or unexpected can be very different. In parts of Cameroon and elsewhere in Africa, for example, it is assumed that people can affect others psychically and physically through the action of witchcraft. Ancestors may bless or curse you according to whether you have performed certain rites and have honoured them sufficiently.

In a cosmology where the activity of the deceased and psychic activities of the living are taken for granted, the boundary between expected and unexpected events and laws governing them are drawn very differently (Bowie 2006, 2011). The term 'miracle' will be redundant or attributed to a different class of events. In the many Middle Eastern and European societies that have thematised the Evil Eye, thought processes, both intentional and unintentional, can have a dramatic effect on someone's health. To complement a baby, for example, may express jealousy and cause it to sicken. An amulet might possess the power to protect its wearer from known and unknown sources of danger (Dundes 1981). For religious people everywhere prayers, rituals, chants, and perhaps specific types of musical performance and dance are expected to be efficacious. God or gods, or other supernatural beings, are assumed to intervene directly in human lives and to have the power to manipulate events, but the extent to which such interventions are considered unusual or miraculous varies greatly. Being subject to such interventions may certainly be an experience, but whether it is a 'religious experience' will once again depend on definitions of 'religion' and the role of 'natural' and 'supernatural' activity within a particular culture. Most theists would only consider a supernatural intervention a miracle if it is the work of God, directly or indirectly. Negative instances of supernatural intervention, such as the biblical Flood, are accorded power and legitimacy but are not miraculous.

A 2011 report by the Pew Research Center on the views of Evangelical church leaders from around the world at a meeting at Lucerne in Switzerland found that 76 per cent of the global evangelical leaders surveyed reported that they had witnessed or experienced a divine healing, and 61 per cent received a direct revelation from God. This survey, and others like it, indicate that a natural/supernatural division is insufficient to capture the specific nuances in the cosmology and understanding of religious believers. Direct mystical experience and divine intervention in the world are expected and commonplace, but only acceptable along strictly defined lines. The survey revealed considerable antipathy towards other religions, but even more towards alternative views of the world that similarly expand the notion of what is normal and natural (astrology and reincarnation) or which suggest alternative methods of accessing supernatural power (yoga). For many Evangelical and Charismatic Christians, the 'laws of nature' provide a framework for daily life, but religious life and experience is judged by the extent to which the individual can also live in a supernatural world in which God's miraculous interventions are continuous, from finding a parking space to healing an incurable illness. Spiritual growth and success can be judged by the frequency and scale of such interventions (Csordas 1997; Luhrmann 2012).

David Basinger (2011: 21) maintains that most theists make a distinction between direct acts of God 'in the broad, fundamental sense that God has created the universe, established the laws that govern the natural order, and continues to sustain these natural laws by divine power', and instances in which God intervenes directly to change those laws. It is generally the latter, such as an unexpected healing like George Ritchie's, that are considered miraculous. A distinction can also be made between personal 'miracles', such as freedom from a destructive habit, that are generally seen as the result of God's grace, and miracles, which are public. A miracle also needs to evoke a positive response. The Roman Catholic Church looks for 'spiritual fruits' when determining whether an event is of supernatural origin or miraculous. These include forms of devotional behaviour approved by the Church, such as 'significant increases in prayer, conversion, sacramental confession, Christian charity' (Klimek 2018: 61). Basinger makes the point that a miracle is always contextual. People can perceive an event very differently from one another. Background beliefs, as well as personal and political agendas play a role in the way an event is experienced and interpreted. For an event to be labelled a miracle it must be 'an instantiation of a recognized pattern of divine action pattern' (Basinger 2011: 22), and these patterns will differ from person to person.

Healing miracles are the commonest form of divine intervention in many religions, and being able to heal others, both while alive and from beyond the grave in some cases, is often taken as a mark of sanctity. Healing miracles played a large part in Jesus's reputation during his earthly ministry according to the accounts of his life in the New

Testament, and Jesus's disciples were told that they too would be given the power to heal and to cast out devils (spirit possession being a major cause of illness). Healing may be psychological, spiritual, or physical, or a combination of these. It can range from an amelioration of illness, or even acceptance of it, to a complete and dramatic cure – the classic miracle healing, as when the blind regain sight and the lame walk.

Writing of the Roman Catholic shrine of Lourdes in the southwest of France, John Eade (1991) noted a tension between the thousands of pilgrims who attend the shrine to bathe in the holy spring waters in the hope of a cure, and the church authorities and the male shrine guardians who control the shrine. He characterised these as a feminine, 'miracle discourse' based on devotion to the Virgin Mary, who appeared to a peasant girl, Bernadette Soubirous in 1858,[14] and a male 'suffering discourse', focused on Christ, the Pope, and male church authorities. On a smaller scale, pilgrimage shrines around the world belonging to different religions commonly display tokens left by grateful supplicants who have experienced a miraculous healing or an answer to prayer. Whether it is a small posy of flowers, a few coins, a photograph, or a handwritten note, the understanding that there is an element of reciprocity in interactions with the divine is a deeply embedded aspect of human religious experience. There is a negative side to the belief that God or divine beings can perform miraculous healings. If someone believes that they have somehow failed when their prayers are not answered, or thinks that they are being punished, medical outcomes tend to be worse than for those with no faith (Hvidt 2011: 316).

The negative and often secret NDE that someone is too afraid or ashamed to relate points to the personalisation that can occur when an individual 'is detached from an interpretive community and from spiritual attainment', relocating a miracle to the 'theatre of the questing self'. Whereas in the Middle Ages a miracle inspired awe, wonder, and faith in God, experiencing a contemporary miracle may be taken as a sign of the God within all of us, a way of believing in the self (Woodward 2000; Twelftree 2011: 13). Even where individuals do belong to an interpretive community, the meaning of an extraordinary event is often disputed. The scientific 'facts' of the case, as Latour (2010) noted, are entwined with those of the 'fetish'. The supernatural, religious, and

---

[14] The Virgin Mary appeared to Bernadette and told her to dig in the earth. She uncovered a spring that gave rise to the healing waters that form the centre of the pilgrimage shrine.

mystical elements of an experience and its interpretation are not easily disentangled from the natural, political, and mundane.

### MIRACLES AND MYSTICAL EXPERIENCE:
### A CASE STUDY

My second case study concerns the small town of Medjugorje in the Herzegovina region of Bosnia and Herzegovina, some twenty-five kilometres southwest of Mostar. In 1981 a figure identified as the Virgin Mary appeared to some local children just outside the town on what became known as Apparition Hill. Apparitions of Mary were not uncommon in nineteenth and twentieth century Catholic Europe (Maunder 2016), as well as in Zeitun in Egypt in 1968.[15] The majority of visionaries have been women and children, but the whole community plays a part in the devotional cults that grow up around the resulting shrines. Scepticism in some circles concerning the authenticity of such visions is shared by the Roman Catholic Church, which may take decades to come to an official view of the status of these events. It has often been pointed out that apparitions tend to occur in times and places experiencing tension, whether war or impending war, social change, threats to the integrity of the church, regional divisions, or religious disputes. It could be argued that a message of peace is particularly needed at such times, or that some form of collective anxiety is being manifested. Uneducated women and children may be the least likely to be believed, but they might also be the most receptive to a miraculous or divine intervention.

What is unusual about the apparitions at Medjugorje is their longevity. For some of the visionaries the apparitions still continue on a regular basis, and have done so for the last twenty-eight years. Apparitions and other mystical experiences are often fleeting and spontaneous, and they often rely on the testimony of a single individual, or small group in the case of shared visions. The continuation and predicable timing of the apparitions in Medjugorje have allowed a variety of scientific studies and tests to be carried out on the visionaries. Extraordinary physical phenomena have also been associated with the

[15] https://youtu.be/tVU8bhbQInw. This site associated with the Holy Family (Joseph, Mary, and Jesus) on their flight to Egypt after Jesus's birth. At Zeitun the apparitions were witnessed by both Christians and Muslims and, as at other shrines, there were numerous testimonies of miraculous healings and conversions. The Zeitun apparitions lasted for some three years and are said to constitute the most widely witnessed paranormal (supernatural) phenomenon in human history.

apparitions, witnessed, and often filmed, by tens of thousands of pilgrims. Most famous among these is 'the Miracle of the Sun'; solar phenomena in which the sun appears to spin, pulsate, change in size, move up and down or in an irregular fashion, change colour, and even on occasion reveal a figure moving about within it.[16] This phenomenon is not unique to Medjugorje, having first been seen by an estimated 70,000 people on 13 October 1917 at the Marian shrine of Fatima in Portugal, and subsequently at many other sites around the globe associated with Marian apparitions. The official views of the Roman Catholic Church have reflected tensions between the Franciscans who ran the parish of Medjugorje and the secular clergy, between Roman Catholic and Orthodox Christians, and between Croatians and Serbians. Popes as well as other senior clergy have been divided over the authenticity of the visions, with Pope John Paul, well known for his devotion to the Virgin Mary, convinced of their divine origin, while Pope Francis has stated his doubts about the identity of the person who appears in the apparitions, while not denying the pastoral fruits that have resulted in terms of conversions and increased devotion.[17]

The various tests on the six visionaries while they were in an altered state of consciousness (during the appearances of the Virgin Mary) concluded that they could eliminate fraud and deception, and that the visionaries were psychologically, physically, and spiritually sound. They ruled out natural causes for the deep, spontaneous, and simultaneous trance states they entered when the visions started, quickly and simultaneously returning to normal when Mary departed. As the examinations were carried out under church direction, even when the teams included independent scientific and medical personnel, the majority of their conclusions were theological, concerning the degree to which the messages received by the visionaries, and their demeanour, conformed to church teaching (Apolito 2005).

The contents of the messages are consistent with those of Fatima, Zeitun, and other Marian visitations. They contain calls for peace, while giving apocalyptic warnings of the end times, and a series of 'secrets' that will be revealed at appropriate points in the future as the events foretold take place. The visions could be seen as manifestations

---

[16] https://youtu.be/8YR6INkTK7Q, accessed 18 August 2019. This phenomenon is often linked to the passage in the Book of Revelation 12:2 which describes Mary as 'a woman clothed with the sun'.

[17] Rome Reports in English published 15 May 2017, https://youtu.be/8FTDWY8SIXo, accessed 18 August 2019.

of collective anxiety rather than divine interventions, but as an explanation this cannot account for the visionaries' altered states of consciousness and the extraordinary physical phenomena witnessed by so many people. There is a recurrent temptation to resort to the binary divisions of subject and object that Latour called into question. The Mary of Medjugorje bears a close resemblance to the image of the Virgin in the local parish church. If it is the Virgin Mary appearing, it would seem that she works through what is culturally familiar. The messages she gives conform to a pattern familiar from other Roman Catholic apparitions, a pattern the child visionaries would have been unfamiliar with. There are elements of the experience that present a challenge to both a religious and materialist view of the world.

Robert Orsi (2006), a scholar who has focused much of his work on popular Catholicism, including Marian shrines and apparitions, emphasises religion as it is actually lived, urging scholars to adopt a middle ground between analysis and practice. Rather than an interpretive view of religion as a way of making sense of the world, Orsi sees it as a network of relationships between heaven and earth, between people, objects, and sacred figures. Describing a visit to the Marian shrine of Knock in Ireland, Orsi prefixed his remarks with the statement that: 'The historical and cultural study of Marian apparitions and pilgrimages immediately draws us into the deepest contradictions of experience and imagination in the modern world' (Orsi 2008: 12). An apparition is the experience of the transcendent breaking into time. The particularity of a place (Knock, Fatima, Lourdes, Zeitun, Medjugorje) contrasts with the no-place, beyond time and space of the sacred. Marian shrines are described as having an 'excess of expression' (ibid.), too many candles, souvenir stalls, people, rosaries, images, and so on. By contrast, Western modernity is described as existing under the sign of absence (ibid.: 13):

> Time and space are emptied of presence ... Drained of presence, religious experience is remade in conformity with modern liberal notions of what 'religion' is: autonomous, a distinct domain apart from other areas of life, private, in conformity with the causal laws of nature, reasonable, interior – all the things that Marian apparitions and what follows from them are not.

The problem for historians and scholars of religion is, according to Orsi, that this presumption of absence means that (2008: 14), 'we have no idea what to make of the bonds between humans and the spirits really present to them within the limits of our critical theories'. The challenge is not to go on talking about shrines and pilgrimages but to understand how people meet their gods and how their gods meet them, how humans and their gods make their ways together through the challenges and excitements of life, how the gods become dwellers in this same modern history, independently of their human counterparts, and what they get up to, and what all this means for the social, political, and psychological life of the contemporary world (Orsi 2008: 14).

The term 'abundant events' is how Orsi describes 'these experiences of radical presence or realness' (ibid.). He proposes studying Marian apparitions as part of Marion devotional culture generally, and shrine and pilgrimage culture in particular. They are dramatic events but within the culture in which they take place they are anticipated, longed for and even expected. Something as extraordinary as the apparitions and related phenomena in Medjugorje are part of a continuum of Marian devotion, the other end of which is a simple prayer or saying the rosary. Both are instances of relationship 'between human beings going about the course of their days and the powerful supernatural figure of the Blessed Mother who is present to them' (ibid.). Orsi points out that, as in any dealings with a powerful supernatural figure, this relationship is not without its dangers. Mary may be a mother who cares for and loves her children, but she also warns, chastises, and challenges them (ibid.: 15). The individual mystical experience of the Medjugorje visionaries makes sense only when embedded within a worshipping community. The messages they receive are ostensibly for the whole of humanity, even if those who receive them are primarily Roman Catholics who are already in a personal relationship with the Virgin. A focus on relationships and the abundance of mystical experiences is a useful way of avoiding debates over authenticity that speak of absence rather than presence.

## CONCLUSION: EXPERIENCE AND TRANSFORMATION

When anthropologist Edith Turner took part in a healing ritual in Zambia in 1985, she was already a convert to Roman Catholicism (Turner 1992). She had lived with the Ndembu between 1951 and 1954 when carrying out fieldwork with her husband, Victor Turner. This first period of fieldwork and experience of Ndembu ritual was the catalyst for the Turners' transformation from Communists to Catholics (Turner 2005). What Edith Turner hadn't realised until her participation in the Ihamba tooth ritual in which she shared the role of healer, was that her belief in the supernatural elements of the Christian faith had remained at a symbolic or metaphorical level. During the Ihamba the healers' role was to reconcile the community and the sick woman through the airing of grievances, and then to remove the tooth (*ihamba*) of a hunter that was said to have entered the patient's body. The tooth demanded to be fed, and, until it could be removed and its demands met, it would continue to cause problems. The Turners had witnessed the ritual in the 1950s, but as observers rather than participants. On this occasion, to Edith Turner's surprise, at the climax of the ritual she saw a grey blob, which she identified as the *ihamba*, leave the patient's body to be 'captured' by one of the healers, and subsequently presented to the onlookers in the form of a tooth. The idea that spirits existed and could take a physical form, or that the healing was anything other than group psychotherapy, had never occurred to Turner until she saw and experienced the ritual from the inside. This direct personal experience was transformational, and became the bedrock of Edith Turner's subsequent academic research on healing and power in different cultures.

Turner did not adopt Ndembu beliefs and practices on her return to Charlottesville, Virginia. She continued to forge her own path within the Roman Catholic Church, but with a new sense of the supernatural. Through her research Turner became aware of the ability of human beings everywhere to heal, to create and transform their lives in relationship with those around them and with the natural/supernatural beings, spirits, and forces. It can take an extraordinary or miraculous event to enable people to recognise the miraculous in the experience of everyday, ordinary existence.

### References

Alvarado, Carlos S. "Out-of-Body Experiences," in Etzel Cardeña, Stephen Jay Lynn, and Stanley Krippner (eds.), *Varieties of Anomalous Experience: Examining the Scientific Evidence*, pp. 183–218. Washington, DC: American Psychological Association, 2007.

Apolito, Paolo. *The Internet and the Madonna: Religious Visionary Experience on the Web.* Translated by Anthony Shugaar. Chicago: Chicago University Press, 2005.

Athappilly, Geena K., Bruce Greyson, and Ian Stevenson. "Do Prevailing Societal Models Influence Reports of Near-Death Experiences," *Journal of Nervous & Mental Disease* 194 (2006): 218–22.

Basinger, David. 2011. "What Is a miracle?," in Graham H. Twelftree (ed.), *The Cambridge Companion to Miracles*, pp. 19–35. Cambridge: Cambridge University Press, 2011.

Beauregard, Mario, Natalie L. Trent, and Gary E. Schwartz. "Toward a Postmaterialist Psychology: Theory, Research, and Applications," *New Ideas in Psychology* 50 (2018): 21–33.

Bowie, Fiona. *The Anthropology of Religion*, 2nd ed. Oxford: Blackwell, 2006.
"Miracles in Traditional Religions," in Graham H. Twelftree (ed.), *The Cambridge Companion to Miracles*, pp. 167–83. Cambridge: Cambridge University Press, 2011.

Bush, Nancy Evans. "Distressing Western Near-Death Experiences: Finding a Way through the Abyss," in Etzel Cardeña, Stephen Jay Lynn, and Stanley Krippner (eds.), *Varieties of Anomalous Experience: Examining the Scientific Evidence*, pp. 63–86. Washington, DC: American Psychological Association, 2007.

Cardeña, Etzel, Stephen Jay Lynn, and Stanley Krippner (eds.). *Varieties of Anomalous Experience: Examining the Scientific Evidence*. Washington, DC: American Psychological Association, 2007.

Csordas, Thomas. *The Sacred Self: A Cultural Phenomenology of Charismatic Healing*, new ed. Berkeley: University of California Press, 1997.

Dundes, Alan. "Wet and Dry the Evil Eye," in Alan Dundes (ed.), *The Evil Eye: A Casebook*, pp. 257–312. New York: Garland, 1981.

Eade, John. "Order and Power at Lourdes: Lay Helpers and the Organisation of a Pilgrimage Shrine," in John Eade and Michael J. Sallnow (eds.), *Contesting the Sacred: The Anthropology of Christian Pilgrimage*. London: Routledge, 1991.

Fitzgerald, Timothy. *Religion and the Secular: Historical and Colonial Formations*. London: Routledge, 2007.

Geertz, Clifford. "Religion as a Cultural System," in Michael Banton (ed.), *Anthropological Approaches to the Study of Religion*, ASA Mongraphs 3, pp. 1–46. London: Tavistock, 1973.

Greyson, Bruce. "Near-Death-Experiences," in Etzel Cardeña, Stephen Jay Lynn, and Stanley Krippner (eds.), *Varieties of Anomalous Experience: Examining the Scientific Evidence*, pp. 315–52. Washington, DC: American Psychological Association, 2007.

Greyson, Bruce, and Nancy Evans Bush. "Distressing Near-Death Experiences", *Psychiatry* 55 (1992): 95–98.

Hanegraaff, Wouter J. *Rejected Knowledge in Western Culture*. Cambridge: Cambridge University Press, 2012.

Holden, Janice Miner. "Veridical Perception in Near-Death Experiences", in Janice Miner Holden, Bruce Greyson, and Debbie James (eds.), *The Handbook of Near-Death Experiences: Thirty Years of Investigation*, pp. 185–212. Oxford: Praeger, 2009.

Hufford, David J. "Beings Without Bodies: An Experience-Centered Theory of the Belief in Spirits", in Barbara Walker (ed.), *Out of the Ordinary: Folklore and the Supernatural*, pp. 11–45. Logan: Utah State University Press, 1995.

Hvidt, Niels Christian. 2011. "Patient Belief in Miraculous Healing: Positive or Negative Coping Resource?", In Graham H. Twelftree (ed.), *The Cambridge Companion to Miracles*, pp. 309–29. Cambridge: Cambridge University Press, 2011.

Klimek, Daniel Maria. *Medjugorje and the Supernatural: Science, Mysticism, and Extraordinary Religious Experience.* New York: Oxford University Press, 2018.

Latour, Bruno. *We Have Never Been Modern.* Translated by Catherine Porter. Cambridge, MA: Harvard University Press, 1993.
   *On the Modern Cult of the Factish Gods.* Durham, NC: Duke University Press, 2010.

Latour, Bruno, and Stephen Woolgar. *Laboratory Life: The Construction of Scientific Facts,* 2nd ed. Princeton, NJ: Princeton University Press, 1986.

Lawton, Ian. *After Life: A Modern Guide to the Unseen Realms.* Rational Spirituality Press, 2019. www.rspress.org

Lehmann, Arthur, and James Myers (eds.). *Magic, Witchcraft and Religion: An Anthropological Study of the Supernatural,* 4th ed. Mountain View, CA: Mayfield Publishing Co., 1997.

Luhrmann, Tanya. *When God Talks Back: Understanding the American Evangelical Relationship with God.* New York: Vintage Books, 2012.

Mackey, James. "Christianity and Cultures: Theology, Science and the Science of Religion," *Studies in World Christianity,* 2(1) (1996): 1–25.

Maunder, Chris. *Our Lady of the Nations: Apparitions of Mary in 20th-Century Catholic Europe.* Oxford: Oxford University Press, 2016.

Masumian, Farnaz. "World Religions and Near-Death Experiences," in Janice Miner Holden, Bruce Greyson, and Debbie James (eds.), *The Handbook of Near-Death Experiences: Thirty Years of Investigation,* pp. 159–84. Oxford: Praeger, 2009.

Moen, Bruce. *Voyages into the Unknown.* Charlottesville: Hampton Roads, 1997.

Moody, Raymond A. *The Light Beyond.* London: Rider, 2005.

Morse, Melvin, with Paul Perry. *Closer to the Light: Learning from the Near-Death Experiences of Children.* New York: Ivy Books, 1990.

Noyes, Russell Jr., Peter Fenwick , Janice Miner Holden, and Sandra Rozan Christian. "Aftereffects of Pleasurable Western Adult Near-Death Experiences," in Janice Miner Holden, Bruce Greyson, and Debbie James (eds.), *The Handbook of Near-Death Experiences: Thirty Years of Investigation,* pp. 41–62. Oxford: Praeger, 2009.

Orsi, Robert. *Between Heaven and Earth: The Religious Worlds People Make and the Scholars Who Study Them.* Princeton, NJ: Princeton University Press, 2006.
   "Abundant History: Marian Apparitions as Alternative Modernity," *Historically Speaking* 9 (7) (2008): 12–16.

Osis, Karlis, and Erlendur Haraldsson. *At the Hour of Death,* revised ed. with Introduction by Elisabeth Kubler-Ross. Guildford, Surrey: White Crow Books, 2012.

Padma-Sambhava. The Tibetan Book of the Dead Or the After-Death Experiences on the *Bardo* Plane. English translation by Lama Kazi Dawa-Samdup, accessed 16 August 2019. www.holybooks.com/the-tibetan-book-of-the-dead-2/. First published in English in 1927, translated by Walter Y. Evans-Wentz, Oxford University Press.

Parnia, Sam, with Josh Young. *The Lazarus Effect: The Science that Is Rewriting the Boundaries between Life and Death*. London: Rider, 2013.

Pew Research Center for Religion & Public Life. "Global Survey of Evangelical Protestant Leaders," 22 June 2011. www.pewforum.org/2011/06/22/global-survey-of-evangelical-protestant-leaders/ (Accessed August 17, 2019).

Ritchie, George G., with Elizabeth Sherrill. *Return from Tomorrow*. Grand Rapids, MI: Chosen, 2007.

Sheldrake, Rupert. *The Science Delusion: Freeing the Spirit of Enquiry*. London: Coronet, 2012.

Sherwood, Jane. *Post-Mortem Journal: Communications from Lawrence of Arabia through the Mediumship of Jane Sherwood*. Saffron Waldon, Essex: C. W. Daniel, 1991.

Shushan, Gregory. *Near-Death Experience in Indigenous Religions*. New York: Oxford University Press, 2018.

Turner, Edith, with William Blodget, Singleton Kahona, and Fideli Benwa. *Experiencing Ritual: A New Interpretation of African Healing*. Philadelphia: University of Pennsylvania Press, 1992.

Turner, Edith. *Heart of Lightness: The Life Story of an Anthropologist*. Oxford: Berghahn Books, 2005.

Twelftree, Graham H. "Introduction: Miracle in an Age of diversity," in Graham H. Twelftree (ed.), *The Cambridge Companion to Miracles*, pp. 1–16. Cambridge: Cambridge University Press, 2011.

Tylor, Edward Burnett. *Religion in Primitive Culture*. Reprint of Volume 2 of Tylor 1891, *Primitive Culture*. New York: Harper & Row, 1958.

Weber, Max. *The Protestant Ethic and the Spirit of Capitalism*. Oxford: Oxford University Press, 2010 [1905].

Woodward, Kenneth L. *The Book of Miracles: The Meaning of the Miracles in Christianity, Judaism, Buddhism, Hinduism, Islam*. New York: Simon & Schuster, 2000.

## 12 Evil, Suffering, and Religious Experience

MICHAEL L. PETERSON

Evil and suffering are part of the common experience of humanity. Whether in the form of natural evils, such as floods or disease, or moral evils, such as violence or murder, we are all familiar with the great negatives of existence. Unsurprisingly, then, the universal human experience of evil and suffering is inevitably related to the important phenomenon of religion in human life. In this brief study, I survey how evil and suffering are understood and engaged by religion generally but particularly select three religions for more detailed exploration: Christianity, Islam, and Hinduism. Without question, it is in the experience of evil and suffering that the intellectual and spiritual resources of a religion are put to the hardest test.

### EVIL AND RELIGION

Many claim that suffering is an important cause of religion, expressing the need for people to control or affect the events of their lives and feel reassured of ultimate wellbeing in the face of hardship, catastrophe, and death. The famous Freudian theory of religion is that it stems from an illusion, borne in wish fulfillment, including the desire to control the real world by means of the wish world. Interestingly, a major Freudian critique of religion is rooted in the ostensible failure of religion along these lines:

> The assertions made by religion that it could give protection and happiness to men, if they would only fulfill certain ethical obligations, were unworthy of belief. It seems not to be true that there is a power in the universe, which watches over the well-being of every individual with parental care and brings all his concerns to a happy ending. On the contrary, the destinies of man are incompatible with a universal principle of benevolence or with – what is to some degree contradictory – a universal principle of justice. Earthquakes

[and other natural evils] do not differentiate between the good ... and the sinner. [And moral evils show] that the violent, the crafty, and the unprincipled seize the desirable goods of the earth for themselves, while the pious go empty away. (Freud 1933: 228ff)

For Freud, nothing displays the utter falsity of religion more than the facts of evil in human experience.

Unfortunately, the Freudian account of the failure of religion in light of the experience of suffering and evil is not only greatly over-simplified but also ignores what Rudoph Otto (1923) presents in *The Idea of the Holy* as an even more basic set of experiences that lie at the root of religion. In Otto's famous theory of the religious development of humanity, the most elemental experience is what he calls the experience of the *Numinous*, which is the feeling of being in the presence of something – a power or being of a different kind from us – which excites mixed feelings of dread, wonder, and awe. The experience of numinous awe seems present in our prehistoric ancestors and does not seem to be disappearing even now because of the troub-ling encounter with evil in the sweep of human existence. The second experience Otto identifies is the impression that there is some kind of morality – that "I ought" and "I ought not" put pressure on human conduct. Yet humankind is also conscious of disobeying the very directives of this morality and consequently conscious of feeling guilt, making the pervasive human sense of morality complex – pertaining to something at once approved and disobeyed. The third element in the development of religion, for Otto, is the identification of the Numin-ous Power about which they feel awe as the guardian of the morality to which they feel obligation.

Nothing could be further from wish fulfillment than the thought that morality is supported by the Numinous Power. But with the con-nection of morality and the *Numinous* comes the sense that ultimate reality is righteous somehow, just, and perhaps benevolent. At this point, evil in human experience is in tension with the longstanding impression of the character of the universe, particularly for the developed religions that have moved beyond primitive animisms and national polytheisms. The awkward facts of pain and evil have to fit into the more complex religious understandings. Peter Berger (1967) writes in *The Sacred Canopy* that every religion provides for its adher-ents categories for processing elements of their experience that seem to be chaotic and destructive, or what he calls "anomic phenomena," most notably the phenomena of suffering, tragedy, and death. In his terminology, religion brings life under a "sacred canopy" by positing a higher meaning and authority:

> The anomic phenomena must not only be lived through, they must also be explained – to wit, explained in terms of the nomos established in the society in question. An explanation of these phenomena in terms of religious legitimations, of whatever degree of theoretical sophistication, may be called a theodicy. It is important to stress here particularly (although the same point has already been made generally with respect to religious legitimations) that such an explanation need not entail a complex theoretical system. The illiterate peasant who comments upon the death of a child by referring to the will of God is engaging in theodicy as much as the learned theologian who writes a treatise to demonstrate that the suffering of the innocent does not negate the conception of a God both all-good and all-powerful. (Berger 1967: 53–54)

Under the sacred canopy, so to speak, religious adherents engage suffering and evil – drawing on the resources of their particular religion for theoretical understanding and for experiential guidance. Thus, what a religious system says about the experience of evil reveals a great deal about what it takes ultimate reality, and humanity's relation to it, to be.

## EARLY CHRISTIANITY AND THE EXPERIENCE OF EVIL

Clearly, the categories provided by a religion give to its adherents a conceptual framework, at whatever level of sophistication, for interpreting and responding to evil and suffering in their experience. A given theodicy, then, as an explanation of evil, develops certain categories drawn from the religion as a way of understanding why the divine allows evil, categories which may be philosophically analyzed and evaluated. Within the Christian tradition, we find various major strands of theodicy for consideration.

Interestingly, the perceived viability of most Christian theodicies depends on the deconstruction of a particular and longstanding approach to theodicy – the idea that pain, suffering, and misfortune are the punishment for sin and wrongdoing. Coming out of ancient Judaism, Christianity, like Judaism, had to come to grips with the import of the deuteronomic code in the early Old Testament – which was based on the general principle that a just God will see to it that righteous people prosper and unrighteous people suffer. Later in the Old Testament, the Book of Job provides a case study that can be seen as affirming the justice and righteousness of God but denying that his justice is meticulously enacted in the details of our circumstances. Like Job, who tried diligently to be righteous according to the known Law, Job's "comforters" had also been schooled in the teachings of the Law of Deuteronomy, which implicitly taught that a moral principle of cause-and-effect governed human affairs. However, when terrible suffering and loss occurred in Job's experience, contrary to his understanding of the principle, he insisted on his righteous obedience and began to question the traditional teaching (Job 3ff). By contrast, Job's comforters insisted on the validity of the traditional principle and argued that his unrighteousness could be inferred from his suffering (Job 4:7). After much debate between Job and his so-called comforters, Job has an experience of God "in the Whirlwind" in which he learned that God is perfectly just but that his justice is not so simplistically played out in human experience (Job 38:1–40:2). For our purposes, the prevailing idea, advocated by Job's comforters, that "there is no innocent suffering," was refuted. Like many religious advances, the implications of this insight were not all seen at once but took centuries to develop.

In the life and ministry of Jesus, upon whom Christianity is founded, these developed insights are poignantly portrayed. The New Testament reports that Jesus healed a blind man and told his followers not to interpret the blindness as the result of any sin (John 9:1–3). When eighteen people were killed by the falling of the Tower at Siloam, Jesus asked rhetorically, "Do you think they were more guilty than all other people living in Jerusalem?" (Luke 13:4). Jesus was intent on helping his followers break through to the higher insight that there is no simple cause-and-effect understanding of suffering, that much suffering is simply gratuitous. A crucial point is that this emerging insight, rooted in Job, eventually provided the category for interpreting Jesus's own suffering and death by crucifixion: that Jesus was the perfectly innocent sufferer. During its early evangelistic period, Christianity offered no complex systematic theodicy but rather affirmed that for believers the sufferings of this world would be outweighed and reframed in the unimaginably wonderful eschatological fulfillment of all things (Rom 8:18–25; 31–39).

## THE CHRISTIAN TRADITION AND THE EXPLANATION OF EVIL

As the expansion of early Christianity solidified and more formal theological and philosophical work began to be done in the medieval period,

Christianity, both West and East, developed more intellectually sophisticated theodicies. In the Western Church, Augustine's theodicy
became dominant and still informs the thought of many theologians
and laity. Augustine weaves various themes together in quite an elaborate response to evil: that God's original creation was good but fell into
sin by the disobedient use of free will, and that all evils flow from this
flaw. Augustine also affirms an aesthetic theme – that the evils we
experience are parts of a greater whole which must still be understood
as good, even as beautiful, under God's sovereign oversight of the world.
Of course, God foreknew that the creature would fall into sin, but
nevertheless "God judged it better to bring good out of evil than to
suffer no evil to exist" (*Enchiridion* 27).

In many ways, subsequent Christian theodicies in the West employ
the Augustinian template of designating some good which is connected
to evils in the world, thus displaying the deep conviction that a proper
explanation for evil is that its existence is necessary to some greater
good as deemed by God. Some of the more prominent greater-good
theodicies designate such great goods as free will, character building,
and deeper spiritual life as worth the price of allowing evil.

In the Eastern Church, Bishop Irenaeus developed a distinctive
theodicy that did not assume as background the V-shaped pattern of
"creation-fall-redemption" assumed in Western theodicies. Instead, for
Irenaeus, the original creation was good and inherently innocent, but
not perfect, and thus was placed on a more gradual developmental path.
Hence, creation's "fall" into sin, according to Irenaeus, was virtually
inevitable because of its inherent and ineliminable immaturity – including the immaturity of fundamentally good human persons who were not
fully morally and spiritually formed that grappled with temptation.
Rather than focusing on the causal genesis of evil, Irenaeus emphasized
eschatological fulfillment of God's plans.

Contemporary philosopher John Hick became a champion of what
he called the Irenaean approach, declaring that God's purpose is to bring
creatures from self-centeredness into moral and spiritual maturity – a
process that requires that persons face opportunities for displaying
virtue or vice and of obeying or disobeying God (2010). According to
Hick, this process meant to bring human creatures who bear "the image
of God" ontologically into the "likeness of God" morally and spiritually. Since, it is logically impossible to create morally and spiritually
mature creatures by divine fiat, Hick reasoned that these creatures will
have to be put in an environment conducive to developing moral and
spiritual maturity. Borrowing the term "soul making" from poet John

Keats, Hick indicates that human persons are in a soul-making process which provides opportunity for moral and spiritual growth.

> For personal life is essentially free and self-directing. It cannot be perfected by divine fiat, but only through the uncompelled responses and willing co-operation of willing individuals in their actions and reactions in the world in which God has placed them. (Hick 2010, 255)

Hence, in a soul-making environment, constituted by a community of moral agents interacting in a variety of special ways, rational creatures must decide regarding how they will treat each other and on what kinds of relationships they will have, which creates the possibility of moral evil as well as moral good. Furthermore, in the case of humans as psycho-physical beings, such an environment necessarily has a physical component – which is a world characterized by physical laws that operate independently of our desires, thus providing an arena for the exercise of free choice but also the possibility of natural evils such as pain, disease, suffering, and deformity. Part of the reason for why natural evils are possible, then, is linked to free will because a relatively independent natural system provides the context for human choice and action.

An important shift in emphasis in Christian theodicy was advocated by philosopher Marilyn Adams, who classifies the mainline tradition in theodicy (of which John Hick's is an instance) as being "global and generic," rooted in general statements (say, about free will or a natural order) meant to justify evil as necessary to the realization of some great good that makes the world better on the whole. Rejecting general cost/benefit analyses, Adams focuses on how it is that God can be good to each individual that falls on the wrong side of such analyses and do not ostensibly benefit from the designated goods. Indeed, Adams coins the term "horrendous evils" to label "evils the participation in which (that is, the doing or suffering of which) constitutes *prima facie* reason to doubt whether the participant's life could (given their inclusion in it) be a great good to him/her on the whole" (Adams 1999: 26). Such evils include, according to Adams, the rape and brutal murder of a woman, psychological torture that destroys personalities, extreme child abuse and murder, the explosion of nuclear bombs over populated areas, etc. In developing a theodicy to address how God can be good to individual persons who experience horrendous evils, her salient point is that, since no finite good can render these evils meaningful, only the infinite good which is God himself can guarantee to each person a life he or she can see as having positive meaning and value. Relationship with God – the

Beatific Vision in classical terms – which is perhaps only realized in the life to come, contains the only elements that can defeat horrendous evils. But, in earthly life, even a sense of identification with the infinitely good God can give a measure of hope.

## ISLAM AND SUFFERING

Although suffering is a universally human experience, the different ways in which suffering occurs vary greatly. The Qur'an as scripture, which claims repeatedly to be the same revelation that God, or Allah, entrusted to such servants as Abraham, Moses, and Jesus, still arises out of its distinctive situation of harsh desert life. Life in the desert is fragile and vulnerable, constantly threatened by drought and famine, and even subject to external attack from hostile tribes. It is perhaps unsurprising, then, that the Qur'an speaks in very direct, concrete language about the particulars of life, and does not venture deeply into more abstract and speculative questions about why Allah allows evil. The direct, concrete language also carries over into the Qur'an's descriptions of the rewards of paradise and the pains of hell.

Yet none of this is meant to suggest that there is no problem of evil and suffering in the Qur'an or that Islam does not face its own problem of evil. Consider the following straightforward statement of the problem in the Qur'an:

> Did you suppose that you would go to Paradise
> untouched by the suffering
> which was endured by those before you?
> Affliction and adversity befell them;
> and so battered were they that each apostle,
> and those who shared his faith, cried out:
> "When will the help of Allah come?"
> His help is ever near.
>
> (Qur'an 2.214)

Such passages express the real-life basis for later theoretical engagement with the problem.

In locating the emphasis of the theoretical problem, one might say that in Judaism the problem was primarily about God's justice, and in Christianity about God's love, but that in Islam it is about God's power and control. The difference in emphasis can be explained, in part, as a difference in how the experience of evil and suffering is processed through the salient categories of the religion. Thus, in Judaism, the question was about the apparent unjust distribution of the benefits and burdens of life, while in Christianity it was about the apparent lack of God's loving purposes in the outcomes of human affairs. In Islam, then, the question becomes about the apparent lack of divine control in light of the strong theological assertions of Allah's omnipotence.

Thus, Islam has its own theoretical problem of evil based on the particular conceptual meanings it gives to Allah's attributes and purposes. In fact, it is possible to detect in Islam three major ways of engaging the problem based upon different points of emphasis and nuance. First, there is clearly a way of construing relevant Islamic teachings to imply that no theodicy is possible and that the activity of seeking a theodicy may even be blasphemous. Emphasis on the absolute controlling power of Allah and on the sheer difference of his infinite understanding from finite human understanding imply both that everything that happens, including evil, is the will of Allah and that no human intellectual attempts to discern God's purposes can be effective.

For example, in the tenth century, Abu al-Hasan al-Ash'ari wrote in favor of the anti-theodicy tradition in Islam:

> [T]here is neither good nor evil on earth, save what God wills and ... things exist by God's will ... [N]or can we pass beyond the range of God's knowledge ... [W]e ought to commit our affairs to God and assert our complete need and dependence upon Him. (al-Ash'ari 1940: 50–51)

In the same vein, Abu Hamid al-Ghazali, a prominent theologian in the twelfth century, argued that God can inflict pain on humans for no reason or for his inscrutable reasons, such that the question of why God allows evil is unanswerable. Further, posing such questions of God displays a lack of trust and must be condemned. Interestingly, this posture toward raising the question of why God allows evil is also seen in certain interpretations of Job's encounter with the whirlwind – again, that a concept of God's infinite controlling power suppresses questions of justice and goodness. One detects in this position an implicit divine command theory – that God's will determines what is just and good (Ghaly 2014: 385).

A second approach which endorses theodicy in Islam is seen in the Mu'tazila theologians who place greater emphasis on God's justice, wisdom, and benevolence than on his controlling power. For these theologians, theodicy is indeed required in order to demonstrate that evil in the world does not detract from God's wisdom and benevolence – indeed, that God always acts from wisdom for benevolent aims. In fact, these theologians even denied that divine omnipotence can supercede or deviate from justice, wisdom, and benevolence conceived in ways consonant with human understandings of those attributes. Further, these theologians denied that God's morality and justice are incommensurate with human standards of morality and justice, and thus affirmed that human investigation into how God remains just in light of evil could be fruitful. Readers familiar with Thomas Aquinas will note that he too emphasized that God's power in action is always guided by his "supreme wisdom" or "right reason" (*recta ratio*) and that his morality and justice are accessible to finite human understanding (*Summa Theologica* 1–2.94; 7.2).

In the theodicies emerging out of the Mu'tazila tradition in Islam, as in many Western Christian theodicies, human free will, granted by God, is identified as the root of moral evil in the world. In his wisdom and goodness, God has given finite human creatures free will in order to give them moral accountability that can be rewarded and punished. Thus, moral evil is not assignable to God acting unjustly but to the wrongful actions of finite human agents. The caveat, of course, is that God is responsible for choosing to create the kind of world that includes morally free creatures who sometimes harm each other (Ghaly 2014, p. 386).

Natural evil, on the other hand, is not humanly caused and, for the Mu'tazila tradition, as for most traditions in Islam, is directly caused by God for specific wise purposes. At this point, an interesting conceptual problem arises regarding divinely caused natural evil because of Islam's keen consciousness of legal justice and compensation. Mu'tazila theologians framed their thinking around the principle of informed consent: it would seem that a morally good being must gain consent from persons before inflicting harm on them. Various answers to this problem covered a range of options – from appeals to God's perfect wisdom, which knows what is best and does not require consent, to assertions that persons who do not consent will be compensated far out of proportion to their suffering, such that no rational person would refuse the suffering. Other possible theories were also offered – for instance, the idea that some suffering is punishment and some suffering is God's offer of an opportunity to earn reward by suffering well.

A third approach to the conceptual problem of evil and suffering was developed by an assorted group of Muslim theologians, jurists, Sufis, exegetes of the Qur'an, and some Ahs'aris diverging from their standard position. This group advocated a middle way between the mainline Ash'aris, who asserted theological voluntarism about divine justice, and the Mu'tazila, who asserted a retributive justice model that was accessible to human understanding. Shaping the thinking of this group was their emphasis on the Qur'anic phenomenon of integrating divine names and attributes for Allah's omnipotence and mercy, which inspired the search for middle ground. The middle ground consisted of affirming, on the one hand, that God's acts are guided by his infinite wisdom for its purposes, such that voluntarism is rejected, and, on the other hand, that these purposes are not guaranteed to be accessible to human intellectual inquiry, such that the use of human standards to assess God's acts is rejected.

Particularly emphasizing revelation as superior to human reason, this group advocating the middle-way approach nonetheless offered some tentative possible reasons that God might have for bringing suffering. For example, God might discipline wrongdoers to correct them and bring them to forgiveness, thus wedding justice and mercy (e.g., Qur'an 4:79; 8:53; 30:41). The following verse in the Qur'an is representative of this view:

> Whatever misfortune happens to you, it is because of the things your hands have wrought, but for many [of them] he grants forgiveness. (42:30)

Another proposal from this group of theologians is the idea that suffering has a purifying effect on the faithful, a point attributed to several prophetic traditions: "No calamity befalls a Muslim but God expiates some of his sins even if it were being pricked with a thorn." Once again, the theme of the relation between justice and mercy is evident here.

One fascinating proposal for why God brings suffering was elaborated by Abū Mansūr al-Māturīdī in his *Book of Oneness*. In a chapter entitled "The Evidence that the Cosmos Has One Who Gave It Temporal Existence," he states the argument that suffering and evil can ground an argument that the world is temporal, not self-existent, which, in turn, entails that there must be a self-existent Creator:

> [I]f the world existed by its own essence, no instant in it would be truer [or more perfect] than any other, no state more appropriate than any other, no characteristic more seemly than any other. But, since it exists with instants, states and characteristics which differ from one another, it is proven that it does not exist by its own essence ... [If the world were self-existent], it would be false to say that moral and physical evils exist. But the fact of their existence shows that the existence of the world came about by something other than itself. (*Book of Oneness* 12.8)

Thus, the presence of degrees of perfection and beauty and appropriate-
ness is evidence of finitude, dependency, and temporality, indeed, of the
fact that finite beings are not in control of their own existence (see
Pessagno 1984: 72–73). Conversely, as the reasoning goes, if the universe
were self-existent, everything would simply be perfect with regard to
points of time and states and qualities of being. The conclusion follows,
then, that the world has a Creator who is self-existent and bestowed
existence on creaturely reality. Some readers will immediately see the
consonance between this reasoning, which employs evil and suffering to
conclude that the world is temporal, and the reasoning of the kalām
cosmological argument, which begins with the universe understood as
having a temporal beginning and concludes that it must have been
brought into being by an eternal, self-existent cause, God, as its Creator.

## SUFFERING AS A PRACTICAL PROBLEM IN ISLAM

Although the experience of evil and suffering of all kinds is universal
throughout the human race, the interpretive categories for evil and
suffering differ across religions, and in turn yield different directives
for practical engagement. The three explanatory approaches already
discussed entail their own distinctive theoretical interpretations of evil
and suffering in human experience, but Muslim scholars in aggregate
agree that believers should display three particular personal responses to
calamity and misfortune of various kinds – an attitude of servitude,
patient endurance, and gratitude. Furthermore, the exact texture and
nuance of these personal responses is much discussed and well defined
within Islamic thought.

Regarding servitude, the first quality of attitudinal response, al-
Qushayrī, quoted his master's saying: "Just as 'lordship' is an eternal
quality of God [may He be exalted], so is 'servitude' a quality of man
that stays with him as long as he lives" (al-Qushayrī 2007: 173). Islamic
scholars indicate that the person who continually raises objections
against the work of specialists such as physicians or engineers because
he fails to understand their point is like the person who lacks a servant
attitude toward God because he fails to understand the divine purposes.
It is unwise, so the logic goes, to think that God must explain his
reasons for every delight or sorrow in our experience. Nonetheless
suffering reveals character – in those who are and are not living in a
state of servitude. The proper posture in the face of suffering and misfortune is to evaluate one's own life for areas in which one may be
failing to observe all Islamic instructions to the faithful.

The second recommended attitude is patience, or patient endurance, understood as refraining from panic or despair when calamity or hardship comes. Patience in this sense also includes not complaining to others about one's misfortune. A famous text regarding a man afflicted with blindness is worth quoting in this regard: "If I test My servant by depriving him of his [eyesight] and he faces that with patient perseverance, I shall compensate him with Paradise" (hadīth no. 5329, vol. 5, p. 2140). Muslim wisdom here also entails that impatience and struggling will not change the negative circumstances, for whatever is decreed by God cannot be changed or reversed. Interestingly, complaining to other humans is not appropriate for the Muslim, while crying out and complaining to God is not forbidden by the Qur'an: "I only complain of my distraction and anguish to God" (Qur'ān 12:86). The Qur'an also refers to the biblical Job's patience (as here defined) and to Job's heart-cry only to God in the face of suffering (Qur'an 21:83).

Gratitude as the third recommended attitude is a feeling of thankfulness because of a benefaction or blessing. Feeling gratitude in times of prosperity and blessing is possible for everybody to practice, but gratitude in times of hardship and suffering is practiced only by the truly faithful, who are showing real piety. As Muslim wisdom goes, those persons who are grateful in prosperity but curse God when their prosperity is removed are not among the faithful, whereas those persons who continue to praise God when their prosperity is removed are displaying true faithfulness. In fact, the truly pious person sees hardship and affliction as a blessing for the refinement of faith and for earning a heavenly reward. The principle here can be clearly stated: "He does not understand religion properly who does not count affliction as a blessing and ease as a disaster" (al-Qayyim 1998: 68). Part of the reasoning here is that the nature of one's love for God is revealed during suffering and hardship – those persons who have utilitarian love for God, because of his blessings, and will depart when the blessings are removed, are distinguished from those persons who love God intrinsically, because of who he is in himself as perfect and righteous.

In summary, at the theoretical level, Islam in general endorses a deterministic principle about God's control of human affairs, including suffering and misfortune, while teaching trust and obedience in that control. At the practical level, Islam largely holds an instrumental view of suffering – that suffering is a means for God to test and develop character, obedience, and love. A final aspect of the Islamic view of evil and suffering is eschatological, affirming God's ultimate victory and ability to give rewards and heaven to the deserving.

## HINDUISM AND UNDERSTANDINGS OF EVIL

For Hinduism, there are many ways of looking at a single object, none of which provides the whole view, but each of which represents a perspective. The well-known Hindu parable of the blind men and the elephant (with versions occurring in Buddhism and Jainism) is actually a metaphor to teach this truth about the divine. A group of blind men, who have no prior knowledge of elephants, encounter an elephant, and each man touches a different part of the elephant to make an identification. One man feels the trunk and declares that it is a rope, another feels the tusk and asserts that it is a spear, and yet another feels the leg and declares it is like a tree, and so it goes, each man disagreeing with the others' descriptions and claiming that his own description is the truth. Of course, for Hinduism, this little story indicates that the divine is unable to be comprehended in finite human categories but that humans nonetheless exhibit the strong tendency of making claims to absolute truth about God based on their finite understanding and limited experience (Goldstein 2010: 492).

The parable in a sense explains diversity within Hinduism itself on many points, but the diversity is nowhere more evident in Hinduism than in the various efforts, often contradictory among the various streams of Hindu thought, to wrestle with the problem of evil and suffering. However, in spite of the range of perspectives on evil that are rooted in a variety of scriptural sources and commentaries, many thinkers maintain that, at the more abstract, theoretical level, the doctrines of karma and rebirth are the heart of the Hindu explanation of evil. Then, on the practical level, Hinduism advocates right perception and right action as the key to living in a world that contains suffering. This comprehensive approach, when explicated more fully, represents the striking differences between Western religious thought generally and the great Indian religious traditions.

The underlying metaphysical vision of Hinduism is often characterized as a particular kind of monism known as panentheism, which holds that ultimate reality is the Divine Ground of Being (Brahman), of which the individual self (*atman*) is but a particular expression. The basic Hindu approach to suffering and evil, then, rests upon other doctrines that are closely interwoven with this view. *Karma* is the Hindu universal law of moral cause-and-effect, whereby the deeds of every person – and, more precisely, the character of every person – receives its exactly proportionate consequences. Whereas sometimes Western theistic religions offer theodicies for suffering that may include a retributive element when combined with a wide range of other elements, Indian thought makes retribution central, perfect, and exact, such that all suffering in each person's life must be explained by that individual's wrongdoing, whether in this or a prior life.

Although common experience tells us that life is often unjust – that sometimes good people suffer and bad people prosper – *karma* is the inexorable law of the universe which guarantees perfect and proportionate consequences. However, karmic effects may be borne out over other lifetimes, since all creatures are caught in *samsara*, which is the cycle of birth–death–rebirth in which all beings will experience a form of existence which is determined by *karma* to be a reflection of the quality of their life in a previous existence. Whereas many other religions, particularly theistic religions, provide ultimate explanations of suffering by reference to what happens after death, perhaps in some eschatological resolution of all things, classical Hinduism explains suffering by reference to conditions before birth. As the Hindu saying goes, "Even as the embodied Self passes, in this body, through the stages of childhood, youth, and old age, so does It pass into another body" (*Bhagavad-Gita* 1983: ch. 2, text 12).

Thus, in the ongoing cycle of many existences, it is possible to rise or fall according to the integrity with which one has previously lived. Swami Adiswarananda addresses the issue of suffering in relation to *karma* and *samsara*:

> Essentially, the law of karma says that while our will is free, we are conditioned to act in certain set ways. We suffer or enjoy because of this conditioning of our mind. And conditioning of mind, accumulated through self-indulgence, cannot be overcome vicariously. A Hindu is called upon to act in the living present, to change his fate by changing his way of life, his thoughts and his actions. Our past determines our present, and our present will determine our future. He is taught that no change will ever be effected by brooding over past mistakes or failures or by cursing others and blaming the world or by hoping for the future. (Adiswarananda, n/d, weekly message 41)

Traditionally, *karma* was seen in social and political terms as playing out in the caste system in which different groups of people were assigned a widely different status and importance. Although officially abolished in India in 1947, the social effects of caste system thinking are still detectable.

According to Hindu thought, the individual self of our ordinary experience is actually a manifestation of the one true reality, Brahman, which entails that individual personhood is part of the realm of illusion (*maya*). In fact, objects of all kinds that are experienced as distinct and separate individuals only amount to "appearance" but are not "reality." Technically, then, even the experience of suffering belongs to the world of *maya* and *samsara*. The foundational Scriptures of Hinduism – the *Vedas*, the *Brahmanas*, and the *Upanishads* – progressively reveal a further and fascinating insight: that suffering is somehow the essence of the universe. The universe expresses the unending process of killing and being killed, devouring and being devoured, such that ritual sacrifice developed in early Vedic Hinduism as a form of identification with the process and a way of trying to bring it into some sort of control.

"Cosmic process," as Swami Radhakrishnan describes it, "is one of universal and unceasing change and is patterned on a duality which is perpetually in conflict ..." (Radhakrishnan 1953: 59). The duality (not dualism) is actually a reflection of different aspects of a single entity seen from different sides of what is essentially a unity, an insight reflected in the parable of the blind men and the elephant. So, ultimately gaining the right perspective and right attitude toward suffering rests on seeing it in relation to the whole, as only relative. To designate the unpleasant experience of suffering as evil still would be to see it as a particular and out of context. Furthermore, suffering can even be beneficial if it serves to cut us off from unworthy objects of our affection. So, true perception is to see the unity behind the variety of manifest forms. While the experience of suffering is real enough, seen in relation to the whole, it cannot be an ultimate reality.

## SUFFERING AS A PRACTICAL PROBLEM IN HINDUISM

As in all religions, the categories in which Hinduism understands the meaning of evil and suffering colors the experience of evil and provides practical guidance for living life. Normally, for worship and devotion, the Hindu believer will select one or several of the thousands of gods or goddesses in Hinduism, usually the god or goddess of his or her village or group, to represent Brahman or a particular aspect of Brahman. Daily prayer and meditation, then, are aimed at living life well and in accord with *karma, dharma*, and *samsara*. But Hindu belief also makes a significant difference for Hindus facing terminal illness and death. Even the aging process is a prod to make apologies and make amends in order to rectify the karmic situation in one's life, in which case debilitation and suffering have a positive, corrective function (Whitman 2007: 607).

The modern medical community is working on developing an understanding of the Hindu psychological frame of mind (which is powerfully affected by belief in *karma, dharma,* and *samsara*) in order to deal sensitively with end-of-life issues for Hindus. Respect must be given by counselors and medical professionals to the strong psychological need to face death with a clear mind in order to strive for a better reincarnation and a chance to move closer to never again being reborn (Thrane 2010: 342).

The ultimate goal of each person, for Hinduism, is *moksha,* which is liberation from the cycle of birth–death–rebirth, is only possible when parts are *seen* to be parts, and Brahman is realized as the sole truth – and this realization may take a long time and many existences to attain. Suffering is only a problem as long as it appears to be a final and inescapable truth – a mistaken perception which causes the individual self to spend itself seeking a solid and secure home in objects that are ephemeral and transitory, still in the realm of *maya.* But when one realizes the famous goal of the *Upanishads* – Atman is Brahman – one sees that the self is not bound forever to the transient world of suffering, and suffering can no longer occur. Consider how Indra comes to understand that the body may suffer while the Self which pervades it is not affected:

> [T]his Self ... will be blind when the body is blind, lame when the body is lame, deformed when the body is deformed. When the body dies, this same Self will also die! In such knowledge I can see no good. (*Chandogya Upanishad* 8.7–15)

Prajapati, who is instructing Indra, explains that the realization of the true Self is like being in a state of dreamless sleep, but it is surely possible that many "as it were" experiences will occur before that state is reached. To be born is to come into contact with evil and suffering, since the material body is full of corruption and potential conflict – a potentiality which is realized if the self gives way to its desires and passions that attach it to the world process.

Achieving *moksha* involves more than achieving right perception; it requires a certain way of living. "The acts done in former births never leave any creature. In determining the working out of karma the Lord of Creation saw them all. Man, since he is under the control of *karma,* must always have in mind how he can restore the balance and rescue himself from evil consequences" (*Mahabharata Vanaparva* 1896: 207.19). *Dharma* is doing whatever is appropriate in the circumstances in which one finds oneself, including one's station in society, without attachment to the results. It is easy to understand why classical Hinduism places considerable emphasis on asceticism (self-denial, privation) as a practical route to getting suffering in its right perspective and moving one toward final release. Of course, not just undergoing but also inflicting suffering is addressed in the *Bhagavad-Gita*, where, as long as causing suffering is part of one's legitimate role or duty, it is in accord with *dharma*, although generally Hinduism recommends *ahimsa*, non-violence.

Interpreters of Hinduism argue that it is not an escapist attempt to avoid the miseries of the present world. The realization that "Atman is Brahman" cannot be attained by pretending that the world does not exist, but only by seeing the world for what it is, in the right perspective, and by acting appropriately in the world. The foundational concept is that suffering is a direct result of *karma*, such that an individual self reaps the fruits of its own deeds and thoughts, in future existences if not in this life. This means that morality is strongly connected with suffering, but it is a quite different connection. The problem of Job as the paradigmatic case of the genuinely innocent sufferer cannot arise because it is ineluctably true that occurrences of suffering are a consequence of activities, not simply in this existence, but in previous ones as well. Thus, the question posed to Jesus – "who sinned, this man or his parents?" – is readily answered, "This man."

## REFLECTIONS ON EVIL AND SUFFERING IN RELIGIOUS EXPERIENCE

The approaches to evil and suffering above, in both their theoretical and practical aspects, provide case studies, so to speak, showing how evil becomes problematical as well as how responses to it emerge based on the intellectual and spiritual resources in the foundation of each different religion. Over time, each tradition must reassert its relevance as new circumstances arise and fresh reflections catalyze new explorations of both the questions posed and the answers given regarding evil and suffering. Despite fascinating differences in theological formulations of the problem as well as responses to it, there is also the common human experience of evil as a concrete reality. Human questioning, then, predictably follows: Why do the innocent suffer and the wicked flourish? Why is the world not better ordered and more just? Why is there suffering and death at all in the universe? How do I face evil and suffering in practical life? How does evil and suffering affect my ultimate destiny? In our brief sample, we can see that responses to evil and suffering across cultures and religions are important ways of engaging with a fundamental fact of human life. For a more comprehensive study of this phenomenon, see John Bowker's classic book *Problems of Suffering in Religions of the World* (1970). As Bowker recognizes, pursuit of this study renews our awareness of our shared humanity and, in turn, alerts us to appreciate the powerful influence of religion in how large portions of the world's population conceptualize, experience, and deal with evil and suffering.

## References

Adams, Marilyn. *Horrendous Evils and the Goodness of God*. Ithaca: Cornell University Press, 1999.

Adiswarananda (Swami). "Hinduism: The Problem of Suffering." Weekly Message Archive of The Ramakrishna-Vivekananda Center, New York City, n/d. www.ramakrishna.org/activities/message/weekly_message41.htm

al-Ash'ari, Abu al-Hasan. *The Elucidation of Islam's Foundation*. Translated by Walter C. Klein. New Haven, CT: Yale University Press, 1940.

al-Qayyim, Ibn. *Healing the Sick on Issues of Fate, Predetermination, Wisdom and Theodicy*. Translated by Nasiruddin al-Khattab. London: Islamic Texts Society, 1998.

al-Qushayrī, Abū al-Qāsim. *Epistle on Sufism*. Translated by A. Knysh. Reading, UK: Garnett Publishing, 2007.

Berger, Peter. *The Sacred Canopy*. New York: Doubleday, 1967.

*Bhagavad Gita*. Translated by Swami Prabhupāda. Los Angeles: The Bhaktivedanta Book Trust, 1983.

Bowker, John. *Problems of Suffering in Religions of the World*. Cambridge: Cambridge University Press, 1970.

Freud, Sigmund. "New Introductory Lectures on Psycho-Analysis," in *The Standard Edition of the Complete Psychological Works of Sigmund Freud*, Volume XXII. Translated by J. Strachey et al. London: Hogarth Press, 1933.

Ghaly, Mohammed. "Evil and Suffering in Islam," in M. Peterson, Wm. Hasker, B. Reichenbach, and D. Basinger (eds.), *Philosophy of Religion: Selected Readings*, pp. 383–90. New York: Oxford University Press, 2014.

Goldstein, E. Bruce. *Encyclopedia of Perception*. New York: Sage Publications, 2010.

Hick, John. *Evil and the God of Love*. New York: Palgrave, 2010.

Otto, Rudolph. *The Idea of the Holy*. New York: Oxford University Press, 1923.

Pessagno, J. Meric. "The Uses of Evil in the Maturidian Thought," *Studia Islamica* 60 (1984): 59–84.

Radhakrishnan (Swami). *The Principal Upanishad*. London: George Allen & Unwin, 1953.

Thrane, Susan. "Hindu End of Life: Death, Dying, Suffering, and Karma," *Journal of Hospice and Palliative Nursing* 12 (6) (2010): 337–42.

Vyasa, Krishna-Dwaipayana. *Mahabharata Vanaparva*. Translated by Kisari Mohan Ganguli. New Delhi: Munshiram Manoharlal Publishers, 1896. For the complete text, see www.mahabharataonline.com/

Whitman, Sarah. "Pain and Suffering as Viewed by the Hindu Religion," *Journal of Pain* 8 (8) (2007): 607–13.

# 13 Naturalism and Religious Experience

## WILLEM B. DREES

Naturalism excludes religious experience. At least that seems to follow from a fairly common science-inspired understanding of reality as shaped by natural laws and of religious experience as referring to exceptional experiences. However, some differentiation is in order.

a. Naturalists indeed do not grant *evidential* weight to claims about religious experiences; they consider claims about religious experiences, whether exceptional or not, as explainable in principle.

b. Naturalists may *interpret* experiences in terms of awe, beauty, order, and even grace; some see such experiences as similar to religious experiences. Those naturalists may designate themselves as religious naturalists.

Before discussing the two main claims, I will describe 'science-inspired naturalism' as the broad kind of naturalism under consideration here. For a nuanced analysis of 'religious experience', I refer the reader to other chapters in this volume. In the context of this article, two particular clusters of experiences will be considered. First, we will consider exceptional experiences, those that seem to be at odds with the natural course of events. Second, we come to experiences that are accompanied by affective responses such as wonder and awe. Thus, after introducing science-inspired naturalism we consider naturalism and exceptional experiences, and naturalism and experiences of wonder and awe, followed by a consideration about the possibility of religious naturalism.

## SCIENCE-INSPIRED NATURALISM

Naturalism, as a philosophical position, can take various forms. Jerome Stone, historian of religious naturalism, defined naturalism as "a set of beliefs and attitudes that focuses on this world." He continues:

On the negative side, it involves the assertion that there seems to be no ontological distinct and superior realm (such as God, soul, or heaven) to ground, explain, or give meaning to this world. On the positive side, it affirms that attention should be focused on the events and processes of this world to provide what degree of explanation and meaning are possible to this life. (Stone 2008: 1; similarly Stone 2003: 89)

The negative claim is a priori. For some, treating reality as one seems philosophically preferable over two or more types. The seventeenth-century philosopher Benedict Spinoza coined the expression *Deus sive natura*, God or nature, as two terms referring in different ways to the same reality.

A posteriori, one might argue for naturalism as an understanding of reality that reflects the success of the natural sciences in developing an empirically well-supported understanding of all phenomena in our world. The sciences provide an increasingly integrated and unified understanding of reality, resulting in predictions which correspond very accurately to empirical results. Scientific understanding has also made it possible to manipulate parts of reality with great precision. Inspired by the success of the sciences, such a science-inspired naturalism is a low level metaphysics that seeks to follow as far as philosophically feasible the insights that the sciences offer (Drees 1996: 11). Unless indicated otherwise, such a *science-inspired naturalism* is what is meant by naturalism in the context of this chapter. As a philosophical position it is itself not science, nor formally implied by the sciences, but it seeks to stay as close as possible to mainstream consolidated science in articulating the way the world might be.

With respect to *ontology*, such a naturalism assumes that all objects, ourselves included, are best understood as made of the stuff described by chemistry in the Periodic Table of Elements. This stuff is described by physicists in terms of atoms, and these in terms of more elementary particles and forces, and beyond that of quantum fields, strings, or whatever. Our knowledge has not reached rock bottom. We may even still be missing major components, as suggested by the search for 'dark energy' and 'dark matter' in cosmology.

A science-inspired naturalistic view of reality need not imply that conceptual language adequate to a particular level of description is also suitable for phenomena at a different scale. The language of biology is different from the conceptual language of chemistry, and economics needs concepts such as money that do not have a type–type correspondence to a particular type of material entity. Emergent entities are real and causally efficacious, even though consisting of simpler components, just as future entities are real and causally efficacious while having been produced by present ones (Drees 1996: 15f.; Humphreys 1997; Goodenough and Deacon 2006; Deacon 2012). Thus, reductionist research programs (understanding a phenomenon as realized by under-lying processes) may well go hand in hand with recognition of emer-gence (appreciating phenomena as going beyond their constituent processes, though realized by them without any additional organizing input).

With respect to *history*, such a naturalism understands all living beings on this planet, including ourselves with our social and mental characteristics, as the result of evolutionary processes on this planet, which itself bears the marks of cosmological history of some fourteen billion years.

Not only does such a science-inspired naturalism follow science in its understanding of reality, it also takes the sciences as providing the strongest example of empirical and mathematical *methods* that we use to acquire knowledge of reality. Such a naturalism involves at least 'methodological naturalism', in the sense that explanations may only refer to causal influences of natural entities, according to natural laws, without adding magic or miracles to it. If something appears not to fit, it is an anomaly to be explained in the future (Perry and Ritchie 2018).

Science-inspired naturalism must be open to *changing* conceptions of reality. A well corroborated phenomenon that at first seems to fall outside the scope of natural possibilities may be discovered to be pos-sible with currently known laws and entities (e.g., superconductivity at higher temperatures than previously known) or might induce scientists to revise their understanding of those laws. Such revisions should respect previous successful predictions, but may present quite different models of reality. This happened when Newton's understanding of gravity as a force working at a distance was replaced by Einstein's general relativity view of gravity as curvature of space-time. These are ontologically quite different, but there is continuity in predictions, say of eclipses of the Sun. Current science is our provisionally best understanding of reality, but not yet the end of our exploring. If we dig deeper, we might need new conceptualities. While we build upon pre-sent day knowledge, research may well lead us to revise previous understandings.

The prominent position given to science is not merely an intellec-tual preference; it is also a *moral* priority, at least according to natural-ists. We have to rely on the best available knowledge, and should not play down scientific insights. Easy examples to support this stance are

306 Willem B. Drees

medical – the insight that a virus, HIV, is the cause of AIDS, supports effective preventive action and hence prevents much suffering. The discovery that even passive smoking is detrimental to health has been important to beneficial changes in policies and lifestyle. Of course, commercial interests or ideological drives may bring some to deny such insights (see Oreskes and Conway 2010). For a science-inspired naturalist (and for many others), science is our best guide, also when bringing insights that appear to be unwelcome.

With respect to one's view of reality, there is some 'room' between science and science-inspired naturalism, as important theories in physics may allow for *multiple interpretations*, and hence multiple ways of developing these philosophically. This is well known for quantum physics, but holds more generally. Hence, though science-inspired naturalism takes science as its basis, it refers to philosophical schemes that are underdetermined by science.

There are certain issues on which science-inspired naturalism need not have a voice. The basic view for science-inspired naturalism is that all events in the world can be understood along the lines of science or future science. However, science-inspired naturalism need not pronounce on elements that are *categorically* different. The primary example is mathematics. In the world as experienced, there are no pure circles or triangles, but nonetheless we may have knowledge of the properties of such objects. Mathematical entities might be understood as the limiting case of abstract reasoning that begins with measuring and counting, if one prefers not to grant these a Platonic type of existence.

Similarly, all social behavior is an appropriate object of empirical scientific study, including our habit of judging behavior as moral or immoral. However, conceptually, one might speak of values that themselves are abstract, 'transcendental' in the way Immanuel Kant understood them. Thus, for a science-inspired naturalist, there may be domains of philosophical reflection that need not be treated strictly naturalistically. A science-inspired naturalist need not be a philosophical naturalist with respect to mathematical entities or normative standards. In light of such challenges to scientific naturalism, Mario De Caro and David Macarthur have in their introduction to *Naturalism and Normativity* argued for 'liberal naturalism' (2010: 9–16; also De Caro and Macarthur 2004: 13–17).

One might relate such limitations of scientific naturalism to traditional arguments for the existence of God, in particular the ontological argument which is conceptual in character, like mathematics, and the cosmological argument that draws on the realization that there is something rather than nothing. Neither of these is excluded by science-inspired naturalism as understood here. Such arguments introduce a concept of God that is not naturalistic but rather 'supernaturalistic', and hence would be dismissed by naturalists on philosophical grounds (e.g., Stone 1992: 28–30; 2018: 12). Such a rejection reflects the a priori emphasis in naturalism. In contrast to the ontological and the cosmological argument, design arguments of natural theology appear to be science-like, in that that their advocates tend to argue that certain phenomena (e.g., functional organs, such as the eye for seeing) provide a basis for conclusions about a causally active designer beyond this world. Such reasoning does not fit the naturalist view of explanations, as I will discuss in the next section.

## NATURALISM AND EXCEPTIONAL EXPERIENCES

The weather today is predicted and understood on the basis of conditions yesterday and our understanding of meteorological processes. In general, scientific explanations explain a phenomenon B on the basis of earlier conditions A and laws that explain the transition from A to B.

Claims about miracles seem to be about exceptional particular experiences. Arguments that treat such experiences as if they provide evidence of an exception to natural processes are at odds with science-inspired naturalism. The experiences may be genuine, subjectively, but they do not support religious conclusions, objectively. First, we will consider this distinction between the first person account, an event as experienced by a subject, and an explanation as a third person account. Second, we will discuss whether the possibility of an explanation of this kind needs to undermine the experience. And, third, we will consider why a naturalist is not giving up on the possibility of such explanations, even if there is a persistent anomaly.

'I experienced a tree' can be said in two ways, descriptively and as a judgment. It can be a description about how something seems to me, without regard to the accuracy of that seeming. I may say 'I experienced a tree, but then I realized I was mistaken'. But experience is also used as an achievement word; 'I experienced a tree' if it not only appeared to me that there was a tree, but that I was awake in the presence of a real tree which I saw or felt. "This second sense includes a judgment on the part of the observer about the accuracy of the subject's understanding of his or her experience" (Proudfoot 1985: 229).

We should not explain away experiences as they appear to the subjects, unless one has reason to believe that the description is intentionally dishonest. However, it is a fair game of science to explain the experiences as they appeared to the subject in a different way than the subject herself does. *"Explanatory reduction* consists in offering an explanation of an experience in terms that are not those of the subject and that might not meet with his approval. This is perfectly justifiable and is, in fact, normal procedure" (Proudfoot 1985: 197). Accepting a subject's experience in the descriptive sense as authentic need not imply the judgment that the self-description is correct.

This combination, of accepting the experience descriptively while suspending judgment, is likely to irritate. It deviates from "normal interpersonal relations" (Dennett 1991: 83). The visiting anthropologist accepts all the accounts of a tribe, but at the same time adopts an attitude of distance and neutrality, whereas the natives do not just want to be taken as sincere; they want to have their beliefs shared. It irritates, just as when a father says he understands how the child feels, while signalling also to the child that she will outgrow those feelings.

If one accepts first person accounts as genuine, in the subjective sense, would a scientific explanation explain the experience *away?* After an explanation some experiences are gone. Once I know that what seemed to me to be a snake in a dark corner was actually a rope, the original experience with its emotional components, such as fear, will fade away. 'It is only ...'. An explanation may liberate from unnecessary fear. It may also be a loss of the innocence of childhood, which diminishes joy and spontaneity, as in the explanation of experiences surrounding Santa Claus. It is 'explained away' once the explanation is accepted by the subject.

Hence, by changing the terms an explanation of an event may change the feelings accompanying those events. Changing the terms is part of what it is to be an explanation, though it is not sufficient. Explaining why opium puts people to sleep by saying that it has a *virtus dormativa*, a sleep inducing power – as happens in Molière's play *Le Malade Imaginaire* – is no explanation at all. "If your model of how pain is a product of brain activity still has a box in it labelled 'pain', you haven't yet begun to explain what pain is" (Dennett 1991: 455). However, even if an explanation uses other terms to analyze the event, this need not make the experience disappear. Opium still puts people to sleep, even if one does not consider the statement that opium has a 'sleep-inducing power' an explanation. A reductive explanation need not imply elimination of the phenomenon.

Such a line of reasoning works less well for religious experience interpreted as an experience with God, as the reference to God is part of the explanation. If there is an explanation of religious experiences in naturalist terms, as expected by naturalists, such an explanation would eliminate the reference to a transcendent being, to God.

Experiences considered subjectively 'religious' can be such that there is no violation of natural laws. As a grandparent it is a source of joy and wonder for me to see my grandchildren develop. Thus, an explanation need not change the experience. We will consider such experiences in the next section. Here we will focus on experiences that seem to resist a naturalistic understanding.

For claims about miracles a naturalist might challenge the evidence. Often, the evidence is testimony. That Jesus walked on water and that after his death he broke bread with some disciples, are of this kind. They are not even testimony in a direct sense; they are elements in religious narratives that tell readers of a most significant and inspiring person, to whom the narrators ascribe religious significance. The narratives were written down much later by people who told a story about what they had heard about this remarkable figure. They did so to convey a particular message; the writings are not documentary in a modern sense, but theological testimony. They may well have been honest in their writings, but by modern standards, the religious meaning trumps truth in the gospels.

It might be that one cannot dismiss the evidence for a phenomenon. Assume that people in a house keep hearing ghosts; the noises are undeniable. A naturalist would not conclude that there are ghosts, but that there is something that deserves further exploration. Perhaps there are mice. Or perhaps there are hidden passageways used by some to trick others. The naturalistic mindset would be to accept the noise as evidence, and engage in further research.

If we were to learn of a guru in the Himalaya's who had been going without food or water for decades, we might at first dismiss this as a legitimizing story by his admirers. But if the ascetic guru were to be transferred to an academic hospital with a major research university, and sceptics were brought in to keep the guru under strict surveillance, and the person would continue to be in good health despite such extreme fasting, we would have to think of other options. Perhaps some humans can absorb sufficient moisture from the air. The hypothesis might arise that some humans are able to do something similar to photosynthesis like the green plants do. Such proposals would go contrary to current knowledge. The science-inspired naturalist would see experiences with exceptional events and other anomalies as reasons to develop one's understanding of the laws of nature and possibilities of nature due to those laws.

This appeal to future developments in our understanding may sound like special pleading, but is the basic scientific attitude, sometimes called methodological naturalism, methodological atheism, or methodological agnosticism. Such explanations exclude reference to divine interventions or other otherworldly elements. Explanations are supposed to draw on natural conditions and processes. If anomalies are persistent, that is an incentive for further research, not a moment to declare defeat and give up the general perspective (e.g., Perry and Ritchie 2018). Exceptional experiences are not accepted as evidence of something beyond the natural.

## SCIENCE AND EXPERIENCES OF WONDER

What about experiences that are not presented as exceptions to the order of nature, but as affectively significant, such as experiences of wonder and awe? Naturalists do not perceive those as at odds with their naturalism. They might even be conducive to their scientific work.

Occasionally, scientists speak with affective terms of their experiences as scientists and their appreciation of the world they study. They may speak of wonder, beauty, and awe to express their attitude towards nature. Let me limit myself here to just one example of someone known for his science communication and his anti-religious polemic, Richard Dawkins. He emphasizes that in his admiration for nature he stands with William Paley, who became well known for the argument found at the beginning of his *Natural Theology* (Paley 1802) that organisms surpass the complexity of watches, and hence are created by a greater 'watchmaker'. In his book *The Blind Watchmaker*, Dawkins writes that "when it comes to complexity and beauty of design, Paley hardly even began to state his case" (Dawkins 1986: 29). Dawkins concurs with Paley on the experience. "The only thing he got wrong (...) was the explanation itself" (Dawkins 1986: 7). The experiences are shared; the explanation differs.

In *Unweaving the Rainbow: Science, Delusion and the Appetite for Wonder*, Dawkins has 'wonder' in its subtitle. In the Preface, he emphasizes the positive message:

> The feeling of awe and wonder that science can give us is one of the highest experiences of which the human psyche is capable. It is a

deep aesthetic passion to rank with the finest that music and poetry
can deliver. It is truly one of the things that makes life worth living.
(Dawkins 1998: x)

As he sees it, understanding does not undermine appreciation –
'unweaving the rainbow' by spectroscopy is not undermining its beauty.
It is rather that an experience, once understood, is thereby also evoking
additional insights; knowledge enriches the experience. Again and
again, Dawkins rejects the view of those that something has to be
unintelligible in order to be appreciated, the "ordinary superstitious
folk" (Dawkins 1998: xi). Among them are religious believers, in particular those who reject an evolutionary understanding of reality.

In an article on "awe and wonder in scientific practice," philosopher
of religion Helen De Cruz has argued that emotions of awe and wonder
have a positive role in the practice of science. Awe, wonder, and
gratitude are positive emotions associated with self-transcendence,
helping us focus on the wider world. Awe, wonder, and curiosity are
major epistemic emotions, that stimulate further research and make
people less likely to neglect novel information. Awe also "provides a
mode of understanding in the absence of full knowledge" (De Cruz
2020: 160).

Many more examples could be produced, and the theoretical understanding of the functions of such emotions can be developed further. For
now, it suffices to note that experiences that some would associate with
religion can be found among scientists with a naturalistic orientation as
well. In his many writings on science, Dawkins provides ample
examples, but it is not limited to science communication, as it is also
found among major research scientists. However, some science-inspired
naturalists go further than merely speaking of awe and wonder; they
understand themselves as 'religious naturalists'. It is to this stance that
we will turn now.

## RELIGIOUS NATURALISM AND EXPERIENCES

To clarify the notion 'religious naturalism', we will first consider the
way 'religion' is used in this context. Thereafter, religious motives in
the work of two religious naturalists, Ursula Goodenough and Charley
Hardwick, will be surveyed, to see how they relate experience and ideas.
Thereafter, we will come to some general considerations about the
possibility of naturalists understanding some of their experiences as
religious experiences.

In *Religious Naturalism Today*, Stone defines religious naturalism as a type of naturalism:

> Religious naturalism is the type of naturalism which affirms a set of beliefs and attitudes that there are religious aspects of this world which can be appreciated within a naturalistic framework. There are some events or processes in our experience that elicit responses that can appropriately be called religious. These experiences and responses are similar enough to those nurtured by the paradigm cases of religion that they may be called religious without stretching the word beyond recognition. (Stone 2008: 1)

Thus, for him 'similar enough' is the basis for labeling as religious some of the experiences of naturalists.

A slightly different way of arguing for the religious character of religious naturalism may be read in the self-understanding of the *Religious Naturalist Association* or *RNA*, formed in 2014. Leaders of this online organization wrote about their self-understanding:

> A religious naturalist, we suggest, seeks to synthesize his/her interpretive, spiritual, and moral responses to the natural world into a coherent whole, a synthesis that functions as his/her version of religious naturalism, where the vocabulary, metaphors, and meanings that emerge from this search are not expected to conform to some external received credo. (Goodenough, Cavanaugh, and Macalister 2018: 311)

There is a certain liberal plurality in their understanding of the movement, as individuals may have different ways of synthesizing their understanding of the world and their moral and spiritual response to it. The authors quote Loyal Rue affirmatively:

> Perhaps the only critical point for religious naturalism is that evolutionary cosmology becomes integrated with ecocentric morality by means of some conceptual device. Whatever metaphors do the trick are fine, so long as they don't compromise the principles of naturalism. (Rue 2005: 364f.; Goodenough, Cavanaugh, and Macalister 2018: 312)

The language of synthesis or integration resonates with the understanding of sacred symbols articulated by the anthropologist Clifford Geertz, though Rue does not refer to him.

> Sacred symbols function to synthesize a people's ethos – the tone, character, and quality of their life, its moral and aesthetic style and

mood – and their world view – the picture they have of the way things in sheer actuality are, their most comprehensive ideas of order. (Geertz 1966: 3)

This emphasis on the integration of ethos and world view is also to be found in the definition of 'a religion' given by Geertz, though in the definition there is a certain 'causal' order, as the worldview ("conceptions of the general order of existence") feed "a system of symbols which acts to establish powerful, pervasive, and long-lasting moods" (1966: 4).

With such a broad understanding of religion as integrating knowledge and moral motivation, almost all naturalists might qualify as religious, perhaps with the exception of those who emphasize the categorical difference and disconnect between our understanding of the world and our appreciation of it, the moods and motivations. All those naturalists would be religious upon a functional understanding of religion. This appropriation as 'religious' might be less attractive to others who have a more substantial concept, as not any integration would do, but only an integration which is sufficiently similar in the way the experiences are understood, to return to Stone's definition. To see how self-proclaimed religious naturalists speak of themselves as religious, we will consider two authors, Ursula Goodenough and Charley Hardwick.

Ursula Goodenough is a biologist who has written a book for a wider audience, *The Sacred Depths of Nature*, on her understanding of 'How Things Are', especially in the light of cell biology, her own area of specialization. With each chapter, she offers reflections to articulate "Which Things Matter" (Goodenough 1998: xiv). The project of religious naturalism, to create a story of nature that serves the global ethos, "can be undertaken only if we all experience a *solemn gratitude* that we exist at all, share a *reverence* for how life works, and acknowledge a deep and complex *imperative* that life continue" (xvii, emphasis added).

In her reflections, she uses religious vocabulary, mostly inspired by Christianity. With respect to ultimate origins, she speaks of an overwhelming universe, frightening in its vastness and apparent pointlessness. She then comes to speak of a "covenant with Mystery" (12); one might be reminded of Rudolf Otto's terminology of a *mysterium tremendum* as well as *fascinans* (Otto 1917: chapters 4 and 7). With respect to the origin of life, she supplements her "covenant with mystery" with "outrageous celebration that it occurred at all" (29f.). Natural emergence is "far more magical than traditional miracles" (30). Following a chapter on the biochemistry in the cell, she quotes William James, linking religion to "our manner of acceptance of the universe": "As a religious naturalist I say 'What Is, Is' with the same bowing of the head, the same bending of the knee. Which then allows me to say 'Blessed Be to What Is' with thanksgiving" (47). After a chapter on organisms, she evokes baptism, being "called by name" (59). "And so I lift up my head, and I bear my own witness, with affection and tenderness and respect. And in so doing, I sanctify myself with my own grace. To the extent that I know myself, I am known" (60). A chapter on evolution triggers reflections on fellowship and community, being connected to ancestors, and hence to all creatures (73). Biodiversity "calls us to stand before its presence with deep, abiding humility" (86). A chapter on consciousness ends with reflections on experiences of inwardness, "being invaded by Immanence," which she considers "wondrous mental phenomena" that are transformative. "It is the path to the holy, taken by seekers before me and seekers to follow, and I give myself over to my mystic potential, to the possibility of becoming lost in something much larger than my daily self, the possibility of transcending my daily self" (102). Religious language recurs in the subsequent chapters. Towards the end, she has an explicit reflection on "our religions of origin," which she presents as different stories woven on the basic structure of the evolutionary epic.

Another religious naturalist is Charley Hardwick, who, in his *Events of Grace: Naturalism, Existentialism, and Theology* (1996), offers a philosophical and theological 'naturalist Christian theology'. His work is less driven by science, though it is driven by the conviction that some such reinterpretation of Christianity is needed in our time. He assumes non-reductive physicalist naturalism, or materialism. He seeks to found Christianity "on much more austere, but also much more transparent philosophical and theological foundations" (Hardwick 1996: xii). Whereas I previously spoke of a functionalist view of religion, it would be more appropriate in the light of Hardwick's proposal, to speak of an existential or valuational view of religion: "the force of basic Christian affirmation is always existential and thus religious" (23). One of the bridges is 'seeing-as' (158–206), thus, to simplify it, interpretation.

With Goodenough and Hardwick, we have encountered two different religious naturalists, who use religious language to articulate their understanding and appreciation of reality, and thus allow religious resources to be intertwined with their experiences, without thereby abandoning a naturalistic understanding of reality. In both cases, we may underline that this regards a religious interpretation or articulation of those experiences; the person who speaks brings that to the experience. This might be a particular instance of a more general insight, that experiences are not purely what comes towards us, as they are intertwined with our expectations and conceptions of reality. Even more it is the case for the religious naturalists, who assume a philosophical naturalism (Hardwick) or science-inspired naturalism (Goodenough) as the frame for their understanding of reality.

This seems to make the philosopher or the scientist a special person, as the one who has such knowledge, the one who is able to mediate the experiences. One of the concerns raised by Lisa Sideris in her *Consecrating Science: Wonder, Knowledge, and the Natural World* is that such science-mediated wonder passes by more immediate experiences with nature evoking wonder (Sideris 2017; for a more extensive discussion, see Sideris 2019 and the essays to which she responds).

Another element, aside of the significance of philosophical and scientific insights shaping experiences, is the move towards a more valuational understanding of religion, which is very explicit in Hardwick's book, but is also present in Goodenough's reflections. Under those conditions, speaking about our experiences in religious terms might be a genuine possibility for a naturalist.

## POSSIBLE BUT NOT NECESSARY

A non-religious (or even anti-religious) naturalist such as Dawkins and a religious naturalist such as Goodenough agree on the science. The difference between them is primarily found in the use of religious language, and with that in affective stance with respect to traditional religious elements. Dawkins writes on Goodenough: "She loves churches, mosques and temples, and numerous passages in her book fairly beg to be taken out of context and used as ammunition for supernatural religion. She goes so far as to call herself a 'Religious Naturalist'. Yet a careful reading of her book shows that she is really as staunch an atheist as I am" (Dawkins 2006: 13). Dawkins is concerned about a too liberal use of the world 'religion', so that people can claim scientists such as Einstein as religious. His primary antagonists are those who hold to a 'supernaturalistic' understanding of their religion, and especially those who on that basis hold on to beliefs at odds with science, such as in anti-evolutionary creationism. Thus, Dawkins' concern that Goodenough's words might be taken out of context and used – abused – for a supernaturalistic religious position.

Let me sum up Einsteinian religion in one more quotation from Einstein himself: "To sense that behind anything than can be experienced there is something that our mind cannot grasp and whose beauty and sublimity reaches us only indirectly and as a feeble reflection, this is religiousness. In this sense, I am religious". In this sense I too am religious, with the reservation that "cannot grasp" does not have to mean "forever ungraspable". But I prefer not to call myself religious because it is misleading. (Dawkins 2006: 19)

Is it merely a misleading use of language? The religious naturalist and the non-religious naturalist accept the same knowledge of the world. They both accept as well that, in principle, all experiences, including those one might label 'religious experiences', may be explainable in scientific terms. And for both, experiences such as those of the beauty of rainbow (Dawkins 1998) are not undermined by increased knowledge of this as a natural phenomenon.

However, the religious naturalists considered here retain something more than a non-religious naturalist such as Dawkins. For Hardwick, there is "objectivity of value" within a non-reductive physicalist framework. Hence, one's language may invoke God, but "the very meaning of 'God' is valuational rather than ontological" (Hardwick 1996: 54). There is no being 'God', nor a causal role for the valuational matrix to which 'God' refers. For Goodenough, her 'covenant with Mystery' has a more persistent agnostic sense, which is at odds with Dawkins' dismissal of 'forever ungraspable'.

For all naturalists, whether religious or not, their experiences seem to be informed by prior convictions, not only their acceptance of science, but their prior understanding of naturalism and their prior affinity with religious symbols and expressions. Thus, religious experiences – their own and those of others – are experiences that are interpreted religiously.

## ACKNOWLEDGMENTS

This chapter was written while on study leave as a fellow at the Center of Theological Inquiry, at Princeton, NJ (USA). It draws liberally on previous publications, such as Drees (1996, 2010, 2018, 2020).

## References

Dawkins, Richard. *The Blind Watchmaker. Why the Evidence of Evolution Reveals a Universe without Design.* New York: Norton, 1986.
  *Unweaving the Rainbow: Science, Delusion and the Appetite for Wonder.* Boston: Houghton Mifflin, 1998.

*The God Delusion*. Boston: Houghton Mifflin, 2006.

De Caro, Mario, and David Macarthur. "Introduction: The Nature of Naturalism," in Mario De Caro and David Macarthur (eds.), *Naturalism in Question*, pp. 1–17. Cambridge, MA: Harvard University Press, 2004.

"Introduction: Science, Naturalism, and the Problem of Normativity," in Mario De Caro and David Macarthur (eds.), *Naturalism and Normativity*, pp. 1–19. New York: Columbia University Press, 2010.

De Cruz, Helen. "Awe and Wonder in Scientific Practice: Implications for the Relationship between Science and Religion," in Michael Fuller, Dirk Evers, Anne Runehov, Knut-Willy Sæther, and Bernard Michollet (eds.), *Issues in Science and Theology: Nature – and Beyond*, pp. 155–68. Cham: Springer, 2020.

Deacon, Terrence W. *Incomplete Nature: How Mind Emerged from Matter*. New York: Norton, 2012.

Dennett, Daniel C. *Consciousness Explained*. Boston: Little, Brown, and Company, 1991.

Drees, Willem B. *Religion, Science and Naturalism*. Cambridge: Cambridge University Press, 1996.

*Religion and Science in Context: A Guide to the Debates*. Abingdon, UK: Routledge, 2010.

"Religious Naturalism and Its Near Neighbors: Some Live Options," in Donald A. Crosby, and Jerome A. Stone (eds.), *The Routledge Handbook of Religious Naturalism*, pp. 19–30. London: Routledge, 2018.

"Why I Am a Science-Inspired Naturalist but Not a Philosophical Naturalist nor a Religious Naturalist," in Michael Fuller, Dirk Evers, Anne Runehov, Knut-Willy Sæther, and Bernard Michollet (eds.), *Issues in Science and Theology: Nature – and Beyond*, pp. 31–37. Cham: Springer, 2020.

Geertz, Clifford. "Religion as a Cultural System," in M. Banton (ed.), *Anthropological Approaches to the Study of Religion*, pp. 1–46. London: Tavistock, 1966.

Goodenough, Ursula. *The Sacred Depths of Nature*. Oxford: Oxford University Press, 1998.

Goodenough, Ursula, Michael Cavanaugh, and Todd Macalister. "Bringing Religious Naturalists Together Online," in Donald A. Crosby, and Jerome A. Stone (eds.), *The Routledge Handbook of Religious Naturalism*, pp. 310–16. London: Routledge, 2018.

Goodenough, Ursula, and Terrence W. Deacon. "The Sacred Emergence of Nature," in Ph. Clayton and Z. Simpson (eds.), *The Oxford Handbook of Religion and Science*, pp. 853–71. Oxford: Oxford University Press, 2006.

Hardwick, Charley. *Events of Grace: Naturalism, Existentialism, and Theology*. Cambridge: Cambridge University Press, 1996.

Humphreys, Paul. "How Properties Emerge," *Philosophy of Science* 64 (1997): 1–17.

Oreskes, Naomi, and Erik M. Conway. *Merchants of Doubt: How a Handful of Scientists Obscured the Truth on Issues from Tobacco Smoke to Global Warming*. New York: Bloomsbury, 2010.

Otto, Rudolf. *Das Heilige: Über das Irrationale in der Idee des Göttlichen und sein Verhältnis zum Rationalen*. Breslau: Terwindt und Granier, 1917.

Paley, William. *Natural Theology, or Evidences of the Existence and Attributes of the Deity Collected from the Appearances of Nature*. London: J. Faulder, 1802.

Perry, John, and Sarah Lane Ritchie. "Magnets, Magic, and Other Anomalies: In Defense of Methodological Naturalism," *Zygon: Journal of Religion and Science* 53 (2018): 1064–93.

Proudfoot, Wayne. *Religious Experience*. Berkeley: University of California Press, 1985.

Rue, Loyal. *Religion Is Not about God: How Spiritual Traditions Nurture our Biological Nature and What to Expect When They Fail*. New Brunswick, NJ: Rutgers University Press, 2005.

Sideris, Lisa H. *Consecrating Science: Wonder, Knowledge, and the Natural World*. Berkeley: University of California Press, 2017.

"Wonder Sustained: A Reply to Critics," *Zygon: Journal of Religion and Science* 54 (2019): 426–53.

Stone, Jerome A. *The Minimalist Vision of Transcendence: A Naturalist Philosophy of Religion*. Albany, NY: SUNY Press, 1992.

"Varieties of Religious Naturalism," *Zygon: Journal of Religion and Science* 38 (2003): 89–93.

*Religious Naturalism Today: The Rebirth of a Forgotten Alternative*. Albany, NY: SUNY Press, 2008.

"Defining and Defending Religious Naturalism," in Donald A. Crosby, and Jerome A. Stone (eds.), *The Routledge Handbook of Religious Naturalism*, pp. 7–18. London: Routledge, 2018.

## 14 Meaning and Social Value in Religious Experience

MARK OWEN WEBB

Whether religious experiences can be good evidence for religious belief has been a topic of concern to philosophers at least since William James's seminal work.[1] He came to the conclusion that they do, in fact, provide evidence for what he calls the "religious hypothesis," but only for the subjects of the experiences; they hold "no authority" for others. In recent years, some philosophers have argued that religious experience is a kind of evidence like other experiential evidence, and should be treated in the same way. The question remains, with no consensus as to an answer. One aspect of religious experience that is frequently overlooked[2] is the fact that these experiences take place in the setting of a religion, which is, in the ordinary case, a social institution. The subjects of the experiences take part in ceremonies and rituals with other people who share, at least in part, their beliefs and convictions. This social setting contributes an important background for understanding what religious experiences are, and so what epistemic value they have.

### DELINEATING THE TOPIC

To begin with, religious experiences can be generally characterized as experiences that seem to the subject to be of some objective reality, and have some religious import.[3] A wide range of experiences fall under this rather vague category. Part of that vagueness comes from the vagueness of the label "religion," as a wide variety of human institutions and practices fall under that category, too. It has been a project in anthropology, sociology, and philosophy to try to define the category, with no end in sight. With some more or less artificial fiddling, we can

[1] James, *The Varieties of Religious Experience.*
[2] Alston, *Perceiving God,* is a notable exception to this neglect.
[3] This is the definition I use in Webb, "Religious Experience."

understand what religious experience is without defining what religion is. Whatever vagueness and/or ambiguity the concept of religion suffers from will be imported into our understanding of religious experience, but we can be precise enough to carry on.

To a great extent, we are at the mercy of the first-person reports of such experiences to make any progress, but that does not mean we have to accept all first-person claims that an experience is a religious one. Two kinds of experience that are often called religious experiences don't really fit well into this discussion, and so I propose to ignore them. One is any experience that has no intentional object. If the experience isn't of anything, then it won't count as a religious experience for our purposes. For example, someone in a religious context might feel a general sense of elation, or guilt, or some other feeling, and so identify it as a religious experience. But if the content of the experience is exhausted without reference to anything but the experiencer's feelings, then it can't, except in the most indirect way, be evidence for the existence of anything.

Similarly, I propose to ignore experiences of ordinary objects that the subject experiences as religiously significant. Seeing god in a flower or the starry sky may be a religious experience in my sense, insofar as part of the content of the experience is the purportedly objective god. Nevertheless, it is hard to distinguish between an experience of the starry sky through which one sees god, and an experience of the starry sky that occasions an experience of god, the first of which would be a religious experience, and the second would be an ordinary experience accompanied by a religious experience. Therefore, it is better for our purposes to leave that category of experience aside.[4]

Another potentially complicating factor is the variety of objects people claim to experience. Many people have claimed to have experienced the God of Abraham, Isaac, and Jacob (and Muhammad, and Bahá'u'lláh, etc.), but those encounters don't come close to exhausting the set of claimed encounters in religious experiences:, Dionysus, Thor, and lots of small-g gods in the ancient world; the dizzying multiplicity of bodhisattvas, saints, angels, demigods, and demons, and the various non-personal beings and non-beings that are the ultimate reality of various Asian religions. For some, the paradigmatic religious experience is the realization of the unity of all things, including the subject. For others, it is the grasping of the emptiness of all things, including the

---

[4] This is the first of the four types of experience according to Richard Swinburne's typology. See Swinburne, *The Existence of God*, pp. 298–99.

subject. Whatever account we give of religious experience has to make room for all this variety.[5]

## RELIGIOUS EXPERIENCE IN ITS SOCIAL SETTING

Since a religion is a kind of social institution or practice, to understand religious experiences requires understanding them in their settings. Even though the experience itself purports to be a one-on-one encounter between the subject and the religious reality, the experience only makes sense in the context of the institution that the subject calls home. Religious experiences are not, by and large, self-interpreting. This is often taken as a special feature of religious experiences that shows why they are epistemically inferior to other experiential grounds of belief, but this is a misunderstanding of how perception works.

Suppose we want to ask what makes an experience suitable grounds for a belief. Historically, when philosophers have asked this about sensory experience, they give a list of reasons why sense-experience can be trusted, including that we can predict future experiences based on past ones; our sense experiences tell a coherent story, in a way that dreams, for example, don't; our individual senses confirm one another, and we can check our own experiences against other people's. The best explanation for these features of our experiences is that they are delivering accurate information about the world. Even when they do fool us, by illusion, hallucination, or the like, one or more of those features will be absent; we can check and correct our beliefs using our other sensory beliefs and the beliefs of others. Religious experiences can't do the same. So it seems that while sensory experience responds to checks and confirmation, religious experience doesn't, so while sensory experience is a legitimate source of belief, religious experience isn't.

This picture oversimplifies what happens both in sensory experience and religious experience. For one thing, it is not necessary for a belief to be subjected to such tests and checks for it to be justified. The vast majority of our beliefs about the world based on sensory experience are never subjected to such tests, and they are nevertheless justified, and suitable for grounding other beliefs. To say otherwise is to court skepticism. If every belief must be subjected to tests to be justified, then the same is true of the beliefs that provided the tests, and a vicious regress is unavoidable. The absence of such checks and tests does not disqualify a source of

---

[5] Keith Yandell offers a fivefold typology precisely to take this variety into account. See Yandell, *The Epistemology of Religious Experience*, pp. 21–32.

beliefs. But it is also true that beliefs based on religious experience are sometimes subjected to tests and checks, just as sensory experiences are. To illustrate, consider this example of a typical religious experience.

> Anna has committed some small wrong (say, petty theft) and feels bad about it. She consults her mother, who says, "You know God doesn't want you to do that. It's a sin. Your conscience is telling you that." Anna decides to pray to God and ask for forgiveness. While she is praying, she feels that God is forgiving her and comforting her, while at the same time giving her courage to confess to the person she wronged, and make amends. When asked about her prayer experience, she says, "I felt God's presence, both convicting me of sin and forgiving me." The members of her church confirm and accept her report as true and genuine, because that is what they would expect to happen, given their tradition's interpretation of the scripture, how it comports with their own experiences, and by the effect it has had on Anna's behavior.

Resources provided by Anna's religious community have entered into the evaluation of the experience in several ways. First, the experience comes to her because of something she does, prompted by guidance from her community. They believe, for lots of reasons, the way to deal with sin is to confess it to God and ask for forgiveness, and that forgiveness will come. Also, when she describes the experience, she uses both ordinary language and the specialized conceptual apparatus of her religion. She describes what she was doing as prayer to God, not just talking in solitude. She describes the feeling as being comforted, not just feeling better. And finally, when she reports her experience, her coreligionists compare it with what they would expect, given their complex picture of God and His relations to the world, a picture developed over centuries. The social setting of Anna's experience provides checks and tests, all of which her experience passes. Compare Anna with another case, Bill.

> Bill is walking down the street in New York City and sees a man who looks like Ben Vereen. Being a big fan of musical theater, he recognizes him, and approaches him. The man confirms that he is indeed Ben Vereen, and after a brief chat about plays and movies, Ben autographs Bill's tourist map, and they part ways. When he gets back to Lubbock, Bill tells his theater friends about his encounter. They accept his story, saying, "Yes, Ben Vereen is known to be very friendly with fans, and he is in New York right now for the new production of *Cats*."

In other words, Bill's experience comes to him because of actions he has taken, that put him in a position to have experiences he might not otherwise have (going to New York and walking outside), and his sensory report is informed by knowledge he already has (what Ben Vereen looks like, plus his memories of Ben's various parts in plays and movies), checked by background facts that are known to his community (yes, Ben was in New York at the time, and the person's behavior comports with what is known about Ben's character), and supported by what they would expect to happen, based on what they know about New York and Ben Vereen.

In other words, sensory experiences are subject to the same kinds of check for coherence with a broader theory as religious experiences are. Both kinds of experience begin with the occurrence of some qualitative state in the subject. Whether it is some feeling of the numinous or some presentation of redness, there is some inner state that can occur without any connection to beliefs or social content. In other words, beliefs based on religious experience are not exhausted by socially supplied resources; there has to be some qualitative content to work on. It is also true that how that qualitative content gets processed is very similar. Socially supplied resources work on beliefs based on sensory experience in broadly the same way that they do religious experiences. Even fairly typical, everyday sensory beliefs are supported by background beliefs and socially supplied information. When I form a simple belief based on my visual experience first thing in the morning, a huge amount of socially provided support goes into the formation of the belief. I identify my surroundings as my own home (this is not a given, since I do sometimes travel and wake up disoriented in strange places). I don't ask myself if this is home, I simply form the belief that it is, informed more or less automatically by my other belief about what I would expect to see in my room. I don't reason to that conclusion; the background information contributes to the content of the belief I form. Since it is unremarkable, I don't report it to anyone, so checks are not needed.

## DOXASTIC PRACTICE EPISTEMOLOGY

Even though lots of aspects of religious experience seem to match up with similar facts about sense-perception, there is still reason to be dubious about it, and so to treat it differently. For one thing, sensory experiences tend to be informationally rich, and provide us with new information almost constantly, whereas religious experiences tend to be informationally scant, and rarely cause their subjects to change their beliefs about the nature of the purported reality they experience. This means that prior theoretical knowledge and background beliefs have a much larger role to play in religious experiences. Also, there seems to be one common view of the physical world (different in details from person to person, to be sure, but almost unanimous in broad outline), while religious experiences figure in wildly different and mutually inconsistent stories about their objects.

So there are significant differences between the two kinds of experiences, and so there may be significant differences between the kinds of beliefs they can ground. We do take our sensory experiences to be good grounds for beliefs about the world, even while we recognize them to be fallible and corrigible. Should we take religious experiences to be good grounds for belief, too, in spite of the differences from sense-experience, or should we reject them as unfit for grounding belief, in spite of the similarities? The question comes down to asking if the experiences are reliable indications of some reality.

The most obvious way to undercut the credibility of an experiential claim is to have evidence that the object of the experience doesn't exist, or, more generally, that the belief formed is simply false. Returning to the example of Bill, above, if I happened to know that Ben Vereen was not in New York at that time, then I have reason to believe Bill's belief is false, and so there was something wrong with the experience that misled him. It may be no fault of Bill's. Perhaps there is a Ben Vereen double wandering around the city fooling Vereen fans. To undercut a belief formed on the basis of religious experience in the same way, I would have to have evidence that corresponding religious doctrine is false.[6] So if a person reports an experience in which she feels God forgiving her, we would have to have reason to believe that God is, in fact, not forgiving her. Staunch defenders of the atheistic argument from evil might say that we do have conclusive reason to believe that God does not exist, so all beliefs about his beliefs, desires, or dispositions must be false. Apart from something like that, though, there is no general refuting defeater for religious belief.

A second way is to find reason to believe that there is something wrong with that way of forming beliefs. Perhaps the mechanisms are defective, and so unreliable. If we know from the past that Bill can't distinguish faces very well, then we won't trust any of his reports about whom he has seen. So how do we go about discovering whether the

---

[6] This is part of what Plantinga means by a de facto objection to religious belief. See Plantinga, *Warranted Christian Belief*, p. ix.

religious-experience way of forming beliefs is defective? We can't just say that it is not like sensory experience. While it is true (as we noted above) that there are significant differences, we also noted that the differences are not as great as they seem on first glance. Even if the differences were huge, we need further argument to show that those differences are disabling for religious experience. In other words, we need reason to think that the characteristics of sense-experience with which we are so impressed are necessary for other kinds of experience in order for them to be good grounds for belief.

Showing that a source of beliefs is reliable is a tricky task, because to do that is to show that the beliefs so formed are true, by and large. Religious experience seems to be in trouble here, because it is, ultimately, the only source for beliefs about God, or emptiness, or Atman, or whatever. We can't let it be a witness in its own case, since its reliability is precisely what is in question. In general, if a source of beliefs is the only source for beliefs of that type, then there is no way for the source to prove itself reliable, on pain of circularity. If the source is not the only one for a particular kind of content, then it can be supported by the other sources for that content. For example, if vision tells us there is a fire in front of us, it can be confirmed by the sound of burning, the smell of smoke, the feeling of heat, and so on. But it's not all clear for sense-perception. True, the senses all support each other, by and large, but what supports the bunch of them? Sense-perception generally seems to be in the same bind; it can't show itself to be reliable without presuming itself to be reliable.[7]

But that's not the end of the matter. We may not be able to show a source of beliefs to be reliable, in a non-circular way, but we can certainly show one to be unreliable. If a source produces two contradictory beliefs, we know one of them is false, even if we don't know which one. If a source of beliefs produces lots of contradictions, then its ratio of true beliefs to false beliefs approaches 50/50, and it's fair to call it unreliable. Wishful thinking, astrology, taking auspices, and such don't have an impressive track record, so the epistemically careful have abandoned them as not reliable. If we show a source of beliefs is unreliable, it's no longer a good idea to rely on it. If we fail to show it to be unreliable, then it has passed a sort of minimal test, and so it may be rational to rely on it after all. Failing to run into contradictions suggests that the source is on to some mind-independent reality. Does religious

[7] William Alston makes this case in *Perceiving God.*

experience fall into that category? Does it escape producing massive contradictions?

Looking at religious experiences within particular traditions, they seem to be more or less consistent. Theravada monks tend to come out of their meditative states with very similar beliefs about the nature of reality as impermanent and unsatisfactory. Christian mystics come away from contemplative prayer with roughly the same story about God's love and majesty. There are anomalies, but that's to be expected from any source of beliefs. But the same question that arises for the senses generally arises for religious experience generally: while the individual religions escape massive contradictions, they do not escape massively contradicting one another. On the Alstonian reasoning I have been deploying, this shows that religious experience tout court is not a reliable way of forming beliefs. But perhaps the individual religious traditions can claim that theirs, at least, escapes contradictions internally, and so it's rational to rely on them. Even if they all escape contradiction individually, they still contradict one another, so they can't all be reliable, but if each is internally consistent, then it can be rational to engage in one of them.

We noted earlier that our five senses prop each other up, evidentially. Suppose that was not true. Suppose, for example, that vision produced a consistent, clear picture of the world, but it didn't match up with the other senses at all. So we see a fire, but we feel cold, hear a buzzing, and smell roses. And just to up the ante, let's suppose that the unreliable senses give us something different every time. So the next time we see a fire, we might feel prickles, hear hissing, and smell skunk. We would quickly come to see that our senses are not, as a whole, reliable. On the other hand, we would come to see that vision is at least constant and consistent and learn to ignore the others. We might do the same if one tradition's religious experiences were constant and consistent, and all the others were unreliable.

Now imagine if each of the senses gave us a constant, consistent picture of the world, but they didn't match up with each other. Each would have some claim to being a legitimate source of belief, and we would have no idea which, if any, was the right one. This is like our situation with respect to religious experience. The analogy with sense-experience is far from perfect; nevertheless, they do seem to be analogous in the epistemically important ways: neither can be demonstrated to be reliable; both sense-perception generally and at least some individual religious traditions' experiential claims escape massive self-contradiction. So it can be reasonable to form religious beliefs on the basis of religious experiences.

## THE COMMON CORE HYPOTHESIS

In spite of the apparent contradictions among religious-experience reports, and the resulting differences in the religious doctrines formed from them, some still believe that all religious experiences are of a single reality, and that the differences are superficial, or otherwise explainable. Since there is so much overlap among the religions on moral values, some think that the metaphysics of the being behind them all is much less important, so it is possible that all the religions are in contact, via religious experience, with the same fundamental reality. One such theory is espoused by John Hick.[8]

The view starts from the idea that religious experiences across the different traditions are equally well grounded, epistemically, and so the believers in them are equally rational. On the other hand, believers in each tradition are aware of this fact, and so are aware that people in other traditions are equally rational. In particular, they are aware that they have no special reason to prefer their own experiential evidence over that of others. But they also have no reason to abandon their own experiences. The only remaining possibility is that all the subjects of religious experiences are in contact with the same reality (Hick calls it "the Real"), and that reality is ambiguous. In particular, it can be experienced as personal, as the theistic religions aver, or as impersonal, as many Chinese and Indian religions assert. Thus, these different experiences can be of the same Real, and those who have the experiences (and those who believe them) can be equally rational. Clearly, the variety of claims about the Real cannot all be true, but the experiences in all their variety are, in some sense, all veridical. Hick's view is that the Real, as it is in itself, is beyond all our categories, and that is why it can be conceptualized in such different ways.

Hick's view has not attracted a lot of support, largely because it is hard to say what the real is, as it is in itself, if none of our concepts apply to it.[9] But one need not be a pluralist like Hick to believe that there is a common core to religious experiences. Even apart from the idea that religious experiences are all of the same reality, there is an idea that they all support a common (admittedly thin) component of religious belief. Take what William James refers to as the "Religious Hypothesis":

> [R]eligion says essentially two things. First, she says that the best
> things are the more eternal things, the overlapping things, the

---

[8] Hick, *An Interpretation of Religion.*
[9] Daniel Howard-Snyder explains the problem in detail in his "Who or What Is God, According to John Hick?"

things in the universe that throw the last stone, so to speak, and say the final word ... The second affirmation of religion is that we are better off, even now, if we believe her first affirmation to be true.[10]

This hypothesis is meager at best, as it gives us no guidance about what those eternal things are, or why they are the best things. This is the general problem with Common Core views. They save the evidential value of religious experiences as to the thin common core, but leave us with nothing to say about the more detailed contents of the experiences. No religious disagreements can be settled this way. No discovery can be made about God, or Brahman, or the Dao, that is not undermined by an equal and opposite experience elsewhere. The best views like this can do is reassure us that those details don't matter. Such a verdict would be a major revision in any religion's self-understanding.

BACKGROUND INFORMATION

One reason that different religious traditions end up with utterly different interpretations of religious experiences is that the background beliefs they bring to the experience are very different. We noted earlier that even my ordinary perceptual beliefs depend on background information, which contribute to identifying the objects in my environment and making predictions about what I will experience in the near future. It's because I have beliefs, formed long ago and lying latent in my cognitive structures, about the nature of glass and tile floors that I confidently expect to hear a crash when I drop a glass in my kitchen. In addition to general knowledge about objects and materials, I also have individual knowledge of my own past that contributes to my identifying this house as mine, and that woman as my wife. Vast theoretical structures about the world and my own place in it are already in place in my mind when I have a new perceptual experience, and it's because of those structures that I am able to form new beliefs so automatically, and incorporate them so effortlessly into my body of knowledge. Much of that structure is provided to me by the social group I grew up in. Some of what I know is based on my own experience, but by far the biggest portion is provided by others. Everything I know about the past, except for the most meager facts about my own biography, I learned in school and from books. The same is true of geography, astronomy, physics,

---

[10] James, "The Will to Believe," p 105.

biology, chemistry, and practically anything else worth knowing. A person who set out to build a body of knowledge based only on what he or she can come to know on his or her own cognitive resources would not be able to get very far.[11]

The same is true, to an even greater extent, about religious experience, and this accounts for a lot of the variety in reports of religious experience. Religious experiences come to people in religious traditions, by and large, and each is quite naturally described in the language of its tradition. Given that religious experiences are frequently vague and not generally rich in detail, it is natural that they would be filled in with background beliefs about the object in question, just as the famous Hidden Dalmatian picture[12] can appear very different after the addition of background information. While this fact seems to undercut the evidential value of the experiences, in that it implies that a lot of reported content doesn't come from the experience itself, it also weakens the objection based on the variety of reports, by providing a non-ad hoc explanation for the variety. So reliance on the testimony of others, and the theoretical models built up over generations, is integral to the understanding of religious experiences.

## MEANING

Perhaps the most important area in which social context provides an important component for religious experience is in the realm of meaning, both in the sense of linguistic (or other semantic) meaning and in the sense of significance. Obviously, linguistic meaning is a social matter, as it is a conventional matter. The same goes for religious language. The meanings of all the key terms used in describing religious experiences are words whose meanings are fixed in the same kind of conventional way as the terms of ordinary language. Many religious terms, in fact, come from ordinary language, and are applied by analogy in religious contexts. How exactly that works is a much-debated question, and one outside the scope of this essay. According to the most popular theories of mental content, the same can be said for the

---

[11] This fact is described thoroughly in Coady, *Testimony.*

[12] The Hidden Dalmatian illusion consists of an array of black spots on a white background, which does not appear to make a picture. When a viewer is told that there is a dog in the picture, they suddenly resolve some of the dots into a shape of a dog. Once you have seen the dog, you can't return to seeing the picture as just an array of dots. It is explained nicely in Gregory's *Intelligent Eye.*

semantics, if any, of mental items. Meaning and reference are fixed partly with the help of others, outside your own head.[13]

There is a concern about how purely religious language and thought, and the religious components of analogical language and thought, can get their meaning, since there seems to be no independent access to the objects so that users of the language can come to agreement about the extension of terms.[14] If there is no public standard for what the terms refer to, then how can we establish any common usage? Analogy does give us a partial inroad, but doesn't answer the worry totally. We might, from a religious experience, form the belief that we had just encountered a very wise, very powerful, holy being, who is also very loving and concerned about us. While the terms "wise," "powerful," and "loving" don't apply to God literally, we can see how they might be extended by analogy. But what about "holy"? We can define the term, but it's hard to see how it connects with any properties that can be represented in the phenomenology of an experience. And there are a whole host of terms that fit together with it the same way. Perhaps they can be inter-defined, but it's not at all obvious how they can be grounded in experience.

It turns out we have other realms of meaning with the same character; they can be inter-defined, but they can't be defined in terms whose meaning comes from outside that circle. Color language – by which I mean the ordinary language of colors we experience, not reflectance or wavelengths – are perfectly meaningful, but there is no way to explain what red is without using color language. That's why inverted spectra and Mary the color scientist are problems for so many.[15] But we still use the language unproblematically, because we have fairly good agreement about the extensions of the terms. In other words, because the vast majority of us see colors the same way, we can agree on how to use the terms, and we can teach them to others. Likewise, moral language is not definable in non-moral language (though naturalists keep trying). But as in the case of color language, there is vast agreement on what is

---

[13] This fact shows us the way to answer Islamophobic concerns about whether Muslims worship the same God as Christians and Jews. If reference is fixed the way most of us think it is, then it is enough that Jesus was intentionally talking about the God of Moses, and so was Muhammad. Differences in theology don't, in general, make for differences in reference.

[14] This concern is parallel to the no-public-checks worry about the epistemic status of beliefs based on religious experience.

[15] See Byrne "Inverted Qualia." For Mary and the Knowledge Argument, see Jackson, "Epiphenomenal Qualia," and the huge literature that followed.

good and bad, right and wrong, virtuous and vicious. This sounds surprising, because our moral talk tends to come into play in the cases in which we disagree, but there is a background of agreement that is vastly bigger than the areas of contention.[16] It's as if we never spoke about color at all except in borderline cases when it is vague or unclear, or when we are talking to colorblind people. Again, the background of agreement makes it possible for us to apply terminology and teach it to new learners.

It seems that we cannot say the same for religious language, precisely because there is no widespread agreement about the objects of experience. There is agreement within particular traditions, and even among closely related traditions, but no universal religious experience, or so it seems, beyond the two components of James's religious hypothesis. James's way of talking about the core of religious experiences gives a way to talk about another aspect of meaning, what we might call "significance." Part of what a community provides for those who have religious experiences is a sense of the importance of those experiences, and related matters, for living their lives. One way it does this is by providing additional reasons to try to be a good person and do good in the world. While it may be problematic to try to make moral value dependent on religious truths,[17] it is certainly the case that religions regularly make recommendations about how to be good. They also provide a cosmic order in which goodness matters; it is no longer just a matter of the individual endorsing values and trying to live by them. The religious community reinforces that connection with moral value, and so helps the individual live up to the values he or she sees as reaching beyond the self. It is no accident that so many religious experiences, especially conversion experiences, come with a recognition of one's previous life as morally inadequate, and a resolution to do better.

In a similar way, religious experiences can provide a sense of meaning or significance to one's life. In contrast to a naturalistic or existentialist view, according to which a human life is not the sort of thing that can have meaning (or if it does, it is chosen by the individual), religions generally offer a story about what matters about human life, and roots that value in something outside of and greater than the individual.[18]

---

[16] In the appendix to *The Abolition of Man*, C. S. Lewis lists a large number of citations from different cultures to illustrate the vast background agreement on values.

[17] See Sayre-McCord, "Metaethics," especially section two, "The Euthyphro Problem."

[18] I argued for something like this in "Religious Experience as Doubt Resolution."

According to the Catholic Catechism, God "calls man to seek him, to know him, to love him with all his strength."[19] This goal underwrites the whole orientation of a Catholic life, in understanding and obeying the will of God. According to Theravada Buddhists, the goal of all life is to bring an end to suffering by seeking enlightenment, and a human life is a precious opportunity to pursue it.[20] This goal underwrites the Theravada Buddhist story about what is good and bad, and the social organizations of monks and laypeople, and their complex relations to one another. In both cases, these claims about the nature of human existence play a fundamental role in their respective views on how we should live. Just as the individual's efforts to do good and be good take on greater richness as part of the cosmic story, so does the individual's life take on greater meaning as part of a cosmic story in which it has a purpose. The religious community provides the individual with the bulk of that story to function as a theoretical framework and background information for interpreting experiences, and also provides behavioral support for efforts to orient one's life appropriately, according to that story.

CONCLUSION

Religious experiences are often conceived of as something that happens to the individual, and are private, inaccessible to examination by others. Nothing could be further from the truth. On examination, we can see that religious experiences happen to individuals in social groups, and the social setting is essential to a great many aspects of the importance of those experiences. Yes, the "experience" part – the qualia or what have you – is private, just in the way that sense-data are private, but there is a lot more than mere qualitative experience happening. Just as sensory experiences start with qualia, and are heavily processed with information from other sources before they eventuate in beliefs, and much of that processing is public and social, so religious experiences are socially embedded. That social embedding provides background information, used to interpret the experience; confirmation, which enriches the experience's evidential value; and meaning, which gives richness to religious belief and purpose to human life.

---

[19] www.vatican.va/archive/ccc_css/archive/catechism/prologue.htm#1.1.
[20] www.accesstoinsight.org/tipitaka/sn/sn56/sn56.048.than.html.

## References

Alston, William. *Perceiving God: The Epistemology of Religious Experience.* Ithaca: Cornell University Press, 1991.

Byrne, Alex. "Inverted Qualia," in Edward N. Zalta (ed.), *The Stanford Encyclopedia of Philosophy.* Winter 2018 ed. https://plato.stanford.edu/archives/win2018/entries/qualia-inverted/.

Coady, Cecil Anthony John. *Testimony: A Philosophical Study.* New York: Clarendon Press, 1992.

Gregory, Richard. *Intelligent Eye.* New York: McGraw Hill, 1971.

Hick, John. *An Interpretation of Religion: Human Responses to the Transcendent,* 2nd ed. New Haven: Yale University Press, 2004.

Howard-Snyder, Daniel. "Who or What Is God, According to John Hick?," *Topoi* 36 (2017): 571–86.

Jackson, Frank. "Epiphenomenal Qualia," *Philosophical Quarterly* 32 (1982): 127–36.

James, William. *The Varieties of Religious Experience.* New York: New American Library, 1902/1958.

"The Will to Believe," in Alburey Castell (ed.), *Essays in Pragmatism,* pp. 88–109. New York: Hafner Press, 1948.

Lewis, Clive Staples. *The Abolition of Man.* London: Oxford University Press, 1943.

Plantinga, Alvin. *Warranted Christian Belief.* New York: Oxford University Press, 2000.

Sayre-McCord, Geoff. "Metaethics," in Edward N. Zalta (ed.), *The Stanford Encyclopedia of Philosophy.* Summer 2014 ed. https://plato.stanford.edu/archives/sum2014/entries/metaethics/.

Swinburne, Richard. *The Existence of God,* 2nd ed. New York: Oxford University Press, 2004.

Webb, Mark Owen. "Religious Experience as Doubt Resolution," *International Journal for Philosophy of Religion* 18 (1985): 81–86.

"Religious Experience," in Edward N. Zalta (ed.), *The Stanford Encyclopedia of Philosophy,* Winter 2017 ed., https://plato.stanford.edu/archives/win2017/entries/religious-experience/.

Yandell, Keith. *The Epistemology of Religious Experience.* New York: Cambridge University Press, 1993.

# Index

For EU product safety concerns, contact us at Calle de José Abascal, 56–1°, 28003 Madrid, Spain or eugpsr@cambridge.org.

www.ingramcontent.com/pod-product-compliance
Ingram Content Group UK Ltd.
Pitfield, Milton Keynes, MK11 3LW, UK
UKHW020341140625
459647UK00018B/2255